It Came From ...

The Stories and Novels Behind Classic Horror, Fantasy and Science Fiction Films

It Came From ...

The Stories and Novels Behind Classic Horror, Fantasy and Science Fiction Films

by
Jim Nemeth
and
Bob Madison

Midnight Marquee Press, Inc.
Baltimore, MD, USA

ISBN 9781644300916
Library of Congress Catalog Card Number 2020936836
Manufactured in the United States of America

First Printing: May, 2020

Dedications

For my husband, Ken Bowden—thank you for … everything. I can't imagine how I got along in life before I met you.
—Jim Nemeth

For Russell—who remains the best thing that ever happened to me. MORE!
—Bob Madison

Table of Contents

Acknowledgments

Writing this book has been one of the greatest challenges and fulfilling achievements of my life. I could not have accomplished this without the assistance of a number of people to whom I must express my sincerest thanks and appreciation.

Foremost, to my co-author, Bob Madison, who unhesitatingly and enthusiastically jumped in and rescued me, and whose friendship remains a constant source of awe and gratitude.

To Gary and Susan Svehla of Midnight Marquee Press, for not only having the faith to say "yes" to this project, but also for your invaluable support, guidance and friendship provided throughout.

To Robert Bloch and Ray Bradbury—the inspiration and assistance provided to me through both personal correspondence and time spent is forever cherished and a debt I could never hope to repay in this lifetime; to try to put into words the impact and untold hours of pleasure your writings have afforded me throughout my life is an impossible task.

To Roald Dahl, Charles G. Finney, Jack Finney, Robert Louis Stevenson, M.R. James, John Wyndham, Daphne du Maurier, Mary Shelley and Bram Stoker for your inspiration, which contributed to this book.

To Jeff Sillifant of *Still Things* and Jack Polito of *Jack Polito Collectibles*, this book would not be what it is but for your incredible supply of photographs, as well as your assistance and support.

To Dwight Macpheson, artist extraordinaire, not only for your talent in regard to this project, but also for becoming more than just a collaborator, but a friend as well.

To Keith Henson and Arel Lucas, for your invaluable help in tracking down the elusive life of Charles G. Finney.

To Lucy Chase Williams, Gibby Brand, Pat H. Broeske, Russell Frost, Richard Heft and Tom Weaver: never hesitating with your support, help, encouragement, inspiration and answers to questions—whether in regard to this project or beyond—your friendship is a blessing for which I am always thankful.

Lastly, to Ken Bowden, for your support, technical help, and being my "rock" through all of this.

To anyone possibly forgotten, please know the omission is not deliberate, but rather the result of faulty—as Agatha Christie's Hercule Poirot would term—"grey matter."

—Jim Nemeth

First and foremost, I would like to thank Jim Nemeth for inviting me to participate in his book. This has been his baby for a while, and when he told me about it, he graciously let me play with it.

Next, I could not have completed my portions of the book without the gracious (and long-suffering) editorial help of noted author and historian, Frank Dello Stritto. He made all of my material exponentially better, though I hasten to add any infelicities of phrase are my own responsibility.

I would also be remiss if I did not mention my immense, personal debt to the late Chris Steinbrunner. Less a friend and more a second father, he was the key influence of my developmental years. Chris was a great man and a dear friend and remains deeply, deeply missed. Not a week goes by when I do not think of him, and am grateful for his memory.

Finally, many thanks to those authors who inspired the work: L. Frank Baum, Pierre Boulle, Edgar Rice Burroughs, Charles Dickens, Walt Disney, Ian Fleming, George Clayton Johnson, Raymond F. Jones, William F. Nolan, Alex Raymond, Joe Shuster and Jerry Siegel, Mary Shelley, and Bram Stoker. I wonder what they would make of it all!

—Bob Madison

Introduction: A Study in Adaptation

The book was better.

How many times have we heard that (or said it ourselves)? It is very often the case. Reading a novel, short story or article, we create mental images that are often superior to even the most polished cinematic representations.

But ... that's not *always* the case. Very frequently, in adapting a work created for one medium (print, comics ... or, as in one case in the following volume, an amusement park) to another, changes are essential in order to make the translation work at all. Even the most faithful adaptations fudge some of the details; it is an unavoidable condition of adaptation.

So, if change is inevitable, what is necessary for a successful adaptation from one medium to another? Though we hoped to come up with some kind of formula for excellence, after examining the films covered in this volume, we realized that there is no one, single answer.

Many of the films covered slavishly copy the source material in all but a few details; others have next to nothing in connection with their literary inspiration other than a title or a few core ideas. Nor is authorial control key here either. Though Ray Bradbury was deeply involved with the making of the film version of *Something Wicked This Way Comes*, the finished product still has a markedly different feel from the original novel.

In fact, what an overview of the films that follow reveals is that the secret of a good (or great) adaptation is to simply make a good (or great) movie.

Television's popular *Shock Theater* helped steer many kids to horror fiction.

Prose and film are not interchangeable, and we short-change ourselves when we expect them to be.

Both of us grew up loving science fiction, fantasy and horror films. Like many genre movie buffs, we frequently sought out the books and stories that influenced our favorite movies, often surprised (if not amazed) at the differences.

Though born in different states and a few, scant years apart, our boyhoods were remarkably similar. Spending our youth on such Saturday night television fare as *Creature Features* and *Thriller Theater*, we made imaginative quests into worlds very different from our own. Where Jim gravitated toward supernatural fiction, Bob dug deeply into literary science fiction. Both of us became devoted readers of

IT CAME FROM ...

genre fiction and then, later on, the history of it.

The love for movies, though, never wavered.

Over the years, while discussing cinema reference books, particularly those covering the horror, science fiction and fantasy genres, we found scant attention paid to literary sources. The initial dream for this volume was a comprehensive history that traces and compares films adapted from other material back to its origins. But such was not to be! The number of science fiction, fantasy and horror films that are adaptations from other media are so varied and repetitive that the challenge was confining ourselves to just a handful of favorite films.

And even that was difficult. Many films on our list—*The Hound of the Baskervilles*, *20,000 Leagues Under the Sea*, *2001: A Space Odyssey*, *The House That Dripped Blood*—were planned, but pruned for space. Also, we tried to limit ourselves to only two pre-World War II films (*Flash*

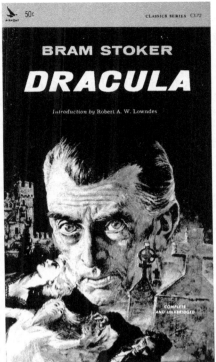

The authors grew up with classics of fantastic literature.

Gordon and *The Wizard of Oz*) because we strove to include more contemporary films that are underserved in genre criticism. Of the movies we didn't cover, let's remember one thing we learned from years of watching movies—sequels happen. Maybe one day in the future we will tackle our remaining favorites.

For clarity's sake, we break the films into three categories—horror, fantasy, science fiction—and then simply list them chronologically. Each chapter is the sole work of one of the authors, with the ringer being special chapters devoted to Dracula and the Frankenstein Monster, where we both delve into not just one, but several of the best, worst, and most popular of their cinematic incarnations.

Enjoy. As for us, we're heading to the movies. Or the local bookstore.

—Jim Nemeth
—Bob Madison

Horror

I've often felt that of the three film genres covered in this book, it is harder to successfully adapt horror. I say this as it's my belief—paradoxically as it may first seem—that the bar set for horror films is lower than for the other genres. Screenwriters both past and present too often seem to believe that all that's necessary to translate horror to screen is to carry over the overarching storyline and all significant scares (or "Boo!" moments as I like to call them). And there, you're done.

That actually sounds easy, right? So why do I proffer that horror is arguably the hardest genre to adapt? Because of having earlier emphasized a *successful* translation. Big difference. A film that merely provides a book's "Boo!" moments are but empty shells, lacking the underlying background and context that frequently makes the literary piece the more satisfying experience. Sure, one can argue that such a film accomplishes its main purpose—to scare audiences—but don't you really want a horror film to capture most everything about the novel or story that makes it so engaging? I do.

Case in point: *The Shining* (1980). This film should have been a slamdunk, enshrined now in cinema history as one of the finest horror film adaptations of all time. With acclaimed director Stanley Kubrick both scripting (with collaborator Diane Johnson) *and* directing the big screen translation of Stephen King's

For a number of reasons, many classic horror movies (such as *The Shining*) were excluded from this book.

IT CAME FROM ...

wildly successful novel, what could go wrong? Well, several things actually. (The film, an obvious candidate for inclusion in this book, didn't make the cut due to our desire to focus on less frequently covered pictures.) In a nutshell, the film's primary problem lay in Kubrick and Johnson's treatment of the novel's three main characters. I'm of the opinion that in emphasizing style and scares over King's deftly developed characters and their all-important motivations, Kubrick transforms the previously relatable and sympathetic Torrances into little more than typical horror movie archetypes:

homicidal maniac, hapless heroine, and victim-turned-unlikely-hero. As a result, audiences lose a vital emotional connection to Jack, Wendy and Danny as established in the novel. And so, *The Shining*, while an undeniably *beautiful-looking* horror picture, nonetheless remains as cold and empty as the reception it received from King fans and the author himself.

There sadly exist many such disappointing horror literature adaptations as *The Shining.* But don't lose all hope, dear readers, as there are always exceptions. Within this section, you'll find three such examples—where screenwriters admirably succeeded not only in capturing the essence of their source material, but in many cases, improving upon it as well. The remaining three entries, in making changes arguably needed for holding film audiences' attention ... fare less well in translation.

So, sit back, dim the lights a bit and enjoy. And just ignore those pesky moans coming from under your bed and the scratching sounds you hear from inside the walls ...

BOO!

The stories and novels behind Classic Horror, Fantasy and Science Fiction Films

A Grave Undertaking:
The Body Snatcher (1945)

Long before celebrities such as Cher, Roseanne, Madonna, et al., made single-name recognition vogue, there were Bela and Boris. Although never billed solely as such, from the 1930s on, anyone even remotely familiar with horror films had only to see the names *Bela* and *Boris* to instantly conjure up images of the devilish duo. Both names were synonymous with the shivers, shrieks and frightfully good fun that awaited moviegoers within darkened, cavernous movie theaters.

Bela Lugosi and Boris Karloff both came to their horrific fame in 1931. Lugosi's *Dracula* and Karloff's *Frankenstein* were huge successes and subsequently cemented each in audiences' minds as "horror actors." Through the succeeding decades, each fought, with varying degrees of success, to escape the inevitable typecasting that can occur from association with a smash hit. Karloff overall fared better here, obtaining work on both stage and screen playing a wider variety of roles. But it was never long, however, before the actor would find himself back playing some variation on a mad scientist or some similarly sinister character. Lugosi, however, was not as fortunate. With few exceptions (such as a small role in Greta Garbo's *Ninotchka*, 1939), Bela was unable to escape from the shadow cast on his career by the very Count he made famous. The actor sadly found himself repeatedly cast in horror pictures of decidedly declining quality.

There is a long-standing debate (to put it *mildly*) as to who was the better actor. While I certainly have a *favorite* (Lugosi), I don't intend to delve into *this* minefield, sensitive among classic monster film fans who can be ... shall we say ... *very passionate* ... in defense of their chosen idol. And to what end? For really, "better" is subjective—is the better actor the one with the wider range, the one with the "chops?" Or is it the one for whom, regardless of the quality of film he finds himself in, always gives 100% and for whom we cannot take our eyes off of, because of the sheer magnetism of his personality? As long as fans of each actor exist, I suspect this debate will rage on.

It was inevitable that Hollywood would attempt to cash in on Bela and Boris' box-office success by pairing the duo together, primarily in horror films. And that's exactly what studios did, a total of seven times. Their first pairing, *The Black Cat* (1934), was a tremendous success, becoming one of the top-grossing films of the year for its studio, Universal. Both Lugosi and Karloff turn in fine performances, while Lugosi is notable here for the rare afforded opportunity at portraying a sympathetic protagonist. Audiences loved *The Black Cat* and demanded more. However, next up was *Gift of Gab* (1934), a forgettable comedy-cum-variety show oddity, where the pair's total screen time amounts

John Gray (Boris Karloff) in a tense moment with Dr. "Toddy" MacFarlane (Henry Daniell) as Joseph (Bela Lugosi) none-too-subtly eavesdrops.

to no more than two minutes at best. Their next horror venture, *The Raven* (1935), is a favorite among many Lugosi fans for his portrayal of Dr. Richard Vollin, who, by film's end, goes off the deep end in no small measure! It's Lugosi at his maniacal best. The underrated *Invisible Ray* (1936) showcases some of each actor's best work with both Karloff and Lugosi turning in restrained (yes, Lugosi reins it in!), nuanced performances. Three years later, Lugosi arguably steals the show in *Son of Frankenstein* (1939) as the broken-necked Ygor, who befriends (for less than altruistic reasons naturally) Karloff's Monster; Boris returns to the role here for a third and final time. *Black Friday* (1940), a gangster crime drama with the barest of science fiction overtones, is a disappointment for all concerned, not the least of which are viewers, for Lugosi and Karloff share no scenes. *You'll Find Out* (1940), a mystery comedy vehicle for Big Band conductor Kay Kyser, is enjoyable fluff, notable to monster fans for featuring not only Bela and Boris, but Peter Lorre as well. Lugosi and Karloff's last pairing would be RKO's *The Body Snatcher* (1945). Featuring one of Karloff's finest performances, the horror classic proved a box-office smash. However, the film ultimately represents a sad coda to the pair's decade-long collaboration, for both Lugosi's health and career were in significant decline at this point in time for the then 63-year-old actor.

The stories and novels behind Classic Horror, Fantasy and Science Fiction Films

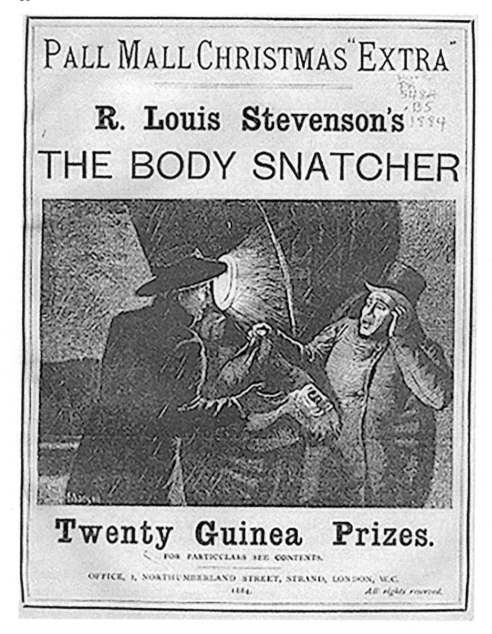

Robert Louis Stevenson's short story of the same name becomes the source material for *The Body Snatcher*. The tale first saw publication in the *Pall Mall* newspaper Christmas "Extra" edition in December of 1884.

Stevenson (1850-1894) was a Scottish writer, born in Edinburgh, Scotland. His fame stems primarily from three enduring writings: the adventure novels

IT CAME FROM ...

Kidnapped (1886) and *Treasure Island* (1883) and the horror novella *Strange Case of Dr. Jekyll and Mr. Hyde* (1886). All three efforts have enjoyed numerous cinematic adaptations. *Treasure Island* stands out in particular, not only for introducing Long John Silver as one of the most iconic characters in fictional literature, but for also serving (in your author's opinion) as the unofficial inspiration (via the Disney theme attraction) to the immensely popular Johnny Depp *Pirates of the Caribbean* contemporary film franchise.

Stevenson was sickly (or perhaps at times indulging in the family's tendency toward hypochondria) from early childhood, where travel to various foreign destinations for recuperative "holidays" was the frequent prescription. Resultantly, he acquired a taste for travel and adventure whose influences would later find their way into his writings.

Consumed from an early age with the desire to write, Stevenson nonetheless bowed to paternal pressure and in 1867 enrolled in Edinburgh University to pursue a curriculum in engineering. The plan was for Robert Louis to follow in the footsteps of several generations of Stevensons in the field. Always a poor (i.e. lazy) student, after a time it was clear that a future in engineering was not in the cards for the aspiring writer. A subsequent pursuit of a career in law met with comparable results, despite Stevenson successfully passing the Bar.

Through his early adult years of the 1870s, Stevenson wrote essays, articles, and volumes on travel which saw print in a number of varied publications. But none were of particular note, nor attracted any significant attention for the writer.

The year 1881 is significant in regard to two Stevenson works. He wrote "The Body Snatcher" as well as saw publication of what would become his magnum opus, *Treasure Island*. The tale was first serialized in *Young Folks* magazine (October 1881–January 1882), seeing publication in book form in 1883. The novel's enthusiastic reception gave Stevenson his much-desired first taste of critical and financial success.

The year 1886 saw the author surpass his previous success with publication of his remaining major works, *Kidnapped* and *Strange Case of Dr. Jekyll and Mr. Hyde*. The former, a historical adventure, is based, in part, on the real-life 18th-century "Appin murder," where James Stewart (no, not the actor!), one of the Jacobite Stewarts of Appin, was unjustly convicted and hanged as an accessory to the murder of Colin Campbell of Glenure. Stevenson attributes the inspiration for *Strange Case* to a dream, one fueled by the writer's long-held interest in the concept of multiple personalities. Both books were successes upon publication and *Strange Case*'s enduring legacy extends through over 100 stage or film adaptations, as well as coinage of the term "Jekyll and Hyde," in reference to anyone displaying conflicting personality traits.

Always in search of warmer climates, owing to his health, he resettled to the Samoan Islands in the South Pacific in 1890. For the short remainder of

Karloff received some of the best notices of his career for his portrayal of "body snatcher" John Gray.

his life there, Stevenson continued to write, but nothing came to match his previous successes. He died four years later in 1894 from a cerebral hemorrhage.

Stevenson wrote "The Body Snatcher" in the summer of 1881, while residing in a cottage in the rural burgh of Pitlochry, in northwestern Scotland. Inspiration undoubtedly came from the sensational real-life murders committed by William Burke and William Hare over the course of the year 1828 in Stevenson's own Edinburgh.

Edinburgh was a leading center of anatomical study in the early 19th century. Dissection classes, taught by resident doctors or independent lecturers, were among the most popular of subjects in the medical schools. Given the constant shortage of anatomical subjects (i.e. cadavers) and the fierce competition among the schools for such, doctors paid a respectable sum for bodies, asking few questions in return. This gave rise to collaborations with "resurrection men," or, grave robbers, who skirted the law to unearth freshly buried corpses to reap the resulting financial remuneration. Burke and Hare were opportunistic common laborers and residents of Edinburgh. Their first taste of the lucrative benefits surrounding the sale of dead bodies came when an elderly paying lodger in Hare's house suddenly died. The pair sold the body to Dr. Robert Knox, one of Edinburgh's leading anatomists/lecturers, who paid the men £7. Encouraged by such relatively easy money, the pair looked for other such opportunities. But due to the shortage of subjects who died of natural causes, Burke and Hare took to murder. Sixteen persons fell victim to Burke and Hare's greed over the course of 10 months, with Dr. Knox the sole beneficiary of the pair's "finds." Their favored technique for killing involved the laying on the chest of the victim, with the primary weight placed

IT CAME FROM ...

on the victim's rib cage to prevent the diaphragm/lungs from expanding, while simultaneously covering the victim's nose and mouth. This method of murder, coined "burking," left no visible signs of foul play upon a body, which undoubtedly contributed to the pair escaping suspicion for as long as they did.

Eventually caught, Burke was convicted and hanged when Hare received immunity for providing State's evidence. Dr. Knox, continuing to claim ignorance of the true source of Burke and Hare's "deliveries," barely escaped prosecution.

As revealed by Claire Harman, in her 2005 biography, *Myself & the Other Fellow: A Life of Robert Louis Stevenson*, upon completion of "The Body Snatcher," Stevenson deemed the tale a tad too horrific to be included in any collection and so was shelved. Stevenson would "resurrect" the story three years later for the 1884 "Christmas Edition" of the *Pall Mall Gazette*, when a previously submitted story fell short of the paper's wordage requirements. It would not be until 60 years later that Hollywood producer Val Lewton would "unearth" Stevenson's body-snatching tale for the big screen.

Val Lewton (1904-1951) was a Russian-American novelist, film producer and screenwriter, best known for a string of low-budget horror films he produced for RKO Pictures in the 1940s. Metro Goldwyn Meyer Studios hired the young Lewton upon his arrival in Hollywood in the early 1930s. Starting out as right-hand man to famed Hollywood producer David O. Selznick, Lewton worked in roles of escalating responsibility, including assistant, publicist, and story editor. In 1942, RKO Pictures hired Lewton to run their "B" movie unit, which was primarily dedicated to horror pictures. Over the next two years, Lewton produced a number of successfully profitable films: *Cat People* (1942), *I Walked with a Zombie* (1943) and *The Leopard Man* (1943). Pressured for a follow-up to *Cat People*, Lewton defied studio expectations and in 1944 delivered *The Curse of the Cat People*, a decidedly *non-horrific*, more child-like "fairy tale" picture instead. For his defiance, and the film's disappointing critical and commercial reception, executives at RKO brought in former Universal associate producer, Jack J. Gross, who as Executive Producer would watch over Lewton from that point.

One of Gross' earliest actions that year was to bring horror film icon Boris Karloff to RKO for a two-picture deal. Lewton was at first skeptical at being saddled with Karloff, but he was eventually won over by Karloff's charm, wit, and graciousness. From that point, Lewton searched for material suitable for Karloff's persona, hitting, at length, upon Stevenson's still relatively obscure "Body Snatcher" tale. After outlining key points in the story's favor to Gross (of greatest weight, most likely, the fact that the story was in the public domain and would not cost the studio to license), Lewton was granted approval to proceed.

Lewton brought in writer Philip MacDonald to write the screenplay after Gross rejected a number of the producer's other choices. MacDonald (1900-

1980) was an English novelist and screenwriter. He gained early fame in the 1920s for introducing the fictional character, Anthony Gethryn, an amateur detective, who would go on to appear in over a dozen such MacDonald's "whodunit" novels through the late 1950s. Arguably the most famous of these is *The List of Adrian Messenger* (1959), which was made into the successful 1963 film of the same name starring such big-name talent such as Tony Curtis, Frank Sinatra and Burt Lancaster; future *Patton* Oscar-winner George C. Scott portrayed Gethryn. MacDonald moved to Hollywood in 1931 and quickly became a sought-after talent, scripting a number of the Charlie Chan and Mr. Moto series movies. In 1939, famed director Alfred Hitchcock tapped MacDonald to adapt the Daphne du Maurier classic, *Rebecca*.

During the summer of 1944, MacDonald began work on *The Body Snatcher* draft, working closely with Lewton on story ideas. In addition to Karloff, Jack Gross and RKO studio heads were keen on adding another iconic horror actor to the film, former *Dracula* star Bela Lugosi. The execs envisioned the potential marquee value resulting from seeing the names "Karloff and Lugosi" together again, a pairing that had proved so successful for Universal the previous decade. Lewton voiced opposition to the idea but relented and worked with scripter MacDonald in creating the role of Joseph for Lugosi.

Lewton submitted a completed draft to the Breen Office, the body responsible for enforcing the Production Code, a series of guidelines that spelled out acceptable/unacceptable content for motion pictures produced in the United States. When the Breen Office deemed the script unacceptable, Lewton took to rewriting the screenplay, incorporating the Office's suggestions. Lewton made such substantial changes to MacDonald's script that the producer was required to share writing credit, which he did under the *nom de plume* of Carlos Keith.

Principal photography on *The Body Snatcher* commenced on October 25, 1944 and completed November 17. The film opened nationwide May 25 the following year to immediate critical and box-office success. The film became Lewton's biggest hit, with Karloff receiving some of the best reviews of his career.

Lewton would go on to produce only a handful of films post-*Snatcher* (most notably, *Bedlam*, another Karloff vehicle), but none approached the success of his grave-robbing tale. Lewton died from a heart attack in March of 1951, at the much-too-early age of 47. Philip MacDonald continued to write, penning scripts for television (*Alfred Hitchcock Presents*, *Perry Mason*), novelizations of films (*Forbidden Planet*), novels under both his real name and numerous pseudonyms, as well as short stories. MacDonald passed away in December of 1980.

Turning now to the comparison of Stevenson's story to its cinematic incarnation reveals great disparity. First, much like M.R. James' tale "Casting the Runes" (discussed in our *Night of the Demon* chapter), many consider "The Body Snatcher" a horror genre classic. I don't quite understand why. Unless,

like "Runes," its status stems primarily from the success of the film it spawned. For Stevenson's tale starts slowly, drags in its middle, and only in its final third or so generates any steam, finally whisking readers up, leading them to a mildly thrilling conclusion.

Characterization is an additional problem. The story is told third person from the viewpoint of a character we learn little about. One expects to become a bit more involved in the life of one's narrator, even in the short story form. But more problematic are our main characters, MacFarlane and Fettes. Here, both are vain, opportunistic, and unsympathetic. Readers find no reason to rally for them, and so, at story's conclusion, we don't really care what happens to them. An exception comes midway in the tale where a fairly absorbing "at the crossroads" moment occurs in the life of a then young Fettes. The lad is presented with an opportunity to turn from a life so inextricably tied to the ghoulish resurrection men, although said choice would most certainly spell trouble with the law and possibly death. Sadly however, under MacFarlane's reasoned logic to stay the course, Fettes ultimately crumbles, and in so doing, seals his pact with the devil. If only Stevenson had infused his story with additional character struggles. Lastly, the tale suffers for its lack of a clearly defined, engaging antagonist. Early on one suspects MacFarlane to be Fettes, but as the story progresses, Fettes quickly becomes as one with his mentor, both now forever linked in an unholy bond. Continuing our antagonistic search, John

Gray does not qualify, given that the totality of his involvement in the story spans a few mere paragraphs. (That Gray is the cause of the pair's undoing at tale's end is more a "gotcha!" moment than anything leading from the plot.) It's simple. A good story needs a good (and clear!) antagonist, and the lack here of one stifles any potential tension that naturally arises between two characters in conflict.

Characterization aside, the greatest problem with Stevenson's tale lies in the author's restraint. It's a bit ironic that, for a tale the author deemed "too horrific," in every instance where Stevenson has the opportunity to really grab readers by the throat and truly horrify ... he holds back. Much like a cruel adult who holds out a treat to a child only to yank it away at the very last second, Stevenson does so with potential shocks. Consider this ... Instead of providing readers with gruesome imagery surrounding dissection, the author merely relates, "The body of the unfortunate girl was duly dissected, and no one remarked or appeared to recognize her." To the extent that the horrors of body snatching are explored, nary a shudder is inspired from "The coffin was exhumed and broken open; the body inserted in the dripping sack and carried between them to the gig." Lastly, MacFarlane's fatal encounter with Gray, a riveting highlight of the film, here receives no elaboration. One day Gray is alive, taunting MacFarlane, and then is gone the following evening, becoming no more than yet another lifeless subject upon MacFarlane's dissection table. Much to readers' dismay, Stevenson time and again sterilizes rich opportunities for shivers. Only with the tale's final paragraph does the author deliver the goods:

> And as Fettes took the lamp his companion untied the fastenings of the sack and drew down the cover from the head. The light fell very clear upon the dark, well-molded features and smooth-shaven cheeks of a too familiar countenance, often beheld in dreams of both of these young men. A wild yell rang up into the night; each leaped from his own side into the roadway; the lamp fell, broke, and was extinguished; and the horse, terrified by this unusual commotion, bounded and went off toward Edinburgh at a gallop, bearing along with it, sole occupant of the gig, the body of the dead and long-dissected Gray.

However, for readers, this comes as too little, too late.

Moving to the film, as discussed in another chapter, an inherent challenge of adapting a short story to film is how to expand enough upon the sparse material to fill a feature-film screen time, all the while remaining true to the spirit of your source. Sometimes the results are abject failures (*The Lawnmower Man*,

Gray inquires after potential fares with the tavern keeper.

1992, based on the Stephen King short story), but there are times, as in the case of *The Body Snatcher*, where the result is utterly sublime. In developing new characters and subplots not found in Stevenson's story, MacDonald creates an extended prologue storyline that seamlessly progresses until it at last dovetails with Stevenson's story near film's end. MacDonald's additions feel germane to the unfolding story and keep with the spirit of Stevenson's tale. The only exception here involves Lugosi's Joseph character—touched on in more detail later.

Foremost of these changes: the substantial expansion of the minor character of cabman Gray from Stevenson's tale into the cinematic Gray to fit Karloff's starring turn. Here, we have the fully realized antagonist missing from the short story. Karloff's Gray proves a superb foil against MacFarlane, whose subsequent encounters provide escalating tension and malevolence, which more logically lead to their fatal confrontation. The scripters also deliver a more fully developed "Toddy" MacFarlane, who, through the gain of a wife and more paternal stance toward Fettes, becomes infinitely more sympathetic. Lastly, our cinematic Fettes transforms into a younger, tad naïve, but more relatable character. This is important in that while perhaps a short story can get

Cabman Gray poses with crippled Georgina Marsh (Sharyn Moffett).

away without one truly sympathetic character, a film does not have this luxury. We must be able to feel for, root for, *someone*. Fettes (and to a lesser degree Mac-Farlane's wife) serves as the film's moral compass, the person who must walk the straight path. Fettes here endures the same "at the crossroads" moment as his literary counterpart, but, while he still aligns himself with MacFarlane on one last "body snatch," Fettes has *not* signed over his soul to the devil. Viewers feel that there is still "good" in the lad, and that, given MacFarlane's death, the youth will correct the course of his life.

Where the film builds from ideas contained within Stevenson's story, in every case it surpasses its source. This is attributable for two reasons. First, given the luxury afforded the film to expand upon background and context, the film brings to each scene a fuller, more emotional experience for viewers. Secondly, as previously discussed, while Stevenson diluted the impact of potentially horrific scenes by holding back, the film *doesn't* shy away from confronting viewers with the ghoulish goings-on. *The Body Snatcher* is meant to be a horror film and thankfully both screenwriter and director deliver. We experience first-hand from Fettes' perspective the sordid details surrounding "deliveries" from resurrection man John Gray; grave digging is depicted as the arduous, secretive and creepy task it is; a superbly chilling scene shows how Gray murderously improvises to provide specimens for the eager doctors. Lastly, the film goes *all* out in depicting the explosive, final confrontation between MacFarlane and Gray.

IT CAME FROM ...

Much credit is due to scripters MacDonald and Lewton for taking the salvageable aspects from a competent-at-best short story and crafting a superb script. Combined with director Wise's sublime work, *The Body Snatcher* is one of the finest horror films to come out of the 1940s (and in this author's opinion, of all time). Its magnificent chills and shudders come through suggestion and subtlety rather than from the too-easy path of overt depictions of violence and gore. Today's filmmakers could learn much from studying this film.

Postscript: I feel the need to briefly touch on what is sure to be a sensitive subject among Lugosi fans: examining Bela's role and performance in the film. Doing so is a difficult challenge, for, in the need to be objective, some of my opinions go against the collective consensus surrounding the actor and this role. But, let's begin.

First, as we learn in Gregory Mank's 2009 book, *Bela Lugosi and Boris Karloff: The Expanded Story of a Haunted Collaboration*, producer Val Lewton was opposed to casting Lugosi in the film. While Lewton initially (and rightly) assumed that Bela would not be up to the challenge from an acting perspective, the producer could not have guessed at the time just how right he would be. For the actor— gaunt, stoop-shouldered and not looking well due to illness—kept blowing takes, unable to remember his lines. For fans of the actor, it's painful to watch him in his few scenes, shuffling slowly and looking unwell; nothing at all like the vibrant, commanding presence of Count Dracula that we remember.

But, as troublesome as Lugosi, the actor, proved to be for the picture, the greater issue lies with his character Joseph. To be blunt, the character is super-fluous. Joseph exists almost as if written into the script as an afterthought, to satisfy some demand of management to shoehorn an actor into the film. Oh, wait. That's exactly what happened. Admittedly, to viewers who don't know the history of the film's production and the reason for Lugosi's insertion, this point is moot. To most, Joseph is nothing more than a minor character, no more or less. But the fact remains that you could remove Joseph from the film with little im-pact. To the argument that Joseph's death provides the catalyst for MacFarlane to finally confront his demon, Gray—to this I simply say that said impetus could have been handled any number of other ways *not* involving Joseph.

Lastly, and herein I truly risk the wrath of Lugosiphiles everywhere (but remember that I am one also!), in all honesty, Bela brings little to his role. Many fans look to his final scene with Karloff and promote his performance here as some of his finest work. In truth, such positive spin is most likely borne of wistful nostalgia and fondness for the actor—as well as this being the final pairing of Lugosi/Karloff—than objective review. It pains me to say it, but any other actor could have done as well in the role. But this point is also moot, as the film should have excised Joseph. Ideally, only characters germane to the story should exist in a film. Adding superfluous characters simply to fulfill some whim (e.g. box-office) cuts away from the heart of good storytelling.

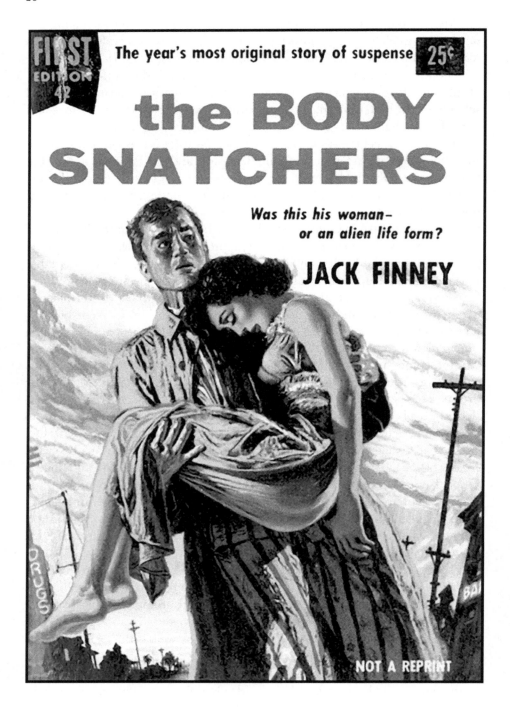

FIRST EDITION 42

The year's most original story of suspense   **25¢**

the BODY SNATCHERS

Was this his woman—
or an alien life form?

JACK FINNEY

NOT A REPRINT

IT CAME FROM …

The Face Isn't Finished:
Invasion of the Body Snatchers (1956)

"There's no emotion—none—just the pretense of it. The words, gestures, the tone of voice, everything else are the same—but not the feeling. He isn't my Uncle Ira." —*Wilma Lentz,* The Body Snatchers.

The loss of one's self, one's identity, everything that comprises who we are as individuals—not just our physical bodies, but our emotions, desires, passions, imagination, our *essence*—is a terrifying concept. Death, of course, is the ultimate loss—the universal absolute. Some fight the inevitable, tooth-and-nail, while some are gracefully accepting; the remainder of us fall somewhere in between. But ultimately, no one escapes his/her encounter with the Grim Reaper. Equally terrifying, to some more so, is a form of "living death:" the erosion of one's mental faculties while still alive. Said degeneration can occur through such avenues as Alzheimer's disease and dementia. Agonizing for all concerned, family and friends helplessly watch as these diseases rob vibrant loved ones of their core humanity. Left behind is little more than an empty vessel, now devoid of what they had once been ... a living zombie, of sorts. The only saving grace of such insidious afflictions is there comes a point where the victim mercifully becomes no longer aware of what is occurring.

This concept of stolen humanity is horrifying enough when occurring naturally. Now, imagine a scenario where something of unnatural origin—oh, let's say an otherworldly alien—involuntarily robs you of your individuality and essence. Compound this horror further with the loss of your physical body, destroyed once duplicated, by aforementioned alien, thus easing its "recruitment" of family and friends in order to exponentially perpetuate an invasion no one suspects. Frightening, no? Writer Jack Finney imagined such a scenario, and his resulting tale, "The Body Snatchers," first saw publication in 1954, serialized in *Collier's*. Hollywood quickly seized on the hot property and released *Invasion of the Body Snatchers* a mere two years later. The film is the first of four (to date) major cinematic adaptations of Finney's tale.

Jack Finney (1911-1995) was born in Milwaukee, Wisconsin. After graduating from Knox College, he moved to New York City and worked for many years as an advertising copywriter. He married Marguerite Guest in 1949 and they had two children. In the early 1950s, Finney and his family moved to Mill Valley, California, a small city a short distance north of San Francisco. Mill Valley would shortly become the inspiration for Santa Mira, the fictional locale where much of the setting for *Body Snatchers* takes place.

Finney's writing career began in the 1940s, writing short stories and serials to such varied magazines as *Collier's, Cosmopolitan, Good Housekeeping*, the *Saturday*

Evening Post, and *Ellery Queen's Mystery Magazine*. Finney's writing during this period was most frequently within the thriller and light fantasy/science fiction genres. Finney later turned his hand toward writing novels when, during the 1950s there came a reduced demand for short stories in the magazine market. His first novel, *5 Against the House*, which tells the story of several college students who set about an attempt to rob a nightclub in Reno, was published in 1954.

Later that year, Finney wrote the story that would set him upon the path of success and later acclaim. *Collier's* magazine published *The Body Snatchers* as a three-part serial in late 1954. Finney shortly thereafter revised and expanded the material, which subsequently saw publication as a Dell paperback the following year. While popular with readers, the tale received a less than welcome reception from critics of the time. The late science fiction writer, Damon Knight, was particularly critical. Writing a rather acerbic review in *Original Science Fiction Stories* magazine (Sept. 1955) Knight summed up the consensus of many science fiction critics of the time, faulting the tale's scientific plausibility.

Finney granted few interviews throughout his life. As such, little is known regarding the author, let alone insights into his fictional works. However, in personal correspondence to famed horror author Stephen King in 1979 (subsequently published in King's non-fiction classic *Danse Macabre*), Finney wrote of his remembrances on the origin of his famous pod tale:

> The book ... was written in the early 1950s, and I don't really remember a lot about it. I do recall that I simply felt in the mood to write something about a strange event or a series of them in a small town; something inexplicable. And that my first thought was that a dog would be injured or killed by a car, and it would be discovered that a part of the animal's skeleton was of stainless steel; bone and steel intermingled, that is, a thread of steel running into bone and bone into steel, so that it was clear the two had grown together. But this idea led to nothing in my mind ... I remember that I wrote the first chapter pretty much as it appeared, if I am recalling correctly, in which people complained that someone close to them was in actuality an imposter. But I didn't know where this was to lead, either. However, during the course of fooling around with this, trying to make it work out, I came across a reputable scientific theory that objects might in fact be pushed through space by the pressure of light, and that dormant life of some sort might conceivably drift through space ... and this eventually worked the book out.

IT CAME FROM ...

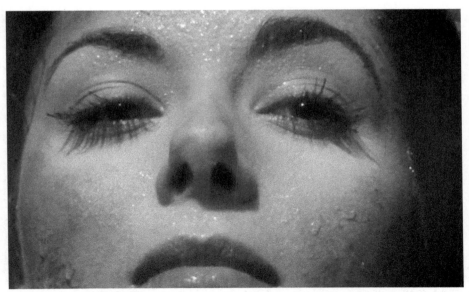

Becky's (Dana Wynter) blank gaze signifies that she has fallen asleep and become a "pod person."

Finney continued to enjoy success as a novelist in the years succeeding *Body Snatchers*. He enjoyed the greatest commercial and critical success of his career in 1970 with the publication of *Time and Again*, a fantasy novel involving self-induced time travel. (Of note: fantasy novelist Richard Matheson's *Bid Time Return*, published five years later in 1975 and made into the 1980 film *Somewhere in Time*, starring Christopher Reeve and Jane Seymour, bears at times a too uncanny similarity in plot.)

In 1954, producer Walter Wanger, seeing the cinematic potential of Finney's tale, pursued 'snatching' up the story's film rights. Upon their acquisition, as well as a deal with Allied Artists studio to produce, Wanger then turned to director Don Siegel to helm the project. Siegel had previously directed Wanger's controversial (but critically acclaimed) *Riot in Cell Block 11* earlier that same year. After signing on to direct, Siegel suggested Daniel Mainwaring, whom Siegel had previously worked with on several films, to pen the screenplay.

Home Mainwaring (1902-1977) was born in Oakland, CA, and attended Fresno College, where he began his professional career as a journalist. Later, he would ply his writing talents in such capacities as a crime reporter for the *Los Angeles Examiner* newspaper, in the publicity departments for the Warner Bros. and RKO film studios, and as a novelist. He published his first novel, the mainstream drama *One Against the Earth*, in 1933. Upon its poor reception, Mainwaring turned to writing within the detective/mystery genre where, for the next decade, he enjoyed considerably greater success. He wrote his first produced screenplay in 1943 for the ultra-low budget film, *Secrets of the Under-*

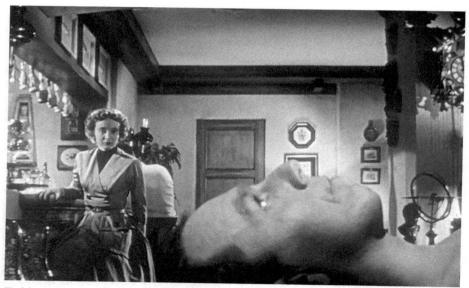

Teddy Belicec (Carolyn Jones) watches in terror as husband Jack Belicec (King Donovan) is replaced by alien beings.

ground. Solely on the basis of this film, the producing duo of William Pine and William Thomas signed Mainwaring to a six-picture deal in 1945. The following year he published his final novel, *Build My Gallows High*, which became a critical and commercial success. Assigned by RKO to adapt his own novel to the screen, *Gallows* became the film noir classic, *Out of the Past* (1947), starring Robert Mitchum. The success of this film cemented Mainwaring's standing as a screenwriter of considerable measure. As noted, Mainwaring paired with Siegel for several films before joining the *Body Snatchers* project. After *Invasion*, Mainwaring continued to enjoy a successful career in film, while simultaneously contributing his talents to the still-then burgeoning medium of television, eventually contributing to such popular shows as *Adventures in Paradise*, *Mannix*, and *The Wild Wild West*.

Mainwaring commenced his work on the *Body Snatchers* screenplay sometime in January of 1955 and quickly turned out a first draft in early February (this being less than a mere two months after the last installment of Finney's serial appeared in *Collier's*!). A month or so of revisions took place, with scripter Richard Collins brought in to assist with the rewrites. The final revised shooting script bears the date of March 17, 1955.

Production commenced on March 23, 1955. Location shooting took place primarily in Sierra Madre, California, northeast of Los Angeles, while the chase and cave sequences took place in the hills of Bronson Canyon. Principal photography completed in a rapid but smooth 23 days.

If only things had gone as smoothly for the film in post-production. A series of previews, held throughout the summer of 1955, produced increasingly dour results. The unfavorable feedback received from participants, as well as walk outs during the screenings, made studio executives rightfully nervous. Additionally, audience laughter during previews only heightened the executives' discomfort; for the powers-that-be held the firm belief that humor had no place in a horror picture. The most significant consequence from these disturbing results came from the studio heads' insistence on making numerous changes to the film. Chief among these: cuts to tighten and clarify the story, the removal of all humor, and—depending on which side of the debate you stand—the egregious insertion of ongoing narration and a framing story in which Miles relates his tale in flashback to a psychiatrist. Siegel and Mainwaring vehemently argued against these changes, insisting that their original vision for the project would be severely compromised. When their arguments fell on deaf ears, producer Wanger wisely convinced the pair that, as the edits would be made with or without their cooperation, it was in their best interests to handle the studio's demands. And so, with reluctance on everyone's part, Mainwaring scripted new scenes and—fortuitously able to bring McCarthy back for a few days' work—Siegel filmed the framing story in mid-September of 1955. The altered film at last premiered in the United States in February of 1956.

Note: I cannot resist the need to address one of the long-standing complaints voiced by the major players involved in the making of the picture—that of the humor contained in the initial print of the film that studio executives insisted be removed, but for which Siegel and Mainwaring steadfastly argued was essential to the story. Siegel related many times over the years his original vision for *Invasion*: that until the mid-film reveal of the true horror of the pods, the audience was to treat as ludicrous the very idea of an alien life-form with the ability to replicate itself into another living organism. Siegel also believed that the removal of said humor compromised this intended effect. Having read the shooting script, I'm baffled. First, some of the "humorous" (reason for quotes will be obvious shortly) lines in question survived into the finished film. Second, and more significantly, of those cut lines: a) there were not *that* many, and b) unless the bar for what defined humor was considerably lower in the 1950s, I don't see what Mainwaring, Siegel, and others are complaining about. The cut lines are only mildly amusing and *might* have inspired a smirk, or perhaps even an occasional chuckle, at best. But to think that these lines actually generated anything resembling genuine laughter to preview audiences beggars belief. In reading the screenplay, the humorous lines add little; they certainly don't add the supposed degree of ludicrousness to the idea of alien pods that Siegel suggested. In viewing the *film*, the exclusions are no loss. It is my opinion that perhaps in their (deservedly so) indignation over studio-imposed changes, Siegel and Mainwaring overly inflated the importance of these "humorous" lines.

While Finney's *Body Snatchers* is not a literary masterwork by any stretch, it is undeserving of the critical stones cast upon it by various reviewers over the decades (yes, we're talking about *you*, Mr. Knight). There is a place within science fiction, or any literary genre for that matter, for highbrow, intellectual tales. There is also a place for stories whose only ambition, as Finney often regarded *Body Snatchers*, may be that of entertaining its audience. If I wanted a "hard" science fiction novel, I would turn to Arthur C. Clarke, Ben Bova, and others. I certainly wouldn't look down my nose at any author such as Finney, who simply wanted to write an exciting, can't-put-it-down, thrilling tale. Whether the novel's scientific posits stand up under scrutiny is immaterial—we're reading Finney for entertainment, not a science lesson.

Much of *Body Snatchers'* success lies in Finney deftly keeping readers alternating between belief and doubt. For until the first true, beyond-a-doubt reveal just short of the novel's halfway point—that of the foursome's discovery of the seed pods developing into human form—readers are not 100% convinced that what is happening is other-worldly. Finney presents readers, through the character of psychiatrist-cum-pod person Manny Kaufmann, with explanations reasoned enough that we come to harbor doubts that what has come before may indeed be nothing more than mass-produced hallucinations! Previously, couldn't the body on the Balicecs' pool table just possibly *be* a dead body? And in his heightened, emotional state, did Miles *really* see a replica of Becky in her father's dark basement? Skillful work here by Finney.

However, upon said discovery of the four developing seedpods, all doubts about what is really happening in Santa Mira shatter, and the story's pace then kicks into high gear toward its conclusion. But sadly, it is here at the novel's denouement that the story comes crashing down like a house of cards. For, from out of left field, Finney throws readers for a loop with … a happy ending. Now, happy endings are, of themselves, not a bad thing in a science fiction novel, but this one ruins *Body Snatchers* for being so logically *wrong* and going against everything that has come before. Let us quickly recap: Becky and Miles stumble upon a crop of seedpods growing in a farm field. He then makes one final, defiant stand by setting the pods ablaze. As a result of this single action, the pods—right then and there, mind you—abandon their entire quest to take over the planet. In the space of an instant, the seed pods in the field break from their roots and rise into the nighttime sky, departing Earth forever, while the human pod people who had pursued Miles and Becky simply turn away and return to Santa Mira to live out the remainder of their too-short lives. Really? *Everything* had been going the pods' way: they had duplicated the bodies of just about every resident of Santa Mira and were well on their way to expanding their sphere of domination into neighboring towns. But because of the continued resistance of *four* humans (who would inevitably *have* to succumb to sleep) and a few scorched seedpods, our insidious antagonists … just give up. Finney's 180-degree turn of logic here is just too much to accept and sours the goodwill generated up to that point as a result.

IT CAME FROM …

One of the alien seedpods transforming in the greenhouse. For 1956 and a lower-budget production, the pods look effectively otherworldly sinister.

By comparison, Siegel's film—and let us ignore the framing story for the moment as that was not part of the filmmakers' original vision—is a very faithful adaption. In fact, only near film's end, when Miles and Becky escape their pod captors and flee into the hills of Santa Mira, do book and film diverge significantly. Happily, the film avoids Finney's regrettable upbeat ending, and in this respect is more satisfying than the novel and the only example of where the film actually improves upon its source. Throw in the framing story and the ending is still not exactly upbeat—the pods retain the upper hand for the moment, merely now their presence acknowledged and action initiated to stop them. Regardless, either ending satisfies more than Finney's, as both remain truer to what has come before.

While the film improves upon the novel with regard to its conclusion, Siegel's picture fails its source overall in one important aspect. Because the film's running time clocks in under 90 minutes, it's a bare-boned, stripped-down-to-the-studs story unfolding. In a way, the film becomes an in-progress "pod." A replication (of Finney's novel) is taking place, but Jack Belicec's reference to the two die-pressings that occur in the making of a medallion is appropriate here:

> Well, usually a medallion shows a face. And when you look at it after die number one, the face isn't *finished*. It's all there, all right, but the details that give it character aren't.

These lines perfectly highlight the film's prime shortcoming. The novel is *there*, all right, but so many of the fine and important details that make

Exhausted Miles (Kevin McCarthy) and Becky (Dana Wynter) huddle close in a cave; a momentary respite from the pursuing townspeople.

Finney's tale a rich, terrifying experience are *not*. Two examples illustrate the point.

The first entails character development and involves our two main protagonists, Miles and Becky. There is only the briefest hint in the film that there is some history behind their relationship. And because they're both involved from the get-go in the mystery surrounding Santa Mira, there's little time for Miles and Becky's relationship to develop into anything beyond superfluous. Compare this to the novel, where Finney spends considerable time not only developing each character individually, but also with rekindling their past relationship. We learn of each's past failed marriages, as well as Miles' apprehension of growing closer to Becky for fear of failing in yet another relationship. This background is not only touchingly personal but also aids in endearing the pair to readers in a way the film never achieves. And because of this failing, when Becky "turns" near film's end, viewers are not the least bit emotionally bothered.

Our second example involves the origin and legacy of the pods. In the film, the horror of the pods lies in their duplication and replacement of humans. But more so, upon completion of the process, while the body and its memories remain, gone are the emotions, the true *essence* of what makes us who we are. Terrifying? Certainly. But what the film leaves out to its regret is pod back-story. Pod

IT CAME FROM …

duplication is not a perfect process, for once pods reproduce, they have a limited lifespan of roughly five years upon replication of the life form. Thus, once they've taken over an entire world and lived out their short lives, said planet, over time, becomes dead and barren—the path upon which our Earth is currently traveling. The novel also chillingly suggests that Earth is not the first planet in our solar system that the pods have visited. For both the Earth's moon and the planet Mars were not always the lifeless orbs they are today. Now this is truly terrifying. It's regretful that Siegel and company couldn't spare an additional minute or so of film time to bring in this additional detail in order to allow audiences to appreciate the full, terrifying threat that the pods represent.

Let us now consider three aspects of the film that, despite having no basis within the source material, deserve mention for being significant detriments.

First, there is simply no avoiding discussion of the film's studio-imposed framing story during any debate surrounding Siegel's film. Now, there is nothing *technically* wrong with the frame—it's admittedly a well-executed sequence. The opening segment certainly gets viewers' adrenaline pumping from its first minutes, while the closing segment provides viewers with the needed glimmer of hope. But, put *together*, the framing story then feels like exactly what it is—a pair of disjointed bookends. Even if a viewer didn't have a clue coming in that it was a sequence shot and tacked on after the fact, one still comes away with a sense of it feeling out of place, for it feels forced and just … doesn't fit well. Additionally, this framing story alerts viewers from its opening seconds that something is amiss. This is diametrically at odds with Finney and Mainwaring's preferred concept, in which readers are *slowly* strung along and allowed to be kept in doubt, regarding events, until well along into the story.

A second, considerable detriment to some (including myself) involves Becky's transformation into a pod person near film's conclusion. Quick recap: Miles and Becky, outwitting the pursuing Santa Mira populace, hide in a cave. Miles, hearing music, goes to investigate, leaving Becky alone. When Miles returns—in what could only have been a matter of minutes—he discovers that his beloved Becky has transformed into a pod person. And with this "reveal," the film logically implodes (in much the same fashion as Finney's happy ending collapses his novel), for it comes out of the blue and is completely illogical for having no precedent. Consider: there were no seedpods in the cave and Becky could have nodded off for only the few minutes that Miles was away. According to what has come before, a transformation takes much longer. Some viewers can get beyond this major glitch in logic, but *this* viewer, who appreciates at least a *small* semblance of continuity of logic in a film, cannot. The remainder of the film is a blur, given my inability to concentrate for the insistent pondering of "How could she have … " Belaboring this point just a *bit* further, some defenders of the film over the years have posited that perhaps there existed a scene, subsequently cut, where one of the Santa Mira townspeople did indeed

leave a seedpod behind in the cave during their search. To this, I offer: 1) the townspeoples' search for Miles and Becky was fruitless, so why would they leave behind a seedpod, 2) watch the film closely: the pursuit of our pair begins back in the town of Santa Mira, then up one of the longest flight of stairs ever seen, followed by running up, down, and across numerous steep hills before arriving at the cave. Who could do all that while carrying a huge seedpod? And 3) in the shooting script, there are no suggestions at how Becky comes to be a pod—there exist no scenes of seed pods being hidden, of her falling asleep near a seedpod, etc. Defenders: there is no *plausible* explanation.

Lastly, we earlier discussed Siegel and Mainwaring's lament of the excised *intended* humor contained in the original version of the film. Perhaps the pair should have been more concerned over what was perhaps *unintended* laughter from preview attendees (for which one cannot lay blame at studio executives). Three such examples quickly come to mind. First, the highway scene near film's end where McCarthy's face, seen in extreme close-up, hysterically shouts into the camera, "They're here already! You're next!" Then, it's the highway scene again, as Miles hysterically pinwheels from the front to back of the truck containing seed pods—carefully watch McCarthy's face here to capture the full comicality of what I'm talking about. Lastly, we have the cave scene, when Miles realizes Becky's transformation to a pod person. Here, McCarthy, in voice-over narration (accompanied by the actor's face completely filling the screen with an embarrassingly over-the-top look of horror), proclaims, "I've

IT CAME FROM ...

been afraid a lot of times in my life, but I didn't know the real meaning of fear until … until I kissed Becky." These three scenes today never fail to inspire bursts of laughter from whatever audience for with I am viewing the film. I cannot believe that audiences in 1956 could not have had the same reaction.

All considered, novel and film are infinitely more similar than not. Remove the film's framing story and the film practically mirrors its source until about the final twenty minutes. Each in its own right is an exciting, taut, competently executed roller-coaster ride until each dampens the overall experience for its audience, done in by its own Achilles heel.

Before we conclude, I'd like to briefly touch upon the three other major cinematic adaptations of Finney's novel. (Warning: spoilers throughout.)

Director Philip Kaufman had a modest hit in 1978 with his *Invasion of the Body Snatchers*. Starring Donald Sutherland and Brooke Adams, the film remains faithful overall to its source material, while updating the location to present-day San Francisco. Unlike the 1956 original, Kaufman provides a downbeat ending, with the pods seemingly victorious in their efforts to take over the city, the first step in their plan for worldwide domination. Kaufman's film contains many highlights, foremost among them the opening sequence, which should be mandatory viewing in film schools to instruct budding directors and screenwriters on the "*show* them, don't *tell* them" truism. For in this two-minute sequence, Kaufman supplies audiences with all needed back-story regarding the pods and how they arrived on Earth, without the use of a *single word* of dialogue. It's simply brilliant.

In 1993, director Abel Ferrara brought us *Body Snatchers*, a competently told, if ultimately unremarkable adaptation. The locale here, updated to a U.S. military base, is actually, a brilliant stroke—for what better place for emotionless, of-one-mind pods to begin a takeover than within the U.S. military, which systematically crushes emotion and independent thinking? Who could spot a pod person here? Ferrara does manage one genuinely horrific moment, however, amidst the gunfire and chase sequences. When pod person Carol Malone (Meg Tilly), delivers the line, "Where you gonna go, where you gonna run, where you gonna hide? Nowhere … 'cause there's no one like you left," hairs stand at attention on the back of this viewer's neck.

Lastly, we have *The Invasion* (2007), directed by Oliver Hirschbiegel and starring Nicole Kidman and Daniel Craig. The only takeaway after viewing this film is the resulting depression from pondering how much money the actors received to appear in this dreck. The less said here the better. All you really need to know is that here the threat initiates not through seedpods but by an alien virus. And transmission of said virus by those infected is through … ready for this? … regurgitation—either onto an intended victim's face (preferably directly into their mouths) or slipped into the unsuspecting victim's beverage.

Yes, really.

Do You Believe in Magic?
Night of the Demon (1957)

Those of a scientific bent routinely dismiss the supernatural and existence of any "things that go bump in the night" ... ghosts, ghouls, vampires and werewolves? Pffft! On the flip side, true believers of such phenomenon cannot be dissuaded otherwise, regardless of provided evidence. This conflict of beliefs has raged probably for millennia. *Night of the Demon* is an engrossing tale whose primary theme touches upon this age-old debate. The film's premise surrounds an American scientist heading to England to participate in a paranormal psychology convention whose main function lies in exposing a local devil cult. Needless to say, the initially skeptical scientist slowly becomes a believer as he finds himself swept up in a succession of mysterious and frightening experiences for which he no longer has easy explanations. His previously unshakable confidence in "science" grows increasingly ... shakable. The film, now considered a classic of supernatural horror, is based on the short story "Casting the Runes," by Montague Rhodes (M.R.) James.

M.R. James (1862–1936) was a British scholar, antiquarian (one interested in, or collector of, items from the period of history before the Middle Ages), and writer of distinction, credited as the originator of the "antiquarian ghost story." He is considered one of the masters of the modern English ghost story, having helped to update the genre by replacing clichéd "fog-swept moat" type components of the form with more realistic and contemporary settings. James mined his background as both researcher and antiquarian to bring a believable realism to his tales.

James' ghost stories are viewed as exemplary examples of the technique of implying the horror—hinting and suggesting at the supernatural events and letting readers' imaginations arrive at far more terrifying scenarios than any explicit depictions could accomplish. In a foreword to the anthology, *Ghosts and Marvels,* James outlines this approach to his writing:

> Two ingredients most valuable in the concocting of a ghost story are, to me, the atmosphere and the nicely managed crescendo ... Let us, then, be introduced to the actors in a placid way; let us see them going about their ordinary business, undisturbed by forebodings, pleased with their surroundings; and into this calm environment let the ominous thing put out its head, unobtrusively at first, and then more insistently, until it holds the stage.

IT CAME FROM ...

James further opined on his desired disposition of said ghosts:

> Another requisite, in my opinion, is that the ghost should be malevolent or odious: Amiable and helpful apparitions are all very well in fairy tales or in local legends, but I have no use for them in a fictitious ghost story.

James' stories were written as "holiday entertainments"—for dramatic oral presentations at annual Christmas gatherings of friends and colleagues. In 1904, a number of these stories were collected and published for the first time in *Ghost Stories of an Antiquary*. "Casting the Runes" was first published in a subsequent anthology, *More Ghost Stories of an Antiquary* (1911).

Little is known surrounding James' personal thoughts on the inspiration for "Runes." The most notable aspect concerning the story's origins revolves around the continued put forth (but to this day unsubstantiated), belief that James based the story's antagonist on the controversial, contemporary figure, Aleister Crowley (1875–1947). Crowley, a British writer and dabbler in occultism and magic, came to be known as the "wickedest man in the world" for his hedonistic lifestyle that flouted many of the moral values of the day. Crowley founded the religion of Thelema, more a spiritual philosophy whose primary tenet is to "Do what thou wilt shall be the whole of the Law." Although he

wrote extensively on a variety of subjects, Crowley's fame today stems primarily from authoring *The Book of the Law*, the "bible" of Thelema.

"Runes," arguably James' best-known work owing to its cinematic incarnation, has enjoyed memorable adaptations in other mediums. The story was adapted for radio presentation in 1947 on the CBS radio series *Escape*. Another radio appearance occurred with a 1974 *CBS Radio Mystery Theater* updated adaptation, titled "I Warn You Three Times." Britain produced notable television presentations including an episode of the *ITV Playhouse* series, as well as a contemporary version by Yorkshire Television, both in 1979. The *film* itself served as inspiration to director Sam Raimi's *Drag Me to Hell* (2009), with plot points involving an item (here, a button) passed to the cursed victim, escalating incidents involving a demon, as well as a set amount of time allotted before the demon's ultimate dispatch of said victim.

IT CAME FROM ...

Seeing the cinematic potential in the story, British screenwriter Charles Bennett (1899-1995) purchased the rights to "Runes" from the James estate and wrote a screenplay, a supernatural thriller keeping very much in the "spirit" (so to speak) of the short story. Bennett had collaborated as screenwriter with Alfred Hitchcock during the 1930s on several of the director's films: *The Man Who Knew Too Much* (1934), *The 39 Steps* (1935), *Secret Agent* (1936), *Sabotage* (1936), and *Young and Innocent* (1937). Bennett followed Hitchcock to America for their last collaboration, *Foreign Correspondent* (1940). Following his association with the famed director, Bennett remained in America where he continued to author screenplays, direct two films, and later became involved in writing for such television series as *The Wild Wild West*, *Land of the Giants* and *Voyage to the Bottom of the Sea*.

Bennett had hoped to direct his own screenplay, but due to an unfortunate case of bad timing, this was not to be. In the biography, *Hitchcock's Partner in Suspense: The Life of Screenwriter Charles Bennett*, Bennett's son, John Charles, reveals his father's memory on this incident:

> On the day I was leaving England to return to the States, a Mr. Hal E. Chester was waiting in the foyer of my residence at Thirty-Nine Hill Street off Berkeley Square. He said, "Look, I can set this picture up with Columbia Pictures. Will you just give me your signature now?" Very tired, I signed the option agreement, and then boarded the plane. Two days later I learned that RKO had given the okay for my screenplay to be shot, exactly as I wanted to make it, and I would be directing my own screenplay. But it was too late: I'd signed this paper on the way out to my plane. I'd signed it away.

Hal E. Chester (1921-2012; as "Hally" Chester) was a child actor before beginning his career as a producer of the series of "Joe Palooka" films in the 1940s. Chester first dipped his producing toe into the waters of monster films with the semi-classic, *The Beast From 20,000 Fathoms* (1953), based on the short story, "The Foghorn," written by acclaimed fantasy and science fiction writer Ray Bradbury.

Chester's choice for director, Jacques Tourneur (1904-1977), is famed for his work in directing a series of low-budget, but effective, horror films in the 1940s for producer Val Lewton, including *Cat People* (1942), *I Walked With a Zombie*, and *The Leopard Man* (both 1943). Tourneur's work on these films, admired for their style, relied more on atmosphere and the subtle suggestion of his cinematic horrors rather than any overt, graphic depiction. This stylistic preference would find Tourneur siding with Bennett in the screenwriter's upcoming dealings with Chester.

Bennett's initial ill-fated encounter with Chester was just the beginning of what would become a strained and combative relationship that would continue throughout the film's production and beyond. For Chester, not content to merely take a producer's credit on the film, took liberties with rewrites to Bennett's script. Again from Bennett's biography, we learn from the screenwriter:

> I had to sit back and watch Chester destroy my picture, rewriting it and taking a screenwriter credit ... here, as elsewhere, it should have read "Screenplay by Charles Bennett, destroyed by another writer!" Hal Chester cut many of the better things out of the picture for the sake of making it cheaply, and the eventual result was a pale shadow of what it should have been.

The most egregious change to Bennett's script came after principal photography on the film had completed. The producer insisted—over the vehement objections of both Bennett and Tourneur—on bookending the film with additional scenes depicting the titular demon. Gone was Bennett's subtle supernatural thriller that allowed audiences to determine whether the onscreen horrors were real or imagined. "The moviemakers added a visible monster, which made me very angry," stated Bennett in his biography. "I had intended a psychological thriller. The monster should have been any pursuing horror that an audience could conjure in its mind. And Karswell (the villain) would throw himself in front of a train in sheer panic and terror."

Despite the writer and director's objections, Chester won out and the film—complete with controversial fire demon—premiered in the UK in 1957 and was well received. But it could not have helped Bennett's opinion of the picture—or the producer's—however, when 13 minutes were shorn from the film a year later for its US release (retitled *Curse of the Demon*). Here, Chester trimmed or eliminated scenes and dialog, including a scene where Holden speaks to Hobart's family. With this key scene now removed, missing were important background details on Hobart and how he arrived at his current state. Also missing were key lines of dialog between Karswell and his mother—dialog which humanized Karswell by showing him to be a man trapped in a situation for which there no longer remained an escape.

It's unfortunate that Bennett's screenplay containing his original concept for *Night of the Demon* is unavailable. It would have provided an interesting read against the shooting script to better judge the true extent of Chester's meddling. Nevertheless—and Chester's fire demon notwithstanding—*Night of the Demon* remains a faithful adaptation of James' short story in that the core plot of "Runes" survives intact into the film: that of an antagonist (Karswell, in both story and film) who brings destruction on his perceived enemies through the passing of a slip of parchment containing runic symbols and the following

John Holden (Dana Andrews) and Julian Karswell (Niall MacGinnis) debate science and the supernatural.

of one intended victim as he races against time to return the slip of paper to its originator before the end of his "allotted time."

When comparing a successful movie against the source from which it originated, one usually finds that certain aspects of the film are an improvement over the story/novel, and vice versa. We have an unusual case here in that, with one notable exception, *Night of the Demon* is superior to its source material in every respect. (To any arguments that slack should be cut to James' story for the disadvantages inherent to the form due to length limitations, this author needs only to consider tales by Poe or Bradbury to realize what can be done with limited words.)

Where to begin? At the risk of raising the ire of M.R. James fans (of which this author is one himself), I am baffled to see how "Runes" is considered a classic of the form given its numerous shortcomings. The pacing of the story is problematic, with the narrative hitting bumps every time James tries to move the action along through extended character conversation. Characterization itself is non-existent beyond James' success in defining Karswell as a thoroughly unpleasant individual. Lastly, the tale fails to generate anything approaching genuine suspense or horror until the very end. Here, at last, James delivers

an "on the edge of your seat" moment with a deliciously suspenseful passage relating our protagonist's attempts to return his parchment back to Karswell. Sadly, this excellent piece of storytelling is a case of too little, too late.

This passage is also the previously mentioned exception of where the source material surpasses its cinematic translation. For in "Runes," our protagonist's efforts to return the parchment are believable, as Karswell unwittingly accepts his ticket case (containing said slip of paper) from our cursed, but *disguised*, hero, Dunning. The equivalent scene in the film is its only failure in translation. For despite his growing terror and resulting haste to depart the train, there is NO way Karswell would have accepted *anything* from Holden, let alone a mere hat and coat. This contrived gimmick to ensure Karswell's comeuppance is a particular letdown given the logical and believable story that has come before.

That particular hiccup aside, *Night of the Demon* does just about everything else right. Taking the kernel of an idea from James' story, Bennett created (Chester's "contributions" notwithstanding) a taut, intelligent, thoughtful script. Combined with Tourneur's masterful execution, the realized film excels in all the areas where the short story falls short—the pacing is brisk, characters are defined and realistic (yes, Holden may be stolid and one-dimensional, but this author knows many such "show me" scientific types) and Tourneur draws upon all his Lewton-era experience to deliver a suspenseful and beautifully atmospheric supernatural thriller.

IT CAME FROM ...

There is one aspect to *Night of the Demon,* not originating from the short story, which deserves special mention. Most "B" pictures of the 1950s and '60s rarely strove to rise above the genre's typical "man vs. monster" and "damsel in distress by said monster" storylines. Such a film existed only to entertain movie-going audiences for its 60-plus minutes' running time. The thought that a "B" picture could involve the audience in an intelligent debate while still entertaining them is almost unheard of. But this is exactly what *Night of the Demon* does, and does so superbly, in a reflection on "magic vs. science" entwined throughout the storyline. This reflection is best exemplified in a scene between Holden and Karswell while on the latter's estate. Karswell articulates his case in support of belief in magic and the supernatural, and one line not only beautifully sums up his argument but also poses questions to which the perpetually argumentative Holden finally has no answers for:

> Where does imagination end and reality begin? What is this twilight, this half world of the mind that you profess to know so much about? How can we differentiate between the powers of darkness and the powers of the mind?

This layer of reasoned, philosophical discussion raises *Night of the Demon* high above the "B" picture, monster movie, and other such limiting labels many would apply to the film.

Shifting from general considerations, let us now turn our attention to the notable and significant differences that exist between James' story and its cinematic offspring.

Critics of the demon's appearance do have some valid points in their favor: the demon *does* look like a phony puppet in some shots (because it is), and for those who like a sense of ambiguity in their supernatural thrillers (*The Innocents* or *The Haunting,* anyone?), the demon's appearance certainly removes any doubt as to whether the strange goings-on are real or imagined. However, one point critics use to bolster their argument, not valid, is the claim that there is no demon in James' short story. Because there is ... of a sort.

To bring us to an acceptance of a demon in James' story, readers must first let go of the notion that all demons have to be fire monsters two stories in height. Demons can take many shapes, sizes, and forms. There is further evidence of a demon's existence when examining the two deaths that occur within the story. In the case of John Harrington's death, the existence of the demon is admittedly only implied. But *something* made Harrington—described as

> "... not an athletic fellow ... " shimmy up a tree in the middle of the night to be found the following morning " ... with the most dreadful face of fear on him that could be imagined."

Even though Karswell is a self-professed Satanist, he also becomes Bo-Bo the clown to entertain the village children at huge parties he and his mother host.

IT CAME FROM ...

With Karswell's death, the demon is more explicit, albeit fleeting, in its appearance. Moments after having the slip of paper returned unbeknownst to him by Dunning and Henry Harrington, Karswell, anxious and uneasy (and *alone*), boards a boat and the following dialogue ensues:

Suddenly the [ticket] official called after him, "You, sir, beg pardon, did the other gentleman show his ticket?" "What the devil do you mean by the other gentleman?" Karswell's snarling voice called back from the deck. The man bent over and looked at him. "The devil? Well, I don't know, I'm sure," Harrington heard him say to himself, and then aloud, "My mistake, sir; must have been your rugs! Ask your pardon." And then, to a subordinate near him, "And he got a dog with him, or what? Funny thing: I could 'a' swore 'e wasn't alone."

Let's just leave it at that what the ticket official thinks he sees *is neither a gentleman nor a dog* ...

Moving on, in the film, there is little doubt attributing the sinister goings-on to supernatural origins. Even if one tried to attribute the appearance of the demon to both Harrington's and Karswell's overactive imaginations or examples of the power of hypnotic suggestion, one would be hard-put to dismiss hoofprint impressions made in the ground (which are *not* seen by characters in the film but by the viewer) or the violent windstorm conjured up by Karswell at a children's party, as it is very real and affects all involved.

In James' story, we are never quite 100% convinced of Karswell's ties to the supernatural, said ties are merely hinted at through one of his writings, *History of Witchcraft*, and a line uttered by a neighbor: "He had invented a new religion for himself and practiced no one could tell what appalling rites."

Additionally, one could attribute John Harrington's death, and even that of Karswell's—a bit of a stretch, admittedly, but credibly—to coincidental accidents.

In "Runes," Karswell (no first name given) is depicted as a loner and very definite sociopath with few redeeming qualities. He is a most unsympathetic character, described as such:

> He was very easily offended and never forgave anybody; he had a dreadful face (so the lady insisted, her husband somewhat demurring); he never did a kind action, and whatever influence he did exert was mischievous.

In the film, Karswell is a surprisingly sympathetic antagonist, hosting annual Halloween parties for the local children, entertaining them with his magic act and pulling adorable puppies out of his hat. If one pays close attention to the film's storyline, one finds that in both instances where he lashes out against his enemies (Professor Harrington and Holden), it is a *defensive* measure; he does so only as a result of perceived attacks (their attempts to expose his devil

Dana Andrews poses at Stonehenge with one of the runic parchments used by Karswell to claim his victims.

cult). Karswell gives his intended victims ample opportunities to stay their fate and only summons the fire demon when his victims ignore his demands to call off the exposé. In fact, one could say that Professor Harrington is especially culpable for his own fate for additionally challenging Karswell to "do your worst." (He did!)

Most pointedly, the film shows Karswell trapped in a situation that he initiated but can no longer escape or control, even if he desired. In attempting to explain this predicament to his mother:

> Karswell: Listen Mother, you believe in the supernatural. I've shown you some of its power and its danger.
> Mother: Yes, Julian.

IT CAME FROM ...

Karswell: Well believe this also. You get nothing for nothing. This house. This land. The way we live. Nothing for nothing. My followers who pay for all of this do it out of fear. And I do what I do out of fear also. It's part of the price.
Mother: But if it makes you unhappy, stop it. Give it back.
Karswell: How can you give back life? I can't stop it; I can't give it back. I can't let anyone destroy this thing. I must protect myself. Because if it's not someone else's life, it'll be mine. You understand, Mother? It'll be mine.

The viewer encounters a sympathetic reflection one seldom finds in a screen "villain."

Lastly, every horror/supernatural film worth its salt must have a female lead (i.e. damsel in distress), and so the character of Henry Harrington— brother to demon victim John Harrington in "Runes"—becomes niece Joanna Harrington in *Night of the Demon*. However, Joanna is not your typical dumb, helpless, and screaming horror movie heroine to whom things (i.e., the monster) happen. On the contrary, Joanna is educated, strong-willed, and her determination to uncover the real cause of her uncle's death becomes the catalyst for much of the action in the film. It's a nice change of pace to have a strong female protagonist.

In the end, *Night of the Demon* may not have been the film that Bennett and Tourneur had envisioned, but Hal E. Chester's decision to include a monster in his film elevated the picture over the years to cult status and ensured the film's posterity through *spirited* "should-the-demon-have-been-included" debates that split fans of the picture to this day.

The stories and novels behind Classic Horror, Fantasy and Science Fiction Films

Some Mothers Shouldn't Be a Boy's Best Friend: *Psycho (1960)*

When a film's reputation, be it good or bad, becomes so ingrained in the public consciousness, dislodging long-held beliefs presents a formidable challenge. Consider the late director Ed Wood. His infamous film, *Plan 9 from Outer Space*, remains universally panned as the worst movie of all time. Could *anything* be said in defense of the film that would change peoples' opinion? Unlikely. Now take *Psycho*, by Alfred Hitchcock. The flip side of *Plan 9*, fans and critics alike fondly regard *Psycho* as an outstanding film. A 97% approval rating on Rotten Tomatoes and the American Film Institute (AFI) ranking the film at #18 on their list of the 100 GREATEST AMERICAN MOVIES OF ALL TIME arguably confirms the film's brilliance, no? Who could argue otherwise? More so, who would dare?

I dare. But first, let's lay some groundwork.

Hitchcock, upon the release of *Psycho* in 1960, found himself on the receiving end of plaudits for the many cinematic "innovations" he brought to the film, such as the audacity of depicting a murder in a bathroom shower, as well as the killing off of a major character less than half way into the story ... among others. Those giving such laudatory remarks were ignorant of the fact that, while Hitchcock certainly added his usual panache in the execution of the screenplay by Joseph Stefano, all the main elements of the film, particularly the "innovations," as Hitchcock himself often credited: came from Robert Bloch's book.

Robert Bloch (1917-1994) was a versatile and prolific writer, at home in the worlds of fantasy and horror, but equally adept at writing thrillers, science fiction, detective/crime, and humor. The author of over 25 novels and hundreds of short stories, many acknowledged classics, has cemented Bloch's reputation as one of the masters of fictional horror. His versatility extended to the field of scriptwriting as well, his talents frequently in demand for writing/adapting stories for radio, television, and film. Bloch's genuine warmth, wit, and unfailing willingness to share his time and talent with fans made him one of the most beloved and respected figures in the world of fantastic literature.

The seed of Bloch's writing career was sown in 1927 when his aunt purchased for him his first copy of *Weird Tales* magazine. The young Bloch thrilled to the bizarre and fantastic tales contained within and over the years came to particularly favor those of (the now) renowned writer, H.P. Lovecraft. Bloch wrote a fan letter to Lovecraft in 1933. Lovecraft responded, to Bloch's surprise, shortly thereafter, and thus began an ongoing correspondence that con-

Author Robert Bloch

tinued until Lovecraft's death in 1937. Initially, the senior author encouraged Bloch to try his hand at story writing and later provided welcome encouragement and feedback to the youthful Bloch's submissions.

Bloch's efforts quickly met with success. He first saw publication in 1934 in the fantasy and horror 'zines, *Marvel Tales* and *Weird Tales*. The latter publication, originally merely a source of unending entertainment to a young boy's dark imagination, in later years practically became Bloch's literary "home" until the magazine's demise in the mid-1950s. Much of Bloch's early work emulated Lovecraft's style and subject matter, often employing the use of Lovecraft's Cthulhu Mythos, an elaborate fictional universe dominated by the titular deity, the monstrous Cthulhu, who once reigned over the Earth. Although long since banished, Cthulhu remains worshiped by a cult of zealous followers who believe in, and work toward, his eventual return.

It wasn't until the early 1940s that Bloch began to move away from his Lovecraftian influences and find his own voice. His fiction, which previously explored the realms of the fantastic and the supernatural, began to take a new direction. The author now turned his focus inward, looking to exploit the limitless terrors inherent within the human animal. By mining the psychology and inner workings of the human brain for material, Bloch brought a level of realism to his work that was all the more chilling for now hitting close to home—for the monster in the room was no longer the vampire or ghoul of old, but could well be the very person standing next to you. Bloch's first published novel, *The Scarf* (1947), expanded upon this theme and established his unique take on literary psychological horror—that of telling his story from the first-person perspective of the villain/antagonist. Bloch would use this effective and lauded technique again in subsequent novels.

Given his new predilection for writing tales detailing the atrocities spawned from the abnormal mind, it's not surprising that Bloch maintained a keen interest in the life and mythos surrounding real-life serial killer, Jack the Ripper. Bloch featured the infamous slasher frequently in his work, first broaching the subject in his now classic 1943 story, "Yours Truly, Jack the Ripper." Bloch revisited the character in the (original) *Star Trek* episode, "Wolf in the Fold" (1967), and in "A Toy for Juliette," his contribution to Harlan Ellison's famed 1967 story collection, *Dangerous Visions*. Bloch ended his long association with Saucy Jacky in 1984 with a full-length novel, *The Night of the Ripper*, an ac-

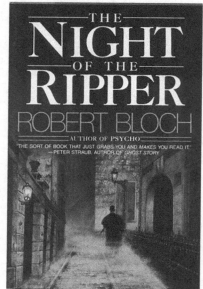

claimed entry in the Ripper canon, notable for weaving such real-life personages as Sir Arthur Conan Doyle, the Elephant Man, and Oscar Wilde into its storyline.

The early 1950s saw Bloch busier than ever with the publication of three additional novels as well as a voluminous amount of short stories. When *Weird Tales* ceased publication in 1954, Bloch's tales continued to find homes in such disparate-themed magazines as *Amazing*, *Ellery Queen's Mystery Magazine*, and *Shock*.

Bloch was shaken near the end of 1957 to learn of the gruesome reports coming out of the small town of Plainfield, Wisconsin surrounding one of its residents, Edward Gein. Gein had become a suspect in the recent disappearance of local female hardware store

Court Told Geir Is Not Competer

Slayer's Hospital Stay Is Extended

NOT COMPETENT TO STAND TRIAL

Edward A. Gein, 51-year-old Waushara County farmer, confessed slayer of two women and looter of at least a dozen graves, is not competent to stand trial, authorities at the Central State Hospital for the Insane have reported to Circuit Judge Herbert A. Bunde. Judge Bunde, who ordered Gein's commitment for a sanity hearing, says Gein's stay at the hospital will be extended and that a formal sanity hearing will be ordered at a time and place to be designated later. This picture was made at the time of Gein's hearing in court at Wautoma. ᴀᴘ ᵂⁱʳᵉᵖʰᵒᵗᵒ)

WISCONSIN RAPIDS (AP) — Circuit Judge A. Bunde said today that authorities at Central S pital for the Criminal Insane have reported to Edward Gein, Plainfield bachelor recluse who killing and butchering two women and looting tl of a dozen more, is "not competent to stand trial."

Judge Bunde, who ordered Gein's commitment for a sanity hearing when the 51-year-old handyman was arraigned on Nov. 21st, said that Gein's stay at the Waupun institution would be "extended" beyond the first 30-day period he ordered.

The judge also said he would order a formal sanity hearing "at a time and place to be designated later."

Committed at Arraignment

The frail-appearing Gein was committed upon his arraignment on a charge of first degree murder in the Nov. 16 mutilation slaying of Mrs. Bernice Worden, 58-year-old Plainfield hardware store operator.

Mrs. Worden's body, dressed out like a deer carcass, was found hung by the heels in the woodshed of Gein's secluded farmhouse on the night of the slaying.

The discovery was only the first in a horrifying series as investigators searching through the cluttered interior of the rambling old farmhouse found ghastly relics of human skin, skulls and other fragments of bodies.

on which we require t of experts to make a "Notice of the time of such further inquiry will be made i future, perhaps within 10 days. Setting of a must necessarily awa come of the inquiry.

"I have today signe extending the commit ward Gein to the Ce Hospital for furth study, examination an tion."

Bloch found horrific real-world events to fire his fiction.

owner Bernice Worden. During a search of his property, police discovered to their horror the decapitated body of Worden hanging in a shed. Authorities additionally found a staggering amount of various human body parts, which Gein accumulated through the years via innumerable exhumations of dead bodies from the graves of local cemeteries. As shocking as Gein's actions must have been to Bloch, the horror must certainly have been heightened for the writer by the fact that he lived, at the time, in Weyauwega, Wisconsin … a mere 40 miles away from Gein!

The stories and novels behind Classic Horror, Fantasy and Science Fiction Films

Local small town papers were reluctant to acknowledge, let alone print, details of Gein's ghastly deeds. As such, Bloch could collect only scant information surrounding the case; Bloch would only come to learn the full account of Gein's horrendous crimes years later. Even so, Bloch came to an idea for a novel. The novel was not based on Gein himself, but on the extraordinary situation of how a seemingly "normal" and respected resident of a small rural town could get away with such unspeakable acts for so long a period of time.

Bloch thus began to give consideration to the major elements needed to tell his story. Foremost, he needed an arresting lead character. In Randall Larson's 1989 *The Robert Bloch Companion: Collected Interviews 1969-1986*, Bloch revealed his thought process behind the development of the man who would become Norman Bates:

> I began to speculate what kind of person this individual might be, and at once came up with the notion that he probably was a schizoid personality and that it would be much more convincing if he himself wasn't aware of his own crimes, rather than have to go through elaborate efforts to conceal them knowingly. What would motivate him? I came up with the Oedipal situation and the transvestite thing, which was pretty offbeat at the time … My feeling was that if he were going to unconsciously impersonate his mother, he'd go all the way. It was also a useful device in the mystification of the plot. If Norman believes his mother is alive and other people see evidence of that, then the reader will believe it too. It worked.

Bloch next needed to devise a way to logically replicate Gein's supreme accomplishment—that of having his lead character's crimes go undetected for an extended period of time. Bloch finally hit on the idea of establishing his character running a motel in a rural, off-the-beaten-path location, providing the believable explanation for his character living a solitary, isolated life. Last-

ly, Bloch conceived a masterstroke—creating an additional character, a female protagonist for whom Bloch would gain readers' sympathy and then shockingly kill off in only the third chapter.

After working out remaining plot and character points, writing went smoothly for Bloch, who completed the novel in roughly seven weeks' time. Simon & Schuster subsequently published *Psycho* in January 1959 to generally favorable reviews, with the novel even earning positive mention in the revered *New York Times*. The book was an instant hit with readers, with its initial hardcover print run selling out quickly. Alfred Hitchcock then released his cinematic adaptation the following year, becoming a box-office success beyond anyone's imagination.

Not one to rest on his laurels (nor that of Hitchcock's film), Bloch's post-*Psycho* career produced an extensive and varied 30-plus-year body of work that included:

- Twenty novels and innumerous short stories.
- Original and adapted screenplays for such films as *Straight-Jacket* (with Joan Crawford), *The Night Walker* (with Barbara Stanwyck), and several anthology films for the British production company, Amicus.
- Numerous teleplays for such popular and acclaimed television series as *Alfred Hitchcock Presents*, (the original) *Star Trek*, *Thriller*, and *Rod Serling's Night Gallery.*

In *The Making of Psycho* documentary feature which accompanied the 50th anniversary DVD release of the film, we learn that shortly upon the publication of *Psycho*, the following information came to the attention of Hitchcock, according to the director's personal assistant, Peggy Robertson:

> We were on *North by Northwest*, and we weren't looking for the next one, particularly. And it wasn't until we finished shooting, and we were preparing for postproduction ... Hitchy would read the *New York Times* book section over the weekend or bring it into the office on Monday. We saw this very good review by [Anthony] Boucher on this book, *Psycho*. So Hitch said, "Call Paramount and get coverage on it." Paramount hadn't covered it, and Hitch went over to England. As he was at the airport, he saw shelves of this book, *Psycho*. He called me and said, "Haven't you got coverage from Paramount yet?" I said, "Paramount didn't cover it." He said, "All right." He got the book and read it going over. He called back from London to say, "I've got our next subject: *Psycho*."

Hitchcock acquired the film rights to the book in short order. This, in turn, should have translated into a great financial boon for Bloch. Sadly, this was not the case due not only to questionable tactics on the part of agents for Hitch-

cock (and, one could argue, Hitchcock himself) but also to Bloch's contract with his publisher. At the time, Bloch and his agent were approached by the MCA talent agency, that presented a blind buy (purchaser not identified) offer of $5,000 for the book's film rights. Bloch instructed his agent to hold out, resulting in a second offer of $9,500. Bloch accepted this offer, eager for both the money and the hopeful boost to his career that the sale might represent. He did not discover that the rights had been sold to Hitchcock until sometime later. Af-

IT CAME FROM ...

ter taxes and agent/publisher cuts, Bloch netted only a little over $6,000 from said acquisition. The author suffered an additional and more anguishing blow when he learned that he would not share in the film's box-office success—his contract with publisher Simon & Schuster did not allow for a percentage of the film's profits upon sale of the film rights. (A point Bloch did not find out until too late and for which he should have fired his agent!)

With the film rights in place, Hitchcock next needed a screenwriter. As Peggy Robertson recalls (again from the *Making of Psycho* documentary):

> We were looking for a writer and someone suggested James Cavanagh, who wrote some of the *Alfred Hitchcock Presents* television shows. I don't remember the meetings they had, but when we got the treatment, we read it, and it was very dull. If you can imagine a dull script written from the book *Psycho*. It just didn't have anything. So then it was decided, we need another writer. "Who are we going to get?" And then names were suggested. And Hitch thought a lot of [talent agent] Ned Brown, and Ned suggested Joseph Stefano.

Hitchcock, happiest when surrounded with people he knew and trusted, was reluctant to meet with neophyte Stefano. For the writer, new to the worlds of Hollywood and scriptwriting, possessed but a handful of credits at this point, none of which Hitchcock was particularly impressed with. However, after some persistence on the part of Brown and other interested parties, Hitchcock relented and agreed to speak with Stefano. The scripter pitched his thoughts in their initial meeting on translating Bloch's novel to the screen. Hitchcock liked what he heard, particularly the writer's idea to expand the role of Mary Crane and open the film with her, rather than with Norman, as does the novel. Shortly after, Hitchcock, sufficiently impressed, hired Stefano as the screenwriter for his 47th feature film.

Joseph Stefano's (1922-2006) interest in entertaining audiences developed at an early age. Adept at dancing, singing, and writing music, he composed the material for a number of high school productions in which he appeared. He took off for NYC mere weeks before his high-school graduation, where he sang and danced in small clubs. Later, he came to write songs for other nightclub performers, as well as for Las Vegas showman, Donn Arden. In the early 1950s, his nightclub/composing experience proved beneficial when hired to write for the *Ted Mack Family Hour*, a weekly variety show that featured cabaret and stage talent.

Later in the decade, Stefano shifted his focus toward writing for film. His first effort was an un-credited contribution to the 1958 Gina Lollobrigida vehicle, *Fast and Sexy*. This led to producer Carlo Ponti tapping the writer to

Joe Stefano

script *Black Orchid* (1958), a Mafia melodrama starring Sophia Loren and Anthony Quinn. Stefano followed this success with a foray into television, co-writing with Leslie Stevens in 1959 the teleplay drama "Made in Japan," an acclaimed entry in the prestigious *Playhouse 90* series (this episode is notable for the debut of future *Star Trek* helmsman, George "Lieutenant Sulu" Takei). Stefano's biggest career assignment came later that year as Hitchcock's choice to adapt Bloch's *Psycho*. On the heels of that film's enormous success, Hitchcock offered Stefano the opportunity to script *Marnie* (1964), the director's expected next film (later, when lead actress Grace Kelly withdrew from the picture, Hitchcock shelved the project and instead commenced work on *The Birds*). Stefano declined the director's offer, as he had already committed himself to write and co-produce *The Outer Limits*, a new science fiction-themed anthology television series created by former *Playhouse 90* collaborator Leslie Stevens. Stefano left the series after only its first season, due to exhaustion and escalating conflicts with network execs. Following his stint on *Limits*, Stefano's career never quite matched the level of success and prestige previously enjoyed. While he continued to work steadily, primarily for television, efforts such as *Snowbeast* (TV movie, 1977) and *Swamp Thing* (TV series, 1990) were hardly of the caliber of what had come before. Stefano even returned to his *Psycho* roots in 1990 with the TV movie, *Psycho IV: The Beginning*, but this attempt to capture lightning in a bottle was but a sad coda to the saga of Norman Bates.

Before commencing work on the *Psycho* screenplay, Stefano spent several weeks in September of 1959 consulting with Hitchcock on the story. There, Stefano reflected on the challenges in translating Bloch's novel to the screen. Of these, Stefano pondered solutions for what he considered to be the two most problematic—both of which centered on his lead character.

First, there was Norman Bates himself. Bloch's novel opens on Norman—a middle-aged (40), unkempt, balding, heavyset drinker—who then remains center stage (more or less) for the remainder of the book. Stefano felt that audiences would not support such an unlikable character for the duration of the entire film. During one of their story conferences, Hitchcock told the writer

IT CAME FROM ...

Janet Leigh reveals character development to director Alfred Hitchcock with the help of her wardrobe mistress.

to imagine Anthony Perkins in the role of Norman (as Hitchcock would soon get Perkins cheaply for his film due to Perkins' contractual obligations to the studio). Stefano thus set to writing Norman as thin, young, and amiable—a character that audiences could much more easily accept and sympathize with.

Even with the problem of his main character's likability thus resolved, there remained for Stefano the issue of maintaining Norman as the film's focus from the start. Keeping the focus on Norman from the beginning would only compound the challenge of Mother's "secret" remaining under (mummified) wraps. And so Stefano conceived the idea to expand the role of victim-to-be Mary Crane and make her, not Norman, the early focus of the film. Stefano also felt it necessary to "soften" Mary's rougher edges from the novel in order to make her a more sympathetic character. By implementing these changes, Stefano felt that audiences would come to care for Marion, which could only heighten the impact of her shocking departure mid-point in the film.

With the main challenges to adapting the novel now resolved, Stefano commenced work on the screenplay. He completed a final draft in early November 1959.

Filming on *Psycho* began on November 30, 1959 and was completed on February 1, 1960; Hitchcock required seven days to shoot the intricate shower sequence.

The stories and novels behind Classic Horror, Fantasy and Science Fiction Films

French theater premiere (From the Collections of the Margaret Herrick Library)

Psycho was a huge hit with the public upon its release on June 16, 1960, breaking attendance and box-office records across the country. Critically, however, the film met with mixed reviews. Some critics were particularly hostile, their negativity believed, by many, to be a result of Hitchcock not allowing the typical preview screenings for reviewers. Critics had to see the film for the

IT CAME FROM ...

first time along with the general public and bruised egos can easily lead to less than objective reviews. Bloch himself was extremely happy with the outcome, relieved that a great majority of his book remained unchanged and intact in the resulting film.

The success of *Psycho* spawned immediate cinematic imitations of decidedly lesser quality. Hitchcock's film opened the door to the entire "slasher" film genre. In perhaps the most extreme example of the adage "Imitation is the sincerest form of flattery," director Gus (*Good Will Hunting*) Van Sant released in 1990 what was, except for some minor deviations, an almost identical, shot-for-shot color remake of the 1960 classic. Then, as now, the public and critics scratched their heads and asked "why?"

The film's success spilled over into Robert Bloch's life as well. Sales of the novel skyrocketed with demand resulting in numerous printings and publication in a number of languages. The most significant effect on Bloch's life, however, was the creation of a permanent and unshakable association between the author and what became his literary "Frankenstein Monster." Bloch would forever after be known as the "Author of Psycho," a label that would stick with the writer and accompany practically everything that bore his name, until his passing in 1994—and beyond. Sadly, the ever-present specters of Norman Bates and his maternal alter ego overshadowed all of the author's post-*Psycho* accomplishments. For it was the rare interview or other media event where the discussion would not invariably turn from Bloch's latest project to some aspect of *Psycho*—be it film, book, or inspiration. Or, in interactions with fans, there inevitably came the confession, "I've not been able to take a shower since!" Bloch reflected on these "admissions" with characteristic wit in his 1993 *Once Around the Bloch: An Unauthorized Autobiography*:

> From time to time people come to me and volunteer the information that after seeing the film they were unable to take a shower. I can only tell them that they're lucky I didn't kill off my victim on a toilet seat.

With invariable good grace, Bloch eventually came to accept, if not necessarily embrace, his PSYCHOtic association and the baggage that came with it.

Now, in comparing Bloch's novel against Hitchcock's film, much of what follows certainly goes against past and current thinking regarding both projects, but it needs stating. In performing research for this chapter, I have been both surprised and saddened—surprised by the continual overwhelming favorable bias accorded Hitchcock's film despite its numerous flaws but saddened by the intensity and pervasiveness of the enmity directed toward Bloch's book.

This dim view in which many regard Bloch's novel is, arguably, unwarranted. Comments directed toward the book over the years range from "pulp trash" and "potboiler novel" to screenwriter Stefano dissing the book for being weak in writing and characterization. Regarding Stefano, one can only speculate that *perhaps* a touch of professional resentment was involved. After all, having to acknowledge that *every* aspect of his screenplay (except the character of the state trooper) had a basis of origin within Bloch's novel, along with Hitchcock's own public comments declaring that Stefano contributed only dialogue and no ideas to the film, could hardly leave the screenwriter with kind feelings toward the source material and its author. Others' comments, when one reads the entire context of their words, hint at opinions based not solely upon the novel's own merits, but rather in unfair comparison against said reviewers' exalted opinion of Hitchcock's film. This supposition gains traction when one considers that the book received generally laudatory reviews upon publication ... i.e., *before* the release of Hitchcock's film.

But, let us be frank. Is Bloch's *Psycho* a masterpiece of literature? Of course not. The novel is admittedly neither *War and Peace* nor *The Great Gatsby*. But that was never Bloch's aspiration, nor should it be readers' expectation. *Psycho* was never meant to be anything more than it is—a can't-turn-the-pages-fast-enough, *psycho*logical horror/thriller. As such, Bloch succeeds admirably, delivering in under two-hundred pages more genuine chills and moments of delicious horror than other authors muster with double the page count. Bloch's mastery at the setup/build-up of suspense, frequently capped by an unexpected (and sometimes rather gruesome) "twist,"—a skill honed over the decades through his innumerous short stories—is in full display here and at its peak. As evidence, we put to you that of the three major shocks shared between book and film (Marion and Arbogast's murders and the revelation of "Mother's" true identity), Bloch's novel outshines Hitchcock in all but one. Shocked? We elaborate shortly.

One area for which the novel is sometimes faulted (by Stefano most noticeably) is characterization, or more specifically, the lack thereof. I argue that this is not the case. Bloch admittedly does not spend page upon page giving minute character and background detail perhaps found in the mammoth doorstop-heavy efforts of a Stephen King or Leo Tolstoy. But then, this is *Psycho*, not *Anna Karenina*. And yet, while readers should have no expectation of in-depth character studies in such a novel—characters here typically exist to serve their plot purpose and little else—Bloch nonetheless delivers to readers a fully realized Norman Bates and even, though she appears in the book for a much lesser duration than her cinematic counterpart, Mary Crane.

Defense of Bloch's *Psycho* is not to suggest that the author does not stumble. Stylistically, the book's frequent stretches of short paragraphs and even shorter sentences try readers' patience for being forced to read the literary equivalent of short, staccato bursts from a machine gun. Bloch leaves the impression at these times that he is more intent on moving the story along as quickly as pos-

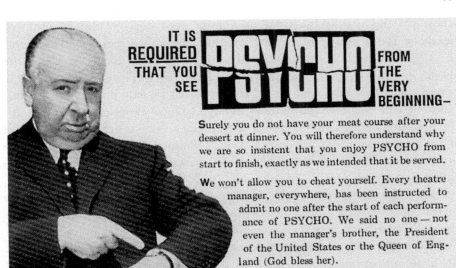

IT IS REQUIRED THAT YOU SEE PSYCHO FROM THE VERY BEGINNING—

Surely you do not have your meat course after your dessert at dinner. You will therefore understand why we are so insistent that you enjoy PSYCHO from start to finish, exactly as we intended that it be served.

We won't allow you to cheat yourself. Every theatre manager, everywhere, has been instructed to admit no one after the start of each performance of PSYCHO. We said no one — not even the manager's brother, the President of the United States or the Queen of England (God bless her).

To help you cooperate with this extraordinary policy, we are listing the starting times below. Treasure them with your life—or better yet, read them and act accordingly.

Alfred Hitchcock

sible in order to get to his destination (a major shock) than allowing readers to revel in the journey itself. However, the effect of these stylistic hiccups is minimal, as elsewhere Bloch opens up his paragraphs, allowing him the luxury to elaborate on the story as needed. It is then that *Psycho* becomes the more complex and engaging tale.

Turning from the book, dissecting Hitchcock's film is a trickier proposition, due to the high regard and esteem in which it is held by … well, just about everyone. But let us ask the same question we posed regarding Bloch's novel. Is Hitchcock's *Psycho* a masterpiece? Unless one's criteria for the term is limited to one superbly directed scene and/or that the film became Hitchcock's biggest financial success, then I put to you that no, Hitchcock's *Psycho* is not the masterpiece that so many fervently declare.

Now, put down those torches and pitchforks (or perhaps more appropriately, butcher knives) for a moment. I am not saying that *Psycho* is a *bad* film. Certainly, Hitchcock's execution of the shower scene is nothing short of brilliant and wholly deserving of the accolades it continues to receive some 50-plus years later. As well, Anthony Perkins' nuanced performance as Norman Bates remains both iconic and mesmerizing. (How Janet Leigh received an Academy Award nomination and Perkins did not is beyond unfair.)

One scene and performance, however, do not an entire film make, and so I put forth that *on the whole*, Hitchcock's *Psycho* is, at best, an average thriller,

The stories and novels behind Classic Horror, Fantasy and Science Fiction Films

whose prestige is overblown due to viewers' obsession—to the exclusion of nearly everything else—upon the film's three previously mentioned moments of shock. Admittedly, upon first viewing, everything taken together—the shocks, the music, et al.—yes, *Psycho* is a fabulous, thrilling experience. One comes away believing that yes, this might well be Hitchcock's finest hour (and one can only envy those lucky enough to have experienced the film for the first time back in 1960). However, the honeymoon is definitely over upon subsequent viewings as the cracks in our relationship with the film begin to appear. For, strip away the three shock scenes and what does one have—a rather pedestrian, noirish mystery that would be a struggle to watch *of itself*, no? Let's be honest: Hitchcock capably executes the scenes that precede each of the shock sequences, but there's nothing that goes beyond ordinary about them. I'd posit that these scenes would have turned out equally well with any other director with a modicum of talent. Running with this point, I'll stick my head out further to postulate that viewers don't truly appreciate the bulk of what they're viewing in Hitchcock's film so much as tolerate it. For, does anyone *really* watch *Psycho* for Marion's theft of the $40,000 and subsequent flight from Phoenix? Or even the oft-praised "quiet" exchange between Norman and Marion in the motel parlor? I argue no. I argue that audiences are not really focusing on the film at this point, merely biding time, awaiting the shower sequence. And then repeat until Mother's dispatch of Arbogast. Then Mother's reveal. That's it.

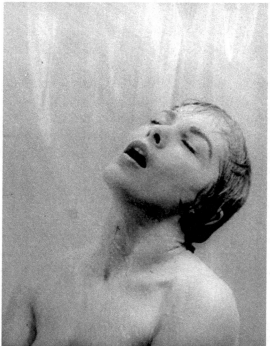

Harsh? Perhaps. But I felt a little tough love was necessary here and long overdue. And returning to my earlier point, I'll grant that filmgoers' enduring interest and affection certainly qualifies the film to *classic* status. But in the end, labeling Hitchcock's film a masterpiece is, as I hope I've established, just too much of a stretch.

Let's now turn a closer eye to significant instances where book or film executes better over the other, beginning with the three shock sequences.

The shower scene: No surprise here. The scene as written in Stefano's screenplay is mundane at best, with Marion dispatched in a single dispassionate sentence. In Hitchcock's hands, however, this one sentence became a legendary 45 seconds of a master class in direction. As volumes of commentary exist regarding the "*Psycho* shower scene," little more needs saying except that Janet Leigh's watery departure undisputedly remains one of the most distinguished sequences in motion picture history. The corresponding scene in Bloch's novel is effective to a point, until Bloch goes overboard by not only having Mother/Norman kill Mary in the shower, but beheading her as well. Bloch here, unable to restrain his usual need to go for something *really* "big," instead only makes readers shake their heads in disappointment for the overreach. While such shocking and gruesome "surprises" work well in Bloch's shorter works, here, restraint would have worked to greater effect.

Arbogast's death: While on *paper* there is little difference in how this scenario plays out—in the novel, Mother slays Arbogast at the front door, while in the screenplay Mother starts her deed at the top of the stairs—Bloch's depiction is the more satisfying, as Hitchcock stumbles badly here. In what to this day stupefyingly remains a prime example of the Emperor's New Clothes, fans and critics alike praise Hitchcock's execution of this sequence, when in fact, it is utterly ridiculous. While one attempts to suspend disbelief when viewing a film, I put to you that no one—especially someone just slashed by a knife across the face—could descend an entire staircase as swiftly as Arbogast does, *backward*, without one hand ever grabbing onto the railing. This gross illogic, combined with Balsam's exaggerated pin wheeling, flailing arms, plays decidedly more comical than terrifying upon each subsequent viewing. Stefano declared Bloch's version unfilmable as written, for revealing Mother's "secret"

upon her descent of the staircase. It seems not to have occurred to Stefano or Hitchcock that one solution could be the simple use of a *Halloween*/Michael Myers-type POV from Mother's perspective. Arguably, the end result would have been considerably more effective than what we have.

Mrs. Bates' "reveal:" One of the finest moments in the book comes when Lila leans forward to address what is actually the wizened, preserved corpse of "Mother." A response comes from *behind* Lila, who turns to find Norman-as-Mother proclaiming, "I am Mrs. Bates." Bloch's sense of misdirection and displacement underscore the eerie surrealism of the moment. Hitchcock's interpretation is considerably less effective. The director undercuts the efforts of both Bloch and Stefano by delivering a scene riddled with cinematic faux pas. First, there is the director's far too heavy reliance on Bernard Herrman's signature "slash" theme to carry the day. Said music plays much too loud, to the point of almost completely drowning out Perkins' declaration, "I am Norma Bates!" That this essential line of dialogue was all too obviously looped in post-production is bad enough. Perkins' noticeably *closed* mouth during much of the line's utterance only compounds the problem. But the *pièce de résistance* comes with "Mother's" struggle with Sam. It's embarrassing to watch Perkins here, with his deliberate and overly exaggerated head movements, intended only to shake the wig from his head for viewers' benefit. It's disappointing that Hitchcock had so little faith in his audience to recognize Norman dressed as Mother that the director would allow this badly executed piece to remain in the film. Only the horrific visage of the desiccated Mrs. Bates intercut throughout keeps this all-important climactic scene from resulting in out-and-out laughter.

An oft-repeated fallacy surrounding Bloch's novel points to its lack of strong characterization. I argue that Bloch's Norman Bates and Mary Crane are more complex, fleshed-out characters than their cinematic counterparts.

Take Norman. Because the novel opens on Norman and he remains (more or less) center stage throughout, we gain significant insight into our antihero— the inner workings of his mind, his life and many interests, as well as important back-story concerning his relationship with Mother. Because Norman doesn't appear until nearly half way through Hitchcock's film, what do we really know about him? Little more than that he is motel proprietor with an interest in taxidermy and has a mother who goes "a little mad sometimes." And it's hardly fair to credit Stefano with a fully realized character here, as the bulk of what we *do* learn of Norman comes from a psychiatrist's expository at film's end. A fully developed character emerges via their words and actions throughout the *entire* story, not from having all their details forced on us at story's conclusion. To be fair, similar explanatory dialogue is conducted by Sam and Lila at novel's end, but at least readers have followed Nor-

Tony Perkins as Norman Bates ... as Mother

man's progression from page one. Remove this expository from book and film and Bloch's Norman remains a fully realized character. One cannot say the same for his cinematic incarnation, however.

Stefano fares little better in his handling of Marion Crane, despite the advantage and luxury of expanding upon the role from the novel and devoting the early part of the film to her. While Stefano does succeed in creating a needed counterpoint to Norman, there is little else to our heroine. Back-story is nonexistent, and what we do glean of Marion "in the moment" isn't particularly revelatory, as it concerns either Sam or her theft of the money. As such, Stefano's Marion Crane never rises above being more than a two-dimensional character. That Hitchcock is able to make *situations* involving Marion interesting doesn't necessarily make *her* interesting (and Leigh's flat delivery doesn't help in this regard). On the flip side, despite existing in the novel for only *two* chapters, there is more to Bloch's Mary Crane than critics are ever willing to give the author credit for. Here, Mary has back-story: a woman who spent her early adult life scraping by and sacrificing in order to support her sister Lila. Stuck now in a menial job, with no perceived hope of living the life she dreams of with Sam, who can blame Mary for having become increasingly embittered toward life? And, as such hardships likely hit close to home for many, it's not hard to grasp why readers come to identify with this character in such a short span. Admittedly, the Mary Crane of Bloch's novel is more cynical and hardened (Stefano would call it "unlikeable") than her cinematic counterpart. But, "likeable" or not, Bloch provides us with a considerably more *relatable* character than Stefano; this, despite the screenwriter's previously outlined advantages.

Even if you haven't come to accept any of the views or opinions thus far expressed regarding Hitchcock's classic, is there anyone who *doesn't* believe

The doctor will see you now.

that the concluding scene of the film—where Simon Oakland, as psychiatrist Dr. Richman, expounds on Mother and Norman—isn't the film's crippling Achilles heel? To start, Stefano and Hitchcock do not play fair with audiences by springing a new character from out of nowhere simply to (all too conveniently) tie up loose ends. Forgiving that, the scene just does not work. It plays far too long, is too static, and Oakland orates as if he more belongs up on a pulpit delivering a fiery sermon to parishioners. It is an understatement to say that

this scene feels decidedly out of place with what has come before. Bloch's novel handles this sequence better. Here, Sam and Lila relate the same material following Sam's discussion with Norman's psychiatrist. Having our two principals discuss Norman's condition, as well as their reflections on the entire experience, just seems the more appropriate conclusion. Bloch even has one last "shock" for readers—following the horror that has just transpired, an unexpected moment of *tenderness* comes when the newly enlightened Lila expresses a measure of sympathy for Norman. This deftly written passage brings Bloch's story to a close with a continuity and sense of satisfaction sorely lacking from Stefano and Hitchcock's translation.

In conclusion, *Psycho*, both book and film, each deserve a fresh look by fans. Acknowledging that Hitchcock's film is not all that we have previously believed does not diminish its stature in the echelon of great American cinema. All great films have their flaws. Conversely, I hope to have shown that Bloch's novel is long overdue for stepping out from the shadow of its cinematic offspring and recognized as one of the all-time great classics of horror literature.

Postscript:

A personal note: never forgetting the kindness and generosity extended to him by his literary mentor, Lovecraft, Bloch in turn "Paid it forward" long before the phrase engrained itself in our cultural vernacular. Throughout his career, Bloch *personally* responded to fans who wrote to him, always taking time to offer his encouragement and sage advice. As I, myself, was a recipient of such personal correspondence from Bloch, I could not forgive myself if I did not take a few words to acknowledge my debt and express thanks to *my* literary

Brilliant marketing prevailed over negative reviews as audiences flocked to see the Hitchcock sensation

mentor. Robert Bloch's talents as a writer not only inspired me to try my hand at writing at a young age, but his words of advice and encouragement later in life kept me going at times when I felt my efforts inadequate and all I wanted was to throw in the towel. A gentleman and class act all the way, my thanks to Robert Bloch will always remain limitless. (Jim)

Hitchcock and entourage during the Australian promotional tour (From the Collections of the Margaret Herrick Library)

The stories and novels behind Classic Horror, Fantasy and Science Fiction Films

This Divided Earth:
The Day of the Triffids (1962)

Tales surrounding the invasion of Earth by otherworldly beings have been a staple of science fiction literature since the genre's inception. One of the very first was Australian writer Robert Potter's little-known *The Germ Growers* (1892), which, in addition to its main alien invasion storyline, contains early echoes of *Invasion of the Body Snatchers* given *Growers'* aliens ability to duplicate human appearance. However, it is English writer H.G. Wells who gained fame, not only for creating the seminal work in this field, but for spawning the entire alien invasion subgenre that followed as well, due to his infinitely more successful novel, *The War of the Worlds* (1898).

In the decades following publication of Wells' landmark work, science fiction authors subsequently put their own spin on Wells' invasion theme, resulting in many acclaimed novels and short stories. Although far too many to list, some of this author's favorites include *Childhood's End* (1953) by Arthur C. Clarke, "Who Goes There?" (1938) by John W. Campbell (the story serving as the basis for the 1951 film *The Thing From Another World*), *The Puppet Masters* (1951) by Robert A. Heinlein, as well as more recent efforts, *Ender's Game* (1985) by Orson Scott Card and *The Alien Years* (1997) by Robert Silverberg.

Science fiction cinema took longer to come to the party. With a handful of exceptions, it wasn't until the 1950s that Hollywood finally embraced the theme of alien invasion—due, no doubt, in great part to the Cold War generated paranoia that had overtaken the country; then, it seemed, Hollywood couldn't churn such films out fast enough. Beloved classics such as *The Day the Earth Stood Still* (1951), *Invasion of the Body Snatchers* (1956), *The Thing From Another World* (1951), *Invaders From Mars* (1953), *This Island Earth* (1955), *Earth vs. the Flying Saucers* (1956), *I Married a Monster from Outer Space* (1958) and Wells' own *The War of the Worlds* (1953), just scratch the surface of the numerous films of the ilk released *just in that decade*. With few exceptions, these films owe thanks to the authors who penned the novels and stories from which they were adapted.

One writer in particular, the British John Wyndham, took Wells' theme and made it his own in the 1950s, publishing not one, but three, acknowledged classic alien invasion novels, two of which found their way to the big screen in relatively short order.

Wyndham (1903-1969) was a science fiction writer whose primary fame stems from four commercially popular and acclaimed novels: *The Day of the Triffids* (1951), *The Kraken Wakes* (1953), *The Chrysalids* (1955) and *The Midwich Cuckoos* (1957), which was adapted to the screen in 1960 as *Village of the Damned*.

IT CAME FROM ...

Wyndham was born and raised in Britain. He labored at a number of different careers during his early adulthood before turning his hand to writing. Wyndham achieved a modicum of success during the 1930s selling stories to American and British pulp science fiction magazines under a number of pseudonyms. He also authored three novels during this period. Two of these, *The Secret People* and *Planet Plane*, with their plots involving underground races of people and Martians, owe much to the classic novels *The Time Machine* and *War of the Worlds*, written by Wyndham's favorite author, H.G. Wells. Wyndham's subsequent output displays both obvious and subtle traces of the renowned fantasy and science fiction writer's continued influence.

John Wyndham

Wyndham's writing career was interrupted when, called up to service in Britain's Royal Signal Corps during World War II, he served as a cipher (algorithm for performing encryption) operator.

Britain's climate, and that of the entire world's, changed irrevocably following the Second World War. Wyndham's homeland was bankrupt and its people were to experience years of hunger and shortages of every kind. The Cold War had begun and the threats of nuclear war and Communism were in the forefront of everyone's minds. It is little wonder that, upon resuming his writing career following his service in the British Army, the direction of Wyndham's writing would shift accordingly, tapping into his country's newly developed fears and paranoia.

Wyndham's new style was an abrupt departure from what had come before. Gone were the gadget-oriented, action-packed adventure yarns of his pulp magazine days, replaced now by more cerebral, character-driven contemplations. A recurring theme of his 1950's output was the exploration of individual and societal effects following a global-wide catastrophe. Disliking the term "science fiction," which others used to label his writing, Wyndham preferred instead "logical fantasy—" where everyday people are presented within familiar landscapes and upon which one great fantastic premise is introduced (another H.G. Wellsian influence). Additionally, a hardly surprising ever-present theme of invasion permeates Wyndham's subsequent output, generated no doubt from his country's recent war-torn experiences. In *Triffids*, the invasion takes the form of carnivorous mobile plants; in *Kraken*, aliens who take residence in the Earth's oceans, and in *Midwich Cuckoos*, in the form of alien children.

Little is known regarding the background for writing *The Day of the Triffids* aside from remarks given in a 1968 interview where Wyndham attributed the origin of his most successful novel to a late night walk when:

> [I] saw some raspberry canes waving in the wind against the sky. The trees and hedgerows were blowing across the road and I thought, by gosh, those'd be nasty things if they could sting you.

Wyndham's resulting tale of mobile, man-eating vegetation first saw publication as an abridged serialization, titled "Revolt of the Triffids," that appeared in *Collier's Weekly* in early 1951. Its subsequent publication as a full and revised novel came later that same year.

Triffids was an immediate commercial and critical success upon publication and remains one of the most respected science fiction novels to this day as evidenced by its frequent publication reissue as well as its number of cinematic incarnations. The BBC produced a six-episode small-screen adaptation, televised in the UK in 1981. This telefilm adhered very closely to the novel. Although while the (thankfully) seldom-seen Triffids were a vast improvement over the 1962 film, they were still a major hindrance in design and execution, bringing unintentional chuckles for their resemblance more toward stubby-legged, lily-topped flamingos than menacing threat to humanity. The BBC produced

yet another version in 2009, which, while benefiting from advancements made in special effects, deserves little attention for resembling more a Hollywood-style alien-vs.-human shoot'em-up action flick than the thoughtful, character-driven story of Wyndham's novel. (As of this writing, previous reports/plans for famed director Sam [*Evil Dead, Spiderman*] Raimi helming his take on Wyndham's classic appear to have fallen through.)

It's a bit of a wonder that Wyndham's novel, with both its unique premise and monster, took over 10 years to see its first cinematic incarnation. But the literary property eventually caught the eye of prolific and controversial producer Philip Yordan, who saw its potential and determined to bring the story to big-screen life.

Philip Yordan (1914-2003) was an American screenwriter and producer, responsible in one or both capacities on such films as *Studs Lonigan* (1960), *The Thin Red Line* (1964), *Broken Lance* (1954), and *Detective Story* (1951), the latter nominated in the Best Writing, Screenplay category at the 1951 Academy Awards. Yordan's writing career remains surrounded in mystery as many continue to doubt the inordinate number of screenplays credited to him. For many suspect that a great number of scripts bearing Yordan's name result from having run a "script factory"—farming out scripts that ended up with his name on them, although written by others. Yordan, however, legitimately acted as the "front" for

Philip Yordan

a number of blacklisted writers, a group that included Bernard Gordon.

Bernard Gordon (1918-2007) was a screenwriter with a troubled past. He joined the Communist Party at the age of 22 due primarily to his view of capitalism as a failed economic system (his opinion influenced largely through the lens of his own personal experiences during the Great Depression of the 1930s) and his disappointment in the Western powers' delayed support of Stalin's stand against Hitler in the early 1940s. When the U.S. government began their Red Party "witch hunts" of the Hollywood film industry in 1947 through the hearings of the House Committee on Un-American Activities (HUAC), Gordon found himself blacklisted shortly thereafter. Gordon was frequently unable to find work in Hollywood or eventually fired from the few jobs he was able to obtain as a result. Gordon moved to Europe, desperate to provide for his family. He spent time in France, Spain, and other countries where it was easier to find work, often through his friendship and association with Yordan.

Yordan approached Gordon in 1960 to come to Spain. There Gordon was to polish an existing but unworkable treatment written for a cinematic version of *Triffids* that Yordan would produce. Gordon informed Yordan upon review that the treatment required a complete rewrite. Gordon was not much more inspired after reading the Wyndham novel, feeling the book lacked dramatic potential as well as a satisfactory (i.e. Hollywood "happy") ending. In his 1999 book, *Hollywood Exile, or How I Learned to Love the Blacklist: A Memoir*, Gordon mused on the pros and cons of writing a screenplay based on existing material:

Writing a screenplay from an existing novel can be at once easier and more difficult than working on an original story. It's easier because the books may contain good character and situation material to be mined instead of invented. It is more difficult because the natural continuity of the novel may have to be abandoned, great stretches of story omitted, characters lost, and a new pattern imposed on the story. On a more meaningful level, of course, a good novel is a creation of words, not of visual images; so a film, no matter how good, however faithful to the novel, can never capture the special magic of the author's words.

Gordon nevertheless accepted the assignment and fell to the task of writing a completely new screenplay. He soon found, however, that he had additional challenges to overcome. Foremost of these was that of location. Yordan, for budgetary reasons, had plans to use foreign (i.e. *cheaper*) actors and locations. As Wyndham's novel takes place entirely within England, this required Gordon to find a way to believably shift a good portion of the story to take place in both France and Spain. Gordon completed a script, despite such challenges, in just four weeks, one that both he and Yordan were happy with.

The Gordon File: A Screenwriter Recalls Twenty Years of FBI Surveillance by Bernard Gordon was published October 2009

Months passed, and Gordon moved on to other projects while Yordan set off to produce the film, to be directed by Hungarian-born Steve Sekely, whose previous film credits were not especially remarkable or memorable. When Yordan at last screened the completed film for the two studios providing financing, both studios rejected the finished product. Primary objections were the film's less than "special" effects and unsatisfying ending. Desperate to save the film (and most likely his reputation with the studios), Yordan hired a film editor to go through the *Triffids* footage to see what could be salvaged. The resulting acceptable footage amounted to only 57 minutes of running time—and Yordan had

IT CAME FROM ...

to deliver a 90-minute film. Yordan again turned to Gordon for help. Given that the cast and crew from the original shoot were now gone, as well as sets torn down, the pair hit on the idea to film another story—one independent and stand-alone, yet still connected to, and interwoven through, the main plot. Filmed at Shepperton Studios, this additional footage featured Janette Scott and Kieron Moore as two scientists trapped in a lighthouse by the Triffids. Freddie Francis, later known for directing numerous acclaimed horror films for the Hammer and Amicus studios, directed. The two film studios, happy with the revised result, released the film in 1962.

Gordon, despite all his work in helping to bring the *Triffids* film to fruition, did not receive a credit on the film. Yordan's dubious stated reason was that his initial deals and contracts with the studios called for Yordan to receive the writing credit. However, Gordon finally received his overdue credit for *Triffids* in 1997 when the Writer's Guild began announcing the restoration of credits to blacklisted writers.

There are conflicting reports regarding Wyndham's reaction to the resulting adaptation of his novel. Some state the author's satisfaction while others his disappointment. Your author is of the opinion that, given: 1) Wyndham's novel is all but unrecognizable aside from the titular plants, and 2) the execution of said Triffids are little more than men in (*very* bad) monster suits, even if one allows for the lower standards of special effects in the early 1960s, one can't possibly imagine Wyndham being happy with the result. For in just about every respect, the cinematic *Day of the Triffids* is an abject disappointment when compared to its source material.

Wyndham's novel is a literate, thoughtful examination into humanity's struggle to survive and rebuild after a phenomenon that results in not one, but *two*, catastrophic threats to survival: almost total global blindness and the Triffids. Each threat *alone* would represent a dangerous and daunting obstacle to overcome. But the two combined presents the human race with the very real likelihood of extinction. The true beauty of the novel lies in how Wyndham's protagonists handle this threat and the resulting challenges that follow. Readers find themselves becoming both engrossed and intimately involved in the characters' struggles against not only the seemingly unstoppable Triffids, but also (and even more so) their fellow survivors.

All characters are well defined, and their interactions with each other play out as believable and relatable. Even the human antagonists here are a refreshing change of pace. They are not typical all-evil villains possessing no redeeming qualities—while their actions here are often deplorable, readers at least understand the antagonists' motivations, which, one can argue, are nothing more than holding a diametrically different viewpoint on how to survive in a new, hostile world. As all sides make valid arguments, who can really claim to have the unassailable, correct one? This ongoing moral debate that winds through the storyline adds additional depth and richness to the book, raising it above the lesser science fiction fare of its time. And lastly, we have the Triffids. Wyndham manages to make characters (albeit thoroughly despicable ones) of even these carnivorous foliage, *stem*ming from their alleged abilities to "hear," sense movement, and communicate with each other, not to mention their possible possession of a level of intelligence! (Those owning Venus Fly Traps beware the next meteor shower!)

Gordon's screenplay adaptation, and its subsequent execution, by comparison (with apologies to Wyndham for doing so), is a depressing, illogical, and unintentionally funny mess. By rejecting a straight-on adaptation, Gordon instead serves up a typical "monster-on-the-loose," "damsel(s)-in-distress" "B" picture common for the period. To be fair, producer Yordan most likely preferred having such a no-brain-required monster flick, as these types of films were usually a sure-fire success at the box office. As a result, lost in the cinematic translation are *any* of the previously mentioned admirable qualities of the book: well-fleshed out characters (let alone any that the audience can come to care about), intellectual moral debates, substantive reflections on the implications of the new world in which the characters find themselves in, etc. You name it, and the film lacks it.

One then becomes befuddled when contemplating Gordon's rejection of his source material. He'd accused the book of being hopeless for being undramatic and lacking a satisfactory ending. This rings as a bit lazy if one assumes that—even living in Spain at the time—Gordon most likely had to have viewed the lauded *On the Beach* (1959) released the previous year. For really, *Beach* is *Day of the Triffids* (novel) without the plants! *Beach*'s screenwriter, John Paxton, did an admirable job of creating dramatic scenes from a novel that follows a number of characters and relates how each handle the imminent end of the world. (Sound familiar?) And you can't get a more unsatisfactory ending than *Beach*, where *everyone* ends up dead! At least in *Triffids*, a remnant of humanity survives and has reason to retain hope for the future. As Paxton was able to deftly handle the challenge of adapting such "undramatic" material with an unsatisfactory ending, Gordon's refusal to attempt the same dooms the cinematic *Triffids* in turn.

Adding to the frustration felt by fans of the

In *The Day of the Triffids* citizens of London watch a meteor shower flash in the night sky, unaware of the resulting effect.

IT CAME FROM ...

Leading man Howard Keel does a credible job, despite often looking like he is about to burst into song.

novel is the fact that the film's first scenes *are* directly from the book and are the best parts of the film. The meteor shower is wonderfully depicted, and Howard Keel's scenes in the hospital nicely capture Masen's (of the novel) growing suspicion, then horror, of what transpired the previous night.

Frustrations aside, let us now examine in greater detail the major disconnects between book and film.

Wyndham's characters are the heart and soul of his novel and their interactions with each other drive the main action throughout. We come to care about many of them, and because we do, the reader develops an intimate connection to them, a rather unique proposition for a science fiction novel. Of the film's many failures in translation, one of the greatest stems from reducing these vibrant characters to one-dimensional monster-movie archetypes that viewers care little about.

As comparison, in the novel, our main protagonist, Bill Masen, is a biologist with a long history of dealings with Triffids. Masen's background here provides logical segues into much of the novel's plot, particularly in understanding how he comes to avoid the blinding effects of the meteor shower. In the film, Masen unfathomably becomes an American naval officer. One sees no particular reason for this shift in occupation, unless to explain his knowledge of navigating through the interior of a ship, as well as his ability to fix a wireless communications radio (merely by replacing a burnt-out part!). Regardless of the cinematic Masen's occupation, the character as written here and played by Keel lacks depth, is not the least bit engaging, and plays as an automaton whose actions are driven more by outside stimuli than from any original thought processes of his own. Hardly the thoughtful, driven, and independent-thinking Masen we have come to appreciate from the novel.

Other major players from the book are even less recognizable in the film. There is Coker, a no-nonsense and at times ruthless bloke in the novel, who at first kidnaps Masen and other sighted survivors and forces them into a sort of indentured servitude. Later in the book, Coker sees the error of his ways and then becomes a valued ally. Coker of the novel is an immensely interesting character. In the film, he becomes little more than a useless old man. Then there is Miss Durrant, a strong-willed religious woman in the novel, who heads a community of survivors at a manor. She butts heads with Masen and Coker at every turn over their beliefs in running the community. Yet in the film, Gordon takes this fascinating firebrand and turns her into a weak damsel-in-distress, lacking any of the spit and fire demonstrated throughout the book. Such a waste.

But perhaps Gordon's greatest sin in translation lies in his decision to completely eliminate the character of Josella Playton—an unforgivable and fatal omission. Josella is a young woman whom Bill rescues early on in the book and from which an intimate relationship develops. And it is this relationship that provides much of the book's powerful emotional impact with readers, as well as being the impetus for much of the action. For Bill spends most of the latter part of the book in search of Josella upon a separation resulting from Coker's misguided "kidnappings." Gordon's excising of Josella from his script leaves a gaping emotional hole in the film for viewers in which no other character or plethora of action scenes can fill.

Early artist's conception of Triffid

Turning our attention now to the Triffids, first-time readers of Wyndham's novel may come away surprised in that our titular carnivorous plants, while an overarching threat throughout, are actually only supporting players within the story. For

IT CAME FROM ...

the Triffids appear only intermittently and even then very quickly, to serve their dramatic purpose and then are gone. Wyndham's decision to minimize the role of the Triffids in no way dilutes their impact on the story or its characters. It also wisely allows the more arresting and (equally frightening) human dramas to unfold. If only Gordon had taken this cue from Wyndham when composing his script.

Regarding our cinematic Triffids, any reviewer must certainly make allowances for critical jading developed as a result of the extraordinary advances in special effects in the decades since the film's release. But, *generous* allowances aside, there is no avoiding the fact that the Triffids as executed in the film are, for the most part, egregiously bad, which, in turn, sinks the film. One can make a good case to lay

Finalized artist's concept

Film version of a Triffid

The stories and novels behind Classic Horror, Fantasy and Science Fiction Films

blame at the feet of any number of individuals: the effects person, director Sekely for not recognizing bad when he saw it, or even Yordan for approving the final cut. But this author feels that responsibility begins with the script. One wants to be generous and afford Gordon some slack in that he could not have initially known that what read well on paper would turn out so poorly on film. However, in his desire to please Yordan with a sure-fire "monster" movie, Gordon populated his script with too many scenes involving Triffids, with said scenes turning out ... well, not quite as hoped. In deciding to deliberately ignore the novel's rich "human" drama in favor of highlighting the Triffids, Gordon could have at least adopted Wyndham's less-is-more approach regarding them. Everyone involved, including viewers, would have been better off.

IT CAME FROM ...

Lobby cards played up both the Eastman color and CinemaScope aspects of the film.

As mentioned previously with regard to the film's lighthouse sequence, all scenes involving the two scientists' battles against Triffids have no counterpart in Wyndham's novel. But these scenes do bear scrutiny for comprising a substantial portion of a film "based" on the book. This new sequence, while a clever way to solve the problem of padding a film when original actors and sets are long gone, adds to the problems of an already crippled film.

However forgiving one attempts to be toward Gordon for writing so many scenes involving Triffids in his original script, the mind boggles at why he made them so plentiful and *visible* here. For when writing these new scenes, Gordon had the benefit of hindsight, knowing that much of the initial film was rejected and excised due to bad Triffid effects! But Gordon, rather than taking to heart what should have been a lesson *well* learned, instead chooses to ignore the past and subject viewers to yet another over-abundance of scenes displaying the (yet again) poorly executed Triffids.

If the Triffids were our only problem in these new scenes, viewers could be a bit more forgiving … after all, the special effects stink throughout the entire film. However, this sequence contains a greater problem than even fake-looking, monstrous plants … the scientists themselves. Our two human characters here (I hesitate to call them protagonists) are overly obnoxious and irritating, with the male, a verbally-abusive drunk, and the female, a helpless mouthpiece

THE RANK ORGANISATION Presents

HOWARD KEEL · NICOLE MAUREY

L'INVASIONE DEI MOSTRI VERDI

(The day of the Triffids)

EASTMANCOLOUR · Sceneggiatura PHILIP YORDAN · Basato sul romanzo di JOHN WYNDHAM · Theatro da STEVE SEKELY · Prodotto da GEORGE PITCHER · Produzione esecutiva PHILIP YORDAN · CINEMASCOPE

for which to scream at every Triffid appearance. One cannot fathom how Gordon could remotely believe that viewers would respond at all positively to the pair. *This* viewer wished that Gordon had instead chosen to allow the hungry Triffids to make a meal of them.

Here's one last (I promise!) and brief point regarding the lighthouse sequence. And I must highlight scripter Gordon's laziness. For the record, when viewing a film, I'm more than willing to suspend disbelief and give myself over to the story unfolding before me. To a point. Especially where coincidence is concerned. Stretch coincidence too far in a film and you lose me. And so we have Gordon, eager to deliver a happy ending to Yordan and audiences. How does he do this? He has our two scientists trapped in a lighthouse, *surrounded by an ocean*, inadvertently discover the secret to destroying the Triffids. And what is this secret? Saltwater. Yes, saltwater. Rushed or not, Gordon couldn't be bothered to attempt to be a *tad* more inventive?

Ultimately, while the Gordon/Yordan *Day of the Triffids* may have been successful in the way they envisioned (box office), fans of Wyndham's novel can only view the film and utter a sigh of what might have been. One holds out the hope that there will yet be a version helmed by Raimi or another, who recognizes the wisdom in remaining faithful to Wyndham's superior source material.

IT CAME FROM ...

Beware of Girls in Red Slickers: Don't Look Now (1973)

We live in a cinematic age where audiences no longer give a second thought to sex scenes in films. More so, it seems today as if that in addition to such traditional building blocks of a movie script such as plot, character, dialogue, et al., we must now add one more: sex. For an R-rated film, I'd argue that it's a requirement. I would be hard pressed to quickly name a recent film I've viewed that did not include at least one such scene. As such, our current generation would find it difficult to envision a time (just a handful of decades ago!) where nudity and explicit "depictions of love" were not only considered taboo, but sources for *cause celebre* as well.

Case in point: Nicolas Roeg's *Don't Look Now,* which did not receive fair consideration from critics or the public at the time of its release in 1973. The film found itself embroiled in controversy even prior to its premiere surrounding its already infamous sex scene—a four-minute, graphically realistic sequence of Donald Sutherland and Julie Christie "going at it"— that almost guaranteed that the core of any review or discussion would center here, at the expense of recognition for the film's numerous other positive attributes. Discourse has rightly corrected over time, however, to center on the film as a whole, with the result that today that many (rightly) regard *Don't Look Now* as one of the finest entries in British filmmaking history. The 1971 story of the same name by Daphne du Maurier is the source of the same-titled film.

Daphne du Maurier (1907-1989) was a British writer of numerous popular novels and stories. Many credit du Maurier with helping to shape the modern Gothic tale by bringing many staples of the genre (foreboding mansions, Byronic heroes, etc.) into modern settings.

Du Maurier was born and raised in London. Her father, Gerald, was a prominent and successful theater actor who later became co-manager of the famous Wyndham Theatre in London. Her grandfather, George, was an accomplished artist and successful author. One of literature's most iconic characters, Svengali was first introduced in his 1894 novel, *Trilby*. The fictional Svengali, a precursor to *The Phantom of the Opera*, uses hypnotism to exert undue control over the titular Trilby, the girl he loves and desires to transform into a successful singer. Du Maurier's fictitious creation has become so ingrained into societal consciousness that today the term Svengali is used to label *any* person who, usually with malicious intent, manipulates and controls another.

Daphne was able to live her early life in privilege due to her family's illustrious heritage. Each year as a child, the du Maurier family would take annual family "holidays"—weeks spent at differing locations outside of London. Near the end of her teenage years, while considering locations for that year's holiday, Daphne, along with her mother and sister, traveled to Cornwall, a peninsula on the southwestern side of Great Britain. Daphne immediately fell in love with the area—with its lush forests and vegetation, as well as its exposure to the sea; she indulged her loves of boating, fishing, and other aquatic activities. Daphne would spend most of her life in Cornwall, using her beloved locale as the setting for many of her novels.

Color by Pat Seg

Image of Dame Daphne du Maurier from 1930

Du Maurier began work on her first novel, *The Loving Spirit*, shortly after her arrival at Cornwall, approaching her 20th birthday. The book, completed and published in 1931, enjoyed critical success and sold well. *Jamaica Inn* (1936), Du Maurier's fourth novel, became the first of her works translated to the screen by famed director, Alfred Hitchcock. In 1938, du Maurier enjoyed her greatest success to date (and subsequently), with the publication of *Rebecca*. Du Maurier's Gothic masterpiece of jealousy, murder, suspense, and that troublesome Mrs. Danvers, was an instant hit with readers, if not critics. Hitchcock's faithful cinematic adaptation, released two years later to much acclaim, culminated the following year with the taking of the Academy Award for Best Picture.

Du Maurier continued to write through the succeeding decades. Of significance from this period is the 1952 short story, "The Birds," a chilling apocalyptical imagining of mankind coming under assault by our feathered friends. Alfred Hitchcock brought the story to the screen a decade later, becoming the director's third and final adaptation of du Maurier's work.

Du Maurier's novels, often regarded as romantic suspense yarns, strike the fine balance of containing larger-than-life situations and characters, while never losing a firm grounding in reality. It was in the short story form, however, that du Maurier allowed herself to delve into "darker" territory, often employing more fantastic premises and interjections of the supernatural. Du Maurier held a strong belief in the "sixth sense"—reputed powers of the mind such as telepathy, clairvoyance, and precognition, which she often incorporated into her stories. "Don't Look Now" incorporates a number of these beliefs, what with the clairvoyant blind sister and John Baxter's power of precognition.

Du Maurier recalled her inspiration for the story in the 1987 collection, *Daphne du Maurier's Classics of the Macabre*:

> I have always enjoyed the challenge and discipline of constructing a short story generally based on some personal experience. In "Don't Look Now," which is set in Venice, I saw the two old women, the twins, who in the story are like a sinister Greek chorus, sitting at a table in Saint Mark's Square. On the way back to my hotel after dark, a child, as I thought, was jumping from a cellar into a narrow boat. These two quite different incidents and the atmosphere of Venice, especially the eeriness of the back streets at night, set me thinking, and ideas began to develop into a story.

"Don't Look Now" has been adapted to other mediums. Radio playwright Ronald Frame adapted the story in 2001 for BBC Radio 4 as part of its Classic Serial series. Frame received kudos for successfully capturing the mood and chills intrinsic to the story. British dramatist Nell Leyshon brought the story to the UK stage in 2007. The production premiered at the Lyceum Theatre in Sheffield, England on February 22, to generally tepid reviews—most complaints centered on a story more focused on the drama surrounding the loss of a child rather than the core themes inherent in du Maurier's tale.

Producer Peter Katz (most notably of *The Wrath of God*, starring Robert Mitchum) approached screenwriters and frequent collaborators Allan Shiach (a.k.a. Allan Scott) and Chris Dobson (a.k.a. Chris Bryant) shortly after the story's publication to write a script based on the du Maurier tale.

Allan Scott (1940-) was born in Elgin, Moray, Scotland, where he lived and was educated, after which he moved to Montreal, Canada to attend McGill University. Chris Bryant (1936-2008) was born in Bolton, a city in the Manchester area of England. In 1957, he emigrated to Canada where he also attended McGill University. The pair met at McGill and became life-long friends and professional partners. Their first collaboration came as stand-up comedians, with the pair traveling together for several years performing their combined act throughout numerous countries. After a time, the two moved to England where they wrote and sold a screenplay on spec. This success, coupled with the sale of additional scripts in short order, brought the pair to the attention of Katz. Scott and Bryant continued to enjoy success after *Don't Look Now*, both together and individually with such films as *The Awakening* (1980; collaboration) starring Charlton Heston, the Jim (Muppets) Henson effort, *The Witches* (1990; Scott alone, here again reunited with director Nicolas Roeg), and the acclaimed TV mini-series *Sword of Gideon* (1986; Bryant, alone), based on the tragic slaughter of Israeli athletes at the 1972 Munich Olympic Games.

Upon accepting Katz's offer to bring "Don't Look Now" to the screen, the pair initially approached the project with the usual trepidations inherent with adapting any short story to the screen: Was there enough workable material in the story to flesh out into a full-length film? In a 2011 interview with journalist Jan Gilbert for Kamera.co.uk, Scott reflected on this unique challenge:

> It was difficult in the sense that it was a short story and there's never enough narrative or clarity about the characters, so you know you're going to have to bring all that along. You always, as an adapter, want to be faithful to what you recognise (sic) as being interesting in the original material, and you want to do it in such a way that the author is not going to be angry with you. It's interesting, when we were making *The Witches* years later, we realized during shooting that we couldn't keep the ending in the novel because film is a whole different experience and we didn't think children would respond to the ending in the book in the film. And that's true all the way through *Don't Look Now* when it came to making any changes. We had to do what felt right for the film experience.

Determining that there was enough material to work with, Scott and Bryant jumped into the project by beginning at the *end*. The pair was particularly impressed with the finale of du Maurier's story and determined to write a screenplay that arrived at that ending. The end result is a film more faithful to

An anguished John Baxter (Donald Sutherland) clutches his drowned daughter Christine (Sharon Williams).

its source than most—the main characters, setting, denouement, and overall plot all survive intact in Scott/Bryant's translation.

The new elements added by the *writers* (emphasis here is important, expanded upon shortly) are germane and faithful to the spirit of du Maurier's tale (yes, even the sex scene). The most significant of these is the opening sequence, which relates Christine's accidental death by drowning. These first few scenes are important to the film in that they not only allowed the screenwriters a way of opening the film more dramatically than the short story (du Maurier's tale opens with John and Laura already in Venice), as well as more solidly establishing from the start the theme of precognition (particularly John's) that winds its way through the film's storyline. Another departure from the source material regards the change of John Baxter's occupation from that of simple Venetian tourist (story) to that of an architectural restorer (film). This change resulted when writers Scott and Bryant read their draft and realized that the midpoint of their script lagged in turns of action. So the pair wrote a suspenseful and exciting scene where John Baxter almost falls to his death in a church due to collapsed scaffolding. Scott further revealed in his interview with Gilbert that to explain how Baxter came to be in such a harrowing situation, he and his writing partner decided upon making the character an architectural restorer in Venice, restoring a dilapidated cathedral. This change in occupation adds credence to other aspects of the storyline as well, such as giving the couple a more logical reason for being in Venice as well as Baxter's interactions with the leading Catholic authority in the city, Bishop Barbarrigo (a new character not found in du Maurier's story). Lastly, there is the sex scene. Its addition, not intended as a titillating romp merely to draw in viewers, is rather a logical extension of the story. As point in fact, the scene as written in the *script* is as

IT CAME FROM ...

*un*titillating as it comes, consisting of merely "They made love." The extended scene as it exists in the *film*, however, came entirely from director Nicolas Roeg, who felt the sequence necessary to not only emotionally balance out the frequent squabbling going on between John and Laura, but to additionally help humanize the couple and make them relatable to the audience.

Bishop Barbarrigo (Massimo Serato) and John Baxter (Donald Sutherland) watch on as another victim of the serial killer terrorizing Venice is dragged from a canal.

Nicolas Roeg had earlier enjoyed a successful career as a cinematographer on such genre films as Roger Corman's *Masque of the Red Death* and François Truffaut's *Fahrenheit 451* (also with Christie) before directing his first film only three years previous. He was brought in to direct *Don't Look Now* after the producer's first choice for the project, American director Larry Pierce, had dropped out. While the overall story elements and structure of *Don't Look Now* came from Scott and Bryant, Roeg's contributions are invaluable: from the masterful intercutting of scenes; the introduction of such elements as water, breaking glass, and the refined use of the color red as recurring motifs; to the expansion of "They made love" into an incredibly delicate and tender four-minute scene. Roeg took an above-average script and created a gripping, suspenseful genre classic.

Principal photography began December 1972 and took roughly 10 weeks to complete with the majority of that time (seven weeks) spent filming in and around Venice, Italy. The film premiered in England on October 16, 1973, in New York City on December 9, 1973, and opened across the rest of the United States in January 1974. The film was a modest success financially, while critically receiving mixed reviews.

Du Maurier over the years voiced varying degrees of satisfaction when asked her opinion of cinematic adaptations of her work. She has had a total of eight of her works translated to the screen, three of them by acclaimed director Alfred Hitchcock alone. (The unevenness of quality in the triumvirate of Hitchcock's adaptations dovetailed perfectly with du Maurier's opinion of them: *Jamaica Inn* was met with cool disappointment (and who can blame her, it's not a very good film), she was greatly pleased by *Rebecca* and hated *The Birds*, due in large part to the director's complete transformation of her material. Of all adaptations, *Don't Look Now* was du Maurier's unequivocal favorite, so much so that, as revealed in Nina Auerbach's 2002, *Daphne du Maurier: Haunted Heiress*, Du Maurier penned director Roeg a letter shortly after the film's release, expressing:

> I know I make the adaptor's work more difficult by too often writing a story as narrator or through a single character's mind, which necessitates further invention on the part of the adaptor, and director, to enable a story and its people to come alive, and here you have succeeded admirably.

As the film is such a faithful adaptation of du Maurier's tale, there are few overarching differences found between the two mediums (pun *intended*). The only significant contrast of note is that while du Maurier's story is told in a fairly linear fashion, the film takes its story down a decidedly *non-linear* path, with viewers frequently not certain whether what they are seeing has occurred in the past, present, or future. Roeg's back-and-forth approach to storytelling can at times be confusing to a first-time viewer, but any such confusion and outstanding questions are ultimately resolved, albeit awkwardly, at film's end (much to John Baxter's eternal regret).

With few broad, sweeping contrasts, let us now examine in detail specific aspects of where film and story differ.

Let's first address the elephant or, coital couple if you prefer, in the room. Much has already been written over the decades regarding *Don't Look Now*'s infamous sex scene from the standpoint of the controversy it generated before and after the film's release and whether said controversy was justified. This author does not intend to add to that debate. We find that the more interesting discussion centers on whether the scene adds or detracts from the film as a whole. (And there has been plenty of discussion regarding *that* over the years as well.)

First, let's clear up a misconception. It's astounding to read reviews or other commentary regarding the film where people assertively declare that the film's lovemaking scene is entirely the province of the film and has no basis whatsoever within du Maurier's tale. *Technically*, this is true if you're referring to the four-minute sex romp between Sutherland and Christie. However, this romp came about when Roeg expanded on three little words from within the screenplay: "They made love," and this certainly originates from du Maurier's story:

IT CAME FROM ...

"Now," he thought afterwards, "Now at last is the moment to make love," and he went back into the bedroom, and she understood, and opened her arms and smiled. Such blessed relief after all those weeks of restraint.

The film suffers for the inclusion of this extended scene regardless of its origin, and is the only case of the film truly letting down the source material. Now, we don't deny or try to take away from any of the accolades accorded this scene. It is one of the most romantic, tender, and realistic depictions of lovemaking ever viewed on film, while at the same time being one of the most incredibly erotic. Combine this with Roeg's ingenious intercutting shots of John and Laura getting dressed in preparation for dinner and you have a truly brilliant sequence. But, brilliant or not, it just doesn't belong in *this* film. As such, this scene has an effect similar to that of slamming on the brakes of an accelerating automobile: all suspenseful momentum is lost, all action (well, non-coital anyway) comes to a screeching halt, and viewers are completely taken out of the story, diverted by this explicit and unnecessary piece of erotica. (As proof, who still does not, during viewing of this scene, temporarily forget what has come before and lapse into mental debate over whether Sutherland and Christie did/did not really "do it?")

Director Roeg himself has, over the years, commented on the necessity of this scene, stating that he felt it integral to the story lest the film contain too many scenes of John and Laura arguing. This argument is hard to accept, despite coming from Roeg himself, when in fact there are really only two such scenes in the film—one, which is indeed a big row, while the other not so much.

The stories and novels behind Classic Horror, Fantasy and Science Fiction Films

John (Donald Sutherland) rushes through the streets of Venice.

What we have here is a case where less would have been more—Roeg should have stuck with his screenwriters' and du Maurier's minimalist approach to lovemaking.

The John Baxter of du Maurier's tale is a stranger in a strange land—a tourist in one of the most beautiful, but by turns sinister, cities in the world. Here, John finds himself increasingly at a disadvantage as our tale escalates for his lack of knowledge of both the city's terrain and language. This inability to navigate the city and fluently communicate with its residents comprise cultural handicaps that lend an additional sense of helplessness to the palpable sense of impending doom that surrounds John as events unfold. And it is precisely because John is a stranger here that even the city itself seems to conspire against our protagonist—acting to provide sanctuary to a serial killer very much in his/her element, while at the same time confounding and twisting John around with its labarythian alleyways and watery dead-ends, ultimately leading John to his fatal destiny.

IT CAME FROM ...

The John Baxter of Roeg's film, on the other hand, is not the hapless tourist, but rather, a restorer of ancient buildings, in Venice for a purpose, and who manages adequately with his rudimentary grasp of both the city's pathways and native tongue. For gaining the ability to open up and expand upon du Maurier's short tale with additional plot lines and characters, it's easy to see the screenwriters' need for John's transformation. But by making Baxter more cosmopolitan, viewers gain a sense that John is better equipped to deal with the circumstances that come his way. The film thus loses from du Maurier's tale an element of sustained tension with this more accomplished John, despite the fact that he is still ultimately unable to avoid his fate.

Du Maurier's tale opens with our couple already in Venice, having had weeks to mourn the passing of their beloved daughter, Christine. The only additional detail du Maurier provides surrounding this tragedy is the briefest mention of Christine's death resulting from meningitis. Given this draught of background character detail, it's hard for readers to fully embrace John and Laura as grieving parents, let alone fully fleshed out characters. Of course, the passing of a child is always a tragic event regardless of the circumstances, and so readers do feel a *bit* of sympathy for our characters, but du Maurier just doesn't provide enough material to allow readers to really *connect* with the Baxters. As such, readers follow the pair as they proceed along their pre-destined paths, but at story's conclusion, John's death, while certainly unexpected and shocking, produces little emotional response. More back-story from du Maurier would have gone a long way toward allowing readers to more fully identify with, and thus care for, John and Laura.

On the flipside, the film's opening sequence—as written by Scott and Bryant, but more importantly, as executed by Roeg—is filmmaking at its best. This sequence should be, if it isn't already, required viewing in film schools, to confirm to up-and-coming directors and screenwriters the truth in the age-old adage that the best cinematic stories move the story forward by *showing*, not telling.

Let's look at this sequence. Overall it contains the barest of dialogue, containing long stretches with absolutely no exposition. And yet look at all that this scene accomplishes. We learn the tragic circumstances surrounding Christine's death, which establishes in viewers the much-needed empathy for John and Laura missing from du Maurier's tale. John's resulting guilt over his inability to save his daughter will critically (and fatally) manifest itself late in the film when he chases the young figure through the streets of Venice, feeling the need to "save" the girl from whatever harm John believes she is fleeing from. Lastly, Roeg skillfully and subtly sets up the previously mentioned recurring motifs that carry throughout the film, as well as establishing the overarching theme of psychic power.

A short terror-take

All this, accomplished in the space of a few minutes of screen time, with perhaps only three or four sentences total spoken. Simply brilliant. If only more of today's filmmakers could execute economy of exposition so masterfully.

In all, *Don't Look Now*, both story and film, are excellent pieces of storytelling. By eschewing excessive violence and gore, too prevalent in other stories and films of the time, du Maurier and Scott/Bryant accomplished their terror the old fashioned way—through the use of mood, setting, and, most importantly, the *suggestion* of terrible things that await. Story and film are both deserving of the acclaim and respect they continue to receive. And yet, with just a few small tweaks to each, both could have been not just excellent … but masterpieces.

Fantasy

This was the most challenging section for our book, because, really, where do horror and science fiction end and fantasy begin?

We relegated *John Carter* to science fiction, but wouldn't it be equally at home in fantasy? And why is *The Day of the Triffids* horror and not science fiction? And just what is *Superman*, anyway?

Trying to sort it all out, we decided to best look at the intent of a given film. If its conceit was a science fictional one, but the goal of the film was to produce shudders, it ended up in horror, like *Triffids*. If it involved other worldly mysticism, but relied on spaceships and Martians to tell its story, then we set it squarely in science fiction, like *John Carter*.

But the true jokers in the deck are our fantasy films. Of all the films we cover, the fantasies in this section are the least easy to classify.

Something Wicked has horrific moments, but it certainly isn't a horror film. *Superman* also has spaceships and aliens, but is never really science fiction. Is *Willy Wonka* a children's adventure, a comedy, or a parable of human greed and ugliness? Is *A Christmas Carol*, with its ghosts and spectral hearses and eternal damnation, a Gothic horror or a holiday romp? Is *The 7 Faces of Dr. Lao* a comedy, or something strangely akin to the tragic? And *The Wizard of Oz* has witches, fright sequences, musical numbers and robotic tin men, but it certainly is neither a science fiction nor horror film.

Unlike horror and science fiction, fantasy is an infinitely more fluid genre. It encompasses everything from (heaven help us) *The Lord of the Rings* to *Winnie the Pooh*, from *Mary Poppins* to *The Twilight Zone*. And while there are arguably more excellent fantasy films than either science fiction or horror films, we somehow only settled on these six for inclusion.

Though they are remarkably dissimilar films, all six are unlike the other movies covered here simply because the emotional reaction they engender is so dramatically different.

While the endings of films as disparate as *Psycho* and *Planet of the Apes* often leave viewers feeling as if they have been whacked in the teeth with a two-by-four, it is only these six films in the collection that offer a real and sustained emotional response.

The emotional frisson packed in these six films is remarkable, and travels throughout the length of them like high energy through a power cable. The horror and science fiction films covered here produce effects, but these six films encourage an emotional response throughout. This depth of feeling is, perhaps, what separates fantasy from science fiction and horror, and is perhaps what makes it so malleable. Without any set formula or catalog of conventions

Sadly *Wind in the Willows* didn't make this volume while *The Lord of the Rings* was deemed too indigestible.

to follow, the fantasy has to rely upon and sustain an emotional response in order to succeed.

It's no accident that fantasy films are often targeted at children, because children are wise enough to trust their emotional responses. It's not surprising that fantasy often hits the middle-aged in a profound way (think of many of Rod Serling's protagonists in *The Twilight Zone*) because that is often a time of longing or regret. The elderly, thinking more of what comes next rather than what happened before, embrace fantasy because they intuit its underlying transcendence. In short, the language of fantasy can be translated in ways that neither science fiction nor horror can adopt.

As always, the challenge was in what to keep out. Both of us rejected *The Lord of the Rings*, as both the films and the source material are indigestible to us (Tolkien will never be a hobbit with me), while the *Harry Potter* corpus was too diffuse and too variable in tone to pick a single film. It's regrettable that neither *Pinocchio* nor some version of *Wind in the Willows* made it into the book, but those are topics for possible future tomes.

These are six very special films, and all are dear to our hearts. We hope you enjoy them, too.

IT CAME FROM ...

Surrender Dorothy:
Sweetness and Cynicism in
The Wizard of Oz (1939)

Most of the films discussed in this book are relative classics, at best. A relative classic is a film that needs a qualifier for classic status. This is a great horror film, or this is a classic science fiction film only means supremacy within their respective genres. Most of the films covered in this book are good, a few are pretty good, and some are masterpieces within their genre. But there is only one film here that can be called great, sans qualifier, and that is MGM's *The Wizard of Oz* (1939)

It would be easy to outline the plot of *Oz*, but at this late date, what is the point? Most people today are born having seen *Oz*; it's coded into their DNA. Moreover, if you haven't seen *Oz*, it would be extremely unlikely that you are reading this book.

Suffice it to say that *Oz* is a masterpiece. It is also a textbook case on adaptations—a movie that enhances the book's strong points, and diminishes its few weaknesses.

Almost every attempt to create a canon of great American film includes a citation for *Oz*, most near the very top. It is beloved by both children and adults, by both men and women. For many of the stars of the film, *Oz* is their sole credit to screen immortality, or, better still, continued cultural relevance. It would seem as if it's nearly impossible to find detractors of the film.

Except, of course, within the denizens of genre film fandom. One recalls with amusement many letters-to-the-editor in publications like *Starlog* commending the bleak and already-forgotten *Return to Oz* (1985) for its *darkness*, while also taking uninformed potshots at *Oz* for its *vaudeville*. Well, vaudeville was extraordinary entertainment for its time, and its influence is still felt to this day … more than can be said for the sorry *Return to Oz*. Hell, there are even those in genre film fandom who begrudge the *songs* found in *Oz*, despite the fact it is one of the most tuneful scores in film history, and produced one bonafide standard, *Over the Rainbow*. Finally, only the most willful of misreadings could judge L. Frank Baum's Oz corpus to be *dark*; indeed, anyone who seriously posits such an interpretation should have their literacy surgically removed.

While the Oz novels had their frights (ditto the 1939 *Oz*), the qualifier *dark* refers to a sensibility that is simply not evinced in the 14 novels by the Royal Historian of Oz, Lyman Frank Baum. Let's start by taking a look at this remarkable gentleman.

L. Frank Baum: The Royal Historian of Oz

Lyman Frank Baum (1856-1919) is one of many *fin de siècle* fantasists who forever changed our imaginative landscape. It is staggering to think that people in, say, 1905 could read Winsor McCay's *Little Nemo in Slumberland*, any one of three Oz books, or any one of a number of fantastic tales by E. Nesbit, when it was all fresh and new. There is a commonality to these three giants, a commitment to other worlds, to the idea that children need independent adventures, and that childhood is a lost world in-and-of itself, with its own rules and rituals.

Baum was one of nine children born to successful parents in Chittenango, New York, only five of whom survived to adulthood. Baum would later recall his childhood as something of a paradise, a lost world returned to only in memory.

Baum became interested in writing at an early age when his father gave him a printing press. Baum published a great deal of small-town journalism, pieces on stamp collecting, and even wrote about raising poultry.

Baum was also besotted by theater, and harbored dreams of the stage. He was something of an amateur actor, and often took a high-profile role in family events. His father had even built a theater for young Baum, where he wrote and performed plays. The theater would later burn down, taking with it most of his early written, theatrical work.

In 1882, Baum married Maud Gage, the daughter of Matilda Joslyn Gage, a women's rights activist. The Baums then led a peripatetic life, moving to Aberdeen, South Dakota, where he owned a dry goods store and worked as editor of the *Aberdeen Saturday Pioneer*. He went on to journalism jobs in Chicago, and wrote *Mother Goose in Prose* in his free time. Illustrated by Maxfield Parrish, *Mother Goose* was a great success. His life would never be the same again.

He followed *Mother Goose* by collaborating with illustrator W.W. Denslow on *Father Goose, His Book*. This success in children's literary fantasy allowed Baum to quit his day job and concentrate more on his daydreams. In 1900, he and Denslow collaborated to create *The Wonderful Wizard of Oz*. It was the best-selling children's book for two years after its initial publication, and has never been out of print.

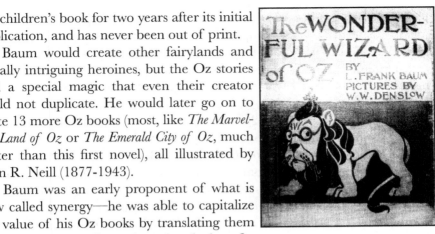

Baum would create other fairylands and equally intriguing heroines, but the Oz stories had a special magic that even their creator could not duplicate. He would later go on to write 13 more Oz books (most, like *The Marvelous Land of Oz* or *The Emerald City of Oz*, much better than this first novel), all illustrated by John R. Neill (1877-1943).

Baum was an early proponent of what is now called synergy—he was able to capitalize the value of his Oz books by translating them into competing media, and reaping the benefits of advertising dollars. Following the publication of the first novel, composer Paul Tietjens and director Julian Mitchell worked with Baum and Denslow to create a musical stage adaptation of *Oz*, with the title simply shortened to *The Wizard of Oz*. This opened in Chicago in 1902 before going to Broadway, where it enjoyed two lengthy runs before touring the country. Baum wrote the first sequel, *The Marvelous Land of Oz*, with an eye to eventually turning it into a Broadway musical extravaganza, as well. It was something of a flop, but his adaptation of *Ozma of Oz* (the third book in the corpus) did well in Los Angeles. Baum's plans for *The Patchwork Girl of Oz* stage show were later jettisoned in favor of a movie version.

And movies were definitely on Baum's mind. He and Maud moved to California, where he became very interested in the burgeoning film industry. He founded The Oz Film Manufacturing Company, and his dream was to create quality films for children (much like Walt Disney). He produced *The Patchwork Girl of Oz* (1914), *The Magic Cloak of Oz* (1914), and *His Majesty, the Scarecrow of Oz* (1914), before finances ran out. Other film versions of the period include *The Wonderful Wizard of Oz* (1910), and *Wizard of Oz* (1925), released just six years following Baum's death.

Perhaps the most daring of Baum's dreams was an Oz theme park, predating Disneyland by decades. In a 1905 interview, Baum said he had bought Pedloe Island, off the coast of California, to create an Oz park, complete with statues of the Scarecrow, Tin Woodman, Woggle-Bug and Jack Pumpkinhead. He dreamt of "a fairy paradise for children," and had claimed to have already selected a young lady to be its first princess, where she would reside in a grand Palace of Oz. Baum himself planned to live on the island ... Sadly, this story, which would be the closest link between Baum and his 20th-century successor, Walt Disney, is probably the merest balloon juice. Contemporary researchers have been unable to *find* Pedloe Island, let alone any documentation of Baum's plans for it. But this sort of thinking certainly places Baum as an innovator in the realm of children's entertainment, who could probably even teach J. K. Rowling a thing or two.

Like many gifted creators of children's entertainment—Kenneth Grahame (1859-1932) and Walt Disney (1901-1966) immediately come to mind—Baum was pulled in opposite poles by his idealized vision of home, safety and small-village charm on one side and by an overweening sense of travel, adventure and expansion on the other. It seems that Baum never fully recovered from his happy years in upstate New York, and sought new and innovative ways to recreate it. Baum longed to return to his own personal Arcadia, one foot in an idealized past and the other foot in an idealized future. His books, and later plays and movies, would be the engines he used to drive him there.

IF THERE'S ONE THING YOU MUST DO THIS SUMMER, IT'S "RETURN TO OZ..."

WALT DISNEY PICTURES

Return To Oz

An all-new adventure fantasy down the yellow brick road.

WALT DISNEY PICTURES presents "RETURN TO OZ"
Produced in association with SILVER SCREEN PARTNERS II
Starring NICOL WILLIAMSON JEAN MARSH PIPER LAURIE
Introducing FAIRUZA BALK Executive Producer GARY KURTZ Music by DAVID SHIRE
Screenplay by WALTER MURCH & GILL DENNIS Produced by PAUL MASLANSKY
Directed by WALTER MURCH Based the Oz/Ozma/Tik/Tiktok Book Color by TECHNICOLOR
DISTRIBUTED BY BUENA VISTA DISTRIBUTION CO., INC. ©1985 Walt Disney Productions [PG]

Disney's *Return to Oz* featured characters like Jack Pumpkinhead, a talking chicken and Ozma.

There are several takeaways from Baum's Oz corpus. First and foremost is a remarkable, unbridled imagination. For Baum and his readers young and old, Oz was a real and tangible place. To this date, Oz enthusiasts obsessively map the terrain, and seek to reconcile the sometimes-contradictory clues about the place Baum presented in the corpus. Baum wrote with complete conviction—the man *believed*.

Next, Baum (no doubt inspired by Maud) was clearly enamored of powerful women, as both protagonists and antagonists in his fiction. The female characters—Dorothy, Ozma, Glinda, Trot, Betsy Bobbin, the Patchwork Girl, Mombi and other witches—are all women to be reckoned with. The only strong male protagonist, Tip, in *The Marvelous Land of Oz*, turns out to be (you guessed it) an enchanted girl, Ozma. (One wonders if his male name was some odd circumcision joke ...)

Baum also exulted in colorful supporting characters. People familiar with Baum only through the 1939 *Oz* know and love the Scarecrow, Tin Man and Lion, but he also created the Woggle-Bug

The Wizard of Oz is a masterpiece of 1930s interior design.

(a giant, intellectual bug, Highly Magnified and Thoroughly Educated, thank you very much), a living couch with a moose head tied to it that flies, a living wooden sawhorse, an evil gnome, a city of living flatware (Utensia), a porcelain girl, a talking chicken and a perpetually Hungry Tiger with a professed taste for babies.

Finally, Baum certainly believed in including a little showbiz razzle-dazzle in his work. Since several of his books were written with an eye to eventual stage or film adaptation, he knew what would "play." His passion for early musical theater would also indicate that Baum would have delighted in the now-fandom-reviled *vaudeville* aspects of the 1939 classic.

Sadly, there is no great, definitive biography of Baum (unlike Disney, subject of Neal Gabler's masterful *Walt Disney: The Triumph of the American Imagination*). The truly interested can read *L. Frank Baum, Creator of Oz: A Biography* if they have the time and inclination for feminist theorizing, but the book is a turgid slog.

Translating *The Wonderful Wizard of Oz* into a viable film property presented two special challenges: creating the world of Oz on film in a convincing manner, and the problem of tone.

As a fantasy, Oz never has to be *convincing*. In fact, the more otherworldly Oz comes across, the more successful that adaptation. The 1933 cartoon version of the novel, directed by Ted Eshbaugh, was only loosely based on the novel. (This eight-and-a-half minute Technicolor cartoon opens in a black-and-white Kansas, much like the 1939 classic.) The animation has that wonderful, frenetic quality one associates with 1930s cartoons, along with a hyper-surrealism that is often delirious. (One wonders what Max Fleischer would have made of Baum and his world.) Animation seldom strives for a sense of human representation, and is often spectacularly unsuccessful when it does; see the Ralph Bakshi *Lord of the Rings*. Filled with Carl Stalling music and zippy gags, the 1933 version has much to commend it.

Without the burden of believability, Baum's own Oz films relied on men in donkey suits, as well as some obvious make-ups. The films of Baum and

Eshbaugh are all readily available on YouTube, and one of the most amazing things about them is how well they work to this day.

No ... the real challenge in adapting *Oz* is one of tone. Baum himself faced this challenge when he initially turned Oz into a musical stage show. He added a waitress and streetcar operator to the cast of characters (!), and included several timely political jokes. His own Oz films often veer between straight fantasies and music hall reviews.

It is in this question of tone where the 1939 film is most successful. A product of its time, *The Wizard of Oz* reflects the mores and aesthetic of a nation emerging from the grips of the Great Depression and putting on its bravest face for the world war to come.

The 1930s were a remarkable time in our once-great popular culture because it was a perfect fusion of cynicism and sentiment. It's no accident that the most representative filmmaker of the era is Frank Capra (1897-1991); the vast majority of his films involve New York wiseacres finding their own innocence and vulnerability, usually when in contact with characters who have maintained their essential American innocence. The zeitgeist of the era was smart and knowing, but with its core decency intact. It's what made scoundrels like Clark Gable vulnerable to children, on-the-make Jean Arthur putty to Gary Cooper, and enabled personas as opposed as Warren William and Mickey Rooney to exist in the same universe. It was *the* perfect historical moment for a cosmopolitan take on a fairy tale.

One of the key architects of the 1939 *Oz* was a man who embodied the many complexities and contradictions of the 1930s: songwriter Edgar Yipsil (Yip) Harburg (1896-1981). Harburg was the quintessential 1930s sharpster, and his body of work is raffish, rakish and jaunty. His words don't walk ... they saunter. One can tell his hat was cocked and his mouth smirked; he's the quintessential New York wiseass between the World Wars—a vanished American everyman who is equal to any occasion. He had smarts, savvy, and his eye on the payoff.

Journalist Peter W. Kaplan, when interviewing Harburg in 1981, wrote:

> Harburg is a giant because when the '30s ended, he crescendos with the most explosively imaginative score in the movies, an Art Deco operetta that defined its moment in culture as surely as the Trylon and Perisphere, and that was *The Wizard of Oz*.

The stories and novels behind Classic Horror, Fantasy and Science Fiction Films

Harburg came from New York, where he went to school with Ira Gershwin. The two were friendly, but separated when Harburg married, had children, and worked first as a newspaper man, and then as co-owner of the Consolidated Electrical Appliance Company. When the Crash came in 1929, Harburg left home and hearth (and wife and children) to reconnect with Gershwin and become a songwriter. Where many Depression-era fathers deserted their families to ride the rails, Harburg left to become a songwriter. How's that for moxie?

Harburg met with a great deal of success, writing the signature song of the Depression, *Brother Can You Spare a Dime?* This led to positions at both Paramount and MGM, where he worked as the lyricist on *Oz*. But more than that, Harburg doctored the *Oz* script, initially by writer Noel Langley. As Harburg's son recalled:

> So anyhow, Yip also wrote all the dialogue in that time and the setup to the songs and he also wrote the part where they give out the heart, the brains and the nerve, because he was the final script editor. And he—there were eleven screenwriters on that—and he pulled the whole thing together, wrote his own lines and gave the thing a coherence and unity which made it a work of art. But he doesn't get credit for that. He gets lyrics by E. Y. Harburg, you see. But nevertheless, he put his influence on the thing.

As Kaplan records in his 1981 interview:

> Hollywood called Yip a Jewish leprechaun, the happy idealist who wanted to write the world as he wanted it to be. And because of that, he knew exactly what he wanted *Oz* to be. He understood it, and he loved it. "They called me in, and they said, 'we're having trouble,'" Yip says. "We've got 10 different versions of this thing here," and I said, "If you ask me, this is what I would do: let me write the score with Harold [Arlen] and let the score tell the story. We'll just cue in all the scenes to fit the lyrics." Harburg wrote fully half of the script—he wrote funnier stuff than what they had. He knew there were laughs in *Oz*.

The contribution of Harburg's sensibility to *Oz* is incalculable. A gifted lyricist who was able to play off the gifts of the performers he wrote for (his *The*

Singing Kid, written for Jolson, showcased the signer's strengths while poking fun at them), Harburg managed to infuse his work with an edgy humanism. Harburg had written for both Ray Bolger (the Scarecrow) and Bert Lahr (the Cowardly Lion) previously, and his *If I Were King of the Forest* includes some of the wittiest lyrics committed to film:

> *What makes the Sphinx the Seventh Wonder? Courage!*
> *What makes the dawn come up like thunder? Courage!*
> *What's makes the Hottentot so hot?*
> *What puts the "ape" in apricot?*
> *What do they got that I aint got?*

Compare, for example, the score of *Oz* to two contemporaneous Disney films, *Snow White and the Seven Dwarfs* (1937) and *Pinocchio* (1940). While *Some Day My Prince Will Come, Heigh Ho!* and *When You Wish Upon a Star* are all lovely melodies, they are also much of a muchness. They are sweet and lyrical, but they lack wit, bite and … moxie.

Perhaps Harburg's towering achievement in the film is the end sequence in the Wizard's reception room. The scene is the core of the film, the payoff to the entire joke. It is also instructive to compare it to Baum's original ending, as it is a distinct improvement.

Most of the changes to Baum's novel in the 1939 film version were questions of concision—extraneous characters are cut, the rescue from the poppy field streamlined, Dorothy's trip home is made easier. But the key change is in the *tone* of the final scene in the Wizard's palace, a tonal shift that marks *Oz* as the archetypical picture of the 1930s.

In Baum's novel, the Wizard provides the Scarecrow with a head full of bran, pins and needles (or, "bran-new brains"), the Tin Man gets a silk heart filled with sawdust, and the Lion receives a potion labeled "courage." All well and good, and the film version pretty much takes this you-always-had-what-you-wanted moral to heart. But what the film has that the novel lacks is that cosmopolitan touch of cynicism to cut the sweetness.

Few films have fired the American imagination like *The Wizard of Oz*.

In Harburg's telling, the Wizard gives the Scarecrow a diploma. He says, "Back where I come from we have universities, seats of great learning—where men go to become great thinkers. And when they come out, they think deep thoughts—and with no more brains than you have ... ! But they have one thing you haven't got! A diploma! Therefore, by virtue of the authority vested in me by the Universitatus Committeeatum e plurbis unum, I hereby confer upon you the honorary degree of Th.D."

With a few lines of dialog, Harburg skewers academicians, pedants, and the notion of deep thinkers—all targets of a more homespun 1930s.

Harburg has the Wizard deliver something more tangible than a potion for the Lion—a medal. "As for you, my fine friend—you're a victim of disorganized thinking. You are under the unfortunate delusion that simply because you run away from danger, you have no courage. You're confusing courage with wisdom. Back where I come from, we have men who are called heroes. Once a year, they take their fortitude out of mothballs and parade it down the main street of the city. And they have no more courage than you have. But! They have one thing that you haven't got! A medal! Therefore—for meritorious conduct, extraordinary valor, conspicuous bravery against wicked witches, I award you the Triple Cross. You are now a member of the Legion of Courage!"

Harburg, a socialist who campaigned against the Great War and would later be brown-listed, can be clearly heard here. Throughout his life, Harburg wondered why the good, common men of America should spill their blood for their capitalist masters, and the mockery here is by turns sweet and acidic.

For the Tin Man, the Wizard provides a mechanical heart-cum-testimonial. "As for you, my galvanized friend, you want a heart! You don't know how lucky you are not to have one. Hearts will never be practical until they can be made unbreakable ... Back where I come from there are men who do nothing all day but good deeds. They are called phil ... er--er--phil--er ... good-deed-doers! And their hearts are no bigger than yours. But! They have one thing you haven't got! A testimonial! Therefore, in consideration of your kindness, I take pleasure at this time in presenting you with a small token of our esteem and affection. And remember, my sentimental friend, that a heart is not judged by how much you love, but by how much you are loved by others."

Of all of the gifts bestowed by the Wizard (yes, including his attempted deliverance of Dorothy—a self-described "cataclysmic decision"), this is perhaps the sweetest of all. But even Harburg's sweetness here is tempered with mockery; but it is the sweetness that lingers.

One wonders what another brilliant filmmaker of the era, Walt Disney, would do with the same materials. I'm sure a Disney animated *Oz* of 1939 (and Walt wanted to follow *Snow White and the Seven Dwarfs* with an animated Oz, only to find the rights already held) would have been as beautiful and accomplished as *Pinocchio*. But it also would have been one more beautiful and lilting Disney vision, lacking the unique qualities of tone brought to it by a man with Harburg's sweetly cynical sensibilities.

Here is the essence of Harburg's genius. The Wizard is worse than a fraud: he's a fraud and a hustler, a liar and self-aggrandizer. ("You are talking to a man who has laughed in the face of death—sneered at doom and chuckled at catastrophe. I was petrified.") An ex-carnival huckster, the Wizard literally blew into town and was mistaken for a Wizard, and was offered the job as the guardian of Oz. ("Times being what they were, I accepted the position.") Despite all of this, the Wizard is also the film's one, indisputable hero.

In keeping with the tone of the era, the Wizard is an operator with a heart of gold, a scoundrel with a soft spot for little girls, lions, and men made of straw and tin. Despite his obvious wealth, power and position, he vows to take Dorothy back to Kansas himself ("the land of E Pluribus Unum!"). This act of kindness does not change the Wizard's inherent psychological make-up—readying his balloon to take Dorothy back home, he cannot help but start delving into his standard carny pitch.

The Wizard is so vividly written that actor Frank Morgan comes very close to walking away with the entire movie. The **Wizard**.

The Italian poster prominately features The Wizard.

original choices for the role—both Ed Wynn and W.C. Fields—would have been cataclysmic miscalculations. Wynn would have had no bite, while Fields would have been too astringent. Morgan, one of the great character actors of the decade, had both necessary qualities of cynicism and sweetness, carrying the emotional tenor of the film almost by himself.

This brings us to one of the most fascinating paradoxes in *The Wizard of Oz*, and the root of its brilliance. The Wizard sells Dorothy, the Tin Man, the Scarecrow and the Cowardly Lion a lie ... a terrible, expensive and rather disappointing lie. However, it is a lie that nourishes, energizes and empowers—it is a lie that becomes a personal myth for all of them. Essentially, Harburg in *Oz* posits that an empowering lie can be better than a mundane truth. He argues, in short, in favor of the great American political, advertising and religious tradition. For that reason alone, *The Wizard of Oz* is a movie not to be missed.

Frightful foreshadowing as Dorothy (Judy Garland) watches Miss Gulch (Margaret Hamilton) transform into the Wicked Witch.

IT CAME FROM ...

Lao Blow: 7 Faces of Dr. Lao (1964)

There is something oddly compelling about the circus.

Amidst the sense of thrills and entertainment, there is often an edge of menace ... or the uncanny. This may be because one of the things the circus does best is lift the veil from the odd, the freakish, the hidden and expose it to the light. A funhouse mirror that imperfectly reflects our own comfortable world, the circus disorients as much as it amuses.

Even more interesting is the notion that "circus folk" are not "normal" like you and I. They are always on the outside, and we have the sneaking suspicion that they are laughing at us. That they have forbidden knowledge that we could never know; that they can see through us, and put a cold hand on our most secret selves, all the while smiling with a clown-like grimace.

Surprisingly, the circus and carnival motif did not figure greatly in fantastic literature until Ray Bradbury's *Something Wicked This Way Comes* in 1964 (covered elsewhere in this book). Previous to this, only two works of any great note come immediately to mind: the short tale "Spurs," by Tod Robbins, the

inspiration for director Tod Browning's infamous and controversial 1932 film, *Freaks,* and the subject of this chapter, *The Circus of Dr. Lao*, by fantasy author Charles Finney.

Charles G. (Grandison) Finney was born on December 1, 1905. He was a novelist (primarily in the fantasy genre), playwright and newspaper editor. He came of noble lineage, and his same-named great grandfather was a famous Presbyterian revivalist preacher of the 19th century (the Billy Graham of his day). Charles Finney, called the Father of Modern Revivalism, often delivered blistering sermons clocking in at two or three hours long.

Finney the author was raised for the first years of his life in Sedalia, Missouri, a somewhat small (pop: 15,000) town, located approximately 30 miles south of the Missouri River and roughly 180 miles from St. Louis. In 1909, the family moved to Parsons, Kansas, where, two years later, age six, Finney fell from a shed and broke his left hip. He spent the better part of a year in traction, tended to by a hired nurse. During this time of incapacitation, the young boy acquired a voracious appetite for reading, as well as daydreaming of one day becoming a hunter or trapper. The following year the family returned to Sedalia. By all accounts, his serious injury notwithstanding, the young future writer appears to have enjoyed a perfectly average boyhood.

Never fond of school in general, Finney endured his time in high school, disliking most all subjects except for English and history. Starting around his junior year, Finney worked summers at the MK&T Railroad where his father was a superintendent. The young Finney performed the grueling work of loading and unloading boxcars, saving for college the 13 cents an hour he earned.

In the fall of 1925 Finney began his freshman year at Missouri University, liking his studies there little more than he did high school. Early into his sophomore year, his hard-earned savings ran out. Not relishing the thought of returning to Sedalia, where money and jobs were scarce and marked by a perceived stigma of poverty, Finney enlisted in the army at Fort Leavenworth, Kansas in 1927.

The new recruit shipped to Tientsin, China, where Finney would spend the next three years. A member of the 15th Infantry, his rank as private earned him a livable $21/month. Finney's initial impression of China was not a favorable one, given the area's poverty, squalor and other deplorable conditions, including the stench arising from open sewers and numerous dead animals strewn about the land. Despite this initial negative impression, the future writer found the local color seeping into his bloodstream, and he would return again and again to this alien terrain in his literary works. The 15th Infantry saw no combat during their time there; their only directive being to keep the railway line open between Tientsin and Peking.

Honorably discharged from service in the winter of 1929, Finney still had no burning desire to return to Sedalia. Seized by a newly acquired desire to try his hand at writing for a living, Finney took a train in February 1930 to Tucson, Arizona to begin this new chapter in his life. In September, as his Army money ran out, he took a job as copy editor of the *Arizona Daily Star*. He would stay there for the next 40 years.

During his long tenure with the *Daily Star*, Finney concurrently pursued his dream of becoming a successful novelist. The year 1935 saw the release of *The Circus of Dr. Lao*, the novel that would cement Finney's place in fantastic fiction. Throughout the succeeding decades, Finney published additional novels, *The Unholy City* (1937) and *The Magician out of Manchuria* (1968), collections of stories, and even a play (*Project Number Six*, 1962), but nothing would match the success achieved by *Lao*. *The Old China Hands*, a memoir of sorts, vignettes of his time in military service in China, was published in 1961 to moderate success. The book became popular with, and acclaimed by, those connected to the military for its honest depiction of life in service.

IT CAME FROM ...

Sedalia-born writer dies in Arizona

Charles G. Finney

By DOUG KNEIBERT
Editor

Charles G. Finney, 78, a notable American writer who was born in Sedalia, died Monday in Tucson, Ariz.

Finney was best known for his 1935 novel, "The Circus of Dr. Lao," The book, which describes the impact of a bizarre circus on a sleepy Arizona town, was voted the most unusual novel of the year by the American Booksellers Association. It has since gone through numerous paperback editions.

Other works by Finney include "Past the End of the Pavement," "The Unholy City," "The Magician Out of Manchuria" and a collection of short stories, "The Old China Hands."

Finney's experiences in China had a great influence on his works. He served there with the U.S. Army from 1927 to 1930. After leaving the Army, he went to work for the *Tucson Star,* where he was a copy editor and financial editor, retiring in 1970.

Born here in 1905, the son of Mr. and Mrs. N.J. Finney, Charles Finney graduated from Sedalia High School in 1924. He last visited Sedalia in the late 1930s.

Mr. Finney's grandfather was the president of the Missouri Kansas Texas Railroad, and his great-grandfather, Charles Grandison Finney, was the most famous American evangelist of the 19th century.

Mr. Finney is survived by his wife, Marie

(Please see FINNEY, page 2)

Finney retired from the *Daily Star* in 1970. Little is known of his later life until his passing on April 16, 1984 at the age of 78, following a long illness.

As with his life, little is known regarding the origins of Finney's most famous opus, *The Circus of Dr. Lao.* The only mention Finney makes concerning *Lao's* origins comes from *The Old China Hands* where the author states he "came back with the makings of a book." Given this lone statement to go on, one can postulate that the titular Lao was perhaps inspired by one or more particularly colorful coolies (indentured laborers) encountered by Finney during his three-year stint in China with the 15th Infantry. Finney completed the book in 1934, where it was subsequently rejected by a number of publishers until published by Viking Press the following year. With illustrations by Boris Artzybasheff, a Ukraine-born artist primarily known for his work for such major American magazines as *Life* and *Time,* the novel went on to receive the National Book Award for Most Original Novel of the Year by the American Booksellers Association.

Beyond this initial recognition, while a steady seller, the book remained a relatively obscure title with the general public until the early 1950s when writer Gwyndolyn Steinbeck (former wife of famed writer John Steinbeck), with collaborator Nat Benchley, dramatized the novel. The result, starring Burgess Meredith in the lead, enjoyed short runs in both Palm Beach and Chicago, but never made it to the Great White Way. The novel gained new life when, in 1953, the *Saturday Review* listed *Lao* as one of the "12 Best Books of Recent Years" (a strange inclusion, given the book was almost 20 years old at the time).

It wasn't until the early 1960s that the novel came to the attention of legendary Hollywood producer George Pal (*War of the Worlds, The Time Machine*) as a potential cinematic property through *Twilight Zone* scripter/fantasy writer Charles Beaumont.

Charles Beaumont (1929-1967) was born in Chicago, IL. A fantasy writer, Beaumont's primary fame stems from his work as one of the original writers for Rod Serling's *Twilight Zone (TZ)* television series. Beaumont would write 22 episodes of the classic series. Additional episodes, actually credited to Beaumont, were in fact ghostwritten by others. More so, he was a novelist, screen/television scripter and prolific short-story writer.

It is surprising how similar the upbringings of both Finney and Beaumont were. Born January 2, 1929 as Charles Leroy Nutt, Beaumont spent the following decade growing up in Chicago, playing football and studying piano. In 1941, the young Nutt had his world turned upside down when he contracted a case of spinal meningitis. Late in the year, Charles' mother moved them to Everett, WA, to both get away from the harsh Chicago winters and to have the boy live with his grandmother and five aunts. Charles was bedridden for two years before recovering. During this time, he became a voracious reader—showing a preference for science fiction and fantasy, he devoured the works of such writers as Baum, Poe, Burroughs and others.

Once recovered, he entered high school in 1944. Finding school boring and unchallenging, the young Beaumont dropped out in 10th grade to join the U.S. Army as an Infantryman. His time in the military was cut short when released three months later with a medical discharge for a bad back. He subsequently moved to Los Angeles. There, he landed a job in the animation department at MGM Studios while simultaneously pursuing an acting career. Meeting little success in landing roles, Beaumont abandoned the craft in 1948, and moved to Mobile, Alabama, where, with his father's help, he found work as a railroad clerk. It is during this time that he met 20-year-old Helen Louise Broun. The pair married in November of 1949 and moved to Los Angeles. While trying to find work as an illustrator, Beaumont supported himself and

Charles Beaumont

his new wife through such varied jobs as dishwasher, movie usher, disc jockey, comic book editor and others. Upon his return to LA at this time, Beaumont joined a number of other genre writers such as William F. Nolan and Jerry Sohl, who called themselves The Southern California Group, a close-knit clan who supported each other in their craft. Included in this group was fellow fantasy writer Richard Matheson (whose later-to-become-classic "Born of Man and Woman" was published in July 1950); Beaumont and Matheson would become life-long friends.

Throughout the 1940s, Beaumont continued to write short stories. While prolific—producing nearly 70-some stories by end of 1949, he had been unable

IT CAME FROM ...

to sell any of them. (That Forrest J Ackerman was his literary agent should probably tell you something.) The rejection dam burst in 1951 with his first professional sale, the short story "The Devil, You Say?" in *Amazing Stories* magazine.

And with that, Beaumont's writing career took off, his stories now regularly published in such pulp magazines as *If*, *Orbit*, and *The Magazine of Fantasy & Science Fiction*. The year 1954 was memorable to the author for two reasons. *Playboy* magazine (yes, that magazine!) chose the Beaumont tale, "Black Country," to be the first work of short fiction to ever appear in its pages. This milestone led Beaumont to become a regular contributor to the "gentleman's" magazine, as well as representing a pathway to publication in other higher-profile, "slick" magazines of the time. The year also saw Beaumont's first screen credit with his story "Masquerade," adapted for the *Four Star Playhouse* television series. The dreadful film, *Queen of Outer Space* (1958), marked Beaumont's first produced screenplay.

Around this time, Beaumont and Matheson, having both just joined the Preminger Stuart Agency, found themselves in demand. Both newcomers to the relatively new medium of television, they decided to collaborate on assignments. For the remainder of the decade the pair wrote teleplays for such television series as *The D.A.'s Man*, *Buckskin*, *Markham*, *Wanted: Dead or Alive*, and others.

The year 1959 saw Beaumont begin his most fruitful and arguably most famous "gig," when Rod Serling made television history with the premiere of *The Twilight Zone* (*TZ*). Given the green light by CBS Television for his new anthology series, Serling, contracted to write 80% of the scripts, needed to look elsewhere for the remaining 20%. Always a champion for the discovery and promotion of new talent, Serling's first attempt at finding potential writers saw him put out a call for unsolicited manuscripts. This idea proved a disaster with the resulting lack of quality material. Serling next turned to more conventional methods for his talent search by inviting established writers in the fantasy and science fiction fields for a screening of the *TZ* pilot episode, after which the writers pitched their ideas. From this, Beaumont and Matheson were chosen. Over the course of *The Twilight Zone*'s five-season history, Beaumont would be credited with 22 of the show's scripts, although other writers ghostwrote some during the period of Beaumont's sickness and decline.

But Beaumont's immense drive and talent during this time was hardly limited to Serling's series. Beaumont continued to write other teleplays (*Alfred Hitchcock Presents*, *Thriller*, *Suspense*) as well as numerous screenplays for Roger Corman (*The Premature Burial*, *Masque of the Red Death*, and *Haunted Palace*) and George Pal (*The Wonderful World of the Brothers Grimm*, and the subject of this chapter, *7 Faces of Dr. Lao*).

In 1963, Beaumont began to show the first signs of ill health. Manifesting itself first through memory loss, it progressed quickly to include the inability to concentrate and an inexplicable, rapid aging, so much so that at the time of his death at 38, he looked like a man of 90. By the end of that same year the disease had progressed to the point where his ability to write had significantly diminished. It was here that fellow writer friends pitched in to help Beaumont out financially by ghostwriting material and giving Beaumont the writing credit. The unfortunate Beaumont declined rapidly and finally succumbed to the disease, later attributed to Alzheimer's or Pick's Disease, on February 21, 1967.

Beaumont, though perhaps not as widely a known fantasy writer such as Matheson, Bloch or Bradbury, nevertheless leaves behind a rich legacy in the field thanks to the aforementioned *Twilight Zone* episodes and horror/fantasy screenplays.

Beaumont's involvement with Pal's *Dr. Lao* was covered in *The Films of George Pal* by Gail Morgan Hickman:

> While [George] Pal was working with screenwriter Charles Beaumont on the script for *The Wonderful World of the Brothers Grimm*, he asked Beaumont, as he asks every writer, if he had any favorite projects he had been unable to sell. Beaumont told him about a curious little novel entitled *The Circus of Dr. Lao* by Charles G. Finney, published in 1935, about a bizarre circus of mythical beasts that suddenly appears in a small Arizona town in the midst of the depression. The book is part fantasy, part allegory, part philosophy, part mythology, and is also one of the finest (and least read) fantasy novels ever written.
>
> Pal was intrigued with Beaumont's description and asked to see the book, but Beaumont instead offered to show him a treatment he had already written on his own. Pal remembers: "So I read the treatment and flipped. It was great, absolutely great. And that's the way it all began."

The final shooting script (if Beaumont had a treatment written during the making of *Brothers Grimm*, one assumes that he must have fleshed out said treatment into a screenplay prior to the onslaught of dementia symptoms), is fairly faithful to Finney's novel, albeit with the change of a few of Lao's mythological creatures, the shift to a more uplifting overall tone (the residents of Abalone leave Lao's circus wiser for their time than in the book), as well as the addition of some plot elements to give the film needed cohesion and direction.

Released in 1964, the film performed poorly at the box office, coming in at #55 for the year. *Lao* fared better with critics, receiving overall positive notices, understandably (for I can think of no other reason) due to the film's make-up and special effects work. Make-up legend William Tuttle received an

Townsfolk soon learn to be careful what you wish for.

honorary Oscar and stop-motion animator Jim Danforth was nominated for his effects work.

A late inclusion to this book, I looked forward to writing this chapter for two reasons: I had never read Finney's novel, and I looked forward to revisiting the film, remembering little of it since my last viewing as a youth (a period of time longer than I'm willing to confess to!). Sadly, more mature reading and viewing have revealed that both works are abject disappointments.

Why some consider the novel a classic is, frankly, baffling. Brief and simply written, it at times reads as if meant as a children's novel, yet its occasional sexual and erotic undertones belies this opinion. On the flip side, said undertones are so fleetingly brief as to dash the hopes of an interesting story arising from erotic thrills.

One of the most maddening aspects of Finney's novel is the way the author tosses aside novelistic conventions that would only help him better tell his story. There are no chapter breaks, nor any gaps used to build up tension or momentum. In itself, I suppose this is not innately a "negative," *if* a story is compelling enough in some way to drive readers forward. But such is not the case with Finney's tale. The only storyline is the arrival of Lao's circus to an out-of-the-way Arizona location and the residents' reactions to its bizarre attractions.

Speaking of characters, Finney's Arizonans are a dull and unengaging bunch—we do not care about any of them and none undergo any significant change (unless you count Kate Lindquist as a result of staring into the face of Medusa!). The mythological residents of Lao's traveling show are slightly more colorful, but each is given short shrift—a few pages at most—and any character background which might elevate them to interesting status is instead pretty much limited to a history of how the mysterious Lao came to capture them.

The novel's conclusion is as disappointing as its preceding story—Lao simply pulls up stakes and leaves Abalone …

Interestingly, a defense by some of Finney's novel lay in proclaiming that a delight lay in its mystery—that the novel leaves more questions unanswered than it answers. To that, I simply say that in general I prefer to finish a book with my questions *answered*, thank you very much. Additionally, praising the novel for its inclusion of interesting "parables" is faint praise. As example, the parable in consideration of who is the more "free"—the sea serpent, caged, but who has traveled the world, or Mr. Eotain, uncaged, but whose life has never ranged past the borders of Abalone—hardly approaches the sophistica-

tion of such parables as the Prodigal Son or the Good Samaritan. Even worse, this parable and all the others are ultimately pointless because they produce no or little resultant change in the character expected to learn from said lesson.

Lastly, and most egregiously, may we address the elephant in the room? The inherent racism contained in the book is, to admittedly politically correct 21st-century eyes, absolutely cringe-worthy. The ease with which the book tosses about various ethnic slurs or Lao's descent into exaggerated, stereotypical Chinese "speech" makes one sadly reflect upon the too-lengthy

IT CAME FROM ...

time in our country's history when such behavior was so readily accepted and even encouraged. As such, said racism only contributes (at least, perhaps, to Left-leaning readers) to the previously described faults in making the book today a difficult read. I would like to think that we, as a nation, have evolved to a more tolerant and enlightened plain. But ...

The film fares little better, but still it is overall a mess. Possessing most of the faults of the novel (with the exception of no utterance of the *Asian* "c" word), the film's saving grace is that screenwriter Beaumont included a plot, however flimsy and derivative. Here, the town's handsome newspaper publisher pursues the love of a beautiful young widow, all the while battling an "evil" wealthy tycoon looking to swindle people out of their homes in the pursuit of greater riches. (Hey, the plot may be thinner than onion-skin paper, but at least viewers have something to engage their attention, unlike readers only having Lao's less-than-extraordinary menagerie.)

Despite said love interest and "will the town be saved" storyline, the characters here, as in the novel, are a dull, uninteresting lot. Not even the talents of a young Barbara Eden or the usually enjoyable Arthur O'Connell can bring energy to their characters. Tony Randall is the lone exception. Playing the titular doctor, as well as each attraction in his circus, seems an odd decision as Randall is unrecognizable as both the Abominable Snowman and Medusa and only provides the

Not even Barbara Eden (above) and Arthur O'Connell (below) can save the film.

voice to the serpent. Yes, each mythological oddity represents one of the doctor's seven "faces," but any other actor could have played said characters with little notice. The answer most likely lay in working as a unique marketing tool. Returning to our aforementioned Yeti, his inclusion here is regrettable. For instead of bringing to life any number of the

The stories and novels behind Classic Horror, Fantasy and Science Fiction Films

novel's other interesting characters—the Chimera, Sphinx, mermaid or the fascinating Hound of the Hedges—we're instead given a Snowman more comical than abominable. An obvious *person* (body double for Randall, as it turns out) in a white gorilla suit that you're quite likely to miss—for his appearances are few, fleeting, and contribute nothing to the film. A great, missed opportunity. Credit, however, must be given Randall for his portrayal of Apollonius of Tyana, the blind seer. Here, the actor superbly captures the sad, "weight of the world" resignation that certainly must accompany one possessed of eternal life, destined to forever reveal the future of others, but all the while prohibited from using his precognitive powers to alter the course of future history. This is brilliant work by Randall.

Speaking of the film's effects, the stop-motion work within *7 Faces* is a double-edge sword. On the one hand, despite the obvious power of readers' imaginations, Finney (and admittedly just about any writer) cannot do these fascinating creatures justice with mere words. The film, however, brings these mythological deities to cinematic life, providing audiences with creatures read about, but seldom or never before seen on the screen. However, time has not always been kind to stop-motion effects from the 1950s and 1960s, and *7 Faces* is hit harder than most. While the film must have been a marvel upon its

Four (and a half) faces of Dr. Lao: a Danforth stop-motion model

IT CAME FROM ...

Tony Randall as (an admittedly fetching) Medusa

re.lease (that animator Danforth was nominated for an Academy Award for his work gives credence to this), but to current-day viewers, most of the SFX are difficult to watch. The rampage of the Loch Ness Monster toward film's end is particularly painful.

As stated earlier, I began this chapter with great anticipation. I end with great disappointment. Finney's novel is a seriously flawed work, lacking both interesting characters and a coherent story. The film is a poorly aged relic, whose only improvement upon its source is the introduction of the most cliché of plots; its special effects, perhaps impressive at the time, are now little more than laughable. In a 2002 Bison Books edition of the novel (University of Nebraska Press), John Marco in his Introduction refers to Finney's book as an "obscure classic." I agree, in part. It deserves to remain obscure.

Pure Imagination: Willy Wonka and the Chocolate Factory (1971)

Though I grew up with a love of books and films of a fantastic nature, my overall preference fell toward the horror genre, particularly those with a supernatural bent. This "horrific" preference does not preclude a love for science fiction, as some of my favorite books (*Childhood's End* and *Rendezvous with Rama*, both by Arthur C. Clarke, *The Martian Chronicles* by Ray Bradbury and most of H.G. Wells' output, to name but a few) and films (*2001: A Space Odyssey*, *Planet of the Apes*, *Close Encounters of the Third Kind* and many others) are very dear to my heart, bearing repeated readings and viewings.

And yet, when it comes to my reading and viewing preferences, fantasy has always been the black sheep of my fantastic family. And I've never quite been able to put my finger on the reason why. I often wonder if it is simply because a great deal of fantasy is geared toward younger audiences (though its resulting appeal may span all ages). Not being particularly fond of children myself, this probably explains a good deal—usually, books or films containing children as major characters are problematic for me. I'd much rather view more "adult" fantasy fare—show me a Harryhausen film featuring Jason or mythological creatures and I'm hooked. But beyond this example and a handful more, there is little fantasy that catches my fancy (say THAT three times quick!).

Original illustration by Roald Dahl for *Charlie and the Chocolate Factory*

IT CAME FROM ...

But, for every preference there are exceptions, and I am … no exception. I would probably be burned as a heretic if I did not profess my adoration for the beloved *Wizard of Oz*. Why? *Oz*, the film, is simply a phenomenon … its magic has cast a spell on audiences for decades and defies description. I've also always been particularly fond of Bradbury's *Something Wicked This Way Comes*, as I write about elsewhere in this book. Explaining *Something Wicked* (book more so than film) is easier … it's the supernatural and horrific (even if Bradbury-ishly watered down) elements. And then there is *Willy Wonka and the Chocolate Factory*—the most perplexing choice of all, as both book and film contain almost as many children as major adult characters! Why *Willy Wonka*? The easy answer lay in my savoring the fiendishly appropriate comeuppances that befall the four selfishly bratty children. But more so, *Wonka* (film more so than book) embodies, as the best fantasy films do, the resulting joy from a belief that anything is possible and limited only by one's imagination. Lyrics from the film ("Pure Imagination," songwriters: Anthony Newley and Leslie Bricusse) wonderfully capture this concept:

If you want to view Paradise,
Simply look around and view it.
Anything you want to do, do it.
Wanna change the world?
There's nothing to it.

There is no life I know,
To compare with pure imagination.
Living there, you'll be free,
If you truly wish to be.

This author wishes to be.

Willy Wonka and the Chocolate Factory is based on the novel, *Charlie and the Chocolate Factory* by Roald Dahl, first published in the United States in 1964.

Dahl (1916–1990) was born in Wales, UK. A multi-faceted writer, over the course of his life Dahl experienced success as poet, essayist, writer for the screen (*Chitty Chitty Bang Bang* [1968], the James Bond film, *You Only Live Twice* [1967], and early drafts of *Willy Wonka*), and television (the science fiction/horror television anthology series *Way Out* [1961], and the David Frost BBC comedy vehicle, *That Was the Week That Was* [1962-1963]), as well as numerous short stories. However, Dahl's greatest fame stems from his authorship of a number of immensely popular children's books, among them *James and the Giant Peach* (1961), *Fantastic Mr. Fox* (1970), *Matilda* (1988), as well as the subject of this chapter, arguably his most famous and enduring, *Charlie and the Chocolate Factory* (1964).

When only three years old, Dahl suffered the loss of both his older sister and father in the space of a matter of weeks. Both losses devastated the young boy and seemed perhaps to have had an indirect impact that continued into his adult life, as the father figure in several of his children's books is either a completely missing or significantly un-influential figure.

Dahl was educated at various schools throughout the UK, lastly at the Repton School in Derbyshire, at the time a boys-only institution. There, the future author spent a miserable four years, being subjected to fagging—a common British practice at the time in private boarding schools, where younger boys acted almost as indentured servants to the older students, who wielded their power and dispensed punishments for the slightest of infractions. His time at Repton held a lasting impression on Dahl, which permeates many of his children's works, where the child of the story must often endure trials or mistreatment initiated by cruel and villainous adult characters (who at least almost always receive a deserving comeuppance).

Roald Dahl

Upon completion of his schooling at Repton, the Shell Oil Company hired Dahl as a clerk, where he worked for several years until the start of World War II in 1939. He immediately joined and served in the Royal Air Force (RAF) for the United Kingdom as a fighter pilot. An injury suffered the following year from a crash forced his withdrawal. Still wishing to serve his country, but no longer able to fly, he was chosen to serve as an air attaché in the United States for propaganda purposes (to help use U.S. sympathies toward their involvement). Fortuitously, his primary way of doing so was through writing. His first book, *The Gremlins*, published in 1943, features the folklorist creatures often blamed by RAF pilots for mechanical hijinks with their planes (think: *Twilight Zone's Nightmare at 20,000 Feet*). He wrote several short stories during this time, drawing upon his experiences as a pilot. One, *Shot Down Over Libya*, was published in the *Saturday Evening Post* in 1942. These stories were subsequently collected in the volume, *Over to You: Ten Stories of Flyers and Flying*, published in 1946.

At a dinner party in 1951, Dahl met his soon-to-be wife, actress Patricia Neal, and the pair wed two years later. Neal, who had earlier that same year starred in *The Day the Earth Stood Still* (1951) would later go on to win the Academy Award for Best Actress in the Paul Newman classic, *Hud* (1963). Over the course of their 30-year marriage (they divorced in 1983), they had five children: four daughters and one son.

Having continued to write short stories since the publication of *Over to You*, these subsequent tales, now eschewing the subject of flying in favor of more dark and decidedly macabre territory, present an extraordinary juxtaposition to his later children's works. In 1957, Shamley Productions, the American production company initiated by famed director Alfred Hitchcock, purchased the rights to a number of Dahl's stories for use on Hitchcock's popular television series, *Alfred Hitchcock Presents*. Arguably, two of the most memorable of these resulting episodes remain the *deliciously* humorous "Lamb to the Slaughter" (1958, with Barbara Bel Geddes) and the nail-biting "Man from the South" (1960, with Steve McQueen and Peter Lorre).

The 1960s was a period of extremes for Dahl. The decade saw the author experience some of his greatest successes, cruelly dampened by several personal tragedies. In December of 1960, Dahl and Neal's only son, Theo, then four months old, was left brain damaged after a taxicab hit his stroller, resulting in hydrocephalus (buildup of cerebrospinal fluid in the brain). It took numerous surgeries to save the boy's life. Significant literary success came the following year, with the publication of his first children's book, *James and the Giant Peach*, which tells the story of an orphan boy who enters a giant (obviously) magical peach, and who, along with several transformed bugs, traverse the world, participating in numerous adventures. Any satisfaction over *James'* success was short-lived, as in November of 1962 tragedy struck the Dahls again upon the death of their eldest, seven-year-old daughter Olivia. Dahl was devastated, resulting in a subsequent life-long dedication to bringing public awareness to the need for measles vaccination. The year 1964 saw publication of arguably Dahl's most beloved and successful novel, *Charlie and the Chocolate Factory*, the story of good boy Charlie Bucket winning his dream of touring the candy factory of its renowned proprietor, Willy Wonka. Seemingly cursed by the Fates, in February of the following year, Dahl's wife Patricia suffered

Dahl and Patricia Neal married in 1953.

The stories and novels behind Classic Horror, Fantasy and Science Fiction Films

a series of debilitating strokes. Unwilling to let his wife succumb to typical loss of speech, Dahl subjected his wife to a new style of therapy involving spending six hours a day re-teaching his wife to speak. While ultimately grueling, the regimen was successful, with Neal recovering enough to return to acting three years later. The year 1967 continued the good/bad pattern for Dahl. The high resulting from the summer box-office success of the James Bond entry *You Only Live Twice*, for which Dahl wrote the screenplay (his first) as a favor to the novel's author, Ian Fleming, was offset by the death of Dahl's mother, Sofie, five months later. The following year saw the release of another Dahl-scripted film, the family-friendly musical fantasy, *Chitty Chitty Bang Bang* (based on the novel by none other than ... Ian Fleming!). Dahl ended the decade mercifully enduring no further tragedies, commencing work on his next children's book, *Fantastic Mr. Fox*, published in 1970.

The succeeding two decades saw Dahl further enrich his literary oeuvre with successful forays into children's books (*Charlie and the Great Glass Elevator* [1972], the sequel to *Chocolate Factory*; *The Witches* [1983] and *Matilda* [1988], among others), the screenplay adaptation of *Willy Wonka and the Chocolate Factory* ([1971]; Dahl wrote the initial script drafts), short stories, poems, and an anthology (*Roald Dahl's Book of Ghost Stories* in 1983). In 1979, the series *Tales of the Unexpected* debuted on British television. Initially, episodes were based solely on Dahl's own stories, with the author introducing. The series subsequently progressed to include stories by other writers.

In November of 1990, Dahl was admitted to the hospital for an unspecified infection. He died shortly thereafter on November 23, in Oxford, England, of myelodysplastic syndrome, a rare cancer of the blood. Rumor has it that the author was buried with an array of articles, including chocolate bars.

Although Dahl officially began writing the story that would become *Charlie and the Chocolate Factory* in 1961, the actual inspiration for *Charlie* may date back to the early days of his youth. Like many children, the author loved sweets, chocolates in particular, with Dahl a regular visitor to a sweetshop in his (then) hometown Llandaff. His chocolate passion only increased during his days at Repton, where the Cadbury confectionery company would regularly send the students an assortment of new chocolates for taste-testing purposes. (What a gig!)

Dahl's shaping of the story of Charlie took three years and saw the story and its characters go through numerous changes. In the story's initial incarnation, titled *Charlie and the Chocolate Boy*, Charlie was a black boy, who after becoming encased in chocolate at Wonka's factory is taken to Wonka's house and there, still bound in chocolate, helps prevent a robbery.(!!) Subsequent drafts held additional changes such as Charlie's transformation from a black to white boy (it is said that Dahl's agent convinced the author to make the change

Wonka (Gene Wilder) commences the prized tour of his Chocolate Factory.

for the sake of potential readership), Wonka with a wife and son, additional Golden Ticket winners/obnoxious children visiting Wonka's factory, as well as the Oompa-Loompas being African pygmies. The tale's ultimate draft, now re-titled *Charlie and the Chocolate Factory*, saw the story come together in its final form. With illustrations by artist Joseph Schindelman, the book appeared in September of 1964 to great acclaim by critics and the public alike.

To date, the book's sales are estimated at over 20 million copies in 20-plus editions in nearly 60 languages. Dahl's enduring tale has been adapted across numerous mediums: two feature films (the 1971 version covered here and the 2005, Tim Burton-directed, Johnny Depp-starring effort, *Charlie and the Chocolate Factory*), audio books, video games, a musical (2013, London and later Broadway), a BBC-sponsored radio presentation, as well as … an opera. Yes! The opera, complete with new music, premiered in 2010 in St. Louis, Missouri. (Imagining Charlie Bucket, Grandpa Joe, Willy Wonka and Veruca Salt—not to mention the Oompa-Loompas—performing *arias* is both simultaneously mind-bogglingly horrific and yet irresistible! Imagine Luciano Pavarotti belting out "The Candy Man"!)

And a little child shall lead them …

Director Mel Stuart (*If It's Tuesday, This Must Be Belgium* [1969]) credits his daughter as the driving force for bringing *Willy Wonka and the Chocolate Factory* to the screen. As he elaborates (with Josh Young) in their 2002 book, *Pure Imagination: The Making of Willy Wonka and the Chocolate Factory*:

It was sometime in the fall of 1969 when my precocious 12-year-old daughter came up to me, clutching a copy of Roald Dahl's *Charlie and the Chocolate Factory*. She announced that she had read the book three times, and, judging from its rumpled pages, I didn't doubt her. But she didn't want any special dispensation from me for that accomplishment. She had bigger things in mind and came right to the point.

"Daddy," she said. "I want you to make this into a movie and have Uncle Dave sell it."

"Uncle" Dave was not a relative, but was a close friend of the family, producer David L. Wolper, chief executive, at the time, of the Wolper Organization—a television and motion picture production company. Stuart convinced Wolper on the project, highlighting the film's potential appeal to both children and adults. Wolper, in turn, struck a unique (for the time) deal with the Quaker Oats company with regard to the then-to-be film, as the food company at the time was looking for projects for which to promote a new, as yet unproduced, candy bar. (Talk about synchronicity!) In return, Quaker would finance not only the purchase of the story's film rights but the entire film as well. Purchase of the film rights to *Charlie* from Dahl involved a caveat: The author insisted on writing the screenplay. Eventually all parties came to agreement and *Willy Wonka and the Chocolate Factory* received the green light. (Ironically, Quaker did not produce their proposed candy bar and ultimately abandoned the idea—thus possessing one of the largest marketing opportunities available and ... no product.)

The Oompa-Loompas were changed from African pygmies in the original story to little orange men with green hair in the film.

IT CAME FROM ...

Dahl began work on the screenplay in early 1970. His resulting first draft was problematic for Stuart and company for a number of reasons. Primary among them was a too-strong adherence to his source novel, resulting in scenes on opposite ends of a spectrum: either too visual (expensive) or not "visual" enough for the

Golden Ticket winners ride the chocolate river upon the Wonkatania.

medium of film. After discussing needed changes with the filmmakers, Dahl set work upon a second draft.

Meanwhile, problems arose on a different front. When news got out of a proposed film adaptation of *Charlie and the Chocolate Factory*, the NAACP complained to Wolper. The organization objected to the perceived racism of Dahl's book: the Oompa-Loompas of *Charlie* were African pygmies, brought from Africa to "work" in Wonka's candy factory. Additionally, there were perceived racial implications found (by some) in use of the words "Charlie" and "chocolate." The filmmakers acquiesced to the organization's demands: Dahl transformed his Oompa-Loompas in both film (green-haired/orange-skinned dwarves) and subsequent editions of his book (dwarves with "golden-brown hair and rosy-white skin"). It was at this point that the film title changed to *Willy Wonka and the Chocolate Factory*. (It remains a mystery as to why "Charlie" was jettisoned from the title yet "Chocolate" survived.)

Second and third script drafts would follow. While waiting on the third, Stuart and Wolper hired David Seltzer, a young writer who had scripted a number of television documentaries for Wolper's production company. Initially brought in for story ideas that were passed along to Dahl, Seltzer would eventually enhance Dahl's delivered the third and final draft. Seltzer, whose *Wonka* script was his first feature film screenplay, would subsequently enjoy a very successful scripting and producing career. Seltzer's other genre-related credits include the classic *The Omen* (1976) and *Dragonfly* (2002). His work on what resultantly became the *Wonka* shooting script involved numerous new or altered scenes from the final draft provided by Dahl.

Principal photography on *Wonka* began on August 31, 1970 and ended on November 19, followed by several months of post-production. *Willy Wonka and the Chocolate Factory* was released on June 30, 1971. While critical reaction over-all was positive, the film received a lukewarm reception from audiences, barely grossing $4 million in box-office revenue in its original release. It was only through a long gestation period, starting with the film's pickup by network television and through the videocassette and cable TV booms of the mid-1980s, that *Wonka* began to collect a growing, devoted audience. Today, the film is considered a venerated "cult classic."

But, while audiences' reaction to the film was tepid at best, what of the story's author, Dahl himself? Reports widely vary as to Dahl's feelings regarding both Seltzer's alterations and the resulting film. The official Roald Dahl website (www.roalddahl.com) is conspicuously silent on the matter aside from mention of having a few "regrets." Other conflicting reports stating the author's opinion range from merely "crummy" (*Storyteller: The Life of Roald Dahl*, by David Sturrock, 2010) to out-and-out disowning the film, with Dahl hating the music, director Stuart, Gene Wilder's performance as Wonka, and Seltzer's changes to the author's original script. Lastly, there is director Stuart, who, in his *Pure Imagination* book, states conversely:

> After the filming began, Roald Dahl found out that we were making changes to his script ... Dahl told me that he had heard that some young writer was adding material to his screenplay and that he was disturbed by the news ... I agreed to fly to London on Saturday and meet with him. When I arrived, I handed him the script. He asked me to wait while he read the screenplay, and went up to his study. An hour passed, and then another ... Finally, Dahl came down the stairs. He handed the script back to me and said that he agreed with the changes.

(Given that for the remainder of his life Dahl refused to sell the film rights to the sequel, *Charlie and the Great Glass Elevator*, I'm inclined to side with those who believe that Dahl was *less* than happy with Seltzer and Stuart's tampering.)

Let's now look at some of the major deviations from his book that Dahl supposedly so "detested," and see who "did it best"—book or film.

Imagine *Willy Wonka and the Chocolate Factory* with no musical numbers—a straight, dramatic interpretation of the novel. Difficult to conceive, no? And yet, a tuneless *Wonka* almost came to be. Director Stuart originally did not envision the film as a musical; even author Dahl only dabbled with the idea of the novel's Oompa-Loompa "poems" fitting into the film musically. It was only due to producer David Wolper's insistence on such (due to the success of recent such films as *Oliver!* at the box office) that the British composing team of Leslie Bricusse and Anthony Newley were brought in.

And the film benefits immeasurably as a result. For the songs are so intrinsic (with some quite indelible—months after my last viewing I cannot banish "Candy Man" from my brain) and add greatly to the emotional context of the film, that their absence would have resulted in something flat and considerably less joyful. (One only needs to endure Johnny Depp's *Charlie and the Chocolate Factory* (2006) to recognize the validity of this point.) The songs are also germane—revealing character background or other insight in much more entertaining fashion than through other potential forms of exposition. All involved

The songs in *Wonka* reveal character motivation or move forward the plot.

were wise in keeping *Wonka* a film with only a handful of musical numbers, "soft-spoken" in nature ("I Want It Now" an exception). Had *Wonka* become a full-blown musical with typical show stopping, "belt-them-out-to-the-back-over-the-balcony," over-the-top numbers, the unfolding Charlie/Wonka relationship—the heart of the film—would have overshadowed.

Regarding the subject of merit attached to the prizes bestowed upon Charlie, book and film each take a point. As a winner of one of the five golden tickets, the film asks us to believe that Charlie is deserving simply because he is a "good boy." Charlie loves his family, works to help put food on the table, and is even willing to share his annual birthday splurge—a chocolate bar—with his family. There is no doubt that he certainly *wants* the golden prize, declaring early on that, "Nobody wants it more than I do," but … is this enough? While Charlie is certainly more deserving of a ticket than the four monstrously behaving children that have come before, how is he more deserving than millions of other "good" boys and girls in the world? What child across the globe wouldn't also lay claim to wanting it more than any other?

Dahl handles this better in the book by depicting the true squalor and poverty under which Charlie and his family live. Times here are so bad that the Bucket family is actually starving and Charlie, so thin and malnourished, resembles more and more a skeleton than a little boy as time progresses. Readers' hearts go out to this Charlie and our emotions match those of the boy's—our hearts break upon each purchase of a chocolate bar whose contents do not contain the oh-so-desired golden foil inside, and we are as gloriously elated when Charlie at last pulls back the wrapping on a Wonka bar and discovers the golden contents inside. Now *this* is a good, lucky, and most deserving winner. In glossing over the struggles endured in the book, Charlie's discovery of the golden ticket in the film is certainly a happy moment, but it's less emotionally satisfying here, as we're shown a boy luckier to win the prize than deserving of it.

Conversely and more striking is Charlie's inheritance of Wonka's chocolate factory. Here, the film greatly improves upon the book with the addition of what I term the "honesty test"—the additional subplot involving the "villainous" Slugworth, who, almost by magic, appears to each golden-ticket-winning child and whispers something into their ear. Later, we come to learn that Slugworth promises each child, Charlie included, a great amount of riches in return for turning over the secret involving one of Wonka's candies, the everlasting gobstopper.

The addition of this subplot is important and necessary. Returning to the subject of merit, in Dahl's book, Charlie wins Wonka's chocolate factory through mere attrition—Charlie literally is the "last child standing," and for this alone Wonka bestows the greatest prize of all. While Charlie is certainly a "good boy" compared to the four rotten brats who preceded him, this just does not feel sufficient enough justification for Charlie to be handed the "keys to the (chocolate) kingdom." In a vein similar to the adage "with great power comes great responsibility," there comes the need for a protagonist to win a great prize from great effort. As such, Charlie's easy win here smacks of being a tad undeserved, for having done little more than "Ooh," and "Aahh," among such other "gee-whiz!" type uttered exclamations throughout the factory tour. With Charlie's winning-through-attrition, we have no real certainty that Charlie's goodness played any role in his winning. Had Charlie been as bratty as the other four children, would he still have won for having been the last child standing? We don't know. Wonka may

Willie Wonka (Gene Wilder) and Charlie (Peter Ostrum).

Director Mel Stuart and friends

have had a hunch about Charlie, but this reader comes away unsatisfied, for Charlie has not been shown to be truly worthy of such a prize.

The movie smartly solves this problem with the aforementioned "honesty test." Near film's end, when Wonka savagely rips Charlie's dream (and chocolate!) away from him, Charlie has the easiest path possible for revenge— simply turn over his everlasting gobstopper to Slugworth. He and his family will then be rich beyond imagining. But Charlie doesn't take this route down the dark side. For he is a good boy, and here *proves* it, by turning down the potential for riches to do the right thing ... return to Wonka his everlasting gobstopper. It's an incredibly selfless act, for which the resulting reward of Wonka's factory is much more emotionally satisfying for having been truly earned.

Lastly, a flaw from the book that the film expands into a bigger handicap is the delayed appearance of our titular chocolate factory owner. In the film, Wilder (Wonka) does not appear until half way into the film. Given that Wilder's iconic performance is the movie's (un)arguable highlight, the film drags in its first half. While a novel can more afford a delayed build up to a main character's appearance, a film does so at its expense, and *Wonka* is a prime example. While Albertson and Ostrum, as Grandpa Joe and Charlie respectively, give it

their best, their appeal is limited, and thus strains one's (at least this viewer's) patience all the more in awaiting Wilder to tumble onto the screen.

Of Tim Burton's 2006 *Charlie*, nothing more needs be said than previously. As of this writing, there are rumors of a proposed Willy Wonka prequel, with actors Donald Glover and the ever-bland Ryan Gosling currently in contention for the title role. I shudder at the mere thought of this project.

Dahl's novel and Stuart's film are beloved classics standing the test of time and deservedly so. Neither are without their flaws, but each have such irresistible appeal that in the end ... who cares?!

Outer Space Jesus:
Superman: The Movie (1978)
and Man of Steel (2013)

Superhero films have now overtaken Westerns as the vehicle for exploring the Great American Myth. This has led to a decidedly mixed bag of films, ranging all over the spectrum from god-awful to near great. We have had retro-cool fantasias (*The Shadow*, *The Phantom*, *Sky Captain and the World of Tomorrow*), dark and cynical junk (pick the Nolan Batman film of your choice), political tracts (the *X-Men* films), stylish and breezy romps (*Captain America: The First Avenger*), noisy and bombastic bores (*The Avengers*), unpleasantly surreal trips (*Popeye* and *Dick Tracy*), over-sexed jokes (*Flash Gordon*), insipid, tasteless fare (either version of *The Fantastic Four*), disgusting and nihilistic garbage (*The Watchmen*), and one lyrical paean to gee-whiz optimism (*The Rocketeer*—the only superhero film following the wave started with 1989's *Batman* to rank as a classic).

But none of them would have been possible without the first great comic book hero, Superman, and the first great superhero film, *Superman: The Movie*. There is a lot to dislike about *Superman: The Movie*. The tone is often disjointed, the superpowers often follow no internal logic, much of it is over-designed or under-realized. It is a masterpiece. Flawed, but fabulous. But it is one of a succession of takes on Superman, each a reflection of its time.

Adaptations of comic books and strips are inherently problematic. As opposed to adapting a novel or short story (or even a self-contained graphic novel), comic adaptations usually have a long history of story beats to incorporate. In having what are sometimes decades of continuity to draw upon, do screenwriters seek to select a single incident, or somehow latch onto the larger character continuity to somehow capture the *essence* of the material? Even when faithful to a particular era of a comic-character's continuity, that doesn't mean the public would want *that* particular iteration. The 1950s Batman comics, for example, are fairly represented by the 1960s television show ... not an approach that would go down well with today's "serious-minded" comic book fans. Sadly.

More difficult still is adapting a character like Superman, who transcends his source material and has entered into American myth. Yes, there are four-color characters that have perhaps surpassed him in popularity and relatability, but in terms of sheer mythic heft, no caped crusader even comes close. How to translate a myth like Superman—a peculiarly *American myth*—into a simple, three-act motion picture? Amazingly, this has been tried twice, with *Superman: The Movie* (1978) and *Man of Steel* (2013), two starkly different films made at different times with different agendas in radically different Americas. What each film says about us, as a people and as a culture, is startling.

Many fine writers, including the late (and sorely missed) Les Daniels (*Superman: The Complete History*), have chronicled the Superman mythos. There are many sources that provide a more-detailed history than can be provided here, but I highly recommend *Superman: The Unauthorized Biography*, by Glen Weldon. Even as a boy, I thought Superman was the great American success story. An immigrant raised in America's heartland, he took our national myth to heart and made himself into the embodiment of all that is good about us. I was also gobsmacked by visions of his lost planet Krypton, which was often portrayed as a 1930s art deco-inspired wonderland. If heaven exists and mirrors our expectations, for me it would resemble the comic's original Krypton to no little degree.

I have always much preferred Superman to his darker counterpart, Batman. This is a prejudice we suspect that Weldon shares, as his book on Superman is relentlessly amusing, affectionate, and reverential. Superman's creators, Siegel and Shuster, says Weldon, saw their creation as quite simply, the ultimate American: "a Gatsby who'd arrived on a bright new shore, having propelled himself there by burning his own past as fuel. The Old World could no longer touch him, and now it was left to him to forge his own path." Throughout the book, Weldon's prose seems charged with a powerful nostalgia for a simpler, and perhaps wiser, America. One that still believed in heroes and other symbols of hope, and, we suspect, one where childish delights were viewed in perspective by adult fans, and not with the soul-crushing scrutiny of today's Perpetual Adolescents.

(A parenthetical note here on the current popularity of Batman over Superman. Weldon is crystal clear in his assertion that, as conceived, Batman is a protector of Moneyed Interests; it is not just tenor and tone that made early Batman the antithesis of Superman, but inherent philosophy as well. Bob Kane, a poor Jewish boy from the Bronx who dreamt of a world of socialites, supper clubs and celebrity, mostly created Batman, and Batman delivered that to Kane in spades. Oddly enough, Batfans tend to find Batman more "relatable" than Superman, arguing that most anyone can become like Batman though application, discipline and hard work. Both Weldon and I dismiss those risible fantasies, arguing that one of Batman's key superpowers is his incredible

Margot Kidder and Christopher Reeve brought a sweetness and charm to their roles, sadly missing from other incarnations.

wealth. Without it, the entire world of Batman would be impossible. Left unsaid in the contemporary discussion of both characters: the strange irony that Superman has steadily diminishing cultural currency in a world of growing economic inequality.)

One of Weldon's strongest passages concerns science fiction writer Larry Niven's 1971 essay on the possible outcomes of Superman having sex with Earth women. The essay, *Man of Steel, Woman of Kleenex*, made excruciating (and amusing) conclusions, and it can still be found and makes for great reading. But Weldon places this now 45-year-old work in contemporary perspective:

> The gag, of course, is the deadpan, painstaking manner in which Niven lays out his thought process. This is where you end up if you take this stuff too seriously, he seems to say: killer sperm from outer space.
>
> Looking back on Niven's humorous essay today, it's impossible to see it as anything but a chilling harbinger of the high-level weapons-grade nerdery that would seize comics in the decades that followed. All too soon, legions of fans and creators adopted Niven's let's-pin-this-to-the-specimen-board

approach and proceeded to leach humor and whimsy and good old-fashioned, Beppo the Super-Monkey-level goofiness out of superhero comics, leaving in their place a punishing, joyless, nihilistic grittiness.

Weldon sees Superman as an ever-changing figure, who always reflects a constantly evolving America. The New Deal crusader of the late 1930s is different from the patriotic boy scout of World War II, and very different indeed from his Jet Age counterpart. What Weldon sees as the core of Superman is not his persona, but his motivation. And that is, simply, that Superman always puts the needs of others over those of himself, and he never gives up. That is the definition of a hero.

Upon finishing Weldon's book, I immersed myself in several decades' worth of Superman comics, and found the experience richly rewarding. Superman comics from the 1930s through the 1950s are great fun. The art would be considered crude by today's standards, but it had an energy and brio that is sadly missing from today's product. Superman co-creator Joe Shuster drew many of the stories of that era, and this steely-eyed, square-jawed avenger is quite a change from the softer, more sensitive Superman of today. But all the Superman artists of that golden age—Ed Dobrotka, Fred Ray and Wayne Boring, for example—bring something unique to the table. (Superman buffs should seek out Weldon's book, which is often laugh-out-loud funny. Here he comments on Superman writer Marv Wolfman's prose: "Wolfman proceeded to slather on the pathos, gilding the emotional lily so fervently it makes Dickens' death of Little Nell read like an expense report.")

The real challenge for Superman's writers during the World War II and the Cold War was how to position a near god-like figure that can do no wrong in the context of a world conflict, without having him in some way resolve it. For example, one World War II story has the Man of Steel explicitly state that he did not join the World War because America's soldiers could do the job without him, and he was better utilized fighting saboteurs and scientifically-created monsters at home. This, of course, is simply another example of how America at the time prized the concept of the Everyman, the average American Joe who was equal to most any occasion. This figure—so central to the American psyche of the time—has been lost, thanks largely to Identity Politics, Political Correctness, and other cancerous notions born of the 1960s. In the 1940s, Superman was a projection of our best selves; in the 2013 film about him, he is a tragic reminder of what we once were.

The Superman found in these earlier comics—so soon after his creation— is part social reformer (Kent is a militant FDR New Deal Democrat) and part super-soldier. He pulls no punches, and the stories are stronger for that. Also fascinating is Lois Lane. While Feminism would like to claim that images of strong women did not exist before the likes of Gloria Steinem, Lane was a strong-minded career woman who, except for super-powers, was his equal in nearly every department. Talented, smart, fearless and adventuresome, Lane is another reminder of perhaps how we had it right before the social upheavals of the 1960s.

Weldon also posits that Superman has long ago transcended the various media that deliver him to us. He has become an idea that is bigger than the comic books, cartoons, TV shows and movies that feature him. It is an idea that has weathered 75 years, and Weldon predicts that will last at least another 75 more. It is this protean quality that makes Superman much like Sherlock Holmes, Dracula or even Ebenezer Scrooge. Each generation can find something new and vital to say about him, and, in doing so, say something about their own era.

Superman: The Movie, of course, was not the first effort to bring the character to the screen. Superman was the focus of 17 Technicolor cartoons produced by Max Fleischer (and later Famous) Studios in the 1940s. Though out of the scope of this essay, I urge Superman buffs to seek out these cartoons. They are among the finest cartoons ever produced, and are not to be missed. (They are currently on YouTube and Amazon Prime, but the re-mastered set from Warner Home Video is perhaps the best way to experience them today.)

Contemporaneous with the Superman cartoons was the splendid radio version. The show would last from 1940 through 1951, and has now passed on into legend. Famous for its focus on core-American values, the Superman radio show had a sense of moxie that is much missed today. One well-remembers

Superman proves that, at one time, comic book heroes smiled.

an episode where Superman scolds Jimmy Olson's mother when she disapproves of the girl Jimmy is dating: "Is it because she … worships differently?"; and the story of how the show actually tackled a Ku Klux Klan storyline is better remembered than the episodes themselves.

Radio producer Robert Maxwell would go on to produce the first season of television's *The Adventures of Superman*, which ran from 1952 to 1958. This series—either when first broadcast or in a seemingly endless cycle of reruns—was the first iteration of Superman for many Baby Boomers. The show starred George Reeves as Superman, Phyllis Coates and/or Noel Neill as Lois Lane, and Jack Larson as Jimmy Olson.

There are many contemporary critics who sneer at Reeves' performance as Clark Kent/Superman, most of them too young to have seen the show during its original run, or even in reruns. A quick view at the comments section of science fiction junk-news site Io9.com, for instance, shows current viewers labeling Reeves as creepy, fey, lightweight or overweight. This is, of course, a sad commentary on contemporary science fiction buffs. In a world where Superman films are grim, ponderous affairs, where superheroes are treated with a weight and reverence denied even the greatest of literary classics, certainly the

IT CAME FROM …

talents of a man like Reeves would seemingly be welcome. However, maybe it's the times, and not the levels of artistry that are off track. Reeves was the perfect Superman for what was fundamentally a different (and better) America. In the absence of Identity Politics, and buttressed by an intelligent and informed middlebrow middle-class, it was possible to attack comic-book material with both sincerity and fun without slipping into pretention and flummery.

Reeves was a player with an easy smile (indeed, a *high-octane* smile), a gentle demeanor and a true Everyman accessibility. His Superman was decent, kind, concerned and engaged. He was also distinctly American, back when American idealism and values actually, to some degree, existed. One well remembers Reeves as an angry Superman chasing away a mob of rednecks who wanted to murder some rather child-like people from the Earth's core. "You're acting like Nazi storm troopers!"

Better still was Reeves' take on Clark Kent. Rather than the high-voiced milquetoast heard on radio, Reeves' Kent is a confident, capable investigative reporter, more than equal to most any occasion. One often wondered why Superman was needed at all—with this Kent on the job, things were already on track for a just resolution. (This is essential if one is going to understand Superman rather than, say, Batman. The benign, decent and crusading Clark Kent is the real human being, and Superman merely the disguise. Batman, though, is the real human being, or what is left of one, and Bruce Wayne merely a convenient fiction.) One of the most intriguing

Reeves' portrayal of Clark Kent has yet to be beat.

aspects of his disguise is that Clark calls Lois "Lois," while Superman calls her "Miss Lane."

The great tragedy of Reeves was his untimely death, deemed a suicide, though clouded by mystery to this day. This incident has haunted many Baby Boomers for decades (for instance, Frank Dello Stritto writes about it eloquently in his recent book, *I Saw What I Saw When I Saw It*), and has fueled the speculations of countless armchair detectives.

The George Reeves Superman has formed a cult of its own; there are many out there who passionately love the show and have never picked up a

TV 'Superman' Kills Himself

HOLLYWOOD (AP)—Television's Superman shot and killed himself Tuesday, leaving no clue to his motive, only moments after his fiancee had a premonition of his death.

Friends said actor George Reeves had been discouraged by not getting other roles after the Superman series ended. But it appeared that his ending his life was a spur-of-the-moment decision.

Police Sgt. V. A. Peterson told of the suicide and its strange prelude.

Peterson said Reeves' fiancee, Lenore Lemmon, 35, and three other persons were in Reeves' house.

Miss Lemmon and a writer, Robert Condon, 45, were house guests.

The fiancee told police that she and Reeves and Condon had retired to their respective bedrooms at about 12:30 a.m. but about two hours later two of Reeves' friends, William Bliss and Mrs. Carol Van Ronkel, appeared at the house and awakened Reeves.

Investigators said the 45-year-old actor became angry because of the lateness of the hour, but apologized almost immediately after a short argument with Bliss. He then excused himself and retired for a second time.

Miss Lemmon said when Reeves left to go to his second-story bedroom she jokingly remarked, "Well, he'll probably shoot himself." A drawer was heard to open, and she said she remarked, "Well, he's getting a gun."

Then a shot was heard. Reeves had killed himself with a bullet in the temple from a .30 caliber luger pistol.

The investigators said from her story they believed Reeves might have been upset because people wouldn't leave the house.

Miss Lemmon said she and Reeves were planning to marry at Tijuana, Mexico, next Friday.

SGT. PETERSON said Reeves had been unhappy about his career and had been trying his luck in some boxing and wrestling ventures. He said he had been scheduled to appear in an exhibition Tuesday at San Diego with light heavyweight champion Archie Moore.

The actor killed himself in the bedroom of his home in Benedict Canyon, an exclusive residential area in the hills above Beverly Hills.

He had starred in scores of the "Superman" films, which are now particularly popular in Japan.

REEVES STARTED in films 20 years ago with a minor role in "Gone With the Wind." He appeared in many featured roles before achieving fame five years ago when "Superman" swept into popularity.

The husky, dark-haired actor complained to a Hollywood writer recently that he wasn't getting enough other roles because he was type-cast as Superman. He realized a handsome income, however, from payments for re-use of the filmed series. He directed many of them.

It was estimated recently that 35 million persons a year watched the series. Reeves told an interviewer that he had received a letter from the emperor of Japan "telling me how much he enjoyed the series."

Superman, for the uninitiated, is a visitor from another planet. Endowed with incredible strength, he is able to leap across oceans and smother atomic blasts with his body. In the series, he disguises himself as a mild-mannered newspaperman, switching to his Superman role only to foil the villains or perform good deeds.

Reeves was born in Woolstock, Ia., and grew up in Pasadena. His mother lives in Galesburg, Ill. He was divorced from his wife, Eleanora, who has since remarried.

GEORGE REEVES
'Superman' Dead

Superman comic or looked at his subsequent cinematic adventures. It is this lure of Reeves, and the mystery surrounding his death, that Hollywood would eventually attempt to tell the story itself. The resulting film, *Hollywoodland*, written by Paul Bernbaum and directed by Allen Coulter, is a hit-and-miss affair, but it does manage to remain affective and poignant. To tell the story, Bernbaum creates a fictional frame to tell the actual facts: Reeves' mother (Lois Smith) hires a down-on-his-luck private detective, Louis Simo (Adrien Brody). She is convinced that Reeves would never have killed himself; Simo takes the case to win back the affection of his ex-wife (Molly Parker) and son (Zach Mills). The trail leads him into the world of Hollywood high-rollers Eddie Mannix (Bob Hoskins), general manager at MGM, and his wife Toni (Diane Lane), who was Reeves' longtime lover. Brody is miserably miscast as the gumshoe, a part more suited to the melancholy talents of someone like the late Robert Mitchum. The framing device of Simo never really takes off, either, and one wonders why Bernbaum thought it necessary. Hoskins maintains a dangerous edge of menace and animal cunning … it would be an intrepid (or stupid) man who tangled with him. Lane is nothing short of magnificent as Toni Mannix, a bottomless pit of doubt, need and self-pity. Her hungers and humiliations

IT CAME FROM ...

are uncomfortably real, and it's stunning for an adult actress to allow herself to appear so naked and vulnerable. Why this performance wasn't considered Oscar-worthy is a great injustice. However, the film belongs completely to Ben Affleck, who plays Reeves in flashback. While not as winning or innocently charming as Reeves himself, Affleck successfully channels the late actor's nonchalance, his easy manner and his doughy sensuality. An inherently decent man in an indecent place, Reeves' life spirals out of control as he loses his career, his self-respect, and his own self-image. It's a complex and ingratiating performance, and Affleck has never been better. Finally, the reason *Hollywoodland* works so well is the reason so many superhero films are disappointing: this film relies upon complex human relationships and often-contradictory emotional attachments. It's an internal drama, rather than an empty spectacle, and it details the inner turmoil of a real super man.

Aside from a few forays into Saturday morning animation and an interesting-if-failed Broadway musical, Superman lay dormant as a property until the late 1970s. It took two Hollywood outsiders—Ilya Salkind and his father, Alexander Salkind—to believe that Superman was a viable property.

The development of what would eventually become *Superman: The Movie* is nearly as interesting as the finished film itself. Guy Hamilton of *Goldfinger* fame was initially slated to direct, only to be replaced at the last minute by Richard Donner. Millions had been sunk into tests for Krypton and flying effects before a single reel of film had been shot. Nearly every major name in Hollywood was floated as a possible contender for the cape—figures as diverse as Paul Newman, Clint Eastwood and Muhammad Ali were all considered, at one time or another. But not until the Salkinds convinced top-tier stars Marlon Brando and Gene Hackman to come on board, as Jor-El and Lex Luthor, respectively, did the project emerge as a legitimate contender to blockbuster status.

The magic that the Salkinds brought to the table—aside from

Christopher Reeve

boatloads of money and the ability to get the thing made—was the initial recognition that they were approaching something close to an American secular
saint. Superman had, by the 1970s, become familiar to millions who had never
opened a comic book in their lives. More importantly, he had come to *mean*
something to people, and that meaning and where it fit into the 1970s zeitgeist
would become the heart of the film.

The Superman character was born in the 1930s, as the film itself says, "a
time of fear and confusion." In 1932, during a period of incalculable poverty and record unemployment, General Douglas MacArthur, on the orders of
President Hoover, attacked World War I veterans marching on the capital,
killing two and burning their shantytown to the ground. By decade's end, the
United States had just barely begun to recover from the Great Depression,
and Americans were slowly getting back to work. On the international scene,
a global conflict loomed.

Out of that toxic soup sprung Superman. And it's important to remember
that Superman was not (and never intended to be) an avenger; rather, Superman's role has always been to restore balance to what was a just (or wanting to
be just) world. Compare his era of origin to the time of this massive recreation
of his myth: the 1970s. America had weathered Vietnam, Watergate, the advent of global terrorism, the continuing erosion of societal and cultural norms
that started in the 1960s, the worsening of the drug epidemic, the degradation
of major metropolitan areas like New York, and the festering wounds that remained from such high-profile assassinations as John F. and Robert Kennedy.

By the end of the 1970s, Americans were mad, they were confused, and
they were *hurt*.

It was the perfect moment for the return of Superman.

And this sense of despair rescued by optimism is really the core of this
fascinating film. Rather than label Superman as a square (much as the hipper,
edgier 1960s take on Batman did), director Richard Donner decided to play
the character completely straight. And that proved to be the final masterstroke.
Superman would be a figure not only of another world, but of another time.
To achieve this, Donner constructed a film that would have three different settings, each with their own individual look and feel.

Donner opens his film with a sequence detailing the destruction of Superman's home world of Krypton. (Here, composer John Williams cribs liberally
from *Pines of the Appian Way*, by Ottorino Respighi.) For years Krypton had
been depicted in the comics, movie serials and television show as a *Buck Rogers*
Wonderland. In this re-visioning, Krypton has become a stark synthesis of the
Ancient World, the North Pole, and Californian crystal worship. It shouldn't
work, but somehow … it is magnificent. This retcon of Krypton would become so iconic in its own right, that it was adopted by the comics, and every
cinematic or television revival of Superman until the ill-considered redesign of

IT CAME FROM …

Christopher Reeve discusses a scene with director Richard Donner.

Man of Steel in 2013. His home planet doomed, scientist-statesmen Jor-El sends his infant son Kal-El into the vastness of space, knowing that he will land on Earth and become its savior.

It is not impossible to see the appeal of this to 1970s America. Though the body politic may be corrupt (whether the Nixon administration or the governing council of Krypton), there are still good people within it. And not only good, but forward thinking and self-sacrificing people.

Kal-El lands in Smallville, Kansas, less an easily identifiable geographical location than an Uber-America. In what is the most beautiful and lyrical sequence of the film, we find that while his nationality may be Kryptonian, America is Superman's religion. Simple farmers who embody great American ideals raise Kal (or Clark Kent, as he is called by his adoptive parents). He is taught civic responsibility, self-sacrifice, self-reliance, and basic morality. To make this work, Donner creates a Smallville out-of-time. If you reckon the timelines of the movie, given how long Superman trains in the Fortress of Solitude to his arrival in Metropolis, the Smallville sequences would have to take place in the early 1960s. But here Donner, with cinematographer Geoffrey Unsworth, creates a Smallville that is a dreamy amalgam of the best of small-town America from the 1930s through the 1950s. It locks Superman not so much in a specific time and place in America, as much as in an *idea* of America.

It is these two sequences—otherworld Krypton and Smallville—that make the contradictory All American Alien Do-Gooder not only possible, but essential.

It is in the final sequence of the film—Superman in Metropolis—that all of this pays off for 1970s audiences. As long-dead Jor-El intones during Superman's education, "They can be a great people, Kal-El; they wish to be. They only lack the light to show the way. For this reason above all, their capacity for good, I have sent them you ... my only son."

As our institutions, customs and social mores crumbled around us, we desperately needed something, someone, to believe in. And Superman—dependable, heroic, incorruptible—answered our call. He may have been a visitor from another planet, but he also brought with him a wealth of American nostalgia—a healing nostalgia for an America that used to be. This notion of "optimism as a form of nostalgia" is a thread that wove its way through several 1970s films (think *Hearts of the West*, *At Long Last Love*, *Lucky Lady*, *The Great Waldo Pepper* ... the list goes on and on), but none more effectively than here. Superman allowed Watergate and Vietnam weary Americans to reconnect with an earlier, untainted version of ourselves.

This is most brilliantly illustrated in the sequence where Lois Lane interviews Superman in her rooftop garden apartment. (Why didn't I go into journalism?) Lane, magnificently played by Margot Kidder, stands in for all con-

Director Donner puts Reeve and Kidder through their paces.

IT CAME FROM ...

temporary Americans with her incredulity at Superman's purity. He doesn't lie, he doesn't drink, he doesn't take advantage ... what gives?, she and we wonder. But that's the point. As a representation of America-Before-The-Fall, Superman is just what he claims to be: truth, justice and the American Way. Lois erupts, "You're gonna end up fighting every elected official in this country!" Superman quietly replies, "I'm sure you don't really mean that, Lois." (Compare this to the inherent self-loathing of Bryan Singer's flaccid *Superman Returns* where editor Perry White asks, "Does he still stand for truth, justice, all that stuff?" In 2006, a character in a mainstream blockbuster cannot even articulate the notion that America once stood for something.)

Superman turns Lois from a cynic (an all-to-easy default position) to a believer (which takes a little more intellectual and emotional muscle). And in doing so, he convinces audiences of the 1970s that, yes, there is still decency ... and here it is. It strips the character to his essence: Superman is more than an alien, and more than a god. He's a guy from Kansas, who does the right thing.

One other stroke of genius in this film is the depiction of Lex Luthor. While many purists bristle that this Luthor is neither the mad scientist nor evil capitalist of the comics, Gene Hackman's Luthor is something better: He is the anti-Superman. Where Superman never lies, Luthor is glibly deceitful. While Superman is partnered with an intelligent and independent career woman, Luthor lives with a vain and stupid parasite. Where Superman takes refuge in the Fortress of Solitude to better himself, Luthor hides in the bowels of Manhattan to hatch his schemes. Where Superman is modest and self-effacing, Luthor plans to refashion the West Coast to his individual specifications. Where Superman has a smart and enterprising chum in Jimmy Olson, Luthor has an incompetent buffoon in Otis. Where Superman uses glasses to disguise himself as a mere mortal, Luthor wears wigs to hide his human physical failings. Where Superman laughs at himself, Luthor laughs at you. Where Superman is big-hearted and warm, Luthor is greedy and indifferent to human suffering. And finally ... where Superman is earnest, representing the best of a vanished America, Luthor is flippant and sleazy and urban, the perfect representative of the America we have become.

The genius of *Superman: The Movie*, though, aside from the stellar performances, superb art direction and photography, and the overall approach, lies in its power as an adaptation. The many writers corralled by the Salkinds to create the initial screenplay drafts (including *Godfather* scribe Mario Puzo— hired and paid for unusable material; essentially an expensive publicity stunt) had trouble finding an overarching plot in which to place the Man of Steel. How to cram the then 40-years-worth of continuity into a single film?

Wisely, Donner and final screenwriter Tom Mankiewicz would eventually create a film that would highlight the essential beats of the Superman mythos. The finished film is less a Superman adventure, and more a meditation on

"You can fly, you belong to the sky ... "

what Superman means. By structuring the film into three distinct parts—Krypton, Smallville, Metropolis—Donner and company were able to use different cinematic techniques to explore these key components of the myth. All three components look different, feel different, and play different. But, taken together, they capture the essence of whom and what Superman is, and what makes him so super in the first place.

For people of this critic's generation (born 1962), the transformative film is usually *Star Wars*. My 15-year-old self saw it in New York that summer (a New York that is so changed that it is itself a galaxy far, far away). I was impressed, but unmoved. Frankly, the furor escaped me.

One year later, I saw *Superman: The Movie* and openly wept. While the special effects were terrific, what blinded me with tears was the simple, emotional heft of the story. *Superman: The Movie* (and, to a degree, its only worthy successor, *The Rocketeer*) is a film of unsurpassed sweetness. It is devoid of irony, or "darkness," or cynicism. It has heart. It not only wears its emotions on its sleeve ... it telegraphs them. This sense of sweetness is found in every aspect of the production, from the lovingly reproduced Americana of Smallville, to the sense of Christian sacrifice of Jor-El, to the honest and emotional performances of the principals. It is helped in no small portion by John Williams' score, which is simply the finest he ever produced. (In fact, not only the finest score for any superhero film, but it must rank as one of the great film scores, ever. Few film scores produce so many, and so varied, emotional responses in the listener.) Williams taps into the emotional core of the film with his *Love Theme*,

IT CAME FROM ...

creating a sense of yearning and loss, the wellsprings of awe and a certain wistful nostalgia can all be heard in this single track. It is impossible for this critic to over-emphasize the emotional power this piece has over him. To hear even the opening strains is to make me 16 again, and to be hopelessly in love with an incorruptible demi-god, a man for whom kindness, compassion and his dedication to good came as naturally as breathing. (Even typing these words, the impetus to weep is great.)

It was, I thought, not only a Superman for my generation, but for all generations.

However, as with all such youthful pronouncements, I was premature. As I hit my 51st year, Superman returned, and the America he found (and the man he was) were radically altered. Could Superman, I wondered, survive the transition into what we laughingly refer to as modernity without losing some vital essence, the very things that made him what he was?

Sadly, the answer for Superman was no. *Man of Steel*, directed by Zack Snyder, is the complete antithesis of the earlier Richard Donner/Christopher Reeve film. Never have I seen a blockbuster film so cynical in its conception, so ham-fisted in its execution or so bleak in its worldview. What should have been an exhilarating romp with a sense of wonder is instead a grim and dour computer game, devoid of life, sentiment, wit, intelligence, or fun.

This creates an interesting aesthetic conundrum. How can Snyder and his producer/writer (Christopher Nolan and David S. Goyer, respectively) take this same material and fashion out of it a film so grim, so lacking in warmth, so devoid of hope, and so ugly to look at? Every artist brings something of him or herself to whatever theme they approach, but surely some themes are, at their core, immutable? Surely the fundamental message of great myths—be it hope or despair, transcendence or degradation—would shine through?

Apparently not. Every choice made by Snyder and company was calculated to leech Superman and his mythos from any sense of grandeur, any sense of fun, any sense of transcendence.

First, let's look at Krypton. In both the comics and the films, the planet is often presented as a kind of paradise. The comics showed us a primary-colored super-science wonderland worthy of *Buck Rogers* comic strips. And the later Superman films with Christopher Reeve opted for a futuristic Greco-Roman splendor, with a sparse purity often associated with Greek drama.

In *Man of Steel*, Krypton is as ugly as the nightmares of H.R. Giger. Its inhabitants wear gray latex drag while moving through what looks like a massive digestive track. Snyder and company have Jor-El die when he is stabbed in the gut by the film's villain, General Zod—saving the explosion for Superman's mother. Before the planet explodes, Zod and his cronies are sent away in what looks like giant, flying penises. Think on that—in 1978, Superman arrived in a crystal star; in 2013, Zod and company arrive in giant dildos. Make the cultural comparison of your choice.

We then see the grown Kal-El finding himself while bumming through the U.S. Reporter Lois Lane has a run-in with him and investigates the story of the mysterious man with strange powers. But soon General Zod and his cadre of Krypton survivors come to earth, looking for Kal-El because it seems that Jor-El downloaded all of Krypton's genetic information into his infant son. With this information, Zod hopes to recreate Krypton on earth … leaving no place for humanity.

Between bouts of tedium, we are treated to flashbacks of Superman's upbringing in Kansas. It would be impossible to offer a more stark comparison between Superman of 1978 and 2013 than to consider the dueling depictions of his all-American upbringing.

In 1978, Pa Kent (a transcendently beautiful Glenn Ford) says to his son:

> When you first came to us, we thought that people would come and take you away, because if they found out about the things you could do, well, that worried us a lot. But then a man gets older and he thinks very differently, better, he starts to see things very clear. And there's one thing I do know, son. And that is, you are here for a reason. I don't know whose reason it is, or whatever the reason … maybe it's … I don't know … but I do know one thing. It's not to score touchdowns.

In 2013, Pa Kent (Kevin Costner—inspired casting for a terribly conceived role) talks to the 13-year-old Clark after he saves a busload of children from drowning:

> Clark: I just wanted to help.
> Jonathan: I know you did, but we talked about this. Right? Right? We talked about this! You have … ! Clark, you have to keep this side of yourself a secret.

IT CAME FROM …

Clark: What was I supposed to do? Just let them die?

Jonathan: Maybe, but there's more at stake here than our lives or the lives of those around us. When the world ... When the world finds out what you can do, it's gonna change everything, our ... our beliefs, our notions of what it means to be human ... everything. You saw how Pete's mom reacted, right? She was scared, Clark.

Clark: Why?

Jonathan: People are afraid of what they don't understand.

Clark Kent: Is she right? Did God do this to me? Tell me!

There in a nutshell is the main problem with this awful film. Superman is who he is because, at his core, he's a guy from Kansas, raised by salt-of-the-earth Americans, who always does the right thing. He is the good man he is because of his earth parents, who school him well in what it means to be a man and a hero. It is what makes Superman a positive character, rather than a dark one.

Losing that moral compass destroys the film and seriously diminishes Superman. If you change Jonathan Kent from warm and optimistic to morally confused and unfocused, everything from that point on will suffer because of it.

The Jonathan Kent in *Man of Steel* looks to suppress his son's abilities, instead of encouraging them. While Ford's Jonathan wanted to prevent Clark from misusing his abilities, Costner's Kent simply wants to keep them from the world, despite the good that they might do.

In a nutshell, this is an America that has lost confidence in its own abilities, and in its own moral compass.

Donner allows Superman to realize, once Jonathan dies, that he cannot save everyone. Snyder has Jonathan needlessly sacrifice himself to protect his son's

Henry Cavill had all the requirements to be a stellar Superman ... except charm

Superman (Henry Cavill) steels himself for yet another battle against Zod's forces.

secret ... leaving his son with a ton of guilt and mixed morals. The distinction is clear.

This change in the essence of Superman's maturation is just one key misstep in this retelling, one that has too many missteps for it to ever recover and truly soar.

Where to begin? First off, Snyder shoots the film with a near complete de-saturation of color. Imagine a black-and-white film poorly daubed with a waxy crayon and you get the effect. Worse still, the thudding, repetitive, and unpleasant score by Hans Zimmer is more reminiscent of the antics at a stoner's rock concert than a glorious science fiction romp.

As for the special effects—they are not that special. When Superman and Zod battle at the climax (seemingly forever), it is all blurred motion and fast cutting, more computer flummery than cinema.

The performances—one of the great strengths of the 1970s version—are nearly invisible. Henry Cavill may be the handsomest man to don the blue-

IT CAME FROM ...

and-red suit, but he lacks the charisma of either George Reeves or Christopher Reeve. His Superman is a cypher. No one else manages to make any impression at all except for Kevin Costner as Pa Kent—and a film is in trouble when the most energetic player is … Kevin Costner.

But the fundamental problem with the seething mess that is *Man of Steel* is one of tone and artistic vision. It seems that Snyder and Nolan wanted to do an "adult" take on Superman, but to them "adult" can only mean gloomy, negative, and nihilistic. I weep for the intellectual and emotional maturity of both men if that is indeed their yardstick of adulthood, because it is both horribly restrictive and blinkered. Transcendent joy is as much an "adult" aesthetic as the cheapest form of tragedy, but try telling that to someone with the emotional sense of a 15 year old.

The filmmakers nail their own coffins finally with their vision of Superman. For nearly 80 years, Superman was the "good guy," the man we looked up to, the person we all aspired to be. This vengeful, glum and, finally, not terribly bright man may be many things, but he will never be … Superman.

General Zod's henchmen

The stories and novels behind Classic Horror, Fantasy and Science Fiction Films

By the Pricking of My Thumbs: Something Wicked This Way Comes (1983)

Literature is rife with "Coming of Age" tales—chronicles of the joys, struggles, and heartbreaks experienced while navigating that frequently rocky path from youth to adulthood. These odes to boyhood (or girlhood!) resonate with readers in a way that few other story types are able. From such enduring book report staples as *The Adventures of Huckleberry Finn* (1884; Mark Twain), *To Kill a Mockingbird* (1960; Harper Lee), and *The Catcher in the Rye* (1951; J. D. Salinger), to more recent efforts as *Boy's Life* (1991; Robert McCammon) and the novella *The Body* (1982; Stephen King; later adapted into Rob Reiner's acclaimed 1986 film *Stand By Me*), it's not hard to see why such stories remain one of the most popular of fiction genres. For when done well, these tales—rekindling fond recollections of a more innocent and optimistic time in our lives—strike a resonant chord in the young boy or girl that (hopefully!) remains in readers of all ages.

Few writers were as facilely adept as Ray Bradbury in recapturing wistful memories of childhood and translating into evocative and poignant literary odes. One, his 1962 classic, *Something Wicked This Way Comes*, is all the greater

achievement for doing so while atypically encapsulated within an overarching supernatural premise. (The novel's title originates from a line spoken by the Second Witch of Shakespeare's *Macbeth* and uttered by Will's father just prior to an encounter with Mr. Dark at the town library: "By the pricking of my thumbs, something wicked this way comes.")

Ray Bradbury (1920-2012) was one of the most acclaimed, prolific, and preeminent writers of fantasy, science fiction, and horror of the past century. The author of over 50 books and nearly 600 short stories— his novels *Fahrenheit 451*, *The Martian Chronicles*, *The Illustrated Man*, and *Something Wicked This Way Comes*— became instant classics upon publication. Bradbury also wrote for the stage, television, and film. Among his many achievements in these mediums, he most notably adapted the Herman Melville classic

Moby Dick (1956) to the screen for legendary actor and director, John Huston. He additionally scripted episodes for the *Alfred Hitchcock Presents* and *The Ray Bradbury Theater* television series. Bradbury was additionally the recipient of innumerous awards and accolades during his life, including an Emmy win and an Academy Award nomination. These selected accomplishments, which many a writer (including this one!) would likely sell his or her soul to be able to claim as their body of work, represent but a small subset of the author's total voluminous oeuvre.

Bradbury grew up in Waukegan, Illinois, a (then) small rural Midwestern town, roughly an hour's drive north of Chicago. By the author's own account, he passed a happy childhood there, surrounded by a warm and close extended family. As a youth, he spent untold hours watching films at the local movie theater, as well as reading at the town library, fueling the young boy's imagination with adventures from the pens of such fantasy and science fiction authors as Jules Verne, Edgar Rice Burroughs and H.G. Wells. Bradbury himself showed an interest in writing—be it poems, stories or other—from an early age. This interest grew to a passion throughout his high school years, giving rise to thoughts of writing as a career. Shortly after his family's move to Los Angeles in 1934, he joined the Los Angeles Science Fiction League (now the Los Angeles Science Fantasy Society), a club where local and visiting writers and fans of the genre met to share, in a communal setting, their common interest in reading, watching, and writing all things science fiction.

In 1938, at the age of 18, Bradbury's first published story appeared in the fanzine, *Imagination*, while his first professional sale would come four years later in *Super Science Stories* magazine. At the age of 24, he turned full-time writer and never stopped, writing daily until his passing nearly 70 years later. When questioned by Sam Weller in an interview for the spring 2010 issue of *The Paris Review* as to why he wrote science fiction, Bradbury explained:

> Science fiction is the fiction of ideas. Ideas excite me, and as soon as I get excited, the adrenaline gets going and the next thing I know I'm borrowing energy from the ideas themselves. Science fiction is any idea that occurs in the head and doesn't exist yet, but soon will, and will change everything for everybody, and nothing will ever be the same again. As soon as you have an idea that changes some small part of the world you are writing science fiction. It is always the art of the possible, never the impossible.

Upon adulthood, Bradbury frequently tapped into his boyhood memories for inspiration, producing tales invoking a distinct pang of nostalgia for a quieter, more idyllic time long since gone. His fondness for the city of his youth nev-

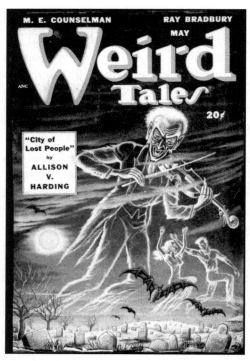

er faltered, as his beloved Waukegan became the fictional 1920s community, "Green Town, Illinois" in such works as *Something Wicked* and *Dandelion Wine*. The true genesis for *Something Wicked This Way Comes* sprang from such nostalgia. From an early age, one of Bradbury's many loves and fascinations involved carnivals and circuses, with all the mystery and trappings they entailed. The carnival/circus motif appears many times in the author's early works, culminating in 1948 when *Weird Tales* magazine published his short story, "The Black Ferris."

"Ferris" is, for all intents and purposes, *Something Wicked*, condensed into about six pages. The story contains all the key elements: two boys from a small town, opposite in personality but best of friends; a recently arrived carnival with malicious intent; a midway ride that can age a person backward or forward in time; and the triumph of the boys over the sinister carnival owner (here, Mr. Cooger, not Mr. Dark). Of note, in the short story the carnival ride is a Ferris wheel; in all subsequent stages of evolution, the sinister time machine becomes a carousel.

Nothing more came of the eventual novel's gestation until 1955. One evening, having just attended a private screening of the latest film of legendary screen star Gene (*Singing in the Rain*) Kelly, Bradbury, infused with excitement, sought to find some way of collaborating with the legendary actor. Searching through his vast collection of material, Bradbury felt certain he had at last discovered *the* vehicle for Kelly when he stumbled upon his old "Ferris" tale. Bradbury spent weeks expanding the short story into a full-length screen treatment. Mere days after having delivered the completed treatment to Kelly, the actor, excited about what he had just read, asked Bradbury's permission to shop the treatment around in hopes of finding potential backers. Kelly returned just a few short weeks later, breaking the news of his inability to find the needed funding.

Disappointed but undaunted, Bradbury then resolved to turn the treatment into his next novel. He spent the next several years reworking the material and Simon & Schuster published *Something Wicked This Way Comes* in 1962 to mixed reviews.

IT CAME FROM ...

In an interview with Robert Jacobs, published in the February 1976 issue of *Writer's Digest*, Bradbury elaborated on the overarching inspiration behind his haunting tale:

> Growing up in northern Illinois is very much like growing up in Oshkosh, or any of those other areas with the carnivals coming through, the autumn weather, with Halloween, and the sense of good and evil in a small town that you don't even recognize. When I got older I wanted to do a story about the traveling carnivals and the autumn weather and the love for the country that you and I have shared together. Illinois is not that much different. And it was about passing existence and sadness and joy. And I sort of put it all in one book. *Something Wicked This Way Comes* just about personifies more than everything else I've done, just about everything I think about life. You know, just the joy of being alive and the sense of passing time and losing friends and death coming and scaring you.

Even prior to its official publication, the book generated considerable buzz in Hollywood, with numerous (but unknown) names expressing interest in the property. Sadly, nothing concrete came out of this initial excitement. It wasn't until the early 1970s, when producers Robert Chartoff and Irwin Winkler optioned the book, that Bradbury first saw his dream of bringing the book to life on the big screen happening. Having confirmed a deal with 20th century Fox, Chartoff and Winkler commissioned Bradbury to write the screenplay, upon which all involved parties bandied about the names of potential directors. One of the more interesting choices to surface was that of Sam Peckinpah, the tough-as-nails director of the acclaimed films *The Wild Bunch* and *Straw Dogs*. Peckinpah held several meetings with Bradbury to discuss the project. A tale Bradbury would relate many times over the years (including to this author, when asked, during some cherished "alone time" at the 1993 *Famous Monsters of Filmland* 35th Anniversary convention in Crystal City, VA) involved his initial misgivings regarding Peckinpah's ability to handle the fantasy elements of *Something Wicked*, given the violent and bloody nature of some of the director's previous work. As the story goes, when asked how he would make the film, Peckinpah replied: "Just rip the pages from the book and stuff them in the camera!" Needless to say, Bradbury's doubts disappeared.

However, after a significant amount of time had elapsed with no further word from Peckinpah, everyone assumed that the director had lost interest. Now, with no big-name director and a change of power occurring over at 20th century Fox, the studio lost interest.

What would you give a man who could make your deepest dream come true?

Ray Bradbury's

Something Wicked This Way Comes

RAY BRADBURY'S "SOMETHING WICKED THIS WAY COMES"
A JACK CLAYTON FILM Starring JASON ROBARDS JONATHAN PRYCE
DIANE LADD PAM GRIER Produced by PETER VINCENT DOUGLAS
Screenplay by RAY BRADBURY Based on his Novel Directed by JACK CLAYTON
Music Composed by JAMES HORNER TECHNICOLOR® DOLBY STEREO
From WALT DISNEY PRODUCTIONS Read the Bantam Book
Lenses and Panaflex Camera by PANAVISION® PG PARENTAL GUIDANCE SUGGESTED
Released by BUENA VISTA DISTRIBUTION CO., INC. © 1983 Walt Disney Productions SOME MATERIAL MAY NOT BE SUITABLE FOR CHILDREN

The project once again lay in limbo until 1976, when producer Peter Douglas (son of screen legend Kirk Douglas) optioned the book. With the assistance of director Jack Clayton (*The Innocents, The Great Gatsby*), friend to the family, Douglas soon struck a deal with David Picker, President of Paramount Pictures. Months later, Clayton confidently turned over to Paramount Board Chairman Barry Diller a revised *Something Wicked* screenplay recently completed by Bradbury. But *déjà vu* raised its ugly head when a power struggle erupted at Paramount between Picker and Diller. Because Picker had supported *Something Wicked*, it was not at all surprising that Diller killed the deal.

With all parties disheartened at this turn of events, Peter Douglas resumed his efforts to find a backer. He met with little success until 1980, when Tom Wilhite, then Walt Disney Studios' Head of Production, struck a deal with Douglas. While the likes of such esteemed directors as David Lynch and Tony Scott were considered for the directing duties, Douglas relentlessly pushed for Jack Clayton. Douglas was eventually able to overcome Disney's concerns regarding the director. (In Sam Weller's 2005 biography, *The Bradbury Chronicles: The Life of Ray Bradbury*, Bradbury takes credit for securing Clayton for the directing duties, in essence blackmailing Disney execs to commit to hiring Clayton in exchange for the sale of rights to his book.) With Clayton now in place as director, *Something Wicked This Way Comes* was at last set to become a motion picture. But first, there would be yet *another* screenplay draft.

Bradbury and Clayton teamed again to rework the material. In an interview with Stephen Rebello for *Cinefantastique* magazine (June-July 1983),

Clayton revealed this insight on reshaping the source material into a workable, believable story for the screen:

> Time had given me a totally new slant on the material. I came to realize that the fantasy of the story must stem from the reality; it must have a context. That's one reason why the town was so important. If it were in any way contemporary, the audience would be wondering why the two boys weren't smoking dope and playing computer games instead of being fascinated by this strange carnival. Giving the fantastic a context also made the human relationships emerge more strongly and clearly, particularly Will and his father. In the book, their relationship is sort of idealized-loving and constant. For the film, I felt there must be some sore spot, some source of friction and antagonism.

With work on the script completed, *Something Wicked This Way Comes* began shooting on September 29, 1981. Production ran smoothly in terms of budget and schedule, and filming wrapped shortly before the Christmas holiday. Disney executives viewed a rough cut of the film and came away alarmingly un-

Something Wicked **author and screenwriter Ray Bradbury poses with cast.**

The stories and novels behind Classic Horror, Fantasy and Science Fiction Films

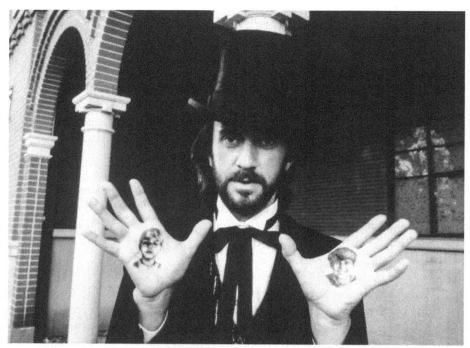

How Mr. Dark (Jonathan Pryce) searches for missing boys in lieu of milk cartons.

derwhelmed. After the studio then received disappointing feedback from a test audience at a preview screening, Disney execs decided that an almost complete overhaul was required. The studio pumped an additional $7 million into the film, to rebuild sets and rehire actors for filming several new, Bradbury-scripted scenes. The bulk of the time and money, however, was spent upon improving the inadequate special effects. Clayton was devastated; the director, now regulated to the sidelines, saw his project torn apart and reassembled, as if a jigsaw puzzle.

The overhauled *Something Wicked This Way Comes* finally premiered in the United States in April 1983 to modest critical and box-office success. The results were disappointing, due, in large part, to the film's inability to find an audience—ironically, the film was too mature in its subject matter to be suitable for typical Disney filmgoers, and yet was insufficiently suspenseful or horrific enough for older audiences who were then cutting their teeth on the then burgeoning "slasher" film genre.

While not quite the film it might have been, through the years Bradbury retained fond memories for *Something Wicked This Way Comes*, declaring it one of the most faithful adaptations of his works to date.

(NOTE: the authors acknowledge that in later years, Bradbury spun a diametrically different version of events surrounding the film's production, con-

IT CAME FROM ...

tradicting even his own words in interviews conducted both before and shortly after the film's release.)

Bradbury's novel is a superlative example of his mastery at producing chills through subtlety and suggestion rather than through any excessively graphic expression (think *The Haunting of Hill House* vs. *The Legend of Hell House*). Perhaps the only aspect for which one could fault the novel is that, while Bradbury's prose is frequently admired and praised for its poetic and lyrical qualities (both of which are in ample supply in the novel), his frequent overuse of metaphors can be difficult for readers to wade through; time taken struggling to understand what an author is saying frequently takes the reader out of the story.

In comparison, the vast majority of the film is equal to the novel. Credit obviously goes to Bradbury for adapting his own work, but more so, director Jack Clayton deserves kudos for his marvelous job in capturing the look, main elements, and *essence* of the book. The opening sequences, establishing the setting and location, are spot-on faithful to the novel and are beautiful scenes. The audience, transported back to the simpler times of the early 1900s and the city of Greentown as depicted in the film, is a place where this author wants to live. The reported $2 million spent by Disney to build an actual, full-functioning "city" set was money well spent. A particular area of improvement for the film is with the dialogue, which is, in large part, cleaned up and refreshingly free from Bradbury's overly poetic and metaphoric influences.

However, in needing to attract as large an audience as possible, the film lacks the book's luxury for subtlety. "Big" scenes are required, and so important and effective passages from the book are replaced, and it is only here—when the film deviates from the source material—that the film suffers in comparison. Two examples vividly illustrate.

The first involves a passage from the novel detailing a thrilling confrontation between Will and the Dust Witch. At first, the Witch attempts to track down and mark Will's house, hunting for the boy as she floats through the night sky in a balloon. The tables eventually turn when Will, fed-up and newly emboldened, springs from his home in pursuit of the witch; the hunter has now become the hunted. It's an exhilarating and atmospherically eerie passage. The myopic filmmakers, however, believing this passage would not work (i.e. too tame) instead replace it with a scene where Will and Jim find themselves in a room suddenly overrun with tarantulas … *hundreds* of them. Sigh.

Our second example involves the demise of Mr. Dark. In the novel, Dark, seeing his plans falling apart and thwarted, uses the carousel to transform into a young boy in an attempt to use the ruse to trick Will's father into meeting his doom. Mr. Holloway, seeing through the disguise, embraces and hugs the now young Dark and quite literally kills the carnival owner with love … anathema to Dark and his ilk. This is not just a moving and affective passage, but more importantly, the *appropriate* end for Mr. Dark. What more suitable way to defeat

The Dust Witch (Pam Grier) bedevils Jim (Shawn Carson) and Will (Vidal Peterson) as Mr. Dark (Jonathan Pryce) approvingly looks on.

the legions of evil and hate than with love? But, rather than trusting the audience to accept this, the filmmakers deliver yet another "big" scene, with Dark meeting his demise on the carousel, trapped on the forward-spinning wheel until dead and desiccated from old age. While this allowed for a somewhat impressive sequence from a special-effects standpoint, the scene is not nearly as emotionally satisfying as its literary equivalent.

While certainly delivering the intended "Boo!" shocks, these two scenes are ultimately disappointing moments, feeling decidedly out of place in a film that up to that point effectively built the tension and suspense through restraint and subtlety, rather than through such unimaginative "gotcha!" gimmicks. It is especially ironic that these scenes—among other departures from the novel—written by Bradbury, decidedly lack that distinctive, special Bradbury "feel."

Special effects are a second significant area where the film fails the novel. One could forgive the resulting shortcomings from departing from the source material if the special-effects sequences were outstanding and breathtaking. Sadly, this is not the case. For the most part, the special effects here are underwhelming and at times outright embarrassing (the demise of the Dust Witch immediately comes to mind). The only exception here is the climactic cyclone sequence, which is a dazzling piece of work! *Something Wicked*'s lackluster effects becomes even more perplexing when one realizes that the film came from the same studio that had released *TRON* just the year before, which was *widely lauded* for its innovative special effects!

IT CAME FROM ...

Let's look now in more depth at the primary area where the film suffers in comparison by straying from its source material.

The characters of Will, Jim, Mr. Holloway, and Mr. Dark escape little changed from the novel, (although Mr. Dark plays a larger role in the film than his literary counterpart). Two other characters, however, were not quite so lucky, and the film suffers greatly from their resulting transformations.

The most egregious change from the novel comes with a complete about face involving the Dust Witch. In the novel, she is a blind, wizened crone, becoming the epitome of the evil witch stereotype: Picture the evil queen from Disney's *Snow White* when she disguises herself as the aged woman. The Dust Witch is a memorably frightening character here, primarily due both to her discomforting visage and the ease with which she works her many evils despite her significant disability. In the film, Bradbury inexplicably transforms the Dust Witch into a beautiful sighted woman, and in doing so, significantly dilutes her overall effectiveness as a menacing figure (really, who's going to run *away* from the beautiful Pam Grier?). Of course, the Witch's newfound beauty isn't the only reason for her diminished ability to invoke chills. For, beyond one suspenseful scene in the town library involving Will's father, Bradbury gives the Witch little else to do beyond petting a tarantula and pursuing the boys in the form of a shapeless mist. Overall, Bradbury's handling of the Dust Witch here is a sad injustice to one of his most memorable literary creations.

Sad though as the Dust Witch's transformation as a character, it doesn't begin to compare to her denouement in the film—a complete and utter travesty in every respect. For in the novel, the Dust Witch meets a fitting end, like that of Mr. Dark; she dies, in essence, from laughter and a smile. Compare this to the film where Tom Fury, the lightning rod salesman, escapes from his bonds and impales the Dust Witch with one of his lightning rods! Tom's action here is totally in-

Pam Grier first enjoyed success in the early '70s for starring in a string of blaxploitation films including *Coffy* (1973) and *Foxy Brown* (1974).

The stories and novels behind Classic Horror, Fantasy and Science Fiction Films

explicable, given that the Witch never directly hurt him at any point during the film. This entire scene (pitiable special effects included) makes absolutely no sense logically and disappoints emotionally for not delivering the *appropriate* comeuppance—a filmgoer gains some sense of satisfaction upon the demise of a cinematic antagonist, but the experience becomes much more emotionally satisfying for the viewer, when it is a *fitting* demise for the character. The film (i.e. Bradbury) does the Dust Witch wrong once again.

Speaking of our lightning rod salesman, one questions Tom Fury's role, not only in the film, but the book as well. In the novel, Tom is a minor character, appearing in an initial chapter to sell his wares, after which—except for a brief mention much later—he disappears completely from the story. Bradbury could (and should) have easily omitted Tom's character without repercussions. Tom's role in the film, however, is not only retained but expanded. This is a questionable move on Bradbury's part as Tom serves no additional purpose here other than for Dark to torture him into revealing when a weather storm will arrive! (Really, couldn't Dark simply open a tent flap and look up at the approaching storm clouds?)

A carnival or circus housing malicious denizens is an established staple of horror literature and cinema.

Overall, *Something Wicked This Way Comes* is a fine film, but ultimately disappointing for its missed opportunities. Sadly, the film found itself in a Catch-22 situation—where the film stays true to the novel, the results are sublime. But in its need to chase after an audience and ticket sales, deviations were made to the source material, all of which collapse upon scrutiny. Yet, had those involved stayed completely true to the novel, the result would have been a beautifully realized film, but most likely would have fared more poorly at the box office than it did.

Regardless, all involved can take solace in the knowledge that *Something Wicked* has many memorable moments and over time has achieved that venerable status of cult classic.

IT CAME FROM ...

The Founder of the Feast:
A Christmas Carol (1984)

Few books are more consistently misread than *A Christmas Carol* (1843) by Charles Dickens (1812-1870). Everyone has seen some adaptation of the story—featuring anyone from Basil Rathbone to Michael Caine to Mr. Magoo—or, more ubiquitous still, some parody or send-up of the tale.

Ask anyone what *A Christmas Carol* is about, and almost certainly they will tell you it's a parable about greed. Ebenezer Scrooge, they will tell you, is a miser, hoarding his money at the expense of his employee, Bob Cratchit, and refusing to use a portion of it for the common good. The spirit of his late partner, Jacob Marley, sends to him the Ghosts of Christmas Past, Present and Future, and they will go on to show him the error of his ways, and he reforms by becoming more generous.

That, however, is not the story Dickens wrote, nor the lesson he wished to impart.

Scrooge-as-miser is a woeful misreading of Dickens' story. The great sin of which Scrooge was guilty was not a niggardly withholding of money, but of personal warmth, distancing himself from the rest of humanity, and refusing his place in the community.

Again and again the mighty Ghosts of Christmas haunt our protagonist with his refusals of human interaction, not mere miserliness. As a boy, Scrooge was left at school during the holidays, alone and unloved. His mother is never mentioned, and his father only in passing ('he is so much kinder now'), but not in any way that demonstrates he loves his son. Worse yet, Scrooge's beloved sister Fan dies early; and Scrooge is later apprenticed to a man who provides one of the few positive influences of his life, Mr. Fezziwig. But the lessons of Fezziwig do not take, and Scrooge turns away his chance at lifelong love by allowing his fiancée,

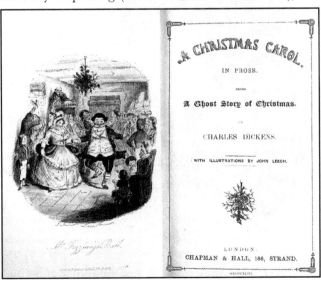

Belle, to leave him. Scrooge devotes himself to business, not simply to grow rich and comfortable, but to fill up his ever-emptying life. He keeps fellow human beings at a distance ... alienating his one relative, his nephew Fred (presumably Fan's child), and closing himself off from his colleagues or employees.

The great tragedy of Scrooge is that we see him as an imaginative boy, delighting in childhood tales of *Ali Baba* and *Robinson Crusoe* ... and we watch that boy almost obliterated by the unimaginative and unforgiving man he becomes. What the Ghosts do, in essence, is connect Scrooge with his inner child. The Ghosts of Christmas do not make a miser generous, rather, they reconnect a broken man to his youthful imagination. The secret of Scrooge after his reclamation isn't that his wallet is open, but that his heart is. A man who was once prematurely old is now forever young.

Few authors wrote of children with the insight and intelligence of Dickens; perhaps that is because he was one of those few adults gifted with a childlike sense of wonder—not a *childish* sense of wonder, for that rare commodity does not exist. Dickens, as Scrooge would, after his visitations, see the world with the clear-eyed view of a child and reprioritize what's important. As Dickens himself writes in the book, "For it is good to be children sometimes, and never better than at Christmas, when its mighty Founder was a child himself."

Though not a children's novel by any stretch of the imagination, *A Christmas Carol* has been read and enjoyed by children for more than a century. This is fascinating because a great deal of children's literature (most notably *Peter Pan*) is about putting away childhood things and parting ways with wonder and childhood passions. That is the way, these books argue, to health.

Dickens, on the other hand, believes in an integration of wonder into the adult for successful and happy maturity. Scrooge becomes whole by adopting the wonders of his vision of the Christmas Ghosts. They are not, like a visit to Neverland, temporary ... but permanent. This is much to our taste, as I like our heroes (and worldview) to incorporate wonder! Bravo Dickens. At 'em Scrooge!

A Christmas Carol predates the first wave of classic children's literature that began with *The Water Babies* (1863) by Charles Kingsley (1819-1875). But the seeds of this transformative mode of literature

John Leech illustration from the first edition

are abundant in Dickens. *A Christmas Carol* is a novel for adults that could be read with keen satisfaction by children, and it is open and honest in its embrace of the invisible world, offering a mode of reconciliation between childhood and adulthood.

We will look at the Gothic sensibilities of *A Christmas Carol* in a bit, but I also wanted to point out how Dickens evokes the fairy tale in his novel. Throughout the book, Dickens invests inanimate objects with thoughts and feelings. Houses are playful, clocks have icy teeth, fires stand up and speak. This animism is a common trope of fairy tales, because it lifts the veil of mundane reality and argues that the world is full of wonders and marvels. In addition, the *Carol* is a *tale to be told*, as the narrator constantly interrupts the story flow with jokes, with various asides, and by reminding you that he is there beside you, in spirit.

Dickens also was responsible for resurrecting Christmas at a time when it was in danger of cultural irrelevance. The Christmas traditions were celebrated between Christmas Eve and January 6th (the Feast of the Epiphany) in mostly rural England. With the advent of the Industrial Revolution, more and more people moved into urban centers, and the old customs were falling by the wayside.

Those customs included drinking and general revelry, feasting, pantomime and plays, caroling, inversion of the social order and ... ghost stories.

Searchers after horror haunt strange, far places. And one of the strangest and furthest is Christmas. While most contemporary epicures of the terrible think Halloween the gold standard for spooky holidays, but such was not always the case. Halloween didn't take hold on the popular imagination as the monster holiday until waves of Scots and Irish immigrants came to the United States. Initially, the idea was for Halloween in the US to become something of a nationalist observation for the Scots and Irish, backpedaling the mediaeval, pagan, scary stuff. Fortunately, most Americans gravitated toward the spooky stuff, and Halloween evolved into the holiday that we celebrate today. (Which is, of course, evolving itself, away from ghosts and goblins, and something closer to *mardi gras*. A great shame.)

But prior to Halloween, fans of the fantastic gravitated to ... Christmas. Going back to the earliest celebrations of Christian Christmas (as opposed to pre-Christian holidays celebrated at year end, like Saturnalia), ghost stories were an integral part of the holiday observance. The days were short, the night was long, the trees were dead, and people huddled around the hearth for both light and warmth. Tales of the uncanny became a natural for this time, when the year itself was dying.

In fact, visions of Christmas and what we think of as the Gothic are just inversions of each other. At Christmas, images that are called to mind include snow, drinks around the fire, thoughts of loved ones distant or now dead, and of benign supernatural visitations. Christmas keeps the cold of the outside world *out*.

In the Gothic, the hearth has grown cold, snow and withered trees litter the landscape, the past and our dead torment us, and the supernatural visitations are decidedly not benign. In the Gothic, the cold of the outside world creeps into our comfort zone, and will not thaw. In fact, Poe's *The Fall of the House of Usher* could be thought of as *A Vincent Price Christmas Special*.

Like the great Gothics, *A Christmas Carol* tells the story of a man haunted by his past, and of past deeds coming back to destroy the present. Like most great Gothics, it involves the death of a beautiful woman (Fan), and of ghosts haunted by past injustices.

The ritual of Ghosts stories at Christmas lasted until at least World War II, with writers as diverse as Henry James (1843-1916), M.R. James (1862-1936), Jerome K. Jerome (1859-1927), and Robertson Davies (1913-1995) keeping it alive. In fact, these tales were already cliché in Dickens' time. As he wrote in his short story *A Christmas Tree* (1850), "There is no end to the old houses, with resounding galleries, and dismal state-bedchambers, and haunted wings shut up for many years, through which we may ramble, with an agreeable creeping up our back, and encounter any number of ghosts … "

A Christmas Tree (1850) is an almost Proustian foray into memory. The narrator sits before his Christmas tree, and various ornaments call to mind Christmases past. His reveries also drift towards the many ghost stories popular during the season:

IT CAME FROM ...

There is probably a smell of roasted chestnuts and other good comfortable things all the time, for we are telling Winter Stories, Ghost Stories, or more shame for us, round the Christmas fire; and we have never stirred, except to draw a little nearer to it. But, no matter for that. We came to the house, and it is an old house, full of great chimneys where wood is burnt on ancient dogs upon the hearth, and grim portraits (some of them with grim legends, too) lower distrustfully from the oaken panels of the walls. We are a middle-aged nobleman, and we make a generous supper with our host and hostess and their guests, it being Christmas-time, and the old house full of company, and then we go to bed. Our room is a very old room. It is hung with tapestry. We don't like the portrait of a cavalier in green, over the fireplace. There are great black beams in the ceiling, and there is a great black bedstead, supported at the foot by two great black figures, who seem to have come off a couple of tombs in the old baronial church in the park, for our particular accommodation. But, we are not a superstitious nobleman, and we don't mind. Well! We dismiss our servant, lock the door, and sit before the fire in our dressing-gown, musing about a great many things. At length we go to bed. Well! We can't sleep. We toss and tumble, and can't sleep. The embers on the hearth burn fitfully and make the room look ghostly. We can't help peeping out over the counterpane, at the two black figures and the cavalier, that wicked-looking cavalier, in green. In the flickering light they seem to advance and retire: which, though we are not by any means a superstitious nobleman, is not agreeable. Well! we get nervous, more and more nervous. We say, "This is very foolish, but we can't stand this; we'll pretend to be ill, and knock up somebody." Well! We are just going to do it, when the locked door opens, and there comes in a young woman, deadly pale, and with long fair hair, who glides to the fire, and sits down in the chair we have left there, wringing her hands. Then, we notice that her clothes are wet. Our tongue cleaves to the roof of our mouth, and we can't speak, but, we observe her accurately. Her clothes are wet; her long hair is dabbled with moist mud; she is dressed in the fashion of two hundred years ago; and she has at her girdle a bunch of rusty keys. Well! there she sits, and we can't even faint, we are in such a state about it. Presently she gets up, and tries all the locks in the room with the rusty keys, which won't fit one of them;

then, she fixes her eyes on the portrait of the cavalier in green, and says, in a low, terrible voice, "The stags know it!" After that, she wrings her hands again, passes the bedside, and goes out at the door. We hurry on our dressing-gown, seize our pistols (we always travel with pistols), and are following, when we find the door locked. We turn the key, look out into the dark gallery; no one there. We wander away, and try to find our servant. Can't be done. We pace the gallery till daybreak; then return to our deserted room, fall asleep, and are awakened by our servant (nothing ever haunts him) and the shining sun. Well! We make a wretched breakfast, and all the company say we look queer. After breakfast, we go over the house with our host, and then we take him to the portrait of the cavalier in green, and then it all comes out. He was false to a young housekeeper once attached to that family, and famous for her beauty, who drowned herself in a pond, and whose body was discovered, after a long time, because the stags refused to drink of the water. Since which, it has been whispered that she traverses the house at midnight (but goes especially to that room where the cavalier in green was wont to sleep), trying the old locks with the rusty keys. Well! we tell our host of what we have seen, and a shade comes over his features, and he begs it may be hushed up; and so it is.

The genius of Dickens is that *A Christmas Carol* manages to be both a Gothic story and a sentimental Christmas tale. It is filled with ghosts and phantasms—not just Marley and the three Christmas spirits, but ghosts of now-dead capitalists, of sister Fan, ghostly hearses, ringing bells, an alternate-reality dead Tiny Tim, and the horrific specters of the dreadful children, Ignorance and Want. Any retelling of *A Christmas Carol* that downplays the Gothic is only half a *Carol*; without darkness, Dickens' light shines less brightly. Accordingly, the very best versions of the story retain a horrific element, in keeping with Dickens and the more traditional sentiments of the season.

Like Sherlock Holmes, any realization of *A Christmas Carol* boils down to the performance of the key character. Scrooge is one of the great characters in the English language, and demands an actor who is somewhat epic, dangerous and larger than life. Aside from his transformation, the ideal Scrooge must reveal his intelligence, his drive, his regret, his fear of death, his somewhat bitter wit and the layers of protection that cover his damaged psyche. The sense of the *Carol* as a performance dates back to its very beginning. By February 1844, eight adaptations of *A Christmas Carol* were mounted, adding songs and additional melodramatic features. It is this sense of theater that has been another key reason for its success and longevity.

IT CAME FROM ...

A Christmas Carol is the most theatrical of Charles Dickens' work. Whole sections of dialogue are infinitely quotable (and have, indeed, entered into the language), and the simple dramatic arc of the story cries out for dramatization. Dickens himself made a performance piece of it, doing public readings of the text over several years, enacting all the parts himself. The closest we have to this type of protean reading was the magnificent one-man show starring Patrick Stewart (born 1940); sadly, his own full-cast dramatization made for Hallmark television is something of a disaster.

It is no exaggeration to say that this writer has spent his entire life closely watching various versions of the *Carol*, so naturally I have some opinions in the matter. For me, the best versions of the *Carol* retain their Gothic sensibility, offering delicious chills along with Christmas sweets. Using that as a yardstick, the most significant versions of the *Carol* include:

Scrooge, made in 1951, starring Alistair Sim (1900-1976) as Scrooge ... This version has been hailed by many as the yardstick by which versions of the *Carol* are measured. However, while we certainly love this film, it is not our favorite. Screenwriter Noel Langley (1911-1980) takes a great many liberties with the original text, providing an extended back-story for Scrooge and introducing many non-Canonical characters. In addition, while Sim is magnificent, we find that none of the Christmas spirits are particularly memorable.

Fans of fantastic film note appearances by Ernest Thesiger (1879-1961) and Miles Malleson (1888-1979). And the settings are impressive. The London streets seem barren and shabby, and Scrooge's apartments appear cold and musty. But ... there is a sense of social realism to the proceedings that co-opt its ability to be truly Gothic. This is *Carol* as social tract, not Gothic story, and it seems unnaturally preachy and thin.

Finally—heresy coming—while Sim is terrific, he is not the definitive Scrooge to our way of thinking. Sim is essentially a great comedian, while we believe a tragedian would best perform Scrooge. Sim's quirky eccentricity, his giddiness upon his reclamation, and his heavily circled eyes make him something of a cartoon.

The great actor Basil Rathbone (1892-1967) essayed the role of both Scrooge and Marley several times on early television, but perhaps never better than as the all-singing all-dancing Scrooge in 1956. This broadcast-live musical, *The Stingiest Man in Town*, was originally part of *The Alcoa Hour*. The kinetoscopes had been counted as lost for decades, and only recently come to light in a terrific DVD transfer that preserves the live broadcast, flubs and all. The show also starred Martyn Green and Vic Damone, and the score, while not stellar, is certainly pleasant.

What is fascinating here is Rathbone's take on Scrooge. This is a particularly virile and argumentative Scrooge, very much in the vein of Stewart's later television take. I think Rathbone a fascinating figure—he was really the first actor to bridge the classical and popular worlds; were he alive today, he would have Ian McKellan's career. Too bad he ended up in some of the films he did. I appreciate *Stingiest Man* more than I like it, but Rathbone is never less than captivating. Where Rathbone shines is that his post-reclamation Scrooge is little different from his frosty Scrooge. His mannerisms and approach are the same … we see here a Scrooge who is still trying to figure out the impact of the Spirits on his life, and post-Scrooge will always be a work-in-progress. While the Christmas ghosts are serviceable, *The Stingiest Man in Town* doesn't stint on the final frights the spirits have for Scrooge. At his gravestone spirits and chains buffet Scrooge as lightning flashes admit spectral moaning. This is Scrooge put through the ringer, and it's a testament to Rathbone's athleticism that he was able to undertake it all so late in life.

There are many animated versions of the *Carol*, but by far the very best features Mr. Magoo. Produced in 1962, *Mr. Magoo's Christmas Carol* offers one of the most faithful adaptations of Dickens' story, and includes some truly champion songs, performed by the likes of Jack Cassidy, Jane Kean, and Paul Frees.

The centerpiece, though, is Magoo as voiced by character actor Jim Backus (1913-1989). This is in every instance a real performance, filled with anger, fear, pathos, and joy. Whole swathes of dialog were lifted verbatim from Dickens, and now it is nearly impossible for this writer to read many of these lines without hearing Backus' voice.

Nearly every version of interest takes some central part of the story and turns it into a showpiece (demonstrating that Dickens' tale is nearly inexhaustible). The highlight of the Magoo *Carol* is definitely the musical number involving Old Joe, the Undertaker, Laundress, and the Charwoman, all of whom have robbed the dead and unloved body of Scrooge. Catchy, funny, and infinitely memorable (and perhaps the only tune to ever rhyme "reprehensible" with "pencil-ble"), this musical interlude is truly Gothic in approach. The Ghost of Christmas Yet to Come (looking more like the Red Death than the Christmas spirit) takes Scrooge to a memorable graveyard, and the deep drum rolls throughout the future sequence are filled with dire portent.

The Albert Finney musical adaptation, *Scrooge* (1970), is a remarkable film. Composer Leslie Bricusse (born 1931) and director Ronald Neame (1911-2010) originally envisioned Albert Finney (born 1936) in the title role, but the actor initially refused without reading the screenplay. The production team then approached Alec Guinness (1914-2000), who opted instead for the plum part of Jacob Marley. (He hated playing Marley as well, developing a double-hernia while wearing his flying harness.) Rex Harrison (1908-1990), still riding high from *My Fair Lady* (1962), was then pegged for the title role, and all seemed a go; until scheduling delays made Harrison's participation impossible. Happily, in the interval, Finney had read the script and, now wanting to do it, came on board.

Alec Guinness and Albert Finney in the 1970 musical *Scrooge.*

Before diving into *Scrooge*, a note on the Rex Harrison Scrooge that might have been. Regardless of the material, Harrison always played some extension of himself. One wonders what this blithe and self-satisfied actor would have made of Scrooge. Always acting on the balls of his feet, preening and mocking, Harrison would have made a deliriously puckish Scrooge, one for whom we might legitimately question his ultimate reclamation. The Finney version is such an embarrassment of riches that it's almost churlish to think of missed opportunities, but one cannot help but wonder.

Though unmemorable as a musical, as a ghost story, *Scrooge* is a champion work. Guinness is spectacularly effective as Marley: spectral, otherworldly, behaving as if he existed within his own ghostly atmosphere. His stylized movements, his halting delivery, his imperturbability all mark him as other-worldly. Marley takes Scrooge on a Christmas Eve flight, where he sees the ghosts of other, unreformed businessmen. These phantoms are truly horrific, with faces splitting into gray globs of malevolence. The horrors pile on with the Ghost of Christmas Yet to Come. For the first time on film, we see the specter's face, and it is a fleshy, molten skull. Scrooge awakens in his coffin before Marley takes him into the pits of hell. There, Scrooge sees his fate: chained to his counting desk, freezing in the only cold part of hell.

This take is interesting for so many reasons it's hard to find a place to begin. Since this is 1970, the Ghost of Christmas Present (the fabulous Kenneth Moore, 1914-1982) gives Scrooge a hit from the Milk of Human Kindness—a nod to the enveloping counter culture. This Scrooge does not dance in flashbacks with Belle, the great love of his life, and much is made of the notion that Scrooge is the victim of his own inhibitions. (The 1960s!) It's only when he loses his dignity and gets high on life, the film argues, that Scrooge becomes his own man. But it is the supernatural aspects of this version that shine the brightest. All of the Ghosts seem otherworldly, and the conception that we are now in the realm of the fantastic seems holistic and sincere. There is haunting stuff here, and it's no surprise that Scrooge emerges a changed man.

Oddly enough, the very best version of *A Christmas Carol* was made for television in 1984 starring George C. Scott (1927-1999). Directed by Clive Donner (1926-2010), who edited the 1951 version, this *Carol* is the most faithful, artful and moving version of all.

After decades of Scrooges re-imagined as cartoons, puppets, women, and even Fonzi (*An American Christmas Carol*, from 1979), Donner and company decided to make a film version that was Dickens, with no added bi-products. Aside from a scene or two for filler (for example, the poor family residing beneath a bridge), this is an almost scene-for-scene adaptation of Dickens' original. Consequently, the ghosts are in full force and the Gothic atmosphere is as thick as the London fog. Several faces familiar to fans of Gothic cinema help the proceedings inordinately.

Brilliantly photographed by cinematographer Tony Imi in Shrewsbury, Shropshire, this *Carol* looks like a ghost story. Scrooge's counting office is suitably moody and grim, and leaving for home, ghostly voices call while a phantom hearse drives by. Chains clank in his home, bells ring, and Scrooge sees visions in the decorative tiles of his fireplace.

The Ghost of Christmas Yet to Come is the creepiest on film (yes, even beating 1970's *Scrooge*). Voiceless, the specter's lone skeletal hand points to a Scrooge future corpse, at the ruin of the Cratchit family, at his gravestone.

IT CAME FROM ...

The Ghost of Christmas Present (Edward Woodward) relates the joys and wonder of Christmas Day to Ebenezer Scrooge (George C. Scott).

There is a signature sound heard when the specter appears, just a mix of muted horn and just-pulled-nails that never fails to unnerve.

The bit with Old Joe the ragman (buying the late Scrooge's belongings) is indeed transgressive. As Scrooge descends into the London underworld, it is almost as if he were journeying to a blighted dimension. Disorienting, too, in the mode of the best ghost stories, is the cutting. Sometimes, as characters loom into the camera, the scene jumps to the next sequence, providing a dream-like quality to the proceedings.

One pitfall that is all to easy for adaptations to fall into is portraying Bob Cratchit as a spineless milksop. Donner neatly avoids this by casting screen villain David Warner (born 1941) in the role, who plays Cratchit as a simple workingman of unusual decency. Susannah York (1939-2011) as Mrs. Cratchit ably supports him. Here, when Bob talks about Tiny Tim's inherent goodness or his hopes for the boy's recovery, York looks aside, as if she is more than used to Bob trying to convince himself of good outcomes that will never come to pass. These are not plaster gods, but real-life people, burdened with care. They are simple in their piety, warmed by familial love, and hopeful of the future. As Dickens writes, there is "nothing of high mark" about them … a cardinal sin of other versions, which portray Bob as little better than an un-ordained priest.

The philanthropists seeking money from Scrooge are wonderfully played by Michael Gough (1916-2011) and John Quarmby (1929-2019)—and they turn these usually sanctimonious nudges into simple humanitarians. Especially noteworthy are the various lip-pursing and lower-register vocals of Gough, who plays to the back rows without ever becoming a cartoon. Roger Rees (1944-2015) is excellent at Scrooge's nephew, Fred. As with Cratchit, many actors make Fred nearly simple-minded in his goodness; here Rees is simply a warm, kind man who feels responsibility toward his uncle. This Fred is all-too-much like people we've actually met; people who are too often too nice for their own good, and who we fear will ultimately be taken advantage of. (Of course, the laugh is on us.)

But perhaps the finest things about this version of the *Carol* are the Spirits. In Dickens, the Spirits are mighty creations, otherworldly visitations that are both great and terrible. Things start with a magnificent, sonorous, stentorian Marley, played with histrionic brio by Frank Finlay (1926-2016). Angela Pleasance (born 1941) is truly … *unnerving* as the Ghost of Christmas Past. There

is something positively inhuman about her, and her line readings sound as if they come from another world. Perhaps even better is Edward Woodward (1920-2009) as the Ghost of Christmas Present. Playing on stilts beneath a rich mantle of green, this is a Ghost of great joviality, but he is also tormented and angry at witnessing man's inhumanity to man. His revelation of the horrid children, Ignorance and Want, residing beneath his robe, is one of the most affecting, chilling moments in television movies. While the Ghost of Christmas Yet to Come (Michael Carter) is little more than a shrouded skeleton, he is a truly terrifying, Gothic figure.

Which leaves us with Scott. This is a Scrooge to be reckoned with. This Scrooge ably defends himself against the accusations of the ghosts, and has a marked sense of humor while relishing his own wickedness. But, at heart, Scott is a tragedian. This is a Scrooge who feels, more than any other, what might have been. Perhaps Scott himself, who had many career ups-and-downs, understood the variable nature of life and how certain roads led to ruin or success.

IT CAME FROM ...

After his reclamation, Scott is transformed. Unlike Sim, who merely tapped into the whimsy patently within him, Scott finds a new lightness of heart, a sense of salvation, and the certainty that he now has the ability to change his life. This is the Scrooge that I would like to know personally.

A Christmas Carol is, along with Washington Irving's *Old Christmas* (1819), the seminal text on the modern Christmas. It could be argued, in fact, that Dickens created Christmas as we know it.

It is at this time of year particularly that this writer finds it impossible not to believe in the invisible world. Just as an ant is innocent of knowledge of the human beings that teem around it, we are unaware of the great mystery that surrounds us. Christmas plugs us directly into great channels of mystery and wonder, leading to a realization of the simple, abundant joy of creation.

The tradition of Christmas has been a boon to this writer that is impossible to measure. Its celebration has made me part of a millennia-long tradition of finding light in the darkness, warming the human heart, and celebrating the wonders of existence. Just as the food and drink of the season underscore the pleasure of our physical, corporeal selves, Christmas nourishes and replenishes our emotional, philosophical, and spiritual selves.

Let's have Dickens have the last word, as he does here in the closing passages of this, perhaps the greatest of all novels:

> Scrooge was better than his word. He did it all, and infinitely more; and to Tiny Tim, who did not die, he was a second father. He became as good a friend, as good a master, and as good a man, as the good old city knew, or any other good old city, town, or borough, in the good old world. Some people laughed to see the alteration in him, but he let them laugh, and little heeded them; for he was wise enough to know that nothing ever happened on this globe, for good, at which some people did not have their fill of laughter in the outset; and knowing that such as these would be blind anyway, he thought it quite as well that they should wrinkle up their eyes in grins, as have the malady in less attractive forms. His own heart laughed: and that was quite enough for him.
>
> He had no further intercourse with Spirits, but lived upon the Total Abstinence Principle, ever afterwards; and it was always said of him, that he knew how to keep Christmas well, if any man alive possessed the knowledge. May that be truly said of us, and all of us! And so, as Tiny Tim observed, God bless Us, Every One!

Science Fiction

Ask anyone who doesn't read (or watch) science fiction what it's all about and they will confidently tell you: *It's all about predicting the future.*

But people actively engaged in the great science fiction enterprise will tell you that is so much hoo-ha. Science fiction was never about predicting the future; it was always about explaining our present.

No great science fiction happens in a vacuum, and the genre always existed as a vehicle in which to better explain how we live now. When it is working on all cylinders, it packs a powerful punch, often like a bucket of cold water clearing away a particularly bad hangover. And when it's bad, it's still instructive, often exposing the guilty thoughts, the failed aspirations, and the prejudices and fears of the people of its time.

Writing about science fiction films, consequently, is often more an exercise in history than in futurism. All of the films covered here, from *Flash Gordon* to *Tomorrowland*, are not only products of their time, but seem impossible to emerge from any other time period. *Dr. No* quakes with Cold War jitters, *This Island Earth* re-imagines the horrors of World War II, *Planet of the Apes* exposes fears at the heart of a rapidly changing America, the futurism of *John Carter* is no match for New Agey religion, and *Tomorrowland* is a meditation on our collective loss in a belief in a better tomorrow. Each a product and reflection of their times, saying more about who we once were than who we are going to someday be.

The challenges with this section were many. It's not that we had a scarcity of material, instead there was simply too much. We very much wanted to do the James Mason versions of Jules Verne's *20,000 Leagues Under the Sea* and *Journey to the Center of the Earth* (we were going to call that chapter *Jules and Jim*), as well as Spielberg's *AI* and Kubrick's *2001: A Space Odyssey*. Also in the hopper were the alternate versions of *The Time Machine*, David Lynch's *Dune*, and Cliff Robertson's *Charley*. Inclusion of these titles, though, would have unbalanced our coverage of horror films, so these movies must wait for future volumes.

Before diving into this section, we did want to share a few thoughts.

Horror films have followed a fairly traceable progression from the earliest years of cinematic horror through today. As the movies became more explicit, horror followed suit, added redder gouts of blood and spicing the whole brew with sex, kinky and otherwise. As the world became more urbanized, the Gothic minarets of the old films gave way to more contemporary settings, bringing horror stories into the cities and suburbs. Decadent and deranged aristocrats became beleaguered homeowners, vampiric counts became anonymous zombies. But—horror films were still recognizable, the family bloodlines were pretty clear.

IT CAME FROM ...

20,000 Leagues Under the Sea (above) and *Journey to the Center of the Earth* (below) must wait for another volume.

Not so with science fiction. There is an insurmountable gulf between *Flash Gordon* with Buster Crabbe and *The Matrix* with Keanu Reeves. Science fiction has changed so much over the years, and changed so *dramatically*, as to be almost an entirely different thing than the article with which both of us grew up. Much of this new material is not to our taste (post-apocalypse porn will never be our bag), but it has remained challenging and engaging. Whereas horror is an effect, science fiction is a conversation. The conversation doesn't always go the way we want it to, but we still want in on the talk until we've had our say.

And we hope you will like what we've had to say.

The stories and novels behind Classic Horror, Fantasy and Science Fiction Films

He'll Save Every One of Us:
Flash Gordon (1936)

For decades, science fiction was synonymous with the names Buck Rogers and Flash Gordon. "That Flash Gordon stuff" was shorthand for any science fictional enterprise, and the debt science fiction owes to both comic strips is vast and largely unpaid.

Buck Rogers, of course, started it all. Debuting on January 7, 1929 and written by Philip Nowlan (1888-1940) and illustrated by Dick Calkins (1894-1962), *Buck Rogers* told the story of an aviator accidently locked in suspended animation, only to awake 500 years later to find a war-ravaged United States. It was a huge success.

Syndicates, initially leery of science fiction until the success of *Buck Rogers*, sought to create a rival feature. Swinging to the rescue was none other than Edgar Rice Burroughs (1875-1950), looking for another medium in which to tell stories of his space-opera hero, John Carter. Burroughs approached United (currently syndicating his *Tarzan*), which passed on the proposal.

But United rival King Features Syndicate started courting Burroughs as early as 1933, selecting artist Alex Raymond (1909-1956) to create the strip. As negotiations over who would own what grew heated, Burroughs continued to work on the project until he got a kill letter from King Features canceling further negotiations. Concurrent with the negotiations with Burroughs, King Features was working on a John Carter knockoff, which debuted at *Flash Gordon* on January 7, 1934. (Ironically, five years to the date after the debut of *Buck Rogers*.) Raymond, who was working *John Carter* until that project was killed, was also developing Flash Gordon.

Artist Alexander Gillespie Raymond was born in New Rochelle, New York. His father was an engineer at the Woolworth Building, and supported his son's interests in the arts. Raymond used his art skills to support his family upon his father's death, dropping out of high school to become an order clerk at a Wall Street brokerage firm. With the Great Depression, Raymond left finance to return to art, working as an assistant to Russ Westover (1866-1966) on the strip *Tilly the Toiler*. He was hired as an assistant at King Features in 1931, and slowly built his reputation helping Chic Young (1901-1973) on *Blondie*. His big break came in 1934, not just with *Flash Gordon*, but with *Secret Agent X-9* (a *Dick Tracy* knockoff), and yet another Edgar Rice Burroughs pastiche, *Jungle Jim*, Raymond's answer to *Tarzan*.

Not only did Raymond liberally recycle Burroughs, but *Flash Gordon* borrows from multiple sources, including *When Worlds Collide*, Sax Rohmer's Fu Manchu, and Wagner's Ring Cycle. A brilliant draftsman who got better the

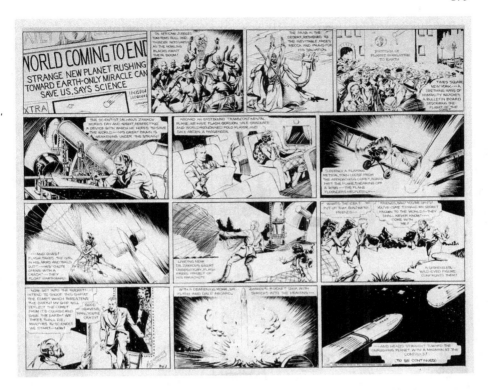

First *Flash Gordon* comic strip

longer he drew, Raymond was only a journeyman writer. Raymond wrote the initial continuity for *Flash Gordon* before the scripting chores went to veteran pulpsmith Don G. Moore. (Oddly enough, despite its many-decade run, *Flash Gordon* never regained the narrative momentum of Raymond's initial story; as his art improved, the narrative took a distant second place to his brilliant illustration.) Raymond would die in a car crash on September 6, 1956.

The initial story of *Flash Gordon* covered in both the comic strip and the film is a simple one. Famed polo-player and Yale man Flash Gordon is on his way home as the Earth is slowly disintegrating, due to the proximity of a previously unknown planetoid. When meteorites seriously damage his plane, he grabs fellow-passenger Dale Arden and parachutes to safety. On the ground, they meet Dr. Hans Zarkov, a scientist who is convinced that the planetoid is inhabited, and that its interference with the Earth is intentional. He intends to travel there in a rocket ship of his own design, and takes Flash and Dale with him.

Once there, they learn that the foreign body is the planet Mongo, made up of multiple kingdoms all under the supreme rule of dictator Ming the Merciless. Flash is sentenced to death, Zarkov exiled to Ming's own laboratories, and Dale slated for his harem. Their only hope is for Flash to escape and rally the other kingdoms into rebellion.

The stories and novels behind Classic Horror, Fantasy and Science Fiction Films

Though both strips were fantastically popular in their day, *Flash Gordon* soon outstripped *Buck Rogers* in terms of readership. This is curious because, in many ways, *Buck Rogers* remains the better (or, at least, more interesting) strip.

Conceived soon after the Great War, *Buck Rogers* is about an aviator and

veteran. Traveling into the future, he literally becomes a "Forgotten Man," a refrain familiar to many veterans who returned home to find a drastically altered country. The world of *Buck Rogers* is one steeped in a global, and seemingly never-ending war. It looked at contemporary fears and imagined threats—uncontrolled gangsterism and the rise of the East— and remolded the problems into a science fictional narrative. His experience as a pilot and soldier would gain greater importance with the start of World War II, where the strip focused most intently on the war in the air. And most importantly, Buck is a man in constant awe of scientific marvels that come at him at an ever-accelerating rate. Like many of his generation, the quick accumulation of scientific wonders were disorienting to the extent of seeming magical. (My grandmother, born in 1894, was a devoted reader of *Buck Rogers*. Born before air travel, she was an adult for two World Wars, the advent of aviation, radio, television, space travel, and dramatic cultural changes; she often said she was born on one planet and would die on one very different.)

The rationale for plot devices in *Buck Rogers* was always a scientific one. Even if the science was absurd and outlandish, the strip attempted to at least pay lip service to science. (And really, is there any significant difference between the inertron of Buck Rogers and the dilithium crystals of *Star Trek*?) The art of *Buck Rogers* was the art of pulp magazine science fiction covers: streamlined art deco with vast machines of gleaming chrome and steel. As an example of what is now considered retro-futurism, *Buck Rogers* can't be beat.

However, *Flash Gordon* served up heaping platters of spectacularly drawn fantasy with only a soupcon of science for flavor. Because the art had its roots in a mythic past rather than an imagined future, the look of the strip became timeless. *Flash Gordon* was a spectacle, a tale of heroes and villains in larger than life settings. Where *Buck Rogers* looked to the future, *Flash Gordon* looked to the past, harking back to Biblical spectacle, crusades, gladiatorial pageantry, and mysterious kingdoms.

Flash Gordon **traded on eroticism; the sexual appetite of Ming's daughter for Flash is a major plot point.**

Though rockets flew over Mongo, how or why they worked was unimportant—how they looked mattered most of all. Where *Buck Rogers* sought scientific explanations for the existence of Atlantis in one prolonged story sequence, *Flash Gordon* served up floating cities, ice planets, lion men, hawkmen who looked curiously like angels, and all manner of monsters with a brazen disregard for internal logic.

The key advantage, though, that *Flash Gordon* had over *Buck Rogers* was sex.

Though *Buck Rogers* presented liberated woman who served as officers in a super-science tomorrow, it was not terribly sexy. *Flash Gordon*, working within more traditional gender roles, was fueled by sex. The story conflict in *Flash Gordon* was one of sexual tensions: a love triangle between Flash, Dale and Princess Aura (daughter of Ming the Merciless), or the pure carnal interest Ming has with Dale. Even more compellingly, Raymond's art was frankly sexual. For much of the strip Flash is less than a handkerchief away from naked, while Dale is always beautiful in her tightly clinging interplanetary frocks.

While *Buck Rogers* engaged the real world in metaphor, *Flash Gordon* ignored it for a hyper-sensual fantasy realm. It is this reliance on passion, on recycling the past and on fantasy that, I think, has given *Flash Gordon* greater longevity. *Buck Rogers* is science fiction, but *Flash Gordon* is a fantasy ballad.

Both *Buck Rogers* and *Flash Gordon* are the pretexts of popular science fiction for general audiences. Both have been imitated and revived, venerated and dismissed, but neither has ever gone away. The idea of science fiction being a general crowd pleaser and a niche pursuit commences with them both, and without them there would be no *Star Trek*, *Star Wars* or DC and Marvel Universes. As such, their central role in science fiction history is secure.

So successful was *Flash Gordon* that Universal Studios decided to adapt the strip into a serial in 1936. Starring Olympian Buster Crabbe (1908-1983) and directed by Frederick Stephani (1903-1962), the serial was successful enough to warrant two sequels (*Flash Gordon's Trip to Mars*, 1938 and *Flash Gordon Conquers the Universe*, 1940), and remains one of the most celebrated examples of the chapter play medium.

Serials were the ideal medium for the adaptation of comic strips. Both were cheap and "disposable" entertainments, and—more importantly—both thrived on long narratives broken into bite-sized nuggets that end with a cliffhanger. No other film covered in this book was as lucky in its medium; the episodic quality of the original text and its cinematic incarnation allow a closer type of adaptation than a simple short story or novel translated into a feature-length film.

Flash Gordon was only the second comic strip adapted into serial form, beaten only by *Tailspin Tommy* (1934), one of the many pop culture aviators inspired by real-life Charles Lindberg (1902-1974). *Flash Gordon*, however, was a very close adaptation of Raymond's initial story and can be considered as the prototype for translating comics materials into film.

Because the grammar of chapter plays and comic strip serials were so similar, the early *Flash Gordon* strips often look as if they were storyboards for the eventual movie serial. The difference, though, is that Stephani managed to replicate the effect of the strip without slavishly copying it "shot for shot." Stephani used surprisingly sophisticated framing techniques to tell his story, creating both greater scope and (when needed) greater intimacy than Raymond's comic panel. Reading the original strip continuity while watching the serial gave me the oddest feeling of experiencing competing but parallel narratives.

The synergy between strip and serial is best felt at the opening crawl at the start of every chapter of *Flash Gordon*. Though already a serial tradition, this narrative update for those who came in late was also a staple of Sunday comic strips. And while the strip would often offer a cliffhanger concerning what was *about* to happen (a ship crashing, for instance), the serial would often close on the catastrophe itself, only to step back in the next episode to provide the vital information on how Flash and company escaped.

Universal bought the rights to *Flash Gordon* in 1935, when the strip was one year old, and shot the film in January and February 1936. Screenwriters Stephani, George Plympton, Ella O'Neill, and Basil Dickey had nearly two years worth of comic strip continuity to work from. *Flash Gordon* retells the first 14 months of Raymond's strip. The movie serial sought to recapture the success of the strip by fidelity to its storyline. A variety of story beats were crafted to transpose the tone and rhythm of the strip into the rhythm of a chapter play, and the budget swelled to an estimated $350,000 in an era when movie serials cost roughly $200,000. (The rights to *Flash Gordon* cost Universal an additional $10,000.)

One of the key differences between *Flash Gordon* on the comics page and the movie screens is the sense of a closed story. The serial tells a complete story, written entirely before production began. The comic strip, in contrast, was still an ongoing story with no end in sight. Things that slowly evolved became more concrete in the movie serial (for example, the certainty that Dr. Zarkov survives the landing—let alone is one of the heroes and not one of the villains—or that

A scene from Universal's *Flash Gordon* serial

The stories and novels behind Classic Horror, Fantasy and Science Fiction Films

Mongo consisted of many kingdoms living under one supreme emperor), and provided newcomers with greater narrative clarity.

Despite compressions and explications, though, the serial *Flash Gordon* is astonishingly faithful to the comic strip. For example, the first of the 13 chapters that comprise *Flash Gordon*, "The Planet of Peril," neatly adapted the first four Sunday pages of the strip into the first 20-minute episode. The second, "The Tunnel of Terror," closely mimics the fourth, fifth and sixth strips. The screenwriters then used a three-Sunday-pages-per-episode model, making concessions, as necessary, when the story expanded in order to draw to a close.

The glories of the first *Flash Gordon* serial are many. Because Stephani actively emulated the look and feel of Raymond's work, there is a great sense of spectacle to the proceedings; one that disdains realism in favor of a type of heightened fantasy. In addition, Raymond's magpie sensibility is superbly suited to the treasures found at the ready in Universal's stock footage library and its prop and costume houses. Raymond's visual memory is a ragbag of history—allowing Universal to raid its store of gladiator costumes, biblical sets, various bits of Orientalia, and even some of the standing sets from its Gothic horror films. The process of recycling becomes blatant in both strip and serial; a sort of delirium is possible watching machinery used in the studio's *Frankenstein* films followed by the impressive number of extras dancing around the 16-foot pagan statue from *The Midnight Sun* (1927).

Where *Flash Gordon* the film improves upon *Flash Gordon* the strip is in the characters, the sense of intimacy and the sense of narrative.

Buster Crabbe is simply terrific as Flash Gordon. With a winning smile and resolute manner, he is much more charming and human than the cold-blooded statue found in Raymond's strip. Stephani aped the comic strip in having Flash clad in little more than tight-fitting black trunks, displaying Crabbe's Olympian torso glistening under several layers of oil. Crabbe dyed his hair blond to be closer to the character in the strip, and so beautiful was Crabbe during the shooting that he recalled wearing his hat at all times "to keep guys from whistling at me."

Jean Rogers (1916-1991) is fetching in her series of diaphanous gowns. Her beauty is luminous, and she seems to shimmer onscreen. In her later years, Rogers commented on Stephani slavishly trying to reproduce the color of her clothes as found in the original Alex Raymond script, despite the fact that the film was shot in black and white.

Frank Shannon (1874-1959) is sober and steady as Dr. Zarkov (dubbed Alexis in the third serial, rather than Hans, as in the strip). Many today chiefly remember Charles Middleton (1874-1949) for his portrayal of space tyrant Ming the Merciless. Middleton's Ming is all tightly controlled fury, his normally guttural line reading becoming nearly incomprehensible when enraged. It is his best performance. Also superb is Priscilla Lawson (1914-1958) as Princess

Frank Shannon as Dr. Zarkov and Charles Middleton as Ming

Aura. In the comic strip, characters are little more than chess pieces moved around the narrative, while the serial invests Crabbe, Rogers, Shannon and Lawson with a vitality and humanity actually missing in Raymond's strip.

The film serial was also able to play-up the heavily sexualized feel of the strip. (So much so, that costumes and situations were drastically toned-down in the second and third serials at the behest of the censors and religious groups.) And while the serial leaned heavily on sex with the eroticized bodies of both Crabbe and Rogers, the film version relied more heavily on romance than sex. The *Flash Gordon* chapter play is as much a love triangle as a space thriller, which renders it more accessible to audiences.

In fact, it was this shift in focus that was the key improvement of the serial over the strip. While both are narrative-driven, the comic strip focuses on the situation and the serial on the characters. We like these people, and it's largely on that basis that the serial succeeds, and makes the idea of two follow-ups so terrific. In fact, without Buster Crabbe's warmth and humor, or Middleton's theatrics, it's possible that the character Flash Gordon would be, in the long run, forgotten.

Happily, that was not to be, as Flash Gordon would return again and again. But before we look at more recent revivals of the character, allow me a self-indulgent, autobiographical interlude.

HOWDY, EARTHFOLKS! BEST REGARDS BUCK ROGERS

COMPLIMENTS OF PHIL NOWLAN AND J. CALKINS

Everything I am I owe to Buck Rogers and Flash Gordon. When I was eight or nine years old—1970 or '71—and growing up in Middle Village, New York, WOR (channel 9) broadcast the *Buck Rogers* serial at 1:00 AM on Friday nights. I caught the first installment quite by accident and was hooked. I saw the remaining 11 chapters over the ensuing Fridays, the experience leaving me with an undying love for science fiction, Mid-century Americana, and Buster Crabbe.

I started looking around me in a more conscious way and realized that all this glorious Mid-century Americana was not only everywhere, but easily accessible. Local television stations regularly ran classic comedies from the 1930s (W.C. Fields, the Marx Brothers, Mae West) after school. I could catch Laurel and Hardy or the Little Rascals, radio stations had programs devoted to music of the 1920s and 1930s, and old pros like Bing Crosby and Bob Hope were still around and in the popular zeitgeist.

Movie serials were re-evaluated. Books on radio shows and comic strips by such authors as Jim Harmon and Don Thompson appeared. Comic strips and early comic books were examined for their artistic and cultural merit. Radio stations around the country started rebroadcasting classic radio shows; in New York, veteran producer (and later friend) Himan Brown (1910-2010) created the all-new *CBS Radio Mystery Theater*, while WRVR-FM started nightly broadcasts alternating *The Shadow*, *The Lone Ranger*, *The Green Hornet*, *Gangbusters* and *Fibber McGee and Molly*. Pulp magazines were reprinted in paperback, and such heroes as The Shadow, Doc Savage, G-8 and His Battle Aces were popular once again. Fanzines such as *Radio Nostalgia* were popular on college campuses and revival houses played classic Hollywood fare late into the night. Public television starting playing movie serials, bringing weekly chapter plays to new audiences of young people. "Golden Age" detective fiction became so popular once again that novelist Bill DeAndrea lamented that the 1970s was "a boom time for dead writers." The past was even mined for new entertainment, resulting in movies like *W.C. Fields and Me* (1976), *The Great Waldo Pepper* (1975), *The Abominable Dr. Phibes* (1971), and the lyrical and brilliant *Hearts of the West* (1975).

In short, we were in the midst of a full-on Nostalgia Craze. The craze even had an in-house organ, *Nostalgia Illustrated Magazine*, spreading the word to the faithful. This mindset was so prevalent that the news media took notice, with stories on this call-back to Mid-century Americana appearing everywhere from *Reader's Digest* to *Newsweek*.

For a kid like me born at the very tail-end of the Baby Boom and the cusp of Generation X, that meant that I had one foot firmly in the pop culture of the 1960s and 1970s, and the other foot deeply entrenched in the 1930s and 1940s. I saw *Logan's Run* (1976) and the television series *The Six Million Dollar Man* (1973-1978), but my bookshelves were filled with Doc Savage, Tarzan, and Conan novels; I saw more Abbott and Costello films and listened to more *Lone Ranger* and *Green Hornet* radio shows than I watched contemporary sitcoms.

One of the sweetest veins of this great revival for me was reading the boyhood memories of people who grew up during the fascinating and fecund

1920s and 1930s. Very soon after first seeing *Buck Rogers*, I badgered my mother into getting me the splendiferous *Collected Works of Buck Rogers in the Twenty-Fifth Century*, a compilation of the classic strips with an introduction by Ray Bradbury. (Who was, in a way, himself the Poet Laureate of Nostalgic Americana). This book was (and is) enormous; roughly the size of a pauper's tombstone. I spent ages pouring over it, thrilling to the adventures of Buck Rogers, a man who belonged to another time. (Trust me, I identified with him even at an early age.) The book also had photos of various Buck Rogers toys from the 1930s, and this really fired my imagination. There were Buck Rogers watches and bicycles, along with pages from Buck Rogers clubs like *The Solar Scouts* and *The Rocket Rangers*. My imagination always took me back to a time when I, as a boy in the 1930s, would play with these magnificent things. I would call my bike a Rocket-Cycle and think of what it must have been like to be a Buck-obsessed youth in Bradbury's Greentown ...

I gulped down the reminiscences of Isaac Asimov reading the early science fiction pulps in his series of *Before the Golden Age* books, and waxed poetic over Philip Jose Farmer's memories of first meeting Tarzan and Doc Savage.

There is a wonderful Portuguese word, saudade, that means nostalgia for something you have never known. While I did not grow up during America's Golden Age of Pop Culture, I felt as if I was catching its immediate rebroadcast, and the difference was only a matter of degree. The appeal of this innocent America was the subject of much debate at the time. The cover story on nostalgia in the December 28, 1970 issue of *Newsweek* started with this evocative paragraph:

> Once upon a time, there was a land of laughing kids and confident grownups called America the Beautiful. In that simpler country—or so at least it seems in rosy retrospect—the Hollywood of the stars and the golden voice of radio, innocent comic books, funny papers and the Big Bands all blared out a message of cockeyed optimism. It was the time of Mickey Mouse watches and Lionel trains, of folksy Fibber McGee and Molly every Tuesday evening, the reassuring *Saturday Evening Post* every Thursday and cheek-to-cheek romance on jukebox Saturday nights. Look for it now only on late-night TV, for it is no more than a dream remembered, an America gone with the wind ...

Newsweek goes on to report that for "the decade that The *Chicago Tribune* has already happily dubbed the 'Second Hand '70s,' nostalgia has become a year-round affair, and 1971 seems to be shaping up as the most poignant attempt to recover the past since 'Our Town's' Emily Webb went back to Grover's Corners to recelebrate her 12th birthday."

But when it came to explaining the why of it all, *Newsweek* punts with the following:

> One answer comes from Alvin Toffler, author of the best-selling *Future Shock*, who believes that "the tremendous wave of nostalgia mirrors a psychological lust for a simpler, less turbulent past." In this view, nostalgia is a psychological time machine: a Jack Benny-model Maxwell, a surrey with a fringe on top, a sled named Rosebud—any "Let's Pretend" device that says, in effect, "return with us now to those thrilling days of yesteryear." When you get there, you will find that nostalgia is also a state of mind oblivious to boundaries—geographical, political, and actuarial. Nostalgia entices Middle America and

IT CAME FROM ...

the Woodstock Nation alike—and sometimes unites the two ('*You* liked W.C. Fields, Dad?')

But something deeper was actually happening. With the 1960s came cultural and societal change that—almost overnight—changed the nation from one thing into something quite different. The sweeping cultural-revolution was so vast, so all-encompassing, and so swift that it left many reeling in its wake. Even as a very young child, I was aware that massive societal-cultural changes were at hand, and that the results were dire.

In retrospect, it's easy to see that *Newsweek* would feel more comfortable talking about societal and cultural change than societal and social collapse. What they could not bring themselves to say was that both Middle America and the many of the Woodstock Nation were realizing that most of this change was not for the better. In this time of change, it is not surprising that many rediscovering (or just discovering) the riches of America's pop cultural heritage turned to its heroes of old. ("In times of fear and confusion," the opening of *Superman The Movie* says, we turn to a "symbol of hope.") Many Depression-era heroes made surprising comebacks in the 1960s and 1970s, including Batman, Superman, Doc Savage and … Flash Gordon.

Flash, it seems, was everywhere in the early 1970s. In 1972 *Heritage*, a Flash Gordon fanzine, appeared. Lasting only two issues, it included fantastic artwork by Mike Kaluta, Larry Ivie, and Gray Morrow. Soon after, Buster Crabbe—Flash Gordon (and Buck Rogers and Tarzan) himself—started making appearances at the annual New York Nostalgia Convention. Crabbe was an incredibly warm and accessible man, and I had the pleasure of meeting him several times.

During this period, PBS starting regularly airing movie serials and Max Fleischer Singalong cartoons on its New York outlet, WNET. The series started with Tom Mix in *The Miracle Rider* (also starting a life-long love of Westerns), but the centerpiece soon became the three Flash Gordon serials. These proved to be so popular that the channel played all-night marathons to incite interest in membership drives.

Flash Gordon hit the paperback racks in 1973 with a series of six books, credited to Alex Raymond but actual-

ly written by Ron Goulart and Bruce Cassiday. They are not particularly good, but they did work to keep Gordon's name front and center.

The mid-1970s also saw the first serious efforts to publish Alex Raymond's original comic strips in hardbound editions. Although originally conceived as products to cash-in on the nostalgia craze, these reproductions garnered high-level interest in the media and mainstream audiences reassessed Raymond's work.

It was also in 1973 that a little-known filmmaker named George Lucas (born 1944) debuted his exercise in nostalgia, *American Graffiti*, a film that represents this entire phenomenon in microcosm. Though only set 11 years prior to its release date, the 1962 America of *American Graffiti* was so alien to the reality of 1973 and it seemed to represent another world. The notion of a "past America," though only 11 years distant at that point, was very potent to a nation racked by the negative side effects of the 1960s. It would be difficult to imagine another time in American history—barring the advent of World Wars—where the opposite ends of only 11 years provided such contrast. (Today, for example, there is very little to differentiate 2009 and 2020, aside from increased political infighting.)

Lucas wanted to take this exercise in nostalgia to the next step and make a large-scale adaptation of *Flash Gordon*, a movie serial he loved as a young film student. His initial dream was to make a Flash Gordon movie that felt like a chapter-play made with *2001*-grade special effects. After putting together a detailed pitch, Lucas tried to secure the rights and was rebuffed. Instead he made *Star Wars* … a Flash Gordon pastiche. (Of course, if he had been successful, we might now have 12 quality Flash Gordon movies to savor, and not have to sit through such trash as *Rogue One* or *The Last Jedi*. Ponder that …) Lucas, of course, would continue to mine Mid-century Americana with his series of Indiana Jones films, which were consistently more appealing to this reviewer than his *Star Wars* canon.

IT CAME FROM ...

That *Star Wars* was "new" does not negate its debt to Mid-century Americana or the nostalgia craze of the 1960s and 1970s. Even in intent *Star Wars* was consistent with the clarion call of the nostalgia craze; in it's May 26, 1977 review of the film, the *New York Daily News* wrote: "Using such interplanetary stalwarts as Flash Gordon and Buck Rogers for inspiration, director George Lucas has concocted a mind-blowing spectacle that sends the audience off onto the wondrously strange world of fantasy and satisfies just about everyone's adolescent craving for a corny old-fashioned adventure movie." The *New York Times*, in a June 5, 1977 article, reported:

> The stylistic thread of *Star Wars* is not the inhuman hardware of outer space but the art deco of the 1930's. "Even Threepio is a 1930s-type art deco robot whose strongest influence is the robot in Fritz Lang's *Metropolis* (1926)," says Lucas.

When covering the film nearly a year later—then still in theaters—the *Daily News* would suggest that the retro-feel of the film was a reaction to the tumultuous 1960s.

The success of the pastiche resulted, ultimately, in a *Flash Gordon* film proper in 1980, but more of that later.

The point of my digression is simply this: Born of America's great era of pop culture, Flash Gordon was kept alive during the renaissance of interest in this fascinating and fecund era. That renaissance spurred a whole generation of genre historians and pop culture curators. That interest was also one of the many spurs that made *Star Wars* possible, which begat *Superman* (1978), *Raiders of the Lost Ark* (1981), and the later Bat-

Flash Gordon (top) influenced *Star Wars* (bottom)

The stories and novels behind Classic Horror, Fantasy and Science Fiction Films

man films, let alone the Marvel Universe. Each and every aficionado of fantastic cinema owes a debt to Flash Gordon, too often dismissed and too large to properly calculate.

He saved every one of us, indeed.

After the magnificent success Flash Gordon's imitators had, it was only natural that he, too, would return to the big screen. The *Flash Gordon* of 1980 was eagerly anticipated by fans of the character who first met him in the 1930s, and who made his acquaintance during the nostalgia craze of the 1960s and 1970s. Plans for a revival Flash Gordon film pre-date *Star Wars*, with various directors, including Nicolas Roeg and Frederico Fellini, working on it before last-minute replacement Mike Hodges stepped in. Produced by Dino De Laurentis (1919-2010) and written in the same camp style employed on television's *Batman* by Lorenzo Semple, Jr. (1923-2014), *Flash Gordon* is a deeply polarizing film for fans of the character.

Played stiffly by Sam J. Jones (born 1954), Flash is an amiable doofus, abetted by a savvy and slightly over-sexed Dale (Melody Anderson, born 1955). Zarkov (Topol, born 1935) is a Holocaust survivor and more aggressively heroic than the bookish Frank Shannon. The sets and costumes are superb, but the sexual content of the strip is played up to almost absurd fetishistic levels, and it leaves a surprisingly dank taste. Where the comic strip and initial chapter play

thrive on romance and passion, the post-Woodstock *Flash Gordon* is little more than kink. Whips, leather, bondage, and sexual torture all play a part in the remake, which cheapens the overall feel of the piece. People who enjoy that style of rock bombast enjoy the musical score by Queen, and the special effects strive for comic strip surrealism that creates spectacle rather than realism.

The key performances in the film are Max von Sydow (born 1929) as Ming and Peter Wyngarde (1927-2018) as his stooge, General Klytus. Also terrific are Brian Blessed (born 1936) as Vultan and Timothy Dalton (born 1946) as Prince

Max von Sydow as Ming in *Flash Gordon* **(1980)** Barin. All are a great deal of fun and make one wonder what *Star Wars* might have been with actors who played with brio and panache.

Oddly, my views on the film have morphed over time. When I first saw the film in first release, its jokey tone, its kitschy score, kinky vibe, and paper-thin characterization appalled me. As I (and it) have grown older, I have grown fonder of it, much as one does for an idiot child. It's easy on the eyes and has style ... and, though horribly flawed, is better than any of the *Star Wars* prequels.

Better still was *The New Adventures of Flash Gordon*, an animated series courtesy of

Buster Crabbe the original Flash Gordon

Filmation that first premiered in 1979. Running for 32 episodes over two seasons, *The New Adventures of Flash Gordon* was a return to the derring-do divinely inspired by the comic strip and movie serial. Though the animation is limited (do not expect the lush treatment found in Disney fare), the show had a certain sense of fun and epic sweep missing from its big-budget movie competition. Previously unused bits were re-edited into a prime time telefilm, *Flash Gordon: The Greatest Adventure of All*, that underscored that the time period was the 1940s and that Ming promised advanced technology to Hitler.

Uncovered in these pages are the *Flash Gordon* television series (1954-1955), the execrable animated series teaming Flash with Lee Falk's Phantom and Mandrake the Magician, *Defenders of the Earth* (1986), or 2007 live-action series that is *Flash Gordon* in name only. Completists may track these down, but be forewarned—it's not worth the effort.

There have been multiple attempts to launch another *Flash Gordon* film over the last decade, all of them languishing in developmental hell without seeing the light of day.

Ultimately, thanks to the original vibrancy of his creation and the renewed interest thanks to the nostalgia craze, Flash Gordon is now too central a character to the science fictional landscape to be erased for good. Though now only present in the very DNA of contemporary fantastic cinema, I think it's safe to agree with Prince Vultan when he exclaims: "GORDON'S ALIVE!"

World War 2.2:
This Island Earth (1955)

All of the three arguably terrific science fiction films of the 1950s—*The Day The Earth Stood Still* (1951), *This Island Earth* (1955), and *Forbidden Planet* (1956)—shudder with visions of World War II. It was six years between the end of the war and the debut of *The Day The Earth Stood Still*; dim enough in memory to no longer be top of mind, but recent enough to fester in the collective subconscious.

The spate of disaster-porn superhero films of recent decades is a direct reaction to the terrorist attacks of September 11, 2001(when a superpower was humbled by some fairly un-super prehistoric screwheads who are probably now more than finished with their promised 72 virgins and are wondering what comes next); it takes a little time for a battered nation to process tragedy through its pop culture. One of the more interesting (and telling) differences between the Greatest Generation and the 9/11 Generation is that the earlier one got over the more momentous and difficult disaster in less than a decade, while our Millennials are still seeking their safe spaces.

The Day The Earth Stood Still is a perverse re-reading of the tragedy of Neville Chamberlain (1869-1940), who sought to find peace in our time by making deals with dictators. Just as pacifist Klaatu exhorts his American hosts to just get along with European interests dedicated to the extermination of the Unit-

IT CAME FROM ...

ed States, one pictures Chamberlain armed with an indestructible robot goon ready to level major cities if his demands are not met. It is never surprising that *The Day The Earth Stood Still* is such a favorite among the Social Justice Warrior faction of science fiction fandom—only a halfwit could stomach its premise.

Forbidden Planet has much weightier things on its mind. A futuristic reading of Shakespeare's *The Tempest, Forbidden Planet* is also a fascinating meditation on genocide and survivor's guilt. Like Europe, the culture of Altair IV is ancient and formidable. When the spaceship that could only be from a "United Earth" arrives there, our space-faring Yanks find that Dr. Morbius and his daughter are the only survivors of an expedition of colonists sent there earlier. They soon get to the bottom of scientific experimentation run amuck, the murder of an entire people, and a man's soul corroded by guilt. It takes but little reimagining for this story to be set with American soldiers entering a remote German town at war's end.

But for me, the most interesting of these pictures is *This Island Earth*. It is certainly the most entertaining of the three. While *Forbidden Planet* is rather windy and something of a slog (when not offensively stupid with its comedic bits), and *The Day The Earth Stood Still* is preachy, pretentious, and just wrong-headed (and Patricia Neal's contempt for the material hangs over the film like flop sweat), *This Island Earth* has a smart, zippy energy, more engaging characters, a better mystery at its core, and better overall production design. It's a winner.

Few films of the era better capture a breathless sense of wonder—of the promise of a super-science tomorrow—more than *This Island Earth*. Unlike most films of the decade, human beings measure up fairly well compared with "superior" alien intelligences, outer space visitors have an agenda other than world domination, and, rather than providing a warning against science, *This Island Earth* celebrates the human capacity for experimentation and thought. On top of that, it is beautifully photographed, competently acted, and the special effects are among the best of any film of that period. And like its other celebrated brethren, it closely connects itself to the global conflict of a decade earlier. (But more on that later.)

Surely a film with so much going for it has to be based upon really good source material? Well ... think again.

The film *This Island Earth* was adapted from a novel of the same name by Raymond F. Jones, serialized in three parts in the pulp magazine *Thrilling Wonder Stories*. Never real-

ly planned as a novel, *This Island Earth* sort of evolved as Jones was putting together a series of interconnected stories in late 1949-early 1950. The book has been reprinted in recent years as a trade paperback by Pulpless with an embarrassing introduction by the late science fiction expert Forrest J Ackerman (1916-2008) and it is, to put it politely, a total dog.

Raymond F. Jones (1915-1994) is a relatively obscure writer from the Golden Age of Science Fiction, toiling mostly under editor John W. Campbell (1910-1971). Like Campbell, he was pro-science, anti-bureaucracy, and a great believer in science fiction as a socially redeeming force. Jones was born in Salt Lake City, Utah, and was turned onto the genre at an early age by reading Wells' *War of the Worlds*. His first published story was *Test of the Gods*, which appeared in the September 1941 issue of Campbell's *Astounding*. Other stories, including *Noise Level, Black Market*, and *Production Test* followed.

Jones was an engineer by trade and, like most engineers, he went where the work was. He was employed at various times as an installer of telephone equipment for Western Electric, a government meteorologist, and as an aeronautics designer. Like many Golden Age writers, Jones thought that science fiction was a guide for our next collective move up the evolutionary ladder. In later years, Jones became more and more disaffected with the genre, writing little after the mid-1950s. A 1951 autobiographical sketch in *Amazing Stories* reads: "I don't believe there is a storytelling medium that can surpass science fiction. But somehow, I think we're missing the boat."

Jones' reputation ebbed with Campbell. The governing aesthetic of his work was often in agreement with Campbell's editorials, while many other writers working under Campbell (Robert Heinlein, for example) made names by writing ideas contrary to those of the celebrated editor. (Both Jones and Campbell were early advocates of L. Ron Hubbard's Dianetics, later rebranded as Scientology, so we can't take their mental acumen too seriously.) Jones' literary star has faded considerably since his heyday, a victim of both a dated prose style and, perhaps, poor agenting. He is completely forgotten by the general public, little better than a footnote to science fiction fans, and is remembered chiefly by film buffs as the man who wrote *This Island Earth*. Sadly, for Jones, *This Island Earth* is one of the few instances where the movie improves immeasurably upon its source material.

The basic setup of *This Island* is the same for both book and movie: Engineer Cal Meacham receives a catalogue and parts, through which he constructs a marvelous extraterrestrial machine, the interocitor. He joins forces with the alien intelligences behind this new technology and becomes embroiled in an interplanetary war.

The resemblances end, however, with these broad strokes. Characters in the novel are crudely drawn, with little or no personality of their own. Joe Wilson in the novel is an anonymous purchasing agent for Ryberg Instrument Corporation, and not Meacham's friend and confidant, as in the film. Meacham is at times a complete dunderhead, unable to believe in an alien influence despite the evidence of his own eyes or the suspicions of Ruth Adams, a psychologist in the book and not the atomic scientist of the film.

It is in this offhanded sexism of Meacham (and Jones) that the book dates most disastrously. Meacham notes that, "It was utterly impossible to think of

Meacham (Rex Reason) and Joe Wilson (Robert Nichols) assess 1950s Super Science.

The stories and novels behind Classic Horror, Fantasy and Science Fiction Films

an M.D. or Ph.D. in that dress. He didn't try." Worse still, at one point, Adams gets Meacham to spy on the late-night goings-on at the plant where: "He felt a little ridiculous—spying on his own shipping department." Moments later, after she is proven right, Meacham takes charge: "He tugged roughly at Ruth's sleeve. Obediently, she followed, slipping through the darkness, stumbling once or twice on the iron stairway leading to the roof."

Meacham, in the novel, is not sent to a well-appointed resort in Georgia for atomic scientists, but, rather to an industrial plant outside of Phoenix, Arizona. In the course of the novel, he squashes a union strike (!), locates alien saboteurs, and marries Adams. He comes across his old college friend, a "big Swede" Ole Swenberg, who turns out to be an alien spy masquerading as human since their college years (!).

For film buffs that enjoyed the character of Exeter, don't bother. Here, Meacham's mysterious employer is Jorgasnovara, (say that twice!) who tells Meacham that the setup is really a secret group called the Peace Engineers. Jorgasnovara explains that the group dates back to the American Civil War, and that it is composed of scientists banding together to end war. Unlike the film, the literary Meacham is sap enough to buy this outlandish folderol. The whole thing falls apart soon after Meacham arrives in Arizona. The Llannan people (Metalunans in the movie) are using human beings to build interocitors much the way "civilized" westerners used native labor to build roads during World War II. (Hence the title.) However, people come and go around the plant freely and no one ever seems to figure out what it is they are building. At the height of intergalactic conflict, not only do Meacham and Adams have time to marry, but Jorgasnovara takes them on a round-the-world tour on a honeymoon-cum-business trip. Swenberg goes alien, holds Meacham and Adams at gunpoint, and the Earth is doomed. Worse still, killers from the planet Gurran (Zahgon in the movie) have infiltrated factory management (!) and Jorgasnovara kills them with thought waves intensified by his interocitor—a machine that can "read" minds. If that's the case, how come he didn't know who was and who wasn't a traitor in the first place?

Finally, Meacham and Adams are taken before the Llannan council after it is decided that Earth is expendable. Meacham manages to double-talk them into protecting our planet (I re-read it yesterday and I've already forgotten how) and then the thing ends rather abruptly. No mutants. No exploding planet. No Monitor. In fact, not much of anything occurs. Unlike the film, the novel *This Island Earth* goes in one eye and out the other.

For years, I have been reading that Jones' novel was "intellectual," and that the film didn't have the "philosophical overtones" that made the book so rewarding. Hogwash. *This Island Earth* the novel is so trite, so filled with improbabilities and inanities, that it's almost impossible to believe that late 1940s readers didn't wrinkle their noses at it.

IT CAME FROM ...

Which brings us to the recent *Pulpless* reprint. I ordered the book with a great deal of anticipation and my disappointment was mighty. Problems arise immediately with a totally witless introduction by the late Forrest Ackerman. Ackerman was Jones' agent, and nowhere does Ackerman offer a single tidbit on the writer, his career or their working relationship. Ackerman's tenure as editor of the kiddie magazine *Famous Monsters of Filmland* was a chronicle of missed opportunities for historical citation, and here Ackerman maintains his old standard. (The opener for his introduction is—I kid you not!—"Catalina Island surrounded by water! All the buildings down town! Now that I have your attention, on to *This Island Earth*.")

Pulpless reprint of Jones' story

There are many, many typographical errors that plague this edition of *This Island Earth*. Not a page (hardly a paragraph) goes by without some maddening mix-up, leading me to believe that the text was re-input by a drunken typist with a bad case of dyslexia. Quote marks appear for no reason, paragraphs break (or fail to) helter skelter, and punctuation is a decorative motif. The original stories that made up the novel can also be found online in archived issues of *Astounding*, and interested readers should look there first.

How did the farrago that was Jones' *This Island Earth* become the supreme piece of 1950s science fiction cinema? Simply by keeping the good, punching up the bad, and forgetting the rest.

This Island Earth is effectively two movies—one, an Earth-bound super-science mystery, the other, an other-world space opera. Both parts are good, but it is the first Earth-bound part that works best. I think the first part of the film resonates most for this viewer because it is not science fiction as much as (to my year 2020 eyes) nostalgia for a vanished, and better, America. This is a film from an era that believed in science as an engine of progress for mankind, and that the universe would eventually become knowable. It also unapologetically celebrates America's primacy as a major world power, and it objectified the power of scientific research. It reflects an America that is working at its peak—research laboratories, clean cities, jet planes, mail delivered on time. It was, in short, an America that *worked*, prosperous, forward thinking, united in ambi-

Scientists were rock stars in the 1950s.

tion, mono-cultural, and aspirational in nature. That all the heroes are brilliant to one degree or another is what gives the film part of its heft, and, frankly, that can-do optimism born of 1950s science fiction that made the moon landing possible is a core component of the American character that has been missing for generations, and we are all the poorer for it.

(One shudders at the thought of today's rabid, politically correct science fiction community getting their paws on something like this. Meacham would probably be a brilliant, disabled, trans-lesbian of color who toiled away for scant reward at a "Womyn's Science Collective," and would probably support the Zahgon fleet to stop the oppressive patriarchy of Metaluna. The mind reels …)

The film opens in Washington, D.C., and we see reporters swarming around scientist Cal Meacham (played by Rex Reason as a cross between Einstein and Tab Hunter). It is impossibly tragic today to watch the news media hover around Meacham as if he were a rock star, but in those Sputnik-era days, American scientists were venerated. Times change. After cagily alluding to some atomic research, he hops into a Lockheed T-33 Shooting Star, headed for Los Angeles. There is something so delicious about our jet-flying super-scientist that is perfectly in keeping with the film's heroic characterization of scientists.

IT CAME FROM …

En route to Los Angeles and the private airfield of his employers, the Ryberg Electronics Corp, Meacham's plane nearly crashes, only to be saved by a mysterious green light (accompanied by a high-pitched hum). At Ryberg, we spend time with him and his assistant, Joe Wilson (Robert Nichols, a great addition to the movie). The laboratory stuff here is wonderful, showing the quietly heroic quest of day-to-day scientists. Meacham and Wilson examine condensers ordered from Supreme (and its unheard-of Unit 16), the size and color of cherry gumdrops. After going through an equally suspicious Electronics Services Unit 16 product catalog (printed on a type of metal, naturally), they decide to build an interocitor. They order the 2,486 necessary parts, and aided by little more than a blueprint, put it together.

The interocitor is a beautiful piece of cinematic design. A rectangular base (like a large television console), topped by a triangular view screen (that can shoot death rays), its logo is a stylized atomic symbol. The atomic symbol appears on all the interocitors, and in other places throughout the film. It was even integral in the film's advertising; far from registering as an object of fear, *This Island Earth* celebrates the liberations found in atomic energy. When the interocitor speaks, it is with the voice and visage of the film's most interesting character, Exeter (Jeff Morrow).

The interocitor was an elaborate test for the engineers.

The stories and novels behind Classic Horror, Fantasy and Science Fiction Films

You don't need to be a rocket scientist to know about the birds and the bees.

Exeter explains that building the interocitor was all an elaborate test, and that Meacham passed. (One guesses that Wilson merely handed him the screwdrivers.) He is invited to board a plane at 5:00 AM, where he will be taken away to a league of fellow scientists working on a secret project for the betterment of mankind. Fortunately, Meacham seems to have no family or friends, and he is off, despite dire warnings from Wilson.

This is terrific stuff. Part *Tom Swift*, part *Rick Blaine*, all 1950s super-science adventure. The pilotless plane lands Meacham in Georgia, where Dr. Ruth Adams (the radiant Faith Domergue) meets him. Meacham remembers skinny-dipping with her during a conference some years ago, but Ruth demurs. She drives him to the "clubhouse," which looks like a resort for scientists. There, he gets the rundown from his new boss, Exeter. Exeter has gathered the world's leading scientists to harness limitless amounts of nuclear power. With that, he wants to drive an international peace accord based on the supremacy of their scientific might. Meacham and Ruth are the tops in their fields (Exeter says that Ruth is "just a step behind you"—but she *is* prettier).

In addition to Ruth, Meacham befriends Steve Carlson (Russell Johnson), a fellow scientist. The three caucus in secret (the interocitor can pick up conversations seemingly everywhere—shades of *Buck Rogers*), and reveal that Exeter is desperate to come up with new sources of atomic energy, and they're the geniuses expected to produce it. They also warn Meacham against Brack (Lance Fuller), Exeter's stooge with a mean streak, and tell him about "the sunlamp," a tool used on some of the scientists to keep them pliant.

And here it's important to mention the small but key role Russell Johnson plays in the film. Long a most valued player in a string of classic science fiction films, Johnson brings a febrile, haunted intensity to Carlson. In fact, while *This Island Earth* is a terrific film, with Johnson in the role of Meacham, it might have been a classic. Reason's Meacham is all chiseled good looks and biceps, with a voice that sounds like he went to broadcasting school in the Holland Tunnel. Johnson, more conventionally handsome and more easily accessible, is much like an idealized version of our real selves. In making Meacham more relatable, the film would have had

Russell Johnson (left) is terrific as Carlson.

an emotional tenor that it now lacks. Such is the benefit of hindsight casting!

Before too long, the three scientists make a break for it, just as Exeter is ordered by his supreme commander, the Monitor, to return to their home planet. The laboratories are destroyed (along with the kidnapped scientists, which makes rather no sense), and Carlson is murdered, to boot. Meacham and Ruth make for a convenient plane and affect their escape, only to have their aircraft sucked into a giant flying saucer.

And it is here that the story abruptly changes tone and becomes an entirely different movie. Part One of *This Island Earth* is pure pulp super-science heroics. It is science fiction in the can-do Americana tone manner of *Doc Savage* and *Jonny Quest*. But with the flying saucer and the trip to Metaluna, it becomes space opera straight out of *Buck Rogers*. Many of the films partisans love both sections of the film, others love one over the other. I think the entire concoction to be delicious, but find the first half infinitely more satisfying.

Aboard the ship—bright and airy with metallic tones, dominated by a spherical disco ball at its center—Exeter apologizes, explaining that "we're not all masters of our souls," a phrase he says he learned on Earth. Whether he is "a devil or a saint" is unimportant, as long as they are on the ship, they should work together as scientists. He also appeals to Ruth, "Don't tell me that as a woman you're not curious as to our destination."

The film then lapses into some colorful but breathless exposition. Exeter's home planet, Metaluna, is in a global war with the planet Zahgon. Zahgon was once a comet and is using spaceship-controlled meteors to bombard Metaluna. Metaluna has a radioactive screen to protect itself from the barrage, but the drain on atomic resources is immense. Hence, Exeter's mission to harness the brainpower of Earth's most advanced scientists. (In the novel, most of the Earth people were too dim to know what they were doing; the film explicitly focuses on our planet's genius population.)

Veterans of the Pacific conflict first seeing the film might well be shaking their heads at this point. The allies made use of island hopping in the Pacific Theater in fighting the Japanese. The allies would land on a smaller island, use its resources and indigenous people to re-harness supplies, and, re-armed, continue the attack.

We are also treated to all kinds of science fictional goodies, like giant depressurization chambers that look like toothbrush holders, vistas of a ruined Metaluna, and grim pictures of bombed-out cities that would have evoked more than echoes of places like Dresden.

Our heroes are soon brought before the Monitor (Douglas Spencer), a haughty dictator who brags that they will relocate to Earth and show these Earthling dinks who's boss. Meacham, rightly, asks if they're so smart, how come they couldn't come up with a new way to generate atomic energy. Next thing you know, Meacham is talking about "the size of our God," and you wonder what the heck happened to such a smart movie. Probably wondering the same thing, the Monitor tells Exeter to shove our heroes into the sunlamp and get to work.

And then, before you know it, the whole thing is over. Exeter promises to save our heroes, as they all get sidetracked by a mutant (a bug-like race that Metalunans use as slave labor), and one-or-two well-aimed Zahgon bombs bring the whole works down on their heads. Exeter and his pals make it back into the spaceship (along with a stowaway mutant to menace the girl), and off we go back to Earth. As they leave, Zahgon finishes off Metaluna, making the planet another in a long list of super-science paradises that vanish without a trace. Like Krypton, Metaluna leaves only one son as survivor. But Exeter, injured in a fight with a mutant, is dying. He watches his planet burn out and die, wondering if it will now become another sun, one that would light and give life to other planets.

IT CAME FROM ...

And here we have one of the most interesting aspects of *This Island Earth*, and that is the conundrum that is Exeter. Just *what* are we to make of him? He seems to truly care for some of the human beings in his program, though others seem to have been unconscionably damaged by his "sunlamp." He openly defies the Monitor again and again, but is too weak a man to do more than fuss and connive. Dying, he lies to the scientists, claiming that he will now explore space ("Our universe is vast—full of wonders!"). Suddenly friends, Ruth says that, "We'll heal your wounds," which leaves Exeter with nothing more to say than, "I'm afraid my wounds can never be healed." And—curiously, much like Meacham—he seems to have no ties that keep him anywhere. While Meacham is able to just pack up his life without a second thought and join Exeter, Exeter is able to watch the destruction of his planet, his culture and way of life, and possibly any friends and family, with nothing more than the pithiest of philosophical pieties. (Obviously a Democrat.)

Much of Exeter's effectiveness comes from Morrow's skilled playing, but one wonders what would have happened with an even better actor and one more trip through the typewriter for the script. There is the potential for something Shakespearean in so divided and conflicted a man as Exeter, but the screenplay (by Franklin Coen and Edward G. O'Callaghan) never does more than hint at his hidden depths. Another missed opportunity that keeps *This Island Earth* from true greatness.

Meacham and Ruth escape, thanks to their captured plane, as Exeter pilots his flying saucer into the ocean. Somehow, despite the murdered scientists, the destruction of an entire planet, and questions of whether or not the Zahgons may now be eyeing Earth ... we have our requisite happy ending.

If my comments on the Metalunan parts of the film leave the impression that I do not unconditionally love this film, think again. I think *This Island Earth* to be the most fascinating science fiction film of the 1950s. But its manifest flaws keep it from being a great film in any general, non-relative sense of the word. The Metaluna portions of the film seem so rushed, and so hastily thought-out, that one has the sense that Universal-International lost faith in the project before its completion. And perhaps this was not unjustified—*Variety* reported that *This Island Earth* had a total payout of $1.7 million, not enough to encourage future investments in big-budget science fiction. It ran on a double-bill with *Abbott and Costello Meet the Mummy* (!), sometimes playing top of the bill, others times, the lower half. Go figure.

However, according to film historians Robert Skotak and Scot Holton, Universal-International did have high hopes for the film. The Metaluna scenes shot by director Joseph F. Newman were deemed lacking in oomph by producer William Alland, who called in accomplished science fiction helmer Jack Arnold to reshoot some of the material. They invested $20,000 in creating the mutant, and reshoots with Arnold must have added much to the final cost. But Arnold's contribution is, frankly, amazingly poor, as the Metaluna sequences are the most ham-fisted in the picture, with some of the clunkiest dialog: ("Our educational complexes, now rubble! Over there was a recreation center!" when I think he meant: "Damn, there goes the school! And the gym!") The only poor performance in the film, Spencer as the Monitor, must then have had the guidance of Arnold, which seems incredible as he was able to tease real performances from actors like John Agar and Grant Williams in different films. One cannot help but wonder what happened?

But all of this is quibbling. One has only to jump deep into the glorious Technicolor of *This Island Earth* to be fully engaged. This is a gorgeous film, with laboratories rich in greens and cobalt blacks, airplanes of navy blue with yellow striping, gleaming metallic spaceships, and the cool-green weirdness of Metaluna. When meeting the Monitor, the room is bathed in a deep purple light, and electric blues of the mutants are vivid. Though *Forbidden Planet* may have the props for overall special effects, in terms of science fiction eye-candy, *This Island Earth* cannot be beat.

It is easy for succeeding generations to laugh at *This Island Earth*. And they did—this wonderful picture was fodder for the theatrical debut of the witless irony that is *Mystery Science Theater 3000*. However, it must be remembered that this is a product of Sputnik-era America. Scientists were heroes, the world (the universe) was ours to control and explore, and a great, big, beautiful tomorrow was just ahead. What was science fiction in the 1950s is now nostalgia for many older Americans. And when I watch the America of *This Island Earth*, I realize that not all lost worlds are floating in space.

The stories and novels behind Classic Horror, Fantasy and Science Fiction Films

Yellow Peril in a Tropic Island Nest:
Dr. No (1962)

"No, no, no, a thousand times, no."—Noel Coward, on being asked
to play Dr. No in the film version of Ian Fleming's novel.

The fascinating thing about literary and cinematic adaptations is that often one doesn't always know what is being adapted. What if a film adapted from a novel takes, as its source, a novel that is itself an adaptation? Case in point, *Dr. No*, the first of the James Bond films. The *Bond* canon is the longest-running film series to never fall into the rut of formula "B" films, and it has consistently flirted with science fictional ideas. This is not surprising, as Bond in general, and *Dr. No* in particular, take their inspiration from a series of inspired fanta-sists who wrote prior to the Great War.

Author Ian Fleming (1908-1964) was often very upfront about his inspi-rations when writing the James Bond thrillers. Such names as John Buchan (1875-1940), Sapper (1888-1937), and E. Phillips Oppenheim (1866-1946) of-ten came up. But the name that came up most regularly in notes, letters and interviews (and most surprisingly, to our 21st century sensibilities) is that of Sax Rohmer.

Born Arthur Henry Sarsfield Ward (1883–1959) in Birmingham to a work-ing class family, Rohmer initially toiled as a public servant before becoming a writer. Rohmer was an incredibly well-read man and amateur Egyptologist;

he also was a working writer in every sense of the term, knocking out magazine articles and comedy sketches.

Rohmer published several stories and a novel before really hitting his stride in 1913 with the publication of *The Mystery of Dr. Fu-Manchu*. This novel was actually a collec-tion of several inter-connected short stories, strung together by one overarching narrative thrust. Secret agent Nayland Smith and his comrade Dr. Petrie work to rid humanity of an evil criminal mastermind bent on taking over the world. The next two novels in the series, *The Return of Dr. Fu-Manchu* and *The Hand of Fu-Manchu*, were also short stories strung together. When Rohmer revived the series 14 years later in 1931, with *Daughter of Fu Manchu*, he turned to full-novel form.

IT CAME FROM ...

Some of these later novels are the best in the series (such as the *Trail of Fu Manchu*), but the sustained narrative structure does seem to knock the wind out of some of them. Rohmer would eventually write 14 Fu Manchu novels (the last, like Fleming's own *The Man With the Golden Gun*, published posthumously and unfinished).

Rohmer also wrote several different series of detective novels, featuring such characters as Gaston Max and Morris Klaw (who featured largely in supernatural mysteries). Rohmer was one of the most well paid thriller writers of his generation, and for laughs would sometimes sign his name $ax Rohmer. He and his wife Rose moved to New York after World War II, and he died in 1959 from avian flu. Sadly, Rohmer was a man of high and expensive tastes, and he and his wife were fairly broke at the time of his death. However, financial

The Bond craze of the 1960s also saw a revival of the many characters that influenced Ian Fleming, including a series of Fu Manchu films.

ups-and-downs were not unknown to the couple, and when hard times hit, Rose would chirp, "Well, back to the kitchen." Rose, along with Rohmer's assistant Cay Van Ash, wrote a splendid biography of the man in 1972, called appropriately *Master of Villainy*. Ash also wrote two Fu Manchu novels of his own, one featuring Sherlock Holmes, and they are equal to those of Rohmer.

It's hard to imagine the full impact of Rohmer's legacy today, after countless imitators (such as the Shadow's Shiwan Khan, Batman's Ra's al Ghul and pulp baddie Wu Fang) and the tides of Political Correctness watered down Fu Manchu. However, it's safe to say that without Fu Manchu and Nayland Smith, there would have been no James Bond, as author Ian Fleming had said that Rohmer's novels were a key influence on his style and his decision to become a writer. Many of the tropes that were invented or perfected by Rohmer have become today's clichés, and the debt the thriller genre (and Fleming in particular) owes him is immeasurable.

Despite their dramatically different prose styles, Rohmer and Fleming had quite a lot in common. Both shared a commitment to his story and his characters—these men *believed*. Both wrote with a sense of integrity to his imagined world: There is never a hint of irony, never less than his 100% commitment as an artist. Neither may have been writing literature, but each wrote as if they were.

Important to both, too, was an insistence on verisimilitude no matter how outlandish the plot or circumstances. Readers of Fleming's letters know how he reached out to experts in the field on a variety of topics to ensure that he got the details right. So, too, with Rohmer, he was a man of great erudition as well. If Rohmer says there's an 18-inch poisonous centipede, rest assured, there is one.

Fleming often looked back on Rohmer as "the reading of my youth," and one assumes that he learned youth's lessons well. Though Fu Manchu's nemesis Nayland Smith is sufficiently intriguing to warrant his attention, we are largely taking the Devil Doctor's word for it. Nayland Smith is a remarkably … *thin* hero. Rugged, worldly (with a hint of exotic knowledge), steadfast; he is little more than an attitude in a tweed suit.

Fleming would correct this problem in his novels with the much more interesting James Bond, and he would do Rohmer one better by creating not only *one* master criminal, but *several*. One of the key pleasures of the Bond novels are the many outlandish, grotesque villains pitted against 007. Men as disparate as Goldfinger, Drax, Largo, and, of course, Blofeld all owe more than a little to the tradition of Fu Manchu.

In addition, both writers understood the synergy of multiple platforms for storytelling. Both Rohmer and Fleming knew that the financial rewards of being a novelist (even a best-selling novelist) were not as important as selling work

to the film industry (or, in Rohmer's case, films, radio, television, and comic strips). It was in this ability to create a sufficiently glamorous hero (or villain) that would support narratives in multiple mediums where Rohmer and Fleming were most alike.

Both writers were also more than comfortable in changing their heroes in order to make them viable film properties. The "Fu Manchu mustache," for instance, is an invention of the film industry. Similarly, what would the film *Dr. No* have been like had Fleming had his way and cast chums David Niven as Bond and Noel Coward as Dr. No? Personally, while *that* film may have been much more satisfying than the finished product, it's unlikely if it would have resulted in the decades-long franchise we know today. If anything, if

IT CAME FROM ...

the film stayed too close to the source novel, *Dr. No* would ultimately have been seen as an old-fashioned film, and never embraced by the culture formed by the Sexual Revolution. In my mind's eye, I imagine the perfect movie realization of *Dr. No* with James Mason as Bond and Basil Rathbone—Rohmer's choice for the role of Fu Manchu—as Dr. No. However, such a film would have closed an era, rather than started one.

As we'll see in the quotes following, it would be hard to imagine two more dissimilar authorial voices than Sax Rohmer and Ian Fleming. Here, too, Fleming has the advantage of coming after and learning from the former's mistakes.

Boris Karloff sports the "Fu Manchu mustache" in *The Mask of Fu Manchu*.

Rohmer often writes in a delirious, ornate, heavily scented style; as if Oscar Wilde and John Buchan collaborated on a thriller while drinking too much absinthe. This is thriller writing for aesthetes, and often too rich a dish for the average reader.

Fleming, on the other hand, knew that nothing dates faster than certain types of stylistic virtuosity, and wrote instead in a spare, muscular prose. As far as his prose line goes, the hard-bitten writers of the Dashiell Hammett/Raymond Chandler school were his inspiration. With few references to current events, and self-contained brevity, Fleming has managed to be more timeless than Rohmer, though seldom more subversive.

I prefer Rohmer's novels to those of Fleming, mostly because of his fearlessness. I often think that Fleming was just a tad more conservative in his imagination, more willing to hold back rather than go completely off the rails. Rohmer, however, had no concept of imaginative self-control; for Rohmer too much is just enough. His bountiful and grotesque imagination is oddly endearing, and is as irresistible and addictive as cherry brandy.

But clearly Fleming never forgot the debt—both of depth of enjoyment and inspiration in his work—that he owed Sax Rohmer. And in homage (if not pastiche!), Fleming paid that back with interest in his most delirious, lurid, over-the-top James Bond adventure, *Dr. No*.

The stories and novels behind Classic Horror, Fantasy and Science Fiction Films

Joseph Wiseman as Dr. No, the first Bond-villain, was just one of a long line of pulpy super-fiends.

It is amazing how much ~~Sax Rohmer~~ Ian Fleming managed to channel into his sixth Bond novel, *Dr. No*. At times, it's almost impossible to tell if Fleming is bowing to the Master, or having a little fun at his expense.

Here, for example, is a close-up look at Fu Manchu, Devil Doctor of Rohmer's imaginings:

> Imagine a person, tall, lean and feline, high-shouldered, with a brow like Shakespeare and a face like Satan, a close-shaven skull, and long, magnetic eyes of the true cat-green. Invest

IT CAME FROM ...

him with all the cruel cunning of an entire Eastern race, accumulated in one giant intellect, with all the resources of science past and present, with all the resources, if you will, of a wealthy government—which, however, already has denied all knowledge of his existence. Imagine that awful being, and you have a mental picture of Dr. Fu Manchu, the yellow peril incarnate in one man.

Not to be outdone, Fleming unveils Dr. Julius No to an incredulous James Bond:

Bond's first impression was of thinness and erectness and height. Doctor No was at least six inches taller than Bond, but the straight immovable poise of his body made him seem still taller. The head also was elongated and tapered from a round, completely bald skull down to a sharp chin so that the impression was of a reversed raindrop—or rather oildrop, for the skin was of a deep almost translucent yellow.

It gets better. Bond cannot tell if Dr. No is 50 or 100; he sports Dali-esque eyebrows and he moves as if his neck and back were fused into a single, unmovable piece. Then comes the *coup de grace*:

The bizarre, gliding figure looked like a giant venomous-worm wrapped in grey tin-foil, and Bond would not have been surprised to see the rest of it trailing slimily along the carpet behind.

Doctor No came within three steps of them and stopped. The wound in the tall face opened. "Forgive me for not shaking hands with you," the deep voice was flat and even. "I am unable to." Slowly the sleeves parted and opened. "I have no hands."

The two pairs of steel pincers came out on their gleaming stalks and were held up for inspection like the hands of a praying mantis. Then the two sleeves joined again.

Even now, some 30 years after I first read the novel, I've never forgotten my shudder at the vision, *see the rest of it trailing slimily along the carpet behind.* Yuck!

But Fu Manchu and Dr. No are not just repulsive physically; they are repulsive mentally. It's not enough that they run criminal organizations and treat human life cheaply—no, no, their homicidal imaginations must be disgustingly ornate. Here are Nayland Smith and his Watson, Dr. Petrie, trapped by the Devil Doctor:

A marmoset landed on the shoulder of Dr. Fu-Manchu and peered grotesquely into the dreadful yellow face. The Doctor raised his bony hand and fondled the little creature, crooning to it.

"One of my pets, Mr. Smith," he said, suddenly opening his eyes fully so that they blazed like green lamps. "I have others, equally useful. My scorpions—have you met my scorpions? No? My pythons and hamadryads? Then there are my fungi and my tiny allies, the bacilli. I have a collection in my laboratory quite unique. Have you ever visited Molokai, the leper island, Doctor? No? But Mr. Nayland Smith will be familiar with the asylum at Rangoon! And we must not forget my black spiders, with their diamond eyes—my spiders, that sit in the dark and watch—then leap!"

Petrie, with a Watsonian gift for stating the obvious, tells us: "He is mad! ... God help us, the man is a dangerous homicidal maniac!"

Fu Manchu is not the only maniac. Like all Master Criminals, Dr. No can't help but be chatty when he feels he has the upper hand:

Doctor No said, in the same soft resonant voice, "You are right, Mister Bond. That is just what I am, a maniac. All the greatest men are maniacs. They are possessed by a mania which drives them forward towards their goal. The great scientists, the philosophers, the religious leaders—all maniacs. What else but a blind singleness of purpose could have given focus to their genius, would have kept them in the groove of their purpose? Mania, my dear Mister Bond, is as priceless as genius. Dissipation of energy, fragmentation of vision, loss of momentum, the lack of follow-through—these are the vices of the herd." Doctor No sat slightly back in his chair. "I do not possess these vices. I am, as you correctly say, a maniac—a maniac, Mister Bond, with a mania for power."

Fu Manchu uses the exotic weapons in his weird arsenal. One of the key threats in his debut novel is The Zyat Kiss. Several characters die mysteriously, until Smith and Petrie are able to finally reveal just what it is:

It was an insect, full six-inches long, and of a vivid, venomous, red color! It had something of the appearance of a great ant, with its long, quivering antennae and its febrile, horrible vitality; but it was proportionately longer of body and smaller of head, and had numberless rapidly moving legs. In short, it was

IT CAME FROM ...

a giant centipede, apparently of the scolopendra group, but of a form quite new to me.

These things I realized in one breathless instant; in the next—Smith had dashed the thing's poisonous life out with one straight, true blow of the golf club!

There is perhaps more than a touch of professional jealousy on Dr. No's part (or Fleming's), as he also tries to dispatch 007 with a poisonous centipede.

With a crash that shook the room Bond's body jackknifed out of bed and onto the floor … There it was crawling out of sight over the edge of the pillow. Bond's first instinct was to twitch the pillow on to the floor. He controlled himself, waiting for his nerves to quieten. Then softly, deliberately, he picked up the pillow by one corner and walked into the middle of the room and dropped it. The centipede came out from under the pillow. It started to snake swiftly away across the matting. Now Bond was uninterested. He looked round for something to kill it with. Slowly he went and picked up a shoe and came back. The danger was past. His mind was now wondering how the centipede had got into his bed. He lifted the shoe and slowly, almost carelessly, smashed it down. He heard the crack of the hard carapace. Bond lifted the shoe. The centipede was whipping from side to side in its agony—five inches of grey-brown, shiny death. Bond hit it again. It burst open, yellowly.

Fortunately, these hellish and exotic menaces are no match for everyday items like golf clubs or shoes. In the course of Fleming's novel, Bond will also face a tunnel full of venomous spiders before he fights for his life against No's giant octopus. In addition, the heroine, Honeychile Ryder, will be offered up to carnivorous crabs. (Whenever friends tell me they wish the Bond films were more serious, "like the novels," I wonder if they've ever read *Dr. No*) … In addition, both doctors share a taste for Caribbean islands: Fu Manchu eventually

The stories and novels behind Classic Horror, Fantasy and Science Fiction Films

Bond and Ryder try to escape detection on Dr. No's island.

holes up in a super-science laboratory hidden in a volcano in Haiti (shades of the film version *You Only Live Twice*), where he becomes a voodoo master, while Dr. No rules a small landmass off Jamaica, which he patrols with a tank disguised as a dragon. Neither man wins points on subtlety. It's these inventions, one more deliciously lurid and outlandish than the last, that makes *Dr. No* such a harem scarem homage to Rohmer and his world. It remains Fleming's most intense fever-dream of a novel, reading more like an artifact of the lurid 1920s than the jet-setting 1950s.

It's important, though, to remember that imitation is the sincerest form of flattery, and that it's clear that Fleming had a great deal of affection for Rohmer. *Dr. No* at times comes to read much like a skilled artist riffing on the obsessions and affections of his youth. For a novel filled with murder and exotic unrelenting menace, it's curiously affectionate in its effort to salute its inspiration.

Dr. No has always been my favorite book in the Fleming corpus because here he goes for broke, and does not care if his creations are unbelievable, or even faintly ridiculous. It's an antic, unfettered romp through Fleming's imagination, untampered by attempts at good taste or self-control.

And, as such, is irresistible. One hopes that somewhere, in the Valhalla of Villainy, Dr. Fu Manchu and Dr. Julius No are happily bent over a cauldron

IT CAME FROM ...

of detestable horrors, cackling with maniacal glee. It's an image that is almost heart-warming.

The film adaptation of *Dr. No* does its best to eschew many of the lurid qualities that Fleming introduced in his *homage* to Rohmer. The screenplay, by Richard Maibaum, streamlines both the storyline and the good doctor, himself.

In the novel, No is, like Fu Manchu, an independent player with his own villainous goals. Maibaum changes this to making No a key agent of SPECTRE (Special Executive for Counterintelligence, Terrorism, Revenge, Extortion), an evil organization with tough management, but I hear the health benefits are terrific. Indeed, No's death at the hands of Bond is one of the key reasons that he is targeted by the organization in the film's sequel, the infinitely superior *From Russia, With Love*.

The weird exotica that make No such a delicious concoction on the page is also toned down in the film. Gone are the poisonous centipede, the carnivorous crabs, the tunnel of spiders and the giant octopus at the end. Perhaps it would be impossible for any film to capture these images without veering too much into the absurd, but to readers of the novel, their absence is keenly felt.

The character of Dr. No is also toned down considerably. His flowing Fu Manchu robes are replaced with a smartly cut Nehru jacket, and his prayin mantis pinchers are now bionic black kitchen gloves. The contact lenses, the fact that his heart is on the wrong side of his body, and the slime have all been sacrificed for a Space Age cleanliness. It may render him more believable, but he is also a lot less fun.

Dr. No, like most films, went down a long developmental road before appearing on movie screens. Fleming knew that the road to big money was in leveraging his secret agent into other media, and he was willing to make concessions to get him into pictures. Aside from Niven, Fleming floated movie stars as diverse as James Stewart (then 53), James Mason (also 53), Cary Grant (58), and … Susan Hayward (45) for the role of Bond. (In Hayward, he would have changed Bond into a Mata Hari–like seductress, an idea not without merit.)

In the end, it was a happy confluence of incidents that led to the James Bond phenomenon of the 1960s, including toning down the more outlandish elements in the novel *Dr. No*, to its happy casting of Sean Connery as the world-famous secret agent. However, one wonders what would have happened had Fleming had his way: a David Niven/Noel Coward *Dr. No* would have been a delirious romp; a blood-spattered drawing room comedy with a sense of insouciant fun.

The Bond films were to become more science fictional as the series progressed, with the jet-packed delirium of *Thunderball* (1965), the Jules Verne fun of *The Spy Who Loved Me* (1977), and the outer space hijinks of *Moonraker* (1980). Bond fans may be even more insecure than comic book nerds in their passion to take these things seriously, but I think Fleming would have found them delightful. And profitable.

We might want to close out with a meditation on the place of James Bond as a prime example of the consolations of junk art.

No one in their right mind would, for a moment, argue that the James Bond films are, well, in a word … good. They are not real in the sense that things happened to the protagonist that change him internally or externally, and certainly not real in the sense that it is possible to make any emotional investment in them. The vast majority of Bond films are laughably terrible, pandering to our cravings for sex, sadism and snobbery—three preoccupations of his creator, Ian Fleming.

The reasons for the sheer awfulness of the Bond corpus are many. The short list would include: Bond is never really a character, but merely a good suit and a set of attitudes; the plotting and scripting of the films often disregard any sense of narrative cohesion, probability, or good taste; aside from many of the villains, the acting is uniformly bad; and, finally, since they are all commentary upon current issues or obsessions of the time in which they were made, the films have aged very poorly indeed.

They are irresistible.

While I enjoy most of the Bond films, I must confess a preference for the Roger Moore films. "Real" Bond fans are already throwing up their hands in exasperation, as the Moore performance is the most deprecated, despised and dismissed of all the big-screen Bonds. "Real" Bond fans are wrong (more on that later), and, in fact, Moore is the only actor who really understood the role.

Bond is not the nicest of men, and most of the Bonds—Sean Connery, Pierce Brosnan, Timothy Dalton and Daniel Craig, especially—have captured that facet of his limited personality fairly well. But real killer instinct is missing from Moore's Bond, mainly because Moore, a limited if effective actor, had too much generosity of spirit and genuine goodwill to pull off Bond's hard edges. Most importantly, Moore got the joke. The phrase world-famous secret agent best expressed the inherent absurdity of the whole idea. (A neat trick, that.) The notion of an indestructible lady-killer in a dinner jacket was catnip for a man with Moore's sense of the absurd.

An excellent and skilled light comedian, Moore made the Bond films something closer to the imaginings of author Ian Fleming, who once admitted to never reading his own Bond books, least he give up on them because of their preposterous nature. In Fleming's mind, Bond's world was part spoof from the get-go.

That is one of the many reasons why adult-adolescents who want a "serious" Bond film (an absurdity equal to the ponderous "adult" Batman films) always amuse me; there is nothing adult about the Bond canon to begin with.

IT CAME FROM …

Fleming himself saw them as a means simply to make ready cash; he wrote them with care and he wrote them with conviction, but he had no pretentions that they were serious.

As Fleming himself wrote: *"I don't regard James Bond precisely as a hero, but at least he does get on and do his duty, in an extremely corny way … My books have no social significance, except a deleterious one."*

Enter Moore, who, with his infectious insouciance, sends up the already absurd. He is, to date, the only Bond who smiled readily and actually enjoyed his line readings. For those who want to revisit the Moore Bond, I recommend the DVDs with his voice-over commentaries, which are infinitely more entertaining than the movies.

When do the Bond films work? Or, to rephrase that, when are they good? The Bond films, like the 1960s from which they sprang, are best appreciated when the politics, aesthetics, and morals are never seriously considered, and when we can consume their empty calories guiltlessly. When we think that amoral characters like Bond (and the political structure he supports) would actually work for the common good, and we think global peace hinges on the correct tailor and the right cocktail. They work best, in short, in the undemanding tatters of our tired imaginations.

I find great consolation in the lightest of Bond films, because here are great resources harnessed for a fully tongue-in-cheek enterprise. I am also tickled at Moore, once one of the world's biggest box-office attractions, carrying the weight of a multi-million dollar film franchise as if he were carrying the mail.

You May Not Like What You Find:
Planet of the Apes (1968)

Of all the essays in this book, none have had a longer gestation period for me than *Planet of the Apes* (1968). I have been actively engaged with this film for 50 years, and even after that long period of time, I still have not gotten my arms completely around it.

I first saw *Planet of the Apes* when I was five years old. I was deeply tickled by it (what a dainty dish for a five year old!), but its deeper philosophical and metaphorical implications were lost on me. Like many of my generation, I was deeply involved in the Apes Craze of the early 1970s, and even attended the all-day viewings of the entire corpus at the premiere of *Battle for the Planet of the Apes* (1973). I was also deeply amused when, attending a revival at New York's Film Forum on my 50th birthday, to observe (for the first time) that the date Taylor records in his final captain's log was my 10th birthday. (How had I not noticed that before?) As I write these words, there is a mini-bust of Dr. Zaius on my desk.

Asked for my assessment of the film over that period of time, my answers would have been all over the map. I have found it alternately optimistic and pessimistic, funny and tragic, very smart and patently glib. I've gone from admiring Cornelius and Zira to gently despising them, and my current thoughts on Dr. Zaius would shock the 20-year-old version of myself.

Given this decades-long engagement, I could not hope to provide a single reading of so vital (and so protean) a text. What follows are my ever-changing thoughts on what I consider to be the finest, most thought-provoking, and most maddening of 1960s science fiction classics.

Planet of the Apes sprang from the fertile imagination of author Pierre Boulle (1912-1994). Not a fantasist or science fiction writer by any means, Boulle's novel is more of a Swiftian satire than a genre novel. As with his other great novel, *Bridge Over the River Kwai* (1952), the film version of the *Planet of the Apes* novel (1963) would follow the overall structure of the original novel, and include many plot points, but result in a profoundly different work. (And like *Kwai*, the final film would be ultimately more satisfying than the book.)

In Boulle's novel, interplanetary travelers Jinn and Phyllis find a manuscript in a bottle floating in space. Inside are the memoirs of Ulysse Merou, who traveled from Earth to a planet orbiting Betelgeuse. There, he and his companions meet mute, animalistic human beings and a race of intelligent apes. Merou is captured, where he soon impresses some sympathetic chimpanzees of his intelligence. But questions of Merou's intelligence and burgeoning theories of evolution make him a political hot potato, and his ape-protectors get him back into space onto his orbiting ship.

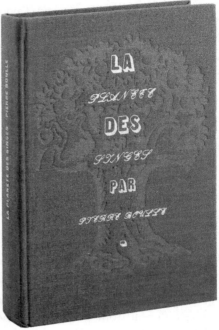

First edition of the original French novel

Merou and his lover, Nova, and their child, Sirrus, return home to earth, now thousands of years later, thanks to speed-of-light travel. And when they exit the ship, Merou finds that intelligent apes have overrun the Earth. Jinn and Phyllis, reading this fantastic tale in space, dismiss it as ridiculous. They, too, are revealed to be apes.

Though this covers the basic plot of *Planet of the Apes* in broad strokes, the overall effect is quite different. The apes in Boulle's novel live in a modern city, drive automobiles and fly planes, and even are beginning space exploration. But several incidents from the novel provide the key plot points for the film.

The plot points and the rhythm of the film closely track the novel. While Taylor travels with Landon in the film, in the novel Merou travels with Levain. The astronauts find an evocative footprint in both tales, and in both the travelers find that savage men have stolen their clothes. The characters in novel and film go for a refreshing swim, only to be hunted down by apes. (In the film, the sequence where ape photographers snap photos of themselves on piles of dead men is close in vibe to the feeling of the novel.) Both Taylor and Merou teach Nova to smile, and both men find sympathetic chimpanzees championing them. (Merou draws a picture in Zira's notebook, as the apes in the novel speak a different language from English; in the film, having the apes speak English is an embellishment that makes much more sense.)

Zaius in the novel and film presents a threat to our lead astronaut ... though in the novel Zaius is a hide-bound establishment tool too stupid to tell one human being from another, while his film counterpart is a more serious foeman. Merou/Taylor both travel with Cornelius and Zira to an archeological dig, complete with relic of a talking human doll. Before heading off to his final destiny, both Merou and Taylor kiss their benefactress (in the novel, she says, "You are really too ugly.").

From the short overview, one would imagine that there is little difference between novel and film, but there is. (More on that later.) Equally interesting is the fact that so much of later *Apes* films borrow liberally from Boulle's novel.

In overall feel, Boulle's novel is more like the later *Escape From the Planet of the Apes* (1971) than the first film in the series. In that film, Cornelius and Zira arrive in then-contemporary America, a place of big cities, space ships, and high technology. Many of the tests that Zira passes in the film were the tests Merou zipped through in the novel, and here the apes are also intelligent enough to study, and then fly, a spaceship. *Escape* also has a different feel in its social satire, quite different from the obvious and sometimes dopey jokes in the 1968 film; not surprising as screenwriter Paul Dehn (1912-1976) conferred with Boulle while penning the screenplay. Dehn also borrowed liberally from Boulle when writing *Conquest of the Planet of the Apes* (1972), which details that apes went from pets to slaves in the distant past, another key part of the novel.

Ultimately, though, the intent of filmmakers throughout the initial films of the *Apes* corpus, and certainly those who made the first film, was something quite different from what Boulle had in mind. Whereas Boulle used his novel as a means to satirically drive home that human beings were just another type of animal that had more in common with the beasts than he is willing to admit, the makers of the 1968 *Apes* made a film that address how precious our own humanity could be. From "we are all animals" to "human beings are special" is a dramatic shift, and to bring that home, producer Arthur P. Jacobs (1922-1973) went to the most famous fantasist at the time working in film, Rod Serling (1924-1975).

Rod Serling is the only American writer as famous for his name, his face and his voice, as for his writing. Serling was born on Christmas day in Syracuse, New York. His father, Samuel Lawrence Serling, owned a wholesale meat business and his mother, Esther, was a housewife. Soon after Rod was born, the family moved to Binghamton, New York, where Rod would spend the rest of his boyhood.

Serling was drafted into the U.S. Army 11th Airborne Division Paratroopers. He made extra money as a boxer; only five-foot four, Serling was classed as a flyweight. He would box 18 fights and lose only one. He was sent to the Philippine Islands during the World War II and was wounded by the Japanese when shrapnel hit him in the leg and the wrist.

IT CAME FROM ...

Behind-the-scenes shot of the ship's crew abandoning their sinking rocketship.

Serling found that writing was an important outlet for him after the stresses and depression he faced during and after the war. He believed writing was a "therapeutic necessity," and that writing about his feelings made him realize that his future was as a professional writer. Serling and his young wife moved to Cincinnati, where he became a staff writer for WLW radio. Serling was not very happy there because radio executives told him that they wanted characters that could "get their teeth into the soil." Serling would later say, "What those guys wanted wasn't a writer, but a plow." Serling continued his freelance fiction writing and collected 40 rejection slips in a row from magazines.

By 1951, Serling was able to sell enough scripts to anthology programs to earn $5,000, and he left the radio station and started writing television plays full time. By 1955, Serling had sold more than 70 television scripts. In January of that year, Serling's teleplay *Patterns* was broadcast. The show was about the infighting inside a large American corporation and won Serling an Emmy award for best writer.

Serling continued writing for television, scoring another hit with *Requiem for a Heavyweight* in 1956. Still, Serling wanted more freedom to write what he wanted. Serling realized that he could write about issues that were important to him if he disguised his ideas as fantasy stories. To do this, Serling created

The Twilight Zone. The show debuted on October 2, 1959 on CBS. The ratings were extremely low, but studio executives thought the show had enough quality to keep it on the air. It would last 156 episodes, ending its run in the summer of 1965.

On one level, *The Twilight Zone* told simple stories of horror and fantasy. But on a deeper level, Serling used the show as a means of writing about things that concerned him. At different times, *The Twilight Zone* explored such themes as racism, nuclear war, mass hysteria, and what is beautiful and what is ugly. Serling wrote 92 of the scripts, the remaining 64 scripts were written by such respected horror and science fiction writers as Ray Bradbury (1920-2012), Richard Matheson (1926-2013) and Charles Beaumont (1929-1967).

The Twilight Zone is now part of television history, and the name itself is a catchphrase. But creating *The Twilight Zone* was not always easy. For his work, Serling won another two Emmy awards, one in 1960 and the other in 1961.

The pace of writing, producing and narrating a weekly television program was grueling, even for a workaholic like Serling. He soon had to start dictating his scripts to his secretary, and he would smoke as many as four packs of cigarettes while working. The grind of writing for television took its toll on Serling. He began to age physically, and his face became prematurely wrinkled. On his 40th birthday, Serling made his first parachute jump since World War II to prove that he was not old. Serling would make comments about feeling older than his age for the last 10 years of his life.

"When I look back over 30 years of professional writing, I'm hard-pressed to come up with anything that's important," he said. "Some things are literate, some things are interesting, some things are classy, but very damn little is important."

In May 1975 Serling suffered a mild heart attack while on summer vacation in Interlake, New York. He stayed in the hospital for two weeks, and was told to quit smoking, work less, and exercise. The following month, Serling was admitted to Strong Memorial Hospital in Rochester for heart bypass surgery. He had another heart attack during surgery and died. He was only 50 years old.

If it seems that we have lingered over the life of Rod Serling at length, it's important to remember two things. First and foremost, Serling was the first fantasist to become a multimedia star. Not only was he famous for writing, but he was famous for his appearances on *The Twilight Zone*, on game shows and commercials, and for his work narrating television specials and documentaries. Second, Serling's humanism and liberality are evident in all of his stories, which have socially or morally relevant themes. And it is that sense of haunted humanism, that same febrile energy and edgy quality found in both his life and work, that brings *Planet of the Apes* to life. His spirit and ethos hang over the finished project like an echo, and his sensibilities and concerns are evident

Kim Hunter (Zira) chats on set with screenwriter Rod Serling.

throughout the screenplay. His vision for *Planet of the Apes* was much more tren-chant and hard-bitten than Boulle's mordant inter-species ruminations.

Serling first became attached to *Planet of the Apes* by the King Brothers; they had acquired rights to the book and wanted to make a cheap feature picture out of it with actors in masks. Serling did a treatment for them and left the project because it would be done on a shoestring. The property then wound up with film legend Blake Edwards (1922-2010), who initially wanted to produce and direct it himself. (If only!) Serling began his epic involvement with the film under Edwards, sticking with the project when it landed on the desk of Arthur P. Jacobs, and it was Serling's script that sold star Charlton Heston (1923-2008) on the project. During his tenure on the film, Serling penned at least three versions of the screenplay, and possibly as many as five.

The finished film follows Serling's overall outline and story arc, as well as the famous *Twilight Zone*-style ending. Before shooting began, screenwriter Michael Wilson rewrote all of the film's dialog, inserting various jokes ("I never met an ape I didn't like") and some obvious social satire. But Serling's impact on the script and the finished product was acknowledged by the crew, as he was photographed several times on the set during production, and the final conception of Taylor is consistent with Serling's driven, troubled heroes.

Taylor is the alpha-male so typical in Serling's scripts for *The Twilight Zone*. Where Boulle's Merou is an everyman, Serling's Taylor is a high achiever left unsatisfied by his success and gradually souring into bitterness. He wears his disappointment and disillusion like armor, but his vulnerability should never be doubted. While *Planet of the Apes* is definitely a product of the Counter Culture of the 1960s, its hero belongs squarely in the Eisenhower era.

Like much of Serling's work, *Planet of the Apes* is all premise and denouncement, with a "gummy" middle section. Also, like the majority of Serling's work, *Apes* is wrenching at the end, but emotionally uninvolving till then. Like many an episode of *The Twilight Zone*, *Apes* is a victim of its own cleverness—neglecting the heart necessary to drive the middle. At the end, largely because of Serling's genius *and* his limitations, *Planet of the Apes* emerges as a polemic disguised as a drama.

How are we, living in the 21st century (heaven help us), to read *Planet of the Apes*? The film is so rich in its subtexts and so loose in its parameters that it could entertain a broad variety of interpretations. I have gone through many different readings myself, and suspect that when I reach my ninth decade, I

Early artist's conception of the famous climactic scene—

IT CAME FROM ...

—and its cinematic realization.

will still be trying to piece it together as I drool into my sippy cup and grope my nurse.

One reading that appeals today as European dominance fades from the world scene is the ultimate degradation of European man. Key to the overall success of the film is not only Heston's performance, but the allusions and associations he brings to the role by virtue of other roles he had played previously. Here, in short, is Moses, Michelangelo, El Cid, Chinese Gordon, and Buffalo Bill Cody, brought low by non-European non-people. The immigration reforms of 1965 were already dramatically altering the country that most of the cast and crew involved in the original film grew up in, and the fears attendant with a dramatic demographic change in the country can clearly be read as a subtext.

Think of it. Replace Heston with any other competent actor of the age, but without the same baggage, then much of *Planet of the Apes* would lose its punch. William Holden (1918-1981), arguably a better actor than Heston and roughly the same age, would not have that baggage. Neither would Gregory Peck (1916-2003), Cliff Robertson (1923-2011) or Marlon Brando (1924-2004)—all of whom would be somehow right, but not right enough. No, it must be not only a representative of European man, but an exemplar of the summit of such men, for the film to have its greatest bite. (On a side note, Zira was first offered to Ingrid Bergman, who regretted turning it down, and Julie

Charlton Heston and Linda Harrison

Harris was slated for the role as late as several weeks before filming began.)

This reading of *Apes* is the ultimate realization of the "stick it to the man" sentiment so common to the Counter Culture era of its production, and sadly still current among many on what Maajid Nawaz now calls "the regressive Left."

Mention of the 1960s brings another possible reading. This reading sees various strains of 1960s society on trial and found wanting. This interpretation finds Cornelius (Roddy McDowall, 1928-1998) and Zira (Kim Hunter, 1922-2002) as progressive 1960s liberals trying to make inroads into an ossified establishment, represented by Dr. Zaius (Maurice Evans, 1901-1989). Like many on the Left of the time, Cornelius and Zira were anti-military, intolerant of religion, comfortable with both heresy and treason, and reckless as to the ultimate outcomes of their activism. That chimpanzees represent this modern Left is made abundantly clear with the character of Zira's nephew, Lucius, who is almost a caricature of student slogans and opinions of the time. In fact, in *Beneath the Planet of the Apes* (1970), chimpanzees would be the sole protestors against the expansive militarism of the gorillas.

This reading appeals especially to young people, who feel as if Cornelius and Zira represent a better and more tolerant future. However, both Cornelius and Zira are timorous and weak, having confidence in their convictions, but doing little to stand by them. Comfortable debating issues confronting ape society, they seem to have little stomach for doing anything about them until an indictment goads them into action. Even when Zaius has Cornelius arrested and silenced, Zira cannot manage to work up sufficient hate for Zaius, and seeks his impressions on Taylor's ultimate destiny.

Another—and the simplest—reading would be to view *Planet of the Apes* as nothing more than gentle, social satire. Screenwriter Wilson's contribution to the screenplay was the dialog playing fast and loose with social mores and concerns, including evolution, religion, and academe. While much of the film in 1968 was good for an easy laugh, such laughter today rings hollow. Many of the institutions *Apes* seeks to take down are toothless or warped beyond recognition today, and one wonders if the laughter is now at our own expense.

All well and good, but where am I in this? Soon approaching my 58th year, how do I regard *Planet of the Apes*, and how do I read it after looking at it for 50 years?

I have two readings dear to my heart, and they for now represent my thoughts on the whole *Apes* corpus. (But touch base with me again in 10 or 15 years—I may have changed my mind again.)

In the first reading, I ponder the extreme paradox that is George Taylor. Taylor hated the world he knew and left it as an astronaut simply to avoid humankind. He muses in his spaceship: "Does man, that marvel of the universe, that glorious paradox who sent me to the stars, still make war against his brother? Keep his neighbor's children starving?" Taylor even seems disdainful of the cultural upheavals of the 1960s, as when he says, "the world we made" was full of "love making, but no love."

In addition to his misanthropy, Taylor is a toad of the first water. Not content with leaving Earth and mankind behind, he has to badger and harass his shipmates upon landing on an (to them) unknown planet. As Serling set up the screenplay, *Apes* begins with a long, slow build so we can get a complete read on Taylor, and it's not pretty.

Taylor abuses Landon mercilessly, belittling his aspirations and certainties, as well as gloating on the hopelessness of their situation and reminding him relentlessly that everyone he knew or cared about is long dead. (It doesn't help that Landon, as played by Robert Gunner, is one of the most colorless and blandly performed roles in a major motion picture of the 1960s.)

In a Serling-esque twist, it is this ogre, this utterly detestable bully, who ends up the mouthpiece defending humanity. And though the dialog is no longer Serling's, the character of Taylor certainly belongs to him. He is a Serling protagonist in everything from his clipped poetic speech, to

The stories and novels behind Classic Horror, Fantasy and Science Fiction Films

his expansive self-loathing, and his quest for meaning. It is perhaps the fullest realization of a type that Serling would revisit throughout his career. In the course of the film, Taylor learns to appreciate his humanity, and then, treasure it. He does not fail to tell Zaius repeatedly that man not only came before the ape but was "better" than they. He is sure man fell because of some planetary catastrophe (initially thinking a meteor storm), before riding off with his renewed sense of self-worth.

And there, in the ultimate cinematic pulling-the-carpet-from-under-our-hero, Serling takes him to the ruins of the Statue of Liberty, showing that Taylor was right to despise mankind in the first place, and his newfound species pride is mis-founded. Serling's Taylor is a man who had nothing, who gains everything back again after enormous travail and suffering, only to lose it all over again. The tragedy is the overall loss of faith; Taylor's universe is absent any real God, human striving is pointless, and time and change are pitiless. The existential tragedy of Taylor is the tragedy of all men: Meaning is uncertain and time will erase us.

The other reading I subscribe to now also comes with another uneasy realization: That not only is Dr. Zaius right, he is the film's only true hero.

Maurice Evans as the imperious Dr. Zaius

(It helps a great deal that actor Maurice Evans very nearly walks away with the whole film with a performance that is deft and multilayered.) No establishment simpleton like the Zaius in Boulle's novel, the film Zaius is a brilliant and capable antagonist. Nor is he in the thrall of simple villainy—like all great heroes, Zaius is convinced of the justice of his cause and takes heroic measures to wrest victory. And that is because Zaius is the only character in the film who truly *sees*, and he sees *everything*. He realizes Taylor's intelligence before Zira does (and erases it as quickly as he can). He knows how dangerous man is, and he is aware that the Forbidden Zone was once a paradise turned wasteland ages ago thanks to man's inherent evil.

IT CAME FROM ...

He realized the threat of man to the environment ("Why, man is a nuisance. He eats up his food supply in the forest, then migrates to our green veldts and ravages our crops. The sooner he is exterminated, the better. It's a question of simian survival.") and later calls Taylor a "walking pestilence."

More interesting still, he knows what is coming. The investigations of both Cornelius and Zira threaten the very foundations of simian theology, philosophy, and society. He sees the societal decay that will result of untrammeled liberalism, and uses the state to safeguard its population. No mere "reactionary" (Taylor disdainfully calls him "chief defender of the faith"), Zaius is engaged in the only enterprise worthy of any true statesman: the care and continued flourishing of his nation and his people.

Dr. Zaius in *Beneath the Planet of the Apes*

If we extend our look at Zaius beyond *Planet of the Apes* to incorporate *Beneath the Planet of the Apes*, we see that Zaius is also brave, sagacious, magnanimous (after he arrests Cornelius and Zira, he pleads for clemency and gets them off), and protective. The actions he takes against Cornelius and Zira give him no pleasure, but he does what must be done. He sees through the illusions created by the mutants, and is the only member of the Ape expedition to understand the threat posed by the Alpha-Omega bomb. When the two are alone, Taylor accuses Zaius of being afraid of him, and he is. He knows that the threat Taylor poses to him and his people is largely existential: aside from human savages depleting food resources in the wild, an intelligent human would destroy simian hegemony.

Zaius is very much a traditionalist as defined by Russell Kirk, author of *The Conservative Mind*. Kirk listed 10 foundational conservative principles, starting with the belief in an "enduring moral order." Zaius believes that moral truths do not change with the times, and neither does human nature. "Conservatives are champions," Kirk wrote, "of custom, convention, and continuity because they prefer the devil they know to the devil they don't know." Like Kirk, Zaius clearly believes that decisions directly affecting members of a community

should be made "locally and voluntarily." Regarding governance, conservatives recognize that human passions must be restrained: Order and liberty must be balanced. Moreover, a conservative "favors reasoned and temperate progress," but does not worship Progress as some type of magical force.

Zaius, in a nutshell.

Zaius is best realized in a snippet of dialog between he and Lucius, Zira's "hippie" nephew. When he destroys evidence of the talking human doll and the rest of Cornelius' archeological dig, Lucius is indigent.

> Lucius: Dr. Zaius, this is inexcusable! Why must knowledge
> stand still? What about the future?
> Zaius: I may just have saved it for you.

When I was a boy, I identified with Cornelius and Zira. Now that I'm an adult, I pray for a Dr. Zaius. This is not a plea for contented ignorance, or for theocratic intolerance. It's simply an acknowledgement that all advances come with a cost, and that an examination of those costs is often the true definition of conservatism.

And it is those twin realizations—the paradox of Taylor and the wisdom of Zaius—that makes *Planet of the Apes* as interesting now as when it was first released, and a cautionary tale now more than ever before.

IT CAME FROM ...

Youth Wasted By The Young: Logan's Run (1976)

Co-authors William F. Nolan (born 1928) and George Clayton Johnson (1929-2015) open their novel *Logan's Run* (1967) with the following dedication:

TO ALL THE WILD FRIENDS
WE GREW UP WITH –
And who were with us when we wrote this book:

To Frankenstein and Mickey Mouse
To Jack, Doc and Reggie and
    The Temple of the Vampires
To Fu Manchu, Long John Silver, Tom Mix and
Buck Jones
To The Iliad and The Odyssey. Superman and The
    Green Hornet
To Jack Armstrong, the All-American Boy, and
    The Hunchback of Notre Dame
To Gunga Din, King Kong and The Land of Oz
To Mr. Hyde and The Phantom of the Opera
To The Sea Wolf, Captain Nemo and
    The Great White Whale
To Batman and Robin, Black Canary, Ted Sturgeon
    And The Ears of Johnny Bear
To Rhett Butler and Jiminy Cricket
To Matthew Arnold, Robert Frost and
    The Demolished Man
To What Mad Universe
To Dante, Dr. Lao and Dick Tracy
To Punch, the Immortal Liar, and
    The Girls in Their Summer Dresses
To The Man in the Iron Mask
To Marco Polo and The Martian Chronicles
To Bogie and The Maltese Falcon
To Flash Gordon, Prince Valiant, Krazy Kat and
    The Dance of the Dead
To Thomas Wolfe
To the Unicorn in the Garden
To Hammett and Chandler and
    You Play the Black and the Red Comes Up

To Pap Hemingway, Micky Spillane and Popeye the
   Sailor Man
To Fancies and Goodnights
To a Diamond as Big as the Ritz, and a Blood Wedding
   In Chicago
To Beauty and the Beast
To The Daredevil Dogs of the Air, The Dawn Patrol and
   The Long, Loud Silence
To Dough Fairbanks, Errol Flynn and
   The Keystone Kops
To Tarzan and The Land That Time Forgot
To Tom Swift, Huck Finn and Oliver Twist
To Citizen Kane, Sinbad and
   They Shoot Horses, Don't They?
To Ali Baba, The Marx Brothers and
   Dangerous Dan McGrew
To The Beanstalk
To The Lone Ranger, Little Orphan Annie and
   The Space Merchants
To The Day The Earth Stood Still
To The Highwayman
To Kazan, The Time Machine and Don't Cry for Me
To Captain Midnight and Lights Out
To Shackleton, Terry and the Pirates, Richard the
   Lionheart and The Rats in the Walls
To The Most Dangerous Game
To Lil' Abner, S. J. Perelman and Smoky Stover
To The Seven Dwarfs and Mandrake the Magician
To Billy the Kid, Geronimo, Stephen Vincent Benet and
   The House of Usher
To The Hound of the Baskervilles and
   The Ship of Ishtar
To Robin Hood, Scarface and Tommy Udo
To Frederick Schiller Faust who was Max Brand
   Who was Evan Evans who was George Challis
   Who was…
To Astounding, Amazing, Fantastic, Startling, Unknown,
   Galaxy, Weird Tales, Planet Stories, Black Mask
   And The Magazine of Fantasy and Science Fiction
To Rhysling, Blind Singer of the Spaceways
   AND, WITH LOVE
To The Green Hills of Earth

IT CAME FROM …

What a list! How evocative! Imagine spending time with a sensibility that encompasses everything from *The House of Usher* to Captain Midnight and the Lone Ranger! Men who appreciate *The Day the Earth Stood Still*, as well as Robin Hood! We must be in store for some good old Tarzan-By-Way-of-Tom-Swift science fictional goodness!

Ah … no. Alas, you have just read the most poetic, compelling, and engaging passage in all the novel that is *Logan's Run*. *Logan's Run* is a brief novel set in 2116, when the people of Earth are not allowed to legally age past their 21st year. When individuals hit 21, or Lastday, they report to a SleepShop where they are painlessly gassed to death. People always know their age by a flower-shaped crystal embedded in the palm of their right hand, which changes color every seven years (yellow, blue, then red) and blinks black and red on Lastday.

Though the vast majority of people (somewhat improbably) willingly accept sleep on Lastday, a number of rebels decide to run. Runners invariably look for a fabled place called Sanctuary, where people can live out their normal span of life.

To maintain law and order, Runners are chased by Deep Sleep Operatives (also called Sandmen), who use a gun with heat-sensitive homing bullets to kill. These bullets, Homers, focus on body heat and set afire every pain nerve in the body, resulting in agonizing death.

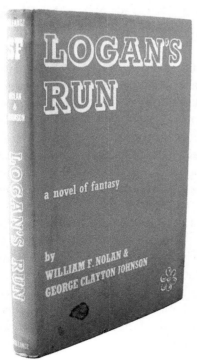

The novel opens with Logan, a Sandman, chasing a Runner named Doyle. Doyle leads a merry chase through Los Angeles, and Logan nearly loses him when Doyle enters Cathedral. (This is the type of book where all concepts have Capital Letters.) Cathedral is a blighted part of town overrun with feral children call Cubs, who get high on a drug called Muscle. (How are these children outside of society? What happened to make Cathedral what it is? *Logan's Run* is one of those books that is always a little dodgy on the details.) The Cubs kill Doyle, but before he expires, he tells Logan about Sanctuary. Sanctuary is a fabled place where people are allowed to grow old and live free.

Logan goes on with his life of empty and rather sordid pleasure—going to parties, glass-walled bordellos; you know, the usual. He also comes across Jessica, Doyle's sister, who tells him about Sanctuary and a

The stories and novels behind Classic Horror, Fantasy and Science Fiction Films

Logan's Run was the pre-*Star Wars* high water mark of cinematic science fiction.

man named Ballard. Ballard seemingly is master of Sanctuary and maybe as old as 40-something. Logan, something of a wretched swine from the get-go, decides to pretend to be Doyle altered by plastic surgery (don't ask) to get Jessica to lead him to Sanctuary. It is coming on Logan's Lastday, and he thinks it would be great to go out in a blaze of legally sanctioned apocalypse, taking Sanctuary down with him. Together they make a break for Sanctuary, utilizing the crazy quilt of underground transportation that takes them through most of the future United States. Along the way, Logan's friend and fellow Sandman Francis pursues them.

Over the course of this picaresque tale, Logan and Jessica have many adventures. They are taken in by prisoners-turned-cannibals in the frozen wastes, temporarily befriend a cyborg named Box, who has them make love so he can create an ice-sculpture of them, are kidnapped by a band of Gypsies who give Logan a super-Viagra so he can copulate multiple times with a band of lovelies, while Jessica is raped by their leader, and, of course, an action sequence that takes place with Logan and Jessica impersonating robots in an animatronic Civil War recreation because ... well, why not?

IT CAME FROM ...

Turns out that Francis is the 42-year-old Ballard, who is working from within the system to destroy it. (How, when he ... oh, never mind.) He controls a supercomputer buried beneath Crazy Horse Mountain (nice to see that project finally got finished) and he leads Logan and Jessica to a launch pad (no, seriously) where they leave Earth for Sanctuary, which is really called Argos, an abandoned space station near Mars. (Again, what "near Mars" means is never fully explained, or how a space station can maintain a growing population, or why people can't see spaceships leaving the planet, or ... oh, forget it.)

Authors Nolan and Johnson each have had significant writing careers. William Francis Nolan, still kicking as of this writing at 90 (take *that*, Sandmen!), has written many books, mostly mysteries and science fiction thrillers. Horror movie buffs know him best for his screenplay *Burnt Offerings* (1976), one of the greatest horror films of the 1970s. Nolan is also an early advocate and anthologist of fellow-author Ray Bradbury (1920-2012), and there are a few brief passages in *Logan's Run* that strive for Bradbury's lyricism.

A native of Kansas City, Missouri, Nolan worked briefly for Hallmark Cards before moving to California. He was part of a bunch of Southern Californian writers in the 1950s and 1960s known informally as The Group, who regularly contributed scripts to such series as *Alfred Hitchcock Presents*, *The Twilight Zone* and *Star Trek*. He has now found Sanctuary in Vancouver, Washington.

Writer George Clayton Johnson was born in Cheyenne, Wyoming. He had a troubled school career, being left behind in the sixth grade and dropping school altogether in the eighth. After a stint in the Army, Johnson settled down to become a writer. His most important work was done for television, where he wrote for *Alfred Hitchcock Presents*, as well as *Route 66*, *Kung Fu*, and *Star Trek*. Short stories appeared in *Playboy*, *Rogue*, and *Gamma*, and Johnson also wrote the initial treatment for what would become the Rat Pack flick *Ocean's 11*.

Johnson wrote seven scripts for *The Twilight Zone*, and three of them, significantly, address aging. *Kick the Can* (1962) involves an old man in a home for the aged who believes the secret of youth is in childish games. *Nothing But the Dark* (also 1962) deals with an old woman terrified of dying meeting Death personified. *Ninety Years Without Slumbering* (1963) is about an old man who believes he will die once his grandfather clock stops ticking. In all three of these tales, there is not only the idea of aging, but, more significantly, of *time running out*. One of the (many) interesting quirks of *The Twilight Zone* is that its young writing staff (Serling, Johnson, Beaumont) were all prematurely preoccupied with time running out. What was it in the zeitgeist (or, within this specialized fraternity of writers) that made them feel time spiraling out of control? Sadly, it is a question that seemed never to be asked of them.

Like Nolan, Johnson was a vegetarian. Johnson was also a strident supporter of the legalization of marijuana, which likely explains a great deal about the vagaries of the finished manuscript of *Logan's Run*.

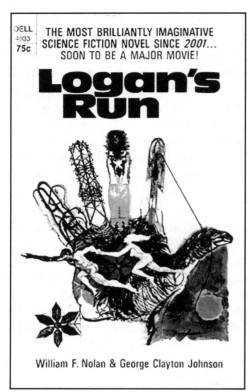

DELL
4033
75c

THE MOST BRILLIANTLY IMAGINATIVE
SCIENCE FICTION NOVEL SINCE *2001*...
SOON TO BE A MAJOR MOVIE!

Logan's Run

William F. Nolan & George Clayton Johnson

According to genre historian Roger M. Wilcox, Nolan tells the story that he and Johnson wrote the book in three weeks while holed up in a booth at Howard Johnson's. (This should surprise no one who has read it.) Nolan desperately needed to make college money for one of his children, and after they were paid for the novel, they were able to parlay that into an even larger paycheck when Hollywood came calling. Science fiction film legend George Pal (1908-1980) initially wanted to make the film version, and by the time various studios became involved, Nolan and Johnson were able to achieve a payday of half a million dollars in the late 1960s.

What this reader finds most astonishing is that this sleazy mess was concocted by two writers clearly in love with so many wonderful pieces of pop culture. How could writers enamored of Superman, Jack Armstrong, *I Love a Mystery*, Hopalong Cassidy, *The Three Musketeers*, and Fu Manchu create a novel so unrewarding, so soulless, so ... lacking in fun?

The buzz around the novel may be a little puzzling to readers coming to it cold in contemporary times, but it's important to remember the particular zeitgeist of its time was literally a new era of science fiction.

Logan's Run made its debut during the New Wave period of science fiction literature. As science fiction became a literary commodity with the magazines edited by Hugo Gernsback (1884-1967) in the 1920s, the genre started working within several, recognizable tropes and expectations. The Gernsback era quickly evolved into a Golden Age, where writers both more serious and sophisticated worked within the genre, fully seeking to make it a legitimate art form.

The New Wave was one of the many cultural blights that plagued the 1960s; it sought to cast aside much of the science fiction canon and re-imagine it into something else. New Wave writers sought a more "modernist" and "experimental" literary approach, often eschewing the hard science (or, at least, the gloss of scientific explanation) that characterized the Gernsback and Golden Ages.

IT CAME FROM ...

As critic Eric S. Raymond (born 1957) writes:

> The New Wave's inventors (notably Michael Moorcock, J.G.
> Ballard and Brian Aldiss) were British socialists and Marxists
> who rejected individualism, linear exposition, happy endings,
> scientific rigor, and the U.S.'s cultural hegemony over the
> SF field in one fell swoop. The New Wave's later American
> exponents were strongly associated with the New Left and
> opposition to the Vietnam War, leading to some rancorous
> public disputes in which politics was tangled together with
> definitional questions about the nature of SF and the direction
> of the field.

Logan's Run is filled (indeed, crammed) with New Wave self-indulgence.
There are snippets of blank verse poetry, key plot points are left unexplained
(or ambiguous), and the "experimental" quality of the story-telling leaves the
reader often scratching his (or her) metaphorical head. Like much New Wave
science fiction, *Logan's Run* reads like a bad jazz riff—there's a melody lingering
in there somewhere, but the musician is so pleased with himself that he forgets
the audience. It is, of course, a perfect entertainment for the era: only a pretentious half-wit would find it commendable.

Also key to the novel's evolution were not only literary developments of
the time, but the youth revolution of the 1960s. The youth culture had already
started its project of dismantling the world that nurtured them, as profound,
sweeping, destructive, and long-lasting as any cultural revolution the Chinese
could concoct. As the prologue of the book has it:

> The seeds of the Little War were planted in a restless summer during the
> mid-1960s,
> With sit-ins and student demonstrations as youth
> Tested its strength
> By the early 1970s over 75 per cent of the people living on earth
> Were under twenty-one years of age.
> The population continued to climb—and
> With it the youth percentage.
> In the 1980s the figure was 79.7 per cent.
> In the 1990s, 82.4 per cent.
> In the year 2000—critical mass.

What is most fascinating about *Logan's Run* (and the film based upon it) is
that, on one hand, it is a product of both the New Wave and the youth movement of the 1960s, and a stunning indictment of it. The dystopia that is this

future world exists solely because it was conceived and then managed by young people ... people too unformed, inexperienced, and naïve to know any better. As Logan considers before his flight to Sanctuary:

> Living is better than dying, Francis. Dying young is a waste and a shame and a perversion. The young don't build. They use. The wonders of Man were achieved by the mature, the wise, who lived in this world before we did. There was an *Old* Lincoln after the young one ...

Clearly Nolan and Johnson, both children of the 1920s, were deeply skeptical of the social changes happening around them. What is inexplicable is that they chose to craft their literary argument in the language of the enemy.

Logan's Run is uniquely terrible in the way that only New Wave science fiction can be. It is prurient and lurid, while also surprisingly ham-fisted in its imaginings. It sacrifices clarity for faux profundity and is sloppily constructed and half-baked. Because of its lack of narrative cohesion, it makes very little impact on the memory, and because, like most New Wave fiction, it is bleak and nihilistic, it does nothing to fire and inspire the imagination.

Logan's Run anticipates many of the tropes ascendant in Cyberpunk, the sad aftermath of New Wave science fiction. The cities of *Logan's Run* seem to be little better than consumerist hellholes, filled with cheap sensation and squalor. Sex has been commoditized, there seems to be little understanding of the past, and there is an obsession with outward appearance and surgically enhanced modes of beauty. Parts of Washington, D.C. are in ruins, and, again, the overall tone is one of scientifically enhanced misery. The conditions in *Logan's Run* seem to be global: Logan has actually visited Venice, Italy and Nairobi, for example, and the one-world government so longed for by the New Left is illustrated as the failure it would and must be.

Surprisingly, the film adaptation of *Logan's Run* would retain much of the criticism of the cultural revolutions of the 1960s, but seen from the standpoint of a glitzy and rather vapid 1970s.

Logan's Run, the film, follows the basic outline of the novel, but with a number of significant improvements. The film was in development for several years after it was initially bought by producer-director George Pal. Pal, one of the most gifted and fondly remembered figures of science fiction film, seems like an unlikely figure to be attached to the project. Pal's films all have a sweet strain of lyrical humanism to them, a deft sense of nostalgic melancholia. It's probable that Pal's *Logan's Run* would have been a very different film indeed—the romance between Logan (Michael York, born 1942) and Jessica (Jenny Agutter, born 1952) would have been sweeter, the friendship between Francis (Richard Jordan, 1938-1993) more real. Alas, it was not to be.

IT CAME FROM ...

Budget overruns, changes in ownership, and other setbacks led to Pal leaving the project to make, instead, the lamentable *Doc Savage* (1975), his last film and his most significant misfire. The project eventually ended up at MGM under the stewardship of Michael Anderson (1920-2018), who earlier scored a great success with *Around the World in 80 Days* (1956). It is perhaps Anderson's gift for organization and planning that marshaled the component parts of the production into a finished picture. Oddly enough, Anderson also directed Pal's *Doc Savage*; for a journeyman director, Anderson's oeuvre has many fascinating byways, including an interesting adaptation of Orwell's *1984* and the television version of Bradbury's *The Martian Chronicles*.

Made on a budget of six or nine million dollars (reports vary), *Logan's Run* never quite achieves the visionary heft to which it aspires. A great deal of it seems rote—as if Anderson and MGM felt there were several check boxes that must be hit to create a science fiction film. Kitschy futuristic music (by Jerry Goldsmith)? Check. Elaborate model work? Check. Futuristic shopping mall set? Insane computer that self-destructs? Check, check, check. (In fact, much of *Logan's Run* was shot in the Dallas Market Center mall in Texas). Many of these elements don't seem "organic," and play more like committee decisions based on perceived genre expectations.

Despite this, the film works significantly better than the novel. It opens with a title card explaining that, thanks to catastrophic wars, overpopulation, and pollution, mankind now lives in a domed city ... and that people may not live past 30. Already, this is a vast improvement on the premise. In the novel,

WELCOME TO THE 23RD CENTURY.
The perfect world of total pleasure.

LOGAN'S RUN

...there's just one catch.

METRO-GOLDWYN-MAYER presents
A SAUL DAVID PRODUCTION "LOGAN'S RUN"
starring MICHAEL YORK · JENNY AGUTTER · RICHARD JORDAN
ROSCOE LEE BROWNE · FARRAH FAWCETT-MAJORS
& PETER USTINOV · Screenplay by DAVID ZELAG GOODMAN
Based on the novel "LOGAN'S RUN" by
WILLIAM F. NOLAN and GEORGE CLAYTON JOHNSON
Music—JERRY GOLDSMITH · Produced by SAUL DAVID
Directed by MICHAEL ANDERSON
Filmed in TODD-AO and METROCOLOR NOW A BANTAM BOOK!

the whole dead-at-21 thing was worldwide, and one wonders how the politics of the entire planet could operate under a single idea. The novel cites the youth uprisings of the 1960s as the start of all of this societal rot, and while in actuality that was devastating to the global culture, it is more likely to result in gated communities rather than domed cities. Also, the concept of a domed city means its inhabitants are prisoners there, as much as they are citizens. Finally, a world where people live to be at least 30 sounds like something that might almost be sustainable (though some of the security guards during Logan's last interrogation look like the wrong side of 50), while a world that is 21 and younger seems incredible, no matter how much computerized coddling.

We first see Logan at the nursery, looking at a newborn baby and wondering if it's his child. With this establishing scene, we know that this Logan is a very different man from the one in the novel ... he's not a jerk.

The film eschews the whole notion of SleepShops and, instead, creates a quasi-religious festival, the idea of Renewal at Carousel. This is perhaps the film's most audacious conceit. Citizens on Lastday gather in this enormous arena, clad in robes, body-stockings, and masks before floating heavenward, where they explode in a shower of sparks before cheering crowds. Supplicants are told that they will be reborn in Renewal ... reincarnated here in the domed city. With the patina of near-religious zealotry, the film makes voluntary self-extinction believable, and confers a greater sense of urgency for those who would stamp out this apostasy.

Logan leaves Carousel to kill a Runner. Here, Runners are a more organized underground, and all carry as their symbol the Egyptian ankh (for

Logan's Run institutionalizes suicide as a religious conceit.

IT CAME FROM ...

reasons never explained). After homicide, Logan relaxes in cinema's most fetching bathrobe, looking for a little anonymous sex. In the future, people on the make are able to teleport themselves into the homes of people on the take, something like a science fictional Tinder. There Logan meets Jessica, recognizes the Ankh, and starts thinking. Fortunately, Francis shows up with some inhaled narcotics and a couple of party girls (the more things change …), and he reverts to form.

In another improvement over the novel, the master computer that runs the domed city directs Logan to find Sanctuary. The computer advances Logan's palm crystal till he is near Lastday as a cover, and Logan's commitment to his society begins to crack when he cannot get an answer if the time erased will be returned to him.

Logan pursues Jessica, trying to convince her that his time is up and he wants to run. She tries to convince her friends in the Runner underground, but they are too leery of a Sandman infiltrating. Fortunately, Logan has another lead: the Runner he murdered during Carousel had his face changed. Logan goes to the same doctor, where a supremely air-headed nurse, played by Farrah Fawcett-Majors (1947-2009), all wide eyes and lip-gloss, helps him. The doctor, played by the director Anderson's son, gets a call from the underground before the procedure, and he seeks to kill Logan. A little operating table tussling later, it's the surgeon who is killed by the cosmetic lasers.

Logan and Jessica escape through a drug-fueled sex club, where they make their way in slow motion through a variety of unclad bodies. This sequence is, frankly, astonishing for a PG film, and indicative of how tightly the movie ratings system has cracked down on sexual content. In 1976, *Logan's Run* was rated for general audiences; today, it would be rated R for violence and sexual content. Time doesn't always move forward.

Logan's friend Francis pursues Logan. The middle section of the film follows many of the same beats of the novel but, again, offering improvements. The Cubs are not feral children on the outskirts of Los Angeles, but rather live in a specific zone for dangerous delinquents. (How delinquency is even possible in such a controlled society is another question, but at least it's something.) They meet the cyborg Box, who wants to freeze them as food for future generations. In fact … all 1,056 Runners who have gotten that far have been frozen by Box; none of them had ever gotten any further. This, too, is more believable than spaceships headed for "near Mars" that are never noticed by anyone. (It's clear that there was a lot of trimming done in this section. Box, played by veteran actor Roscoe Lee Browne (1922–2007), barely has five or six lines. And the sculpture tool is in his hand … clearly he sculpted Logan and Jessica before trying to kill them; none of that, though, makes it into the final film.)

The final segment feels like another movie entirely. Logan and Jessica see the sun for the first time, and are outside for the first time as well. As the movie

opens up, we realize just how claustrophobic the preceding sections of the film have been, and how liberating it is to see our characters in natural light.

Like the book, Logan and Jessica amble through the ruins of Washington, D.C., stopping to gaze on the Lincoln Memorial. They stop at the Capitol and there, the film gets a much-needed jolt of wit and whimsy. They meet the Old Man (Peter Ustinov, 1921-2004) who lives in the Senate with his many cats. The Old Man has a passion for T.S. Eliot, as most of his dialogue is cribbed from *The Old Possum's Book of Practical Cats*. He tells Logan and Jessica of parents and children living together and loving one another, and then dying; the normal life cycle.

Jessica wants to go on to Sanctuary, and again, the film touches on the idea of devotion to a religious ideal. While the denizens of the city believe in Carousel and Renewal with religious fervor, Jessica believes in Sanctuary. Logan realizes both ideas are just so much horse puckey and wants to go back to the city and liberate the minds of the people that live there. Before they go, Francis returns, and Logan kills him.

Logan, Jessica and the Old Man make it back to the domed city, Ustinov making subtle *sotto-voce* comments the length of the journey. Once more in the city, Logan and Jessica are captured. When the computer downloads Logan's memories, it cannot cope with its findings and self-destructs, causing the city to explode and break apart. (Because … ?)

Logan's Run ends with the young people of the world stepping outside for the first time, where they meet Ustinov (who presumably spends the rest of his life doing schtick for them), now masters of their own destiny. This is a significantly more upbeat ending than that novel, as this solution saves *everyone*, rather than just Logan and Jessica. The caveat, of course, is that the world is now the domain of young people who have lived on computers, are incapable of interpersonal relationships, are socially awkward, know nothing of the past, and are terribly under-educated. You know, Millennials.

So *much* of *Logan's Run* works because of the game performances by the leads. Agutter is splendid, and her innocence and vulnerability provide the heart of the film. York plays very effectively; he seems callow and callous in the beginning reels, and slowly matures before the camera. It is a deft performance. While spectacularly popular in the 1970s, York's career stalled in the 1980s—too handsome, too earnest, and too likable for an increasingly cynical age.

The two standouts are Jordan and Ustinov. Jordan, a particularly gifted actor, brings much more to Francis than is found in the screenplay. In fact, his playing very effectively could be read as subtly coded sexual jealousy of Agutter; same-sex relations are normalized in this future, and York and Jordan do everything together. York's Logan walks away not only from the accepted faith of Carousel, but he leaves Jordan for Agutter. Jordan's Francis is not simply an avatar of law and order, he is, more dangerously, a man spurned.

Ustinov strolls through *Logan's Run*, making faces, mumbling comic ditties, and providing a human focal point for the viewer amidst the very different people of Logan's world. He doesn't exactly *save* the movie—it doesn't need saving—but he is certainly the key player.

What are we to make of the 1976 *Logan's Run* today, two complete lifetimes later, as tabulated in the original novel?

The first thing that is most striking is that the film version is a very Hugo Gernsbackian vision of a New Wave idea. Made by and large by people whom the 1960s had left behind, Anderson and company create a post-1960s world as conceived by The Greatest Generation. Where the novel keeps details loose and fairly vague, the film works overtime to connect the dots. It eschews the proto-Cyberpunk cityscape for that trope of classic science fiction, the domed city, and provides a more concrete rationale for the situation.

Where the novel is rather gritty and sleazy, the finished film is glossy and sleazy, as if Radley Metzger (1929-2017) had directed *Things To Come*. The movie throws in several scientific rationales (the city is powered by sea water, for example, or the palm crystals no longer work outside the city) to better ground the story. Most important, the film underscores that Man will overcome and emerge triumphant, while that sentiment is more ambiguous in the novel. In fact, in the movie *everyone* wins, as Logan liberates the planet from both its machines and its religious mania, and mankind is once again in control of its destiny. (It's impossible to believe that the makers of *Wall-E* did not have *Logan's Run* in mind when crafting its finale.)

Remarkably, *Logan's Run* and *Star Wars* were released only a year apart. They seem like movies not only from different studios, but from different universes. *Logan's Run* is clearly an "A" picture, but an "A" picture by a studio that considered science fiction "a thing," a conglomeration of various component parts, and not an organic entity. *Star Wars* was made for $11 million (only $2 million more than one estimate for *Logan's Run*), but the attention to detail, the "lived-in" feeling of the world it created, make it seem like a much (much!) more expensive picture. And while the original *Star Wars* relied heavily on models, they had a weight and gravity not seen in the more window-display miniatures in *Logan's Run*.

But more than effects, what makes *Logan's Run* such a product of its time are the internal politics on display. By the time the film was made, many of the cultural revolutions of the 1960s were going on a decade old, and had already ossified into a type of empty-headed entitlement; the beginning of the Me Decade. With its messages about the dangers of the Youth Movement and where it will all lead, and its Glitter Rock décor (the whole film looks like a David

IT CAME FROM ...

Set designers stand like giants in miniature future city; the film would go on to win a Special Achievement Academy Award for its visual effects.

Bowie concept album), *Logan's Run* wants to have its cake and eat it, too—criticizing what it is fetishizing. It is both a stunning indictment of its period, and a sleazy reflection of it.

If all of this carping makes *Logan's Run* sound like a bad film, I'm leaving the wrong impression. While *Logan* is no masterpiece, it improves upon the book in nearly every particular. It is certainly more interesting, more immediate and more thought provoking than anything in the *Star Wars* canon. And, more important, experiencing the film itself is often oddly involving and visceral in ways that contemporary blockbusters cannot engage. Because the world of *Logan's Run* was constructed in-camera, and not through CGI, it has an intimacy missing in green-screen blockbusters. The effects sometimes scream *fake*, but that's not the point. The cinema of the fantastic should look … fantastic, and not a flat, simulacrum of reality, whatever that happens to be.

Many of the pre-*Star Wars* science fiction films of the 1970s (e.g., this, *Silent Running*, *Zardoz*, *Fantastic Planet*) are movies that are experienced more than watched. It's impossible to experience *Logan's Run* and not think it's something different, something wonderfully odd, and something that's now incredibly precious. Sure, it's a mess, but it's an awfully compelling mess.

For many people of Generation X (born 1960-1980), the picture that comes to the mind's eye when thinking of cinematic science fiction are visions of worlds that look much like *Logan's Run*. As this viewer enters his 58th year, I don't look at the film as an artifact of yet another retro-future, but rather, as a vision of youth.

The Other Martian:
John Carter (2012)

The history of Hollywood adaptations of beloved properties is littered with sad stories. Perhaps none are sadder than the tortured history of bringing Edgar Rice Burroughs' cherished Martian books to the screen. The lack of critical and audience appreciation for *John Carter* is the only fitting coda to a decades-long story of missed opportunities, narrative appropriation, and regrettable lapses in public taste.

It's not as if the effort had not been made. First published in serial form in 1912, Burroughs' *A Princess of Mars* created a template by which all later Planetary Romances would be judged. It told the story of Civil War soldier John Carter being magically transported to Mars, where he encounters a world filled with wonders and terrors alike. So successful was Burroughs' foray into science fiction that he would eventually write 10 sequels and branch out with separate science fiction series about Venus and the strange world at the Earth's core.

Oh. He also wrote a successful series about an English lord raised by the great apes. You may have heard of the hero of these books (and movies and radio shows and comics) as well: Tarzan.

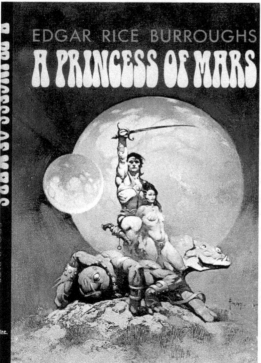

During my misspent youth—back when dinosaurs ruled the earth—I spent most of my summer vacations reading the works of Edgar Rice Burroughs (1875-1950). Whether they know it or not, many people enter the world of science fiction, fantasy, and heroic fiction by way of Burroughs; his literary influence is astronomical. His readers are fiercely protective of his reputation, and his lack of standing in the greater canon of genre fiction (and literary fiction) is inexplicable.

The literati who dismiss Burroughs do so at their own peril, as a compelling case can be made that Burroughs is one of the most successful and influential writers of the 20th century. I say without shame and in complete candor that some of the people I met in my ramblings through ERB's corpus are among the most important literary friendships that I have ever made. Tarzan of the Apes, John Carter of Mars, and the explorers of the subterranean world of Pellucidar, where intelligent reptiles live at the Earth's core, are as real to me to this day as many actual human beings that I have met in later life. And some of them even make better friends.

No one will argue for a moment that ERB was a prose stylist, or that his insight into human nature was a rare and subtle one. More damning to his literary reputation are his sensibilities and taste for high adventure; most modern novels are simply slices of life that may best be labeled *why we are miserable now*. (I have come to think that the short-fiction found in *The New Yorker* are stories shorn of their beginnings and endings.) ERB had no patience for this type of thinking or that type of narrative. He wrote adventure stories—set in some of the most exotic places on and off of the planet—and they were unabashedly plot-driven. If you want to know the plight of unhappy men in a midlife crisis, or women struggling for identity in a world redefined by feminism, look elsewhere. Want to learn how a Civil War soldier miraculously transported to Mars befriends four-armed green giants and battles rampaging, carnivorous white apes, then you've come to the right place.

Minds as brilliant and creative as Carl Sagan (1934-1996), Gore Vidal (1925-2012), Ray Bradbury (1920-2012), William Joyce (born 1957) and Jane Goodall (born 1934) have all credited him as an influence, and his contribution to global popular culture is incalculable.

Whatever the faults or strengths of his particular novels, what is most remarkable about his work is the *experience* of reading Burroughs. The adventure novels of ERB have the remarkable quality of affecting the reader in ways unexpected and serendipitous. Aside from (not so) simple narrative pleasures as a compelling storyline and absolutely unfettered imagination, it is impossible to read his works without a sense of delight and wonder. In the world of ERB, all bets are off and most anything is possible. There is a sense of energy, drive and, for want of a better word, *pep*. Burroughs is a tonic; read him and grow young again.

And … ERB *believed* in adventure. Much of the literary establishment has written off Burroughs not only for his prose, but also for his abundant output and for his choice of genre. Burroughs was no hack, churning out novels at a penny a word. Rather, he lived in an imaginative landscape that was as real to him as the workday world is real to us. His Martian society, the (mostly invented) African jungle of Tarzan, and the land at the Earth's Core all share a sense of … conviction. In his way, Burroughs was a serious novelist—as his worlds mattered to him; there was a compelling urgency to his vision that is evident in his fiction.

Burroughs' success is doubly amazing when one considers that his first novel, *A Princess of Mars*, was written as a lark. A keen fan of the pulps and

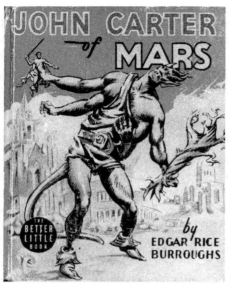

genre fiction, Burroughs read a particularly pallid story and thought he could do better. His maiden effort began a publishing powerhouse that chugs along to this day.

Like many other imaginative world-builders (talents as diverse as Ian Fleming, Walt Disney, and Charles Schulz come to mind), Burroughs realized that conceiving and executing his dream was only a first step, and that real success came from diversifying his efforts. In nearly no time at all, Burroughs' works (particularly Tarzan) were adapted to the screen, and later to comic strips and radio. He wisely invested in real estate, buying the ranch that would eventually become the city of Tarzana, California. He also became his own corporation, allowing his company to hold copyright to his fiction. It was this foresight that allowed Burroughs and his heirs to maintain some level of quality control on the brand. So pervasive was Burroughs' influence, so extensive was his grip on the popular imagination, that his very success was one of the many reasons that *John Carter*, quite a terrific movie, failed at the box office ...

Burroughs' Mars novels have not only inspired other similar works, but they have been pillaged and raped as well. Others have ripped off so much of what Burroughs created with his seminal science fiction series that now the originator looks like an imitator.

When soldier John Carter arrives on Mars, he finds that the different atmosphere affects his physical prowess. Already a fine physical specimen (he is a top solider serving in the Confederacy), Carter is now able to leap incredible distances and perform tremendous feats of strength. Two teenage Burroughs fans in Cleveland, Jerry Siegel and Joe Schuster, borrowed these powers and the scientific rationale for them when they created Superman. Siegel and Schuster improved upon the concept by rooting it in our everyday world, rather than far-off Mars. Where John Carter goes to another planet to display "powers and abilities far beyond those of mortal men," Superman comes to Earth, to our rural and urban America, to confound us with his newfound abilities. It is this reversal that made Superman infinitely more accessible than the baroque (but delightful) John Carter, and this is a big part of his appeal to this day.

Looking for a new venue to cross-pollinate his imagination, Burroughs urged United Features Syndicate in 1931 to create a John Carter comic strip.

Syndicate head George Carlin dismissed the enterprise, writing, "Production of the Martian strips would seriously handicap the Tarzan feature." Two years later King Features Syndicate approached Burroughs. They had corralled artist Alex Raymond and writer Don G. Moore to visualize Burroughs' Martian landscape for an ongoing comic strip. With typical enthusiasm, Burroughs threw himself into the project, working with his longtime illustrator J. Allen St. John to create a sample based on the second John Carter novel, *The Gods of Mars*. King Features offered a contract for 50 percent of the gross, but Burroughs demanded all spinoff rights, including movie serials, Big Little Books, and radio shows. Negotiations dragged on … until King Features finally responded with a letter stating, "It seems impossible for us to arrange syndication under terms which suit you."

Three days later, King Features and Alex Raymond published their first *Flash Gordon* strip.

Decades later, when George Lucas dreamt of a space opera, his initial impulse was to helm a big budget version of *Flash Gordon*. As recorded in *SF Review* (12/77), Lucas said: "Originally, I wanted to make a Flash Gordon movie, with all the trimmings, but I couldn't obtain the rights. So, I began researching and found where (Flash Gordon creator) Alex Raymond got his idea: The works of Edgar Rice Burroughs, especially his John Carter series of books."

Consider this: On Mars John Carter meets a princess leading a rebellion, fights an evil empire, meets a variety of aliens, and traverses a desert landscape. Much like *Attack of the Clones*, Carter finds himself in an enormous open-air arena where he fights gigantic monsters. Lucas, too, echoes Burroughs in many of the words/concepts he created. In *Star Wars*, a beast of burden is a bantha, while Burroughs has a banth. On Mars, kings are called a Jed or Jeddak … and Lucas had his Jedi knights. Burroughs called a padwar a low-ranking officer, while Lucas had a Padawan as an apprentice Jedi. And both are full of Sith, one a Martian insect, and the other a dark practitioner of the Force.

However, perhaps the most egregious offender in the John Carter rip-off sweeps is *Avatar*. James Cameron's film, with its military man on a strange plan-

The stories and novels behind Classic Horror, Fantasy and Science Fiction Films

et and falling in love with an alien woman, is an ERB film in all but name only. As Cameron told one journalist: "This story could've been written in the '30s. It could have been an Edgar Rice Burroughs type story or a Rudyard Kipling story or a Western, absolutely. But it's an adventure story of a guy from one culture dropped into another culture."

He elaborated in another interview:

> The big irony of this film is, you know, we're doing this story that takes place out in the rain forest, a very simple story, almost classic in a sense, almost an Edgar Rice Burroughs kind of adventure, and yet it's being done with the most advanced technology in the history of film. So there's this weird juxtaposition. I take the actors to Hawaii and we're out on some muddy trail someplace learning how to shoot a bow in the woods and not get bitten by mosquitoes so that they'll have enough of a sense of memory of what it's like to move through a rain forest so that when they come back to this very sterile stage environment, they can recreate that.

Cameron's ode to Burroughs was a remarkable success ... for Cameron. The great challenge to anyone adapting Burroughs henceforth would be finding a way to emerge from the shadow of its own imitators.

The drive to bring John Carter to the screen started early. Enthused (if not impressed) by the initial success of Tarzan films during the silent era, Burroughs wished for a screen adaptation long before the talkies. Despite this enthusiasm, he could never find any takers on the property. The first real opportunity for a John Carter film came from an unlikely source: a key animator from Warner Bros.' successful *Merry Melodies*. Animator Bob Clampett was born in 1913 in the heart of Hollywood (he grew up next door to Charlie Chaplin), and he began working as a cartoonist in the felicitously named Harman-Ising studio in 1931. Though still a very young man, Clampett saw that animation had greater potential than short gag-driven comedies. Clampett grew up on Burroughs' books, and he went to Tarzana Ranch to meet with him and discuss his big idea: a series of animated cartoons based on John Carter. Burroughs responded with characteristic zest.

Clampett quickly partnered with the author's son, John Coleman Burroughs, and the two worked (nights and weekends, for Clampett) putting together detailed color sketches and sculpted models. The two envisioned a series of nine-minute cartoons that could stand alone, or be later incorporated into a feature-length film. (This, years before Disney's *Snow White and the Seven Dwarfs*.) The two also created six minutes of test footage to accompany a detailed studio pitch ("WHY has the public THRILLED to the Mars books for 25 years?

IT CAME FROM ...

Because ACTION and ROMANCE are the keynotes of the BURROUGHS name. Because the MARS STORIES are CHOCK-FULL of ACTION and ROMANCE!"). This footage, readily found on YouTube, is nothing short of fabulous. The use of color, the sense of scope and scale, the sense of derring-do and adventure; to this day it is how I envision the world of John Carter in my mind's eye, much the way the Fleischer Superman cartoons still define that character for me.

Clampett explained:

> We would oil paint the side shadowing frame-by-frame in an attempt to get away from the typical outlining that took place in normal animated films. In the running sequence, for example, there is a subtle blending of figure and line, which eliminated the harsh outline. It is more like a human being in tone. We were working in untested territory at that time. There was no animated film to look at to see how it was done.

Executives at MGM, riding high on their Tarzan films, took the bait. So strong was MGM's reaction that Clampett quit his job at Warners to ready himself for the John Carter project. And then … it just fell apart. MGM cancelled the project at the last moment, citing that audiences in middle America would not understand, or appreciate, the planetary adventures of a Civil War soldier. The studio countered with an offer to produce animated Tarzan adventures, but Clampett had lost his taste for the enterprise. In the end, Clampett would return to Warners, and John Coleman Burroughs, who became a talented artist over the course of the project, would go on to illustrate his father's work. The loss of the Clampett/Burroughs animated John Carter series is one of the great tragedies of fantastic cinema.

Nearly as great a loss was the abandoned possibility of one of fantastic cinema's greatest auteurs and die-hard Burroughs fan, Ray Harryhausen, taking on

The imagery created by Burroughs in his Mars novels inspired people as diverse as Ray Bradbury, Carl Sagan, George Lucas and Bob Clampett.

the John Carter series. Following his success with *Jason and the Argonauts* (1963), Harryhausen campaigned to get the series off the ground, but he could never find the funding. In addition, the Mars books would require so many effects shots (the Tharks, the white apes, thoats, Woola) that it would not be a manageable project.

One can almost, in the mind's eye, see what a Harryhausen *John Carter* would be like. Shot largely in the Spanish desert, with Kerwin Matthews perhaps as John Carter, Harryhausen's film would have included all the strengths and weaknesses found in his impressive oeuvre. Too short to do the story justice, rather flaccid except for dynamic animation sequences, a Harryhausen *John Carter* would be remembered for its audacity and hand-made quality ... but it never came to pass.

In the 1970s, Raymond Leicestershire created character and set designs for a production that never came to fruition. Nothing survives of that effort.

But still, the shade of John Carter continued to haunt filmmakers. In the 1980s, Disney executives approached *Die Hard* director John McTiernan about a big-budget version, floating Tom Cruise as star. It remained unrealized. A fierce bidding war for the property occurred in 2004 between Paramount and Columbia, with Paramount winning. They threw three talented filmmakers at it over the course of the next two years: Robert Rodriguez, Kerry Conran and Jon Favreau, but none of them were able to make a viable pitch.

Of the three, let's take a moment to consider what Kerry Conran would have done with John Carter. There are few critics who enjoyed his sole feature film *Sky Captain and the World of Tomorrow* more than me. Kerry's overarching aesthetic sensibility was born of 1930s action films; here is a man more influenced by the 1933 *King Kong* than by *Star Wars*. Conran's concept reel for *John Carter* is easily available on YouTube, and like Clampett's test, it is definitely worthy of examination. Conran's *John Carter* would have been more dreamscape than landscape, a handful of live actors roaming a computer generated wonderland. Where Andrew Stanton's *John Carter* was ultimately influenced by graphic depictions of Burroughs created during his great revival of the 1960s and 1970s, Conran would have made a film visually more in keeping with classic 1930s Hollywood. Again ... an unrealized John Carter provides a devastating loss to imaginative cinema.

Conran was off the project when Paramount leadership changed hands (illustrative of what would happen with the finished product at Disney), where the latest project would change studios and land in the lap of Burroughs fan and Pixar animator/director, Andrew Stanton. The travails faced by Stanton in getting *John Carter* made are now the stuff of legend. There is no better record of the whole fiasco than *John Carter and the Gods of Hollywood*, by Michael D. Sellers. This volume is highly recommended; for a close-up look at Hollywood dysfunction, it is hard to do better.

Here finally was a film nearly 100 years in the making … and one cannot help but ask, was it worth it?

Well … yes. Stanton's *John Carter* is not perfect, but so much of it is simply wonderful. Stanton (and screenwriters Mark Andrews and Michael Chabon) provides a worthy framing device, which features Edgar Rice Burroughs himself. The plot incorporates the frame of the initial novel in the series, as well as materials from the second and third novels. The visuals are superb, the narrative sweep impressive, and dramatic stakes are high. The Tharks are magnificent (it is perhaps the only time I have been able to stomach Willem Dafoe), the arena scene is Burroughs made flesh, and the much-appreciated overall lack of irony separate it from noisy junk like the Marvel films or the Snyder Batman films.

More interesting, Stanton was determined to film *John Carter* on real exteriors, on real sets, with help from animation. This gives the film a physical heft that so many contemporary science fiction films lack, grounding it in a 3D reality sadly missing in current fantasy films. Portions of *John Carter* feel more

The screenplay for *John Carter* liberally borrowed elements from the first three novels in the series to team both the Tharks and the Red Martians as the main antagonists.

The stories and novels behind Classic Horror, Fantasy and Science Fiction Films

like *Ben Hur* or *Lawrence of Arabia* than *Ender's Game* or *Tron*. By any reasonable yardstick *John Carter* should not have just been a hit, it should have been a blockbuster, and right now we should be well on our way to having enjoyed two or three more films in the series. What the hell went wrong?

As one Hollywood commentator has said, *John Carter* didn't fail, Disney murdered it. And when the studio finished putting the film in its coffin, disdainful Millennials gladly buried it.

The first culprit is Disney CEO Bob Iger, who inherited the film already in production when he came on board. Whereas Disney historically created its own films, Iger broadened the portfolio of studio activity by actively seeking new intellectual property. During the *John Carter* production process, Iger fired producer Dick Cook, the film's in-house champion. Iger was also actively seeking purchase of both Lucasfilms (owners of both *Star Wars* and *Indiana Jones*) and Marvel. This new model—Disney as owner of Pixar, DreamWorks, Jerry Bruckheimer Films, Lucasfilms, and Marvel properties—was the direction that interested him, and nurturing a new brand was simply not on his agenda. He quickly slashed marketing investments on *John Carter* as well.

Further, in an act that could only be called sabotage, Iger issued a doomsday announcement that *John Carter* was a financial disappointment, requiring a multi-million dollar write-down on Disney's part. This announcement came a scant 10 days into the film's run, a movie which normally would have a 100-day theatrical run at a point when more than 50% of the revenues and all other sources were still to be collected, and while still vulnerable to negative impact. (Who, in the general audience, would actively go to a movie disowned by its own studio as a colossal flop?)

From a purely business standpoint, the money lost on *John Carter* was nothing to Disney, proportionally. But the announcement allowed Iger to draw focus away from *John Carter* and realign it to the upcoming *Avengers* and future *Star Wars* films. (The fact that he screwed Stanton, the Burroughs heirs, and the core Carter fans cost him no loss of sleep, I'm sure.)

Iger replaced Dick Cook with Rich Ross. He put Ross in place under the new mandate for Disney to become more of a distribution hub servicing client producers, rather than being a content generator. (Somewhere, not only is Walt Disney turning over in his grave … he is on a rotisserie.) Ross came aboard two months prior to *John Carter* going into production, but he was uninvolved with the production, other than hiring professional PR flack MT Carney to spearhead the marketing of the film, a decision with catastrophic effects.

MT Carney was a marketing goddess brought in by Ross and Cook, who made the decision to change the title of the film from *John Carter of Mars* to, simply, *John Carter* … in an effort to appeal to women. (Let the supreme stupidity of that sink in for a moment … a project that was bought to appeal to male adventure fans was neutered to appeal to … young girls. I'll retire to Bedlam.)

Worse still, her instincts were spectacularly off on every facet of the campaign. Social media was largely silent, nothing was done to build buzz, there was no outreach to Burroughs (or science fiction) fandom, the marketing visuals were dull and … the sole images that seemed to penetrate to the public were largely the arena fight, making viewers think *John Carter* was nothing more than *Attack of the Clones* and water. Soon after *John Carter*, Carney returned to New York and non-Hollywood accounts. But the damage was done.

Equally inexplicable was the critical and fan reaction to the film. Take, for instance, David Denby in his review for *The New Yorker*, in the March 26 issue.

John Carter (Taylor Kitsch) finds Dejah Thoris (Lynn Collins) to be a warrior in her own right, and not just a damsel to be rescued.

The stories and novels behind Classic Horror, Fantasy and Science Fiction Films

Modern technology makes the outlandish visions of Edgar Rice Burroughs possible: here we see for the first time the white apes of Mars, one of the most enduring images of the early novels. The hero-in-arena concept Burroughs originated was later stolen for *Star Wars: Attack of the Clones*.

One is used to a certain amount of fatuity in the genre opinions of mainstream critics (and, sadly, genre critics, as well). Denby seemed constitutionally unable to take the film on its own terms—a planetary romance with no pretentions to art. Fatuity, however, seems to be Denby's stock in trade during his review. His bias is clear in the second sentence: "Andrew Stanton's *John Carter*, based on an ancient novel by Edgar Rice Burroughs (written at about the same time as *Tarzan*), begins with a battle on Mars ... "

Hold the phone. "An ancient novel by Edgar Rice Burroughs??" One wonders how he would describe a film adaptation of *Hamlet*. "Based on the

IT CAME FROM ...

super-duper ancient play by William Shakespeare?" What did he say about *Troy?* "Based on *The Iliad,* which is so old that we can't even imagine its age?" Pfui. Later on in his review, Denby also adds: "I wouldn't trust the sanity of any critic who claimed to understand what goes on in this movie." Frankly, I would not trust the intelligence of any critic who couldn't. Denby is the author of quite an excellent book on bad behavior called *Snark.* Sadly, I don't think he took his own writing to heart.

More egregiously tone deaf were the responses from many in the science fiction community, who one imagines would at least know better. (Or, at least, know something of the history of their genre.) The number of genre critics who wrote off *John Carter* as a rip-off of either *Avatar* or *Star Wars* is literally gob-smacking. Indeed many bragged about their ignorance of the source material. The number of ever-ridiculous YouTube pundits who used the words 'ancient' and 'old timey' are enough to diminish your faith in human nature. A parenthetical note on the revolting locution "old timey." Millennials use it indiscriminately, employing "old-timey" to describe everything from classic American cinema to the Italian Renaissance. For many contemporary science fiction fans, I believe "old-timey" can be defined either as (1) anything pre-2000 or (2) anything worthwhile and irony-free. Nostalgia has a rather bad name today; it is associated with backwards thinking, slowed development, or an escape from reality. Actually, "old-timey" is a meaningless phrase that often leaves this author reaching for the nearest weapon (or heaviest dictionary)— and its practice should not be encouraged.

Soon after the premiere of *John Carter,* I caucused with several science fiction fans, all of whom were in their mid-twenties at the time of the film's debut. Without exception, not one of them had intended to see it, one openly deriding "anything that old as inherently cheesy." I am often amazed at how contemptuous science fiction fans are of the rich and varied history of their genre, and how closed they are to engaging with the classics. For those who would rather see a film like *Star Wars: The Last Jedi* than a sequel to *John Carter,* I have nothing to add other than Lord love you and good luck. But by and large, contemporary culture is suspicious of anything older than the milk in its refrigerator.

Fortunately, devotees of Burroughs have the finished film, regardless of its success (or lack of it). *John Carter* hit this critic in a particularly vital place, and it's impossible for me to consider it outside of my devotion to Burroughs' novels. I cannot think about Burroughs without remembering the summers of my youth. I make it a point to at least revisit one of his novels every year, or, if possible, read one I have not come across before.

If you are immune to the call of literary science fiction, you would do well to visit the film version of *John Carter.* It represents the best of what the genre once was.

The stories and novels behind Classic Horror, Fantasy and Science Fiction Films

The Sun Won't Come Out Tomorrow: Tomorrowland (2015) and the Current Malaise

We live in an era where cinematic adaptations have evolved from novels and plays and into a brave new range of potential properties. Video games have been turned into films (*Super Mario Brothers*- 1993), old radio shows (*The Lone Ranger*, 2013, and *The Shadow*, 1994), television series (everything from *The Flintstones*, 1994, to *The Untouchables*, 1987), even animated cartoons have been turned into live-action cinema (*Transformers*, 2007, *Beauty and Beast*, 2017). It would seem that most anything is grist for the Hollywood mill.

But perhaps the strangest manifestation of this adaptation mania is the urge to turn theme parks and rides into cinematic narratives. Disney had an unusual bit of luck with the vapid and flaccid *Pirates of the Caribbean* franchise, built on their celebrated ride, and tried again with the infinitely more interesting and subtle *Tomorrowland* (2015).

If the book you hold now has been about anything, it is an exploration of what it is that makes a good adaptation. Does fidelity to the source material mean success? Surely not, as the film *Planet of the Apes* (1968) is arguably better than its source material, Pierre Boulle's interesting *La Planète des singes* (1963). Is it only adapting from good (or better than good) sources? One wouldn't think so, as *This Island Earth* (1955) is a crackerjack film based on the most wretched and disposable science fiction hackwork.

Perhaps great adaptations are largely matters of tone; a discussion between an original artist (the author) and an interpretive one (the artisans who make a film). Or, perhaps, not. It seems to me that the key to a good (or great) adaptation is something that can stand on its own, and also has within it something of the tone and ambition of the earlier work.

Tomorrowland is remarkable for any number of reasons, and that question of tone is the core of its success. *Tomorrowland* has no wish to "adapt" the theme park that names it; rather it seeks to have a detailed conversation of the historical moment that produced the Tomorrowland park, the changes in our national psyche (mostly for the worst) since that historical moment, and what it would mean to get it back.

It is also—and this is perhaps the most amazing thing of all about *Tomorrowland*—a remarkable example of an *anti-adaptation*, a stunning and effective denunciation of another work. Because while *Tomorrowland* takes its name from the Disneyland theme park, the film is director Brad Bird's impassioned takedown of William Gibson's seminal cyberpunk story, *The Gernsback Continuum*.

The Gernsback Continuum is a 1981 short story by William Gibson original-ly published in the anthology *Universe 11*, and later reprinted in the author's short-story collection, *Burning Chrome*. Cyberpunk was the harbinger of doom for literary science fiction, which soon found itself mired in fashionable but empty nihilism, cultural Marxism, virtue-signaling, and confusing political correctness, and an aesthetic that could only be called *failure chic*.

Cyberpunk stories are often set in a near future, where the streets are dirty, and it's always raining and 3:00 in the morning. They often feature advanced technologies in the hands of gangsters or street people, or ubiquitous evil corporations driving consumerist dystopias. Where much previous science fiction gazed at the stars, cyberpunk was obsessed primarily with the gutters. Cyberpunk is not only in opposition to the gee-whiz aesthetic of so much 1930s science fiction, but also downright antagonistic towards it. The aspirational sentiment found in everything from "Doc" Smith's *Lensmen* books to *Star Trek* is not in evidence in cyberpunk; in fact, such a sentiment would be unthink-able. If the *Superman* mythos originated in cyberpunk, the story would begin and end with the destruction of Krypton—and that would be "bad ass." In a cyberpunk canon, *Buck Rogers* awakens 500 years hence only to be cannibalized by zoned-out zombies in jerry-rigged dune buggies.

You can have it.

The poisonous seeds of cyberpunk (and the resulting dissolution of science fiction) are found in the larger, "intellectual" Postmodernism movement.

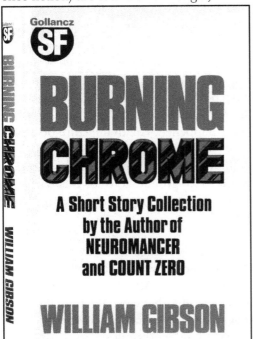

Postmodernism rejects grand nar-ratives, ideologies, and denigrates such ideas as objective truth, cul-tural superiority, and a shared common humanity. Culture, iden-tity, and even facts all become rel-ative. The great strides we have made, thanks to the Postmodernist "liberations" of the 1960s, are the bragging rights of the morally and culturally bankrupt. The end of an American communal identity, national pride, self-respect—all of these things became passé, thanks to this revolutionizing of the whole fabric of American society. Many of our societal ills are the results of, or reactions to, this wicked cant: BLM terrorists, TSA, and

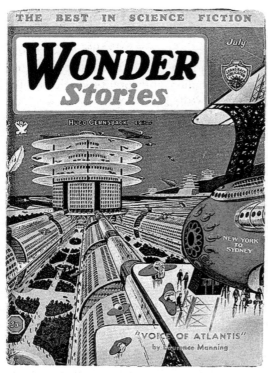

NSA over-reach, burnt-out cities, multigenerational welfare plebes, Islamic terrorist apologists, the dissolution of institutions like marriage, civic-mindedness ... all of that is the glorious legacy of Postmodernism. If a science fiction novelist of 1933 conceived our current reality, it would be received as the direst of dystopias ... a perception that is inherently correct.

It is useful to review the narrative of *The Gernsback Continuum*, because in it can be found many of the story-points of its brighter mirror image, *Tomorrowland*. The major difference is that *Tomorrowland* bemoans our creeping and ever-escalating societal decay, while *The Gernsback Continuum* celebrates it.

The Gernsback Continuum concerns a successful and unnamed freelance photographer. He is hired by a publisher to take photos for an upcoming book by pop culture historian, Dialta Downes, called *The Airstream Futuropolis: The Tomorrow That Never Was*. Downes is a devotee of what she calls American Streamlined Moderne (and the publisher calls Raygun Gothic)—or, the science fiction-inspired art deco that had a popular American vogue in the 1930s, culminating in the 1939 World's Fair. As Downes says, "Think of it as a kind of alternate America: a 1980 that never happened. An architecture of broken dreams."

The narrator spends his time photographing the ruins of this lost art deco Utopia around California, which seems to be ground zero for this particular dream. His take on much of this architecture in sneering condescension, mixed with a touch of Leftist political hysteria:

> When I isolated a few of the factory buildings on the ground glass of the Hasselblad, they came across with a kind of sinister totalitarian dignity, like the stadiums Albert Speer built for Hitler. But the rest of it was relentlessly tacky: ephemeral stuff extruded by the collective American subconscious of the 1930s, tending mostly to survive along depressing strips lined

with dusty motels, mattress wholesalers, and small used-car
lots. I went for the gas stations in a big way.

His take on the gas stations is of particular interest to connoisseurs of vin-
tage science fiction:

> They put Ming the Merciless in charge of designing Califor-
> nia gas stations, favoring the architecture of his native Mongo;
> he cruised up and down the coast erecting raygun emplace-
> ments in white stucco. Lots of them featured superfluous cen-
> tral towers ringed with those strange radiator flanges that were
> a signature motif of the style, and made them look as though
> they might generate potent bursts of raw technological enthu-
> siasm, if you could only find the switch that turns them on.

Parenthetically, the Ming the Merciless crack is a nice, snappy line, but it
makes little internal sense. Gibson's beef with the Gernsback school is not only
the philosophy, but the aesthetic. The aesthetic of *Flash Gordon* has always been
the default setting of most Planetary Romance: a mix of medieval and late
19th century-Pan-Europeanism. The comic strip apotheosis of the Gernsback
aesthetic is *Buck Rogers*, particularly as drawn in the 1930s by Dick Calkins and
Rick Yager. But "Killer Kane" is not quite as snappy as "Ming the Merciless,"
so we'll have to give the point to Gibson.

Back to the story—enmeshing in all of this delicious futurism, the narrator
starts to see visions. Massive single-wing airplanes out of *Tom Swift*, along with
whole futuristic cityscapes:

> The books on the 1930s design were in the trunk; one of them
> contained sketches of an idealized city that drew on *Metrop-
> olis* and *Things to Come*, but squared everything, soaring up
> through an architect's perfect clouds to zeppelin docks and
> mad neon spires. That city was a scale model of the one that
> rose behind me. Spire stood on spire in gleaming ziggurat
> steps that climbed to the central golden temple tower ringed
> with the crazy radiator flanges of Mongo gas stations. You
> could hide the Empire State Building in the smallest of those
> towers. Roads of crystal soared between the spires, crossed
> and re-crossed by smooth silver shapes like beads of running
> mercury. The air was thick with ships: giant wing-liners, little
> darting silver things (sometimes one of the quicksilver shapes
> from the sky bridges rose gracefully into the air and flew up to
> join the dance), mile-long blimps, hovering dragonfly things

The stories and novels behind Classic Horror, Fantasy and Science Fiction Films

that were gyrocopters ... Behind me, the illuminated city: Searchlights swept the sky for the sheer joy of it. I imagined them thronging the plazas of white marble, orderly and alert, their bright eyes shining with enthusiasm for their floodlit avenues and silver cars.

Concerned for his mental health, the narrator meets with his friend, Merv Kihn, a "free-lance journalist with an extensive line in Texas pterodactyls, redneck UFO contactees, bush-league Loch Ness monsters, and the Top Ten conspiracy theories in the loonier reaches of the American mass mind." Kihn tells our nominal hero that what he sees are "semiotic ghosts," a sort of ectoplasmic residue from the mass consciousness. Kihn tells him not to worry too much about it, and that the visions will soon fade. However, driving back to Los Angeles, the narrator has one more vision, one that nearly drives him over the edge. It is of a futuristic couple on the side of the road, and he describes them as having "all the sinister fruitiness of Hitler Youth propaganda"(!):

They were blond. They were standing beside their car, an aluminum avocado with a central shark-fin rudder jutting up from its spine and smooth black tires like a child's toy. He had his arm around her waist and was gesturing toward the city. They were both in white; loose clothing, bare legs, spotless white sun shoes. Neither of them seemed aware of the beams of my headlights. He was saying something wise and strong and she was nodding, and suddenly I was frightened, frightened in an entirely different way. Sanity had ceased to be an issue; I knew, somehow, that the city behind me was Tucson—a dream Tucson thrown up out of the collective yearning of an era. That it was real, entirely real. But the couple in front of me lived in it, and they frightened me.

Terrified beyond belief by a vision more reminiscent of *The Jetsons* than Leni Riefenstahl, our narrator again runs babbling to Kihn, who has a novel cure in mind. Kihn tells our narrator that he can cure himself of these visions of our better selves by immersing himself in current popular culture: our soap operas, game shows, and pornography. Getting back to Los Angeles, and getting the book pictures out of the way, the narrator goes to a showing of *Nazi Love Motel*. It seems to do the trick. When a newspaper salesmen murmurs, "Hell of a world we live in, huh?," our narrator tells him it could be worse. "It could be perfect."

So. What seems so cloying about Gibson's story is his celebratory wallow in *failure chic*. He laces signs of our societal decay throughout the story, and serves them as a favorable contrast to a Gernsback future. Gibson's world of choice is peppered with the following references: "dead" restaurant food, casual drug use, cattle mutilation, crumbling pharmaceutical products, beer can-strewn roads, rattlesnakes and cannibal hippies, old brothels, amphetamine psychosis, crushed cigarettes, bad Spanish Modern architecture, sleazy popular culture, Nazi porn, and closing with a news dealer with "bad teeth and an obvious wig."

As our narrator says:

> And as I moved among these secret ruins, I found myself wondering what the inhabitants of that lost future would think of the world I lived in. The 1930s dreamed white marble and slipstream chrome, immortal crystal and burnished bronze ...

What, indeed, one must ask ...

Sadly, for over 30 years, science fiction has largely followed Gibson's lead. In accordance with most Postmodernists, decay is somehow more "authentic," good riddance to a dying cultural West, and dreams of shared community and sweeping technological progress (a better world reaching for the stars) are met with snickers in our Ivory Towers. The dream of a better tomorrow—that jetpack age first glimpsed in the 1930s and lasting to the end of our aborted Space Age—died at the hands of Postmodern academics and the young people they intellectually poisoned. The rot spread throughout our culture, and shows no signs of abating.

It is instructive to contrast the inspiration for *Tomorrowland* (the place and the film) with Gibson and the state of Postmodern science fiction.

When Tomorrowland first opened in Disneyland in 1955, Walt Disney invited visitors into a "vista into a world of wondrous ideas, signifying Man's achievements ... a step into the future, with predictions of constructed things to come. Tomorrow offers new frontiers in science, adventure, and ideals. The Atomic Age, the challenge of Outer Space, and the hope for a peaceful, unified world."

An old-fashioned futurist of the Gernsback stripe, Disney viewed tomorrow through a gleaming prism that borrowed heavily on Buck Rogers. Born of a generation that lived through the Great

The stories and novels behind Classic Horror, Fantasy and Science Fiction Films

---

TOMORROWLAND

On the Autopia, the Freeway of Tomorrow, young and old will thrill to a ride in one of the Autopia cars, and no trip to Disneyland will be complete without a ride on one of the 14 speed-boats in Tomorrowland Lake.

The TWA Rocket Ride to the Moon will also be a thrilling experience. The Luna and Diana each accommodate 104 passengers and are at your service.

In Tomorrowland you can also see the "20,000 Leagues Under the Sea" exhibit. Here you will find the Nautilus and the giant squid that were immortalized in Walt Disney's recent motion picture.

From Space Station X-1 you will be able to see the planet Earth as though you were 500 miles up in the sky.

Long Beach Independent July 16, 1955

Depression and two devastating World Wars, Disney was incapable of imagining anything other than a better tomorrow. Walt Disney has been described as one of the great futurists, and he certainly was an advocate of cutting-edge technology. Throughout his career, he employed often-experimental techniques to get the results he wanted. Nor did he think human imagination should have boundaries; this is a man who said, "If you can dream it, you can build it." That phrase, more than anything, perfectly encapsulates the vision of *Tomorrowland*, the movie and the place, and stands as a stunning rebuke of Gibson and our contemporary mindset. We no longer have time, energy, or room for visionaries that say, "It's fun to do the impossible."

It is hard for us in 2020 to remember how influential Disney was during the Space Age. On *The Wonderful World of Disney*, the great man would often gush about space ships, monorails, and the coming interplanetary age. His imaginings carried over to reality—concepts created at Walt Disney found real-world applications during the Space Race. He mused: "Tomorrow can be a wonderful age. Our scientists today are opening the doors of the Space Age to achievements that will benefit our children and generations to come. The Tomorrowland attractions have been designed to give you an opportunity to participate in adventures that are a living blueprint of our future."

That blueprint reflected the aesthetic of 1930s pulp magazines. The theme park was initially underfunded at its debut, but several corporate sponsors helped by adding pavilions of their own. In this way, the nascent Tomorrowland was much like the 1939 World's Fair (often cited as the greatest in the history of fairs); the 1939 Fair sought to imagine the world of 1980; Tomorrowland presented a vision of life in far-off 1986. Disney imagined a Moonliner, a House of the Future, and Autopia—envisioning supercars and highways.

Tomorrowland got a major facelift in 1967, employing many of the devices and plans that Disney had created for the historic 1964 World's Fair. With its improved rocket imagery and gleaming white lines splashed with brilliant color, it is this incarnation of Tomorrowland that has entered into myth; the purist distillation of Disney's future aesthetic. (The 1964 Fair also plays a role in the film *Tomorrowland*.)

IT CAME FROM ...

Tomorrowland in 1967

Tomorrowland would get a facelift again and again throughout the ensuing decades, but an underlying challenge with each redesign was that our vision of the future had changed … for the worse. In a time when most people are energized by post-apocalyptic landscapes, what was Disney to do? With no positive vision for the future, the park has instead slipped into crass commercialism, and Tomorrowland is little more than a mediation on all things *Star Wars*.

But in its heyday, Tomorrowland was all about the collective effort to build a better tomorrow. It said that we had the ability, the will, and the communal responsibility to build Utopia—and that this dream of today would inevitably become the reality of tomorrow.

If only.

It is no surprise that the inspiration for Bird's cinematic version of *Tomorrowland* found little acceptance in the science fiction climate of 2015. Though it narrowly squeaked into first place at the box office its opening weekend (barely beating out a sequel, *Pitch Perfect 2*), each succeeding week saw its fortunes decline dramatically. (The film has grossed a total of $93.4 million in North America and a worldwide total of $209.2 million against an estimated cost of $330 million.) This is a great shame since *Tomorrowland* is not only an enjoyable and beguiling romp, but it is the only summer blockbuster in recent memory that actively asks something of its audience, and even questions the nature of what a summer blockbuster means.

Tomorrowland confounded expectations by relying heavily on theme and message to propel the story, with special effects eye-candy as only a secondary concern. More important, unlike the vast majority of summer films, *Tomorrow-land* seeks to actually say something, and the message is not one that contemporary audiences wanted to hear.

The plot of *Tomorrowland* reads like an inverted *Gernsback Continuum*: Casey Newton (Britt Robertson) is an extremely bright young woman chomping at the bit to use her intelligence to make the world a better place. Her father (Tim McGraw) is an engineer at NASA, who will soon be out of a job, as the space agency rapidly moves away from the early 1960s promise of actually doing space exploration.

After being arrested for trying to halt the shutdown of a NASA launch site, Casey finds a pin that, whenever she touches it, shows her visions of a glossy, high-tech Utopia—Tomorrowland. As she seeks to learn more about this Buck Rogers-inspired paradise, she meets a mysterious child, Athena (Raffey Cassidy), who leads her to Frank Walker (George Clooney), an ex-boy genius who first entered Tomorrowland when he brought his home-made rocket pack to the 1964 World's Fair. (In a particularly poignant moment, we see young Walker going to the Fair alone by bus—something unthinkable for American children today.) The trio face dangers from both our world and the world of Tomorrowland as they try to find their way back in, and seek to pull our own world back from the brink of self-destruction.

There is a brief interlude where Casey and Athena battle homicidal robots in Blast From the Past, a science fiction-themed antique shop. One of the killer robots is named Hugo, in homage to Hugo Gernsback, and the shop is festooned with visions of a tomorrow that never came: personal rocket ships, robots, ray guns, and all manner of trinkets from everything from *Buck Rogers* and *Flash Gordon* to *Lost in Space* and *Star Wars*. After these semiotic ghosts are destroyed (to use a Gibsonian phrase), the girls make their way to Paris, along with a reluctant Walker.

In Paris, Casey learns of a group of inventors, visionaries, and dreamers called *Plus Ultra*. Founded by Gustave Eiffel, Jules Verne, Nikola Tesla, and Thomas Edison (or, as the Academy would have them, the ultimate DWEMs: dead white European Males). After a harrowing journey, Casey makes it into Tomorrowland, but opens it up so that everyone who dreams of a better tomorrow is able to enter.

As of this writing, *Tomorrowland* has a 50/50 rating among Top Critics on that most basic tool for movie buffs, RottenTomatoes.com. This is not surprising, considering how it seems that no two critics see the same movie. *Tomorrow-land* is a critical and cultural Rorschach test—tell me what you think of it, and your aesthetics are laid bare.

Many critics were savage, following what Harold Bloom calls the School of Resentment. For example, Charles Paul Freund at Reason.com has condemned the film as an Ayn Rand fable for Objectivism. In this reading, only the elite

are allowed to enter Tomorrowland, and the fruits of its discoveries are not for the masses. (Barry Hertz at the *Globe and Mail* wrote of director Brad Bird: "Unless you're preternaturally gifted—unless you're part of the 0.01 percent of us who are truly special, whose self-made superiority is undeniable—the writer-director behind *Tomorrowland* can't be bothered.") Other critics, John Nolte at Brietbart.com for example, dismiss *Tomorrowland* as a liberal save-the-Earth-from-global-warming screed, too mired in science fantasy to even enjoy the label of science fiction. Some perceive the future-vision of *Tomorrowland* as based on a white-male aesthetic, and is thus automatically suspect; others feel that the inclusive, multinational vision it presents is merely a liberal sop. In short, responses to *Tomorrowland* are all over the map.

Even the critical arm of the science fiction community seems immune to the messages of *Tomorrowland*. Critical assessments in tightly cloistered fan communities are often driven by agendas or allegiances that make little sense to the uninitiated, but even by that yardstick, *Tomorrowland* has taken a licking. For example, in an insight of staggering vacuity on the science fiction news blog io9.com, Charlie Jane Anders dismisses the film as so much "Baby-Boomer nostalgia at its most dreary," and opines that the film ultimately "winds up feeling so much like you're listening to a cranky rant about how things were so much better 50 years ago."

Well ... yes, that's really the point. And it is a point that the viewer takes *con amore*, or not at all. *Tomorrowland* asks—directly, to the viewer's face—why were we more optimistic 50 years ago when we had less than when we now have more? (At one point, Clooney says, "The future looked different when I was a kid.") And why, more importantly, are we glutting ourselves on apoca-

Tomorrowland **traded on an optimistic future that is now taboo in the current American cultural landscape.**

lyptic rubbish like *Mad Max: Fury Road*? And why does our current world look so drab, so colorless, so … ugly?

Because, as *Tomorrowland* leader David Nix (Hugh Laurie) says, we like things that ask nothing of us. We, as a people, as a culture, and as a nation of former dreamers, have given up. We would rather watch the world burn than save it, and woe to us for our self-fulfilling fantasies, predetermining our own failures. *Tomorrowland* holds up a mirror to our contemporary culture, and the reflection is not at all a pretty one.

It is a simple and sad reality of our culture that we have lost the taste for imagining a Big Future. These imaginings were once the national pastime of writers, moviemakers, pulp magazine artists, and young people (and people young at heart) everywhere. Our visions of tomorrow were suffused with a bright metallic art deco glow. The Big Future had a raw energy, a gee-whiz feel for boundless possibility, and a sense of expansion. It may have been junk, but it was glorious junk. And somewhere along the way, we just turned our backs on it.

Tomorrowland is an attempt to turn science fiction and pop culture away from its current nihilistic obsessions and channel that energy into something that celebrates life and imagines the Big Future. The failure of this film is—and I kid you not—the failure of an America that no longer dreams big. An America that consumes negativity because negativity asks nothing of its audience; an America that has broken itself down into groups of powerless, self-defined victims; and an America that has drifted dangerously from its can-do moorings and is currently sailing away into aesthetic and intellectual irrelevance.

It is instructive to look at two other science fiction films released that same summer that have done terrific box office. *Avengers: Age of Ultron* has grossed over $1.3 billion worldwide, while the post-apocalyptic fantasia *Mad Max: Fury Road* has garnered $378.4 million worldwide.

Mad Max: Fury Road is more of the same as other films in the series—leather-clad roughnecks duke it out over gasoline in a post-nuclear wasteland. It is, in short, another brutal tale of survival in a future world of moral decadence. *Avengers: Age of Ultron* is perhaps more insidious as its messages lie at the rotten core of a loud superhero spectacle. One of the centerpieces of the film is a building collapsing under the brunt of an attack from the Hulk—and the audience is treated to seemingly endless scenes of white-dust covered survivors, tears darkly streaking their faces, in yet another junk film reference to September 11. It would be inconceivable for the heroes of *Tomorrowland* to so fetishize such a national tragedy, and it's a mystery as to why we, as a nation, have never been able to come to grips with it. Perhaps *Age of Ultron* provides its own answer. At the end, hero Vision (played by Paul Bettany, sounding like Peter Lawford and looking like Gumby) and villain Ultron (voiced by James Spader) agree that mankind is "doomed."

Tomorrowland has generated more critical meditations than ticket sales, and it is this ongoing discussion that may give the film legs and relevance (if not success) for years to come. Perhaps *Tomorrowland* will act like one of the pins in its own narrative, generating visions of a possible super-science tomorrow for those drowning in our drab environs. *Tomorrowland* says that things do not have to be the way they currently are, and that each and every one of us has it in our power to make that gleaming tomorrow, if we have the heart and the hands to build it.

Look at the response to *Tomorrowland*, however, and that may be one supposition where optimism would not actually pay off.

Love Bites:
The Many Faces of Dracula

With the following chapters on *Dracula* and *Frankenstein*, two of the most well known and enduring novels in the fantasy/horror genre, we thought it would be fun to look at not just one, but several of the best, worst, and most popular of their film adaptations.

The basic storyline of each novel is so well known to readers of this book as to make a synopsis redundant. However, if you haven't read, or recently reread, Mary Shelley's *Frankenstein* or Bram Stoker's *Dracula*, you are doing yourself a disservice. They are the cornerstone classics of the Gothic Horror canon, and each rewards multiple readings.

IT CAME FROM ...

Nosferatu (1922)

Perhaps the finest movie interpretation of *Dracula* was also the earliest: *Nosferatu.* Actor Max Schreck (1879-1936) portrayed the vampire as pestilence incarnate, and with his sharp talons, pointy ears, rat-like teeth, and bald pate, Schreck's Count Orlock was hardly a creature welcome in the drawing room mystery plays of the time.

Produced by Prana Films, an artistic collective that folded after this single production, *Nosferatu* was the focus of widow Florence Stoker's wrath for nearly a decade. Though freely adapting the novel *Dracula* (names are changed and the narrative is streamlined), the film is unmistakably a retelling of Stoker's book. Designed as an "art film," *Nosferatu* was Murnau's response to the horrors of post World War I Germany. It was an enormous success upon its release, and sustained a Continental vogue.

This enraged Mrs. Stoker, who received no royalties from the film. Not only was she outraged by the frankly horrific nature of the film (so much so that contemporary historians wonder if she ever actually *read* her husband's

Bram Stoker's widow sued the filmmakers of *Nosferatu* (1922) over copyright infringement, and all prints of the film were ordered to be destroyed. Luckily, a few copies survived.

novel), but money was tight for the widow at this time, and *Dracula* was virtually her husband's sole legacy to her. Her legal pursuit of Prana led to naught. The company dissolved before she could receive any money from them. She had to content herself with the promise that the negative and all existing prints of the film would be destroyed.

Fortunately for cinema buffs, this Dracula escaped to America. In its original state, the film featured color-tinted scenes and a modernist musical score, composed by Hans Erdmann. It has recently been restored, both in Europe and the United States, and can now be seen in something approximating its original glory.

Nosferatu is a masterpiece of mood. The scenes in Castle Dracula have a vivid, otherworldly feel, while the boat trip is wonderfully creepy. The moments where Dracula makes his way in his new home, coffin under his arm, dance with surrealism. It would be more than 50 years before Dracula films could match its artful imagery.

Surprisingly, *Nosferatu* is still able to generate scares in contemporary audiences. That is probably because a palpable air of disease and decay seems to permeate the film, as if some toxic substance was unspooling on the screen. This sense of the "reality" of *Nosferatu* came into play in the 2000 film *Shadow*

IT CAME FROM ...

of the Vampire, whose conceit is that Schreck really was a vampire. A high-camp joke that never quite comes off, *Shadow of the Vampire* is rapidly fading from the popular zeitgeist, while *Nosferatu* seems as powerful as ever.

Nosferatu is responsible for one of the great misconceptions of Dracula lore: that the Vampire King can be destroyed by sunlight. In Stoker's novel, Dracula's powers are minimal during the day, but sunlight will not destroy him. It was only after *Nosferatu*, when the rat-faced vampire vanished in a puff of smoke at the film's finale, that the lethal effects of sunlight were grafted onto the legend.

Schreck—whose name, coincidentally, means "terror" in German—is simply marvelous as the repugnant Orlock. Like Dorian Gray's attic portrait, Orlock seems to grow uglier as his sins escalate. His talons grow longer, the rat-like configuration of his face grows more pronounced, and his movements become yet more stylized. Though he does not physically resemble Stoker's description, Schreck probably comes closer to the author's idea conceptually than any other actor to play the role.

The film makes considerable use of location shooting—Dracula's castle is indeed a *real* castle—and the brooding Germanic countryside is more effective than any other Transylvania committed to celluloid. Here is Dracula captured on film in his homeland, only 25 years after his literary debut.

Schreck left the promise of a secure place in the business world to become an actor. He worked with Max Reinhardt before entering films, and continued to act until the year of his death. Schreck's crowning achievement, *Nosferatu*, is now considered one of the masterpieces of German silent cinema. The make-up used continues to linger in the consciousness of moviegoers, and has been adapted for everything from Tobe Hooper's *Salem's Lot* (1979), to the vampire mockumentary *What We Do in the Shadows* (2014). The film's high regard has only come in recent years, long after Murnau or Schreck were alive to enjoy its rediscovery.

Actor Bela Lugosi: still the most iconic screen Count.

IT CAME FROM ...

Dracula (1931)

A deeply flawed film that started a strain of Gothic cinema that continues to this day.

When actor Bela Lugosi (1882-1956) fled to the United States to continue his career as an actor, he had no idea that he would become America's premiere bogeyman. Lugosi entered the states when he jumped ship in New Orleans, later making his way to New York and its Hungarian theater community.

There, Lugosi won several parts in well-reviewed shows, starting with *The Red Poppy*, which opened at the Greenwich Village Theater in December 1922. His impassioned performance as the Spanish Fernando—a role that the Hungarian-speaking actor had to learn phonetically—took New York by storm. According to legend, Lugosi's onstage lovemaking was so passionate he broke one of co-star Estelle Winwood's ribs. Winwood, in later interviews, both verified and denied the tale.

Whatever the truth, it was certain that Lugosi's studied intensity marked him for stardom. The actor worked in several shows, including *The Werewolf* and *Arabesque*, before landing the title role in the 1926 production of *Dracula*, loosely based on Bram Stoker's novel.

When *Dracula* premiered in Broadway's Fulton Theater, neither the critics nor the audience realized that they were witnessing the creation of one of modern theater history's great signature roles. Though Lugosi was generally praised for his work, the thought of a supernatural protagonist on the Broadway stage was a concept that took a while to settle in. The passion that Lugosi brought to the part—he so mesmerized actress Clara Bow at a performance of *Dracula* that it was the start of a stormy romance between the "IT" girl and the undead Valentino—along with his intensity, strange intonation, and charisma, made Dracula acceptable to critics and audiences alike.

And the rest is history. *Dracula* both secured and destroyed the actor's future career. Lugosi went to Hollywood to repeat his stage triumph in the Universal Pictures version, directed by Tod Brown-

Lugosi takes a bite out of Broadway (and Dorothy Peterson).

ing. Sadly, Browning fumbled the ball badly with *Dracula*, which is unusually slow, stagey, and … pedestrian. Browning initially sought Lon Chaney for the role, but following the death of his most important collaborator, it seems as if Browning lost his taste for the project. Whatever the reason, it's clear that *Dracula* meant little to Browning.

Brilliant publicity shot for *Dracula* (1931) involving (l-to-r) Bela Lugosi, David Manners, Helen Chandler, Dwight Frye, and Edward Van Sloan, in character

The finished film is such a hodgepodge of both effective moments and missed opportunities that modern audiences often don't know how to grade it. The early scenes with Lugosi and Dwight Frye (as the luckless Renfield) in Castle Dracula are wonderful, if stagey. The film continues its powerful hold through the boat trip to England, up until the discovery of the now insane Frye. But after that, the film never recovers, relying heavily on its stage inspiration. Things are described—Dracula turning into a bat, a wolf, an opaque mist—but never shown. Worse still, the rest of the cast never match Lugosi's intensity or investment in the material.

While Lugosi worked in the American version of *Dracula* during the day, actor Carlos Villarias starred in a Spanish-language version shot on the same sets at night. Director George Melford managed to create a much more fluid,

Carlos Villarias and Lupita Tovar

erotic, and exciting film than Browning, missing only Lugosi's charisma. While Villarias is an adequate stand-in, he is never more than a pallid imitation of Lugosi. (Melford even included out-take footage of Lugosi in his film.)

While Lugosi's hypnotic hand gestures often make him look like a human spider, Villarias' efforts to copy him only make the Spanish actor look like a malefic chipmunk. Though many critics find this alternate version technically better than Browning's finished film, it is the Lugosi version that was the more influential film.

That's because with *Dracula*, Browning and Lugosi created the contemporary horror film. Like an earlier tradition of Gothic literature, most "monsters" in Hollywood films of the era were explained away as involved contrivances on the part of the villain. It was only with *Dracula* that a supernatural anti-hero was allowed to take center stage, starting a tradition of monstrous movies that continues to this day. *Dracula* is the first modern horror film, and Lugosi, the genre's first star.

Receiving only a pittance for his work in the film, Lugosi waited for better offers to come in. They never did. Lugosi learned, as many later actors did, that Dracula is a tough act to follow. He made a tragic miscalculation in turning down the part of the Monster in *Frankenstein*, allowing future rival Boris Karloff to step into the role and eclipse Lugosi's star entirely. Together, Lugosi and Karloff starred in some of the horror genre's best-remembered films, including: *The Black Cat* (1934), *The Raven* (1935), and *The Invisible Ray* (1936).

After the early 1930s, Lugosi could only secure supporting parts at the major studios. But he continued to be treated as a star by independent operations, like Monogram Studios and PRC, where he made such forgettable potboilers as *The Devil Bat* (1941), *The Invisible Ghost* (1941), and *The Ape Man* (1943). Lugosi continued to play *Dracula* in stock and vaudeville shows throughout the 1940s and early 1950s. He repeated the role on film only once, in 1948's affectionate romp, *Abbott and Costello Meet Frankenstein*. In the early 1950s, Lugosi committed himself for treatment for medically induced drug addiction. Lurid photos from the era show the actor an emaciated shell of his former self—the Vampire King now a victim. Amazingly, he survived the rigors of his cure, left the hospital, and married for a fifth and final time.

Unfortunately, during this period, young Edward D. Wood, Jr., who would later win infamy as movieland's worst director, befriended the desperate-for-work Lugosi. Lugosi appeared in several forgettable features for Wood, including *Glen or Glenda* (1953), *Bride of the Monster* (1955), and he later shot footage that was slipped into *Plan 9 From Outer Space* (1959), Wood's tribute to his own incompetence.

Always eager for a comeback, Lugosi returned with a vengeance after death. With the advent of the Monster Craze in the late 1950s, Lugosi's image once more became valuable currency. His legend has continued to grow with time, perhaps reaching its apex when Martin

The stories and novels behind Classic Horror, Fantasy and Science Fiction Films

Landau won an Academy Award for his portrayal of the elderly Lugosi in Tim Burton's *Ed Wood* (1994).

Other actors would play Dracula (both John Carradine and Lon Chaney, Jr. did forgettable turns during Lugosi's lifetime), but they had large boots to fill. The Hungarian actor jealously holds the part from beyond the grave, staking a claim on the vampire that no other actor has managed to jump.

Actor Bela Lugosi *is* Dracula to the popular imagination. Never before—or since—has an actor become so defined by a solitary part. The identification was so great that for the rest of his life the actor was often billed as Bela "Dracula" Lugosi. No other actor's face, voice, inflections, or body language holds greater supremacy over the part than those of the Hungarian expatriate. Nor has any other actor so obsessively identified with the role; Lugosi was buried in his Dracula cape after playing the Count in two films and for decades on the stage.

Many actors to later essay the role found themselves hobbled by the long shadow of Lugosi. When Martin Landau played *Dracula* in a revival of the Edward Gorey production of the Broadway play, he found that audiences would accept nothing but the Lugosi conception. (And this, 10 years *before* Landau won the Academy Award for playing Lugosi in Tim Burton's *Ed Wood*.) Gary Oldman, a terrific actor who made his mark in challenging roles, frankly admitted that the voice he used in *Bram Stoker's Dracula* was "pure Lugosi."

As Dracula, Bela Lugosi has appeared on toys, games, model kits, and magazine covers. Any television or radio commercial employing Dracula also employs Lugosi, for it is the actor and not the part that other players use. Posters, greeting cards, record albums, Halloween costumes, iron-on patches, candy boxes, and bubble gum cards have all borne Lugosi's likeness.

In the gallery of pop icons, Lugosi's hold over his role is unshakable. Mention Sherlock Holmes to the casual fan, and images as diverse as Basil Rathbone, Peter Cushing, Jeremy Brett, or Benedict Cumberbatch may come to mind. Tarzan is little more than a generic muscleman, and Johnny Weismuller, Buster Crabbe, and Gordon Scott all blur in the memory. It is the costumes of both Batman and Superman that resonate with audiences, and not particular performances. But show a photograph of Bela Lugosi to anybody on the street, and the identification comes immediately: *that's* Dracula.

IT CAME FROM ...

Dracula (1958)

Like the Lugosi *Dracula* more than 20 years previous, the Terence Fisher (1904-1980) version of Stoker's novel starring Peter Cushing (1913-1994) and Christopher Lee (1922-2015) is a not very good film that has had a tremendous cultural impact.

Created at a critical time for the struggling English film industry, *Dracula*, like its predecessor *The Curse of Frankenstein* in 1957 (also starring Cushing and Lee), brought much needed attention to the British film and its production company, Hammer. Released at a time of loosening film mores, specifically concerning sex and violence, *Dracula* was able to stun viewers in ways the Lugosi version could not.

This was both good and bad for the company, as the use of vibrant color, along with judicious violence and hints of sex, made for several early potent genre pictures by Hammer. But as time progressed, Hammer became lazy in its product, releasing films that became increasingly tawdry and violent.

Of Hammer's early films, *The Curse of Frankenstein*, *Dracula*, and *The Mummy* (1959) are easily the best, the production company falling into a rapid decline with the advent of the 1960s. (Though out of the scope of this volume, *The Mummy* is quite a wonderful film, with Cushing at the top of his game, and comes highly recommended.) Aside from a fresh take on the character and the novel, it is difficult to see why Hammer's initial *Dracula* film made such an impact. Though not as stagey as its 1931 predecessor, it feels equally "cramped:" Dracula never leaves the Continent, his number of "wives" is reduced to one

The stories and novels behind Classic Horror, Fantasy and Science Fiction Films

(admittedly buxom) vamp, and the vast majority of the action takes place indoors. This gives the adaptation a loose kind of *Classics Illustrated* feel, but Hammer's initial *Dracula* borrows as little from Stoker as the 1931 version. The studio would continue to bleed the concept dry until the early 1970s, with each film becoming more ridiculous and irrelevant than the last. The total collapse of Hammer's Dracula series is a shame, because Hammer's first Dracula sequel, *The Brides of Dracula* (1960), is a minor classic of Dracula and horror cinema. Actor Peter Cushing, always Hammer's Most Valuable Player, carries both films, and his absence is felt in their immediate sequels. With his return to the series in the last two films, playing his own grandson (!), Cushing could easily have carried a film or television series centered around the supernatural exploits of the Van Helsing family, and left Dracula on the sidelines. Sadly, that was not to be ... but one can almost imagine an alternate universe where such a series of films, heavily flavored with exotic menace of the type delivered by Sax Rohmer, carried monster fans through the 1970s.

Though actor Lee would go on to play Dracula in more films than any other actor, he makes little impression, despite the affection held for his performance by many Baby Boomers. The total line-count for his seven Dracula films equals less dialogue and screen time than Bela Lugosi had in his initial, 1931 performance. Perhaps this was for the best because Lee's (few) line readings in the latter films are dull and windy, as if he knew he had to do little but mumble to receive his check. Wisely, Hammer's scenarists and directors elected to keep him mute (in *Dracula: Prince of Darkness*) or taciturn in most of the remaining films. Over time, Lee grew to hate his Dracula films, and publicly whined for a chance to play the part as written by Stoker. He received his chance in Jess Franco's ill-fated *Count Dracula*, a major embarrassment to all concerned. Lee actually mouthed some of Stoker's dialogue in this film, and showed that the character as originally conceived was completely and totally out of his limited range. Lee's turn as *Count Dracula* is bland and lifeless, lacking terror or resonance, and remains the worst performance by any actor as Dracula in a serious adaptation of the novel.

IT CAME FROM ...

Count Dracula (1970)

Jess (Jesus) Franco (1930-2013) was a Spanish film director with over 100 film credits, primarily low-budget entries in the horror and/or erotica genre. In 1969, he embarked on his latest project—an effort to bring to the screen a version of *Dracula* that more closely followed Stoker's book than any to date. Actor Christopher Lee, who had grown increasingly frustrated with the progressively bloody and violent direction Hammer *Dracula* series was taking, and who shared Franco's desire to realize a faithful adaptation, readily jumped on board with the project.

And indeed, the entire opening sequence detailing Harker's journey to, and subsequent time at, Castle Dracula is considerably faithful to Stoker and promisingly sets viewers up for what is to come. But Franco ultimately frustrates as, upon the Count's arrival in England (unforgivably eliminating the key sequence of his voyage aboard the Demeter), the film begins to unravel due both to the film's limited budget as well as unsuccessful deviations from the source material.

Not to say that all of Franco's changes are without merit however, as the film improves upon the novel in two respects. First, character Arthur Holmwood is completely removed from the film, replaced instead by Quincey Morris serving as Lucy's fiancé. Having one less character for viewers to focus on actually serves the film well. Secondly, Franco's film considerably abridges the novel's lengthy battle over the life of Lucy Westenra. Truth be told, Stoker is long-winded to the point of tedium far too often in his narrative, and the novel's sequence detailing Dracula's ongoing attacks on Lucy, and Van Helsing and company's efforts to save the girl, is a prime example. The film thus tightens up a much-needed aspect of the narrative by editing down this too-long sequence.

Dracula (Christopher Lee) bids Jonathan (Frederick Williams) welcome in Jess Franco's *Count Dracula* (1970).

Soledad Miranda and Christopher Lee

If only Franco's other deviations resulted in improvements. Some departures are merely head-scratching and/or annoying but ultimately of little consequence: the Count's ruse in luring Mina to an opera performance to attack her, Jonathan Harker being bitten (!) with no subsequent ramifications to the story, and Van Helsing suffering a stroke, confining him thenceforth to a wheelchair.

Other deviations, however, are more significant and have ramifications. The first involves the character of Renfield, played by the late, famed German actor, Klaus Kinski. Here, aside from screaming and moaning, Renfield is mute (at least until the very end of his life when he far too conveniently utters the one word that allows our heroes to know the Count's plans). By rendering Renfield speechless, lost are the novel's interesting, often philosophical, exchanges between the character and Dr. Seward. And it is through these very exchanges we come to realize that Renfield is *not* merely the raving, life-consuming maniac as portrayed in so many films, but a sympathetic, tortured individual, who fears not just for his physical life, but for the fate of his immortal soul as well. In Franco's film, as Kinski's attempt at characterization through mime is less than successful, we lose this subtlety and nuance of character. Kinski's Renfield thus becomes little more than superfluous. Our second major change involves the

IT CAME FROM ...

film's finale. Here, Harker and Morris (minus the wheelchair-bound Van Helsing) journey to Dracula's Castle ahead of the Count. Upon the arrival of Gypsies driving the cart containing Dracula's coffin, Harker and Morris proceed to drop fantastically phony-looking "boulders" down from their hiding spot, killing some and sending the others scurrying away. Approaching the still-resting vampire, our heroes set fire to the coffin in which Dracula ages to bones as the flames slowly consume him. To say that this finale is wholly unsatisfying is a gross understatement. Ignoring the novel's exhilarating climax—complete with chase sequence, battles with Gypsies, and finally Dracula's gory but fitting denouement—was a bad decision by all concerned, resulting in an ending that lands with a thud duller than those from the phony boulders.

Damaging as these deviations are to Franco's film, they become trivial when compared to the director's execution of the passage from Stoker's novel where our heroes encounter an army of rats at Carfax. Here instead—with faithfulness to the source material understandably moot at this point—in a scene that truly needs to be seen to be believed, our heroes are "attacked" by a collection of … taxidermied animals. (Yes.) Alternating close-ups of a stuffed owl, boar, ferret, mounted swordfish (yes), and other unidentifiable animals are either shaken in place or moved slightly toward the camera, accompanied by ridiculous "animal" shrieks as well as music appro-

priate to three men being attacked by … well, stuffed animals. And that's the *highlight*. The whole sequence is so completely ludicrous that the film never recovers—the remainder of Franco's picture is little more than a blur, as memory of this unforgettable scene lingers on in viewers' minds long after the end credits.

Briefly, even given the above, which is a *lot*, Franco's *Count Dracula*'s greatest fault lies in that no one onscreen brings even the slightest bit of energy to the project, ultimately leaving the film as dead and lifeless as any of Dracula's victims. No performance here is worthy of positive note, not even that of the usually dependable Herbert Lom as Van Helsing. While it is nice to see Christopher Lee delivering actual lines for a change in a turn as Dracula, his typical stiff and wooden delivery brings nothing to the role, not even that of a dead and lifeless vampire. The *only* good news to be gleaned here is that, unlike many other Dracula films, none of the main actors attempt a regional accent that in the end comes off sounding terribly unconvincing.

Dan Curtis' Dracula (1973)

In 1973, producer/director Dan Curtis, creator of the *Dark Shadows* Gothic soap opera of the 1960s, collaborated with famed fantasy writer/scripter Richard Matheson to bring their take on the Dracula legend to the small screen in this made-for-television adaptation. Veteran actor Jack Palance, who had previously worked with Curtis on a version of Robert Louis Stevenson's *The Strange Case of Dr. Jekyll and Mr. Hyde*, returns to the genre in the role of the iconic vampire.

For roughly the first third of the film, scripter Matheson remains faithful to his source. The film's depiction of Harker's journey to Transylvania, through his subsequent imprisonment at Castle Dracula, is among the finest put to film. However, upon the climax of this segment, Matheson throws viewers the first of many surprising deviations from the novel. For, rather than his expected escape from Castle Dracula, Harker instead falls victim to Dracula's three vampire wives!

Turning the tables on Harker's fate is only a prelude to the additional surprises awaiting viewers. Matheson and Curtis substantially up the ante by completely eliminating the characters of Jack Seward, Renfield, and Quincey Morris! As such, only Van Helsing and Arthur Holmwood remain as our story's vampire hunters. Upon first viewing, my reaction was to consider this execution of beloved characters nothing less than blasphemy. To be sure, regret over the loss of Morris was short lived—as detailed elsewhere in this chapter, I have long considered the character thoroughly unnecessary to the story. But Seward and Renfield are another matter completely. They represent a significant portion of the novel and their occasional philosophical discourses refreshingly break up Stoker's at times too dry narrative. However, as the film wears on, this Stoker novel purist grudgingly comes to the realization that losing Seward and Renfield actually worked—*given* the caveat of a television production that, with commercials, needed to hit the mark at two hours. Such an abridged version of Stoker's sprawling, verbose tale would have to make substantial cuts somewhere, and as the Seward/Renfield arc is *relatively* self-contained, it was a masterstroke on Matheson's part to eliminate them. The end result makes for a leaner and tauter story that at the same time remains full, coherent, and eminently satisfying.

Not all of Matheson's changes from the novel are successful, however. Having Harker become a vampire himself early on results in no advancement to the tale. After becoming a meal to Dracula's wives, Harker then disappears from the story until near film's end, where he is then very quickly dispatched by Arthur. As such, this "surprise" turn feels more a gimmick than any attempt to be germane to the story. Additionally, as we have already seen this in 1958's

Dracula (Jack Palance) meets a decidedly pointed end at the hands of Van Helsing (Nigel Davenport) as Arthur (Simon Ward) watches on in Dan Curtis' *Dracula* (1973).

Horror of Dracula, this rehashed ruse is disappointing coming from a talent such as Matheson. Turning next to the film's climax, Matheson again borrows elements from *Horror of Dracula*, but sadly, not the best ones. Here, viewers are neither treated to an exciting fight sequence, nor the vampire's disintegration to dust. Rather, Palance's Dracula is first exposed to incapacitating-but-not-lethal (?!) rays of the sun followed by the *coup de grâce* via impalement. Whether an artistic choice or one dictated by budget, the decision to stray from Stoker's thrilling end chase sequence results in one of the most lethargic end confrontations in the Dracula canon. Lastly, in the film's most egregious stray from Stoker, Matheson introduces a romantic love story involving Dracula and Lucy. In viewing Lucy as the reincarnation of his former love of centuries ago, this story arc closely mirrors the Curtis/*Dark Shadows* romance between Barnabas Collins and Josette du Pres. (Really, *idea*-wise, Curtis' *Dracula* must have been Matheson's easiest writing gig ever.) Of any departure from Stoker's novel, it is giving Dracula a love interest that infuriates most. Why? To say that it is "not in the book" is too easy. In the most obvious sense, having Count Dracula pine for a lost love burdens the vampire with yet an additional vulnerability for enemies to exploit. But of greater consequence, the King of the Vampires becomes a

diminished character through loss of one of his greatest attributes. For no longer is Count Dracula a loathsome, preternatural figure to be feared, he is now simply an Undead in love (shudder)—a fate worse than a stake through the heart. Let's be clear: Few literary creations are as unabashedly evil as Stoker's Count Dracula, and it should

Jack Palance as the Count in Dan Curtis' *Dracula* **(1973)**

remain that way. Let Barnabas pine for his Josette and allow Louis, Edward Cullen, and others of their ilk to wallow in angst, guilt, and other such emotions unbecoming a true vampire. But leave Stoker's Dracula alone.

Overall, Palance's turn as the Count misses the mark. Credit is certainly due for the measure of nuance he brings to scenes involving Lucy/his past love. However, while Palance delivers on the "menace" required for the role, it is overdone, with the actor coming across more like a grimacing mobster

thug than a measured, dignified Transylvanian nobleman. No additional cast member brings anything of worth to the table. Nigel Davenport's turn as Van Helsing is a particular disappointment. The actor brings none of the needed intensity toward hunting down and ridding the world of Dracula that we expect from the leader of the vampire killers; instead, Davenport dispassionately goes through the prescribed motions. Lastly, the sequence where Dracula uses a wolf to gain entrance to the Westenra house is nicely done and genuinely thrilling. Although straying from the novel by having Arthur involved and Mrs. Westenra *not* dying, the fact that this oft-ignored, horrifically chilling passage from the novel is included at all is much appreciated.

IT CAME FROM ...

Count Dracula (1977)

This British Broadcasting Corporation (BBC)-produced version, first airing in the UK in 1977, is a lesser acknowledged but terrific entry in the cinematic Dracula canon. French film actor Louis Jourdan (*Gigi*) dons the cape of the centuries-old Count.

In this writer's mind, the BBC's *Count Dracula* ranks as not only one of the *overall* best Dracula films ever, but also one of the most faithful adaptations of Stoker's classic as well. All the major pieces are here: Harker's initial journey to Transylvania, Dracula's voyage to England, the action in England, and turned full circle as our heroes pursue the Count back to his native land. The film's loyalty to its source material extends to the novel's "smaller" scenes as well. Included in this category is the appreciated inclusion of one the novel's last attacks on Lucy. Here, Dracula, in dog-as-wolf form, appears outside Lucy's bedroom window. After literally scaring the girl's poor mother to death, the Count then materializes inside the room to claim the young girl. Such scenes, often omitted in other adaptations, here add an additional layer of pathos to the drama, allowing viewers to become more emotionally involved with the characters than is usual for such a film.

However deserving of its praise for fidelity to Stoker's novel, the film does take liberties with the source material. As a Stoker novel purist, I tend to take a dim view of cinematic deviations from the book. However, being a purist does not mean being blind to the novel's faults and I must confess that the film's com-

bination of characters Arthur Holmwood and Quincey Morris into *one* character (Quincey Holmwood) significantly improves upon Stoker. For one of the novel's shortcomings is its overabundance of characters— Stoker gives readers *seven* primary protagonists to deal with, which, in turn, only serves to spread readers' attentions and sympathies too thin. Of our band of heroes, Quincey Morris is, truth be told, superfluous. His

Louis Jourdan brought a measured, calculated menace to the BBC-produced *Count Dracula* **(1977).**

contrived "heroic" death at novel's end is truly the only significant role the character plays (which is handled in the film by Holmwood receiving critical, but not fatal, wounds during the climactic finale). By wisely removing Morris from the story, the film allows viewers to concentrate on just the essential char-

IT CAME FROM ...

acters who all serve critical roles. (In a less significant deviation from the novel, the film makes Lucy and Mina *sisters*—a thoroughly head-scratching alteration, as this 'sisterhood' produces no discernable effect to the storyline.)

The only significant aspect of the film to fail in justice to the novel is the severely abridged sequence of Dracula's voyage to England aboard the Russian schooner, the Demeter. Here, viewers receive little more than the storm-beaten Demeter's arrival and landing at Whitby harbor, followed by a too-quick close-up of the deceased Demeter captain lashed to the wheel of his ship. As such, this sequence is considerably disappointing. The full passage in the novel—thanks to entries in the Captain's log—detail the events of the Demeter's full voyage, from the ship's departure from Varna until shortly before the ship's arrival in Whitby. Given the natural claustrophobic nature of a month-long voyage at sea, compounded by the *Ten Little Indians*-style disappearance of crewmembers, results in a growing sense of "impending doom" felt by both the Demeter crewmen and Stoker readers. It is a wonderfully atmospheric and chilling literary passage. That the filmmakers chose not to include this entire sequence (possibly for budgetary reasons) is a significant missed opportunity for *Count Dracula* to not only have further raised hairs on the back of viewers' necks, but to *stake* a claim to the title of *best* Stoker adaptation as well.

Louis Jourdan brings a more measured interpretation to the role, a welcome respite from the histrionic performances seen in other films. Jourdan's Count carries an air of assured confidence and coolness, although perhaps too much so—a *bit* more emotion on Jourdan's part (i.e., he doesn't rage against his vampire wives as in the novel when they almost feast upon a hypnotized Harker; here, the Count merely speaks gently to them, not even amounting to an admonition) would break up a *too* static performance. The efforts from supporting players are bland at best but adequate. Two notable exceptions here: Frank Finlay turns in one of the more effective portrayals of Abraham Van Helsing, perfectly capturing both the serious and unintentionally humorous aspects of Stoker's character. Jack Shepherd's portrayal of Renfield is simply superb—easily the best portrayal of the character ever delivered on screen. Here is not the leering lunatic of other films (with apologies to Dwight Frye, whom we love!), but an intelligent, philosophical, tortured soul. Shepherd's nuanced performance delivers to viewers a multi-layered and sympathetic Renfield not previously seen. Lastly, of special note, one small scene deserves mention. During one of his attacks upon Lucy, as Dracula lies upon the supine girl in bed, the vampire's cape spreads fully out across the entire bed so that Jourdan resembles more a bat, with wings outstretched, feasting upon its prey. Simply terrific.

Dracula (1979)

It's curious how the versions of *Dracula* that have had the greatest impact—1931, 1958, 1979—have been mixed-bags themselves. While John Badham's *Dracula* has many terrific elements (including a turn by Broadway star Frank Langella, simply the finest, most gifted actor to ever play the classic vampire role), it is ultimately not 100 percent satisfying.

The Badham/Langella *Dracula* was the result of a Broadway revival of the original play (and inspiration for the Lugosi version) by Hamilton Deane and John L. Balderson. Langella made such a hit with it, that he was nominated for a Tony and took Broadway by storm. Coupled with Langella's full-bloodied performance were sets created by legendary illustrator, Edward Gorey (1925-2000), who won a Tony for his costumes. This 1977 production was an unqualified success, and such was the mark that Langella made in the part that the show, which had been commonly referred to as *Edward Gorey's Dracula*, soon became known as *Frank Langella's Dracula*. (The original Edward Gorey cover for *Playbill* was soon discarded in favor of one featuring a photo of Langella's Dracula.) Due to the character's few scenes, additional dialogue was lifted from the 1931 film to pad Langella's stage time.

The play opened at the Martin Beck Theater to mixed reviews and packed houses. Critics generally found the production design inspired and Langella a revelation, but found the Deane-Balderston script anemic. Played largely for its camp quality, Langella and company managed to infuse the play with genuine melodrama, romance, and scares along with a sense of style and fun. Langella's stage performance was grandiloquent and theatrical, complete with rich flourishes and evocative gestures. (He wore a series of different capes throughout the performance, each with different weights sewn into the hem to produce specific effects.)

Langella realized that playing to the vanity inherent in the role made his performance more effective. At New York City's Dracula Centennial Conference in March, 1997, Broadway actress Anne Sachs (Lucy) remembered that Langella enacted their seduction scene as if he were playing to a reflection of himself. Isolating Dracula by rendering him a prisoner of his own charm and good looks made him all the more attractive.

Langella was also the first actor to make Dracula sexy, and the fact that he could play Dracula as both a character part and romantic idol is a testament to his ability. He played the part hundreds of times on stage, and modified his performance for the 1979 movie version.

Universal, spurred by the play's New York triumph, quickly planned a remake of their Bela Lugosi classic. Director John Badham decided to discard the evocative production design of Gorey, and to increase the story's romantic

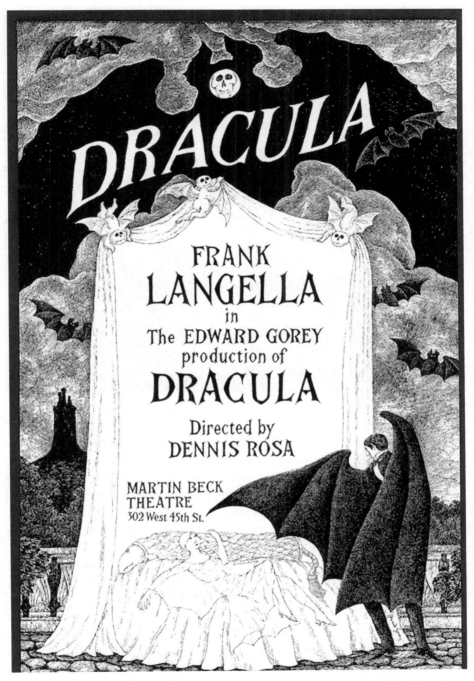

Frank Langella first spread his vampire wings in the Broadway production designed by famed illustrator Edward Gorey.

The stories and novels behind Classic Horror, Fantasy and Science Fiction Films

Frank Langella in Universal's big-budget *Dracula*, 1979

possibilities. Langella left the show, allowing such accomplished actors as Raul Julia and David Dukes to take the Broadway spotlight.

Where Langella was purposely hammy and grandiloquent on Broadway, he toned down his performance for the film version, going instead for an understated, romantic menace. One of the fascinating things about the film performance is that Langella manages to make his eyes … *quiver*, as if Dracula is always seeing something not quite visible to human eyes.

Badham needed a star to match Langella's talents and recruited Laurence Olivier to play Dr. Van Helsing. Kate Nelligan, then at the beginning of a distinguished career, played Lucy, and character actor Donald Pleasance was tapped to play Dr. Seward. Although a modest hit, Universal's *Dracula* was not the box-office champion they had anticipated. Perhaps hoping to trade on the vogue that fantasy films were enjoying at the time (such as the phenomenally successful *Star Wars*), Universal did not realize that their *Dracula* was too old fashioned and atmospheric to be appreciated by the youth market.

Despite that, *Dracula* is a fascinating if not completely satisfying film. Badham opted for a rich, lush look of Victorian Gothic Revivalism. The production design is excellent, with Carfax (Dracula's home) and Seward's sanitarium looking especially evocative. Maddeningly, Badham never allows us to fully see the sets, so little visual tastes are all we get of what must have been a sumptuous meal. This handsome film has the feel of a Merchant Ivory Production, and provides a glorious recreation of *fin de siècle* England, becoming the kind of gold-plated production that went completely beyond the garage-level capabilities of Hammer. Badham's *Dracula* ranks with Coppola's later version as the most lush and lovely realization of the novel to date.

Sadly, the original, lush Technicolor version of the film is not available to current collectors. Cinematographer Gilbert Taylor shot the movie in rich, autumnal tones. In its original incarnation, Badham's *Dracula* was glorious to look at. However, the director originally wanted to shoot in black-and-white— Badham was allowed to completely desaturate the color for later LaserDisc and DVD releases. As an artistic choice, it is defensible, but it's simply the *wrong* choice. Badham turned a gorgeous movie into a black-and-white "B" programmer.

Badham further stacks the deck against himself by staging his actors all too often at the far ends of his compositional frame (look, especially, at the initial confrontation between Dracula and Van Helsing), so we don't even always see the actors. Another missed opportunity was that Badham chose to adapt the play, rather than the novel. Had they adapted the novel instead, their film would have had more opportunities to strut its lush production design and employ a greater epic sweep in the narrative. Because of that, there is no sequence in Transylvania, a misstep that even Browning avoided in 1931. (Perhaps the Transylvania sequences, where Dracula is at his most monstrous, would have undercut any attempts to make him a romantic figure.)

Like the Lugosi film, one of the main reasons to see this version of *Dracula* is the lead performance. Langella's turn is often dismissed by a core-group of horror films aficionados and that is somewhat understandable: he does not resort to the sort of cheap, horrific hugger-mugger found in the Hammer films. As a romantic reimagining of the play, Badham's film is unbeatable. Aided by a memorable score by composer John Williams, Frank Langella's *Dracula* was the movie that the character often deserved, but so seldom received.

Langella's Dracula moved the character further down the path of romantic anti-hero started by actor Jack Palance. Reconceived as a tragic lover and not a bloodthirsty fiend, Dracula was ready to stalk the popular imagination once more.

But that would have to wait for Francis Ford Coppola.

Bram Stoker's Dracula (1992)

Francis Ford Coppola, director of the acclaimed films *The Godfather* and *Apocalypse Now*, brought the James V. Hart-scripted version of the Stoker classic to the big screen in 1992. With an all-star cast featuring Gary Oldman in the leading role, never before had such a lavish, big-budget treatment been accorded the Count. The film performed respectably at both the U.S. and overseas box offices and received overall positive critical reviews.

Within the first few paragraphs of Stoker's novel, Jonathan Harker enters into his journal: "I read that every known superstition in the world is gathered into the horseshoe of the Carpathians, as if it were the centre of some sort of imaginative whirlpool." Similarly, Coppola manages to gather into one film just about everything I consider wrong with filmmakers' modern-day "flourishes" in bringing the literary Count to life. It would be less upsetting had the film had been touted as a *reimagining* of the novel, or just titled *Dracula*. But I take umbrage at a filmmaker with the audacity to title his film *Bram Stoker's Dracula*, and further, crow over his picture's "loyalty" to its source no less, when in fact, it is nothing of the sort. If looking for a Gothic romance that features a vampire, this film fits the bill nicely; however, as a faithful representation of Stoker's novel … not so much.

And so let's look at the film's "fidelity" (insert intense sarcasm here) to Stoker. First, our film opens on the origin of Dracula's vampiric life, a tableau that has no basis in the novel. However, Hart takes this admittedly interesting premise too far by mistakenly linking his vampire to the historical, real-life "Dracula," Vlad Tepes. Tepes was the 15th-century Prince of Wallachia, renowned for impaling his enemies (and his own law-breaking citizens) upon wooden spikes. That it has been established since the 1970s, upon discovery of Stoker's working notes and papers surrounding his writing of *Dracula* that the author merely borrowed the name of the 15th-century ruler and did *not* base his vampire Count on the historical Vlad, makes the film's perpetuation of this disproved connection all the more infuriating.

More infidelities against Stoker: Dracula's vampire wives actually feast upon Jonathan, and it appears that our good doctor, Jack Seward, is a drug addict. As neither plot development serves any part in the subsequent drama, both reek of screenwriter gimmickry intended merely for viewer titillation rather than, say, to advance the story.

But of all Hart's sins in translation, the most egregious is the introduction of a love story between Dracula and Mina, whom the vampire believes to be the reincarnation of his long-lost love, Elisabeta. Count Dracula … *in love* … is certainly a concept at odds for a film claiming to be loyal to its source material (not to mention anathema to Stoker novel purists). The implications of a Dracula capable of love have been detailed in our earlier discussion on Dan

Gary Oldman in *Bram Stoker's Dracula* (1992)

Curtis' television adaptation. But we feel compelled to add that while the idea of a Dracula with a "softer" side was a detriment to Curtis' film, at least said idea was contained, ultimately amounting to but a small part of the overall story. Screenwriter Hart, however, takes this concept and runs to the hills with it so that in short order Dracula's love for Mina becomes the film's overarching story. As a result, Hart unforgivably manages to transform one of literature's most malignant and evil creations into little more than a lovesick wolf pup. One just cannot take the King of the Vampires seriously after he nearly comes to orgasm (yes!) while under the covers with Mina. Now, there's no longer a need for Van Helsing and company to hunt down the vampire—for love has already driven a stake through his heart.

But, enough of the negative, let's now look for some good—those aspects of Coppola's film that improve upon Stoker's novel. Upon multiple viewings of the film and long contemplation, I came to the surprising realization that in *no* way does the film actually improve upon the book. How can this be? As just discussed, the most obvious answer lies in that simply none of Hart's deviations from the source material work to the film's advantage. But more than that, to the argument made by some that Stoker's tale, having never looked better on the big screen somehow equates to *surpassing* Stoker's novel, this author … couldn't disagree more. Here, great photography and smart direction merely serves the source material well and should not be confused with *improving* upon said material.

Sir Anthony Hopkins

With the exception of Oldman, who overall delivers well, performances across the board can only be considered subpar—a point simply *boggling* considering the talent (and salaries) involved. Winona Ryder, Richard Grant, Cary Elwes, and Billy Campbell are all unremarkable save for their bad accents, and Keanu Reeves' almost universally panned performance needs no further elaboration here. The brilliantly inspired casting of singer Tom Waits as Renfield results in a major missed opportunity, as the script sadly confines the wonderfully eccentric Waits to portraying merely the typical fly-eating lunatic. One longingly ponders what Waits could have done with the role had Renfield been written as the more nuanced character of the novel.

Lastly, special mention is reserved for Anthony Hopkins. In his role as Abraham Van Helsing, Hopkins turns on the ham and in the process nearly ruins every scene in which he appears. That the Van Helsing of Stoker's novel and most cinematic incarnations is strictly serious, but at times *unintentionally* funny, appears to have been lost (or, I suspect, deliberately ignored), by the actor. Rather, Hopkins plays his lines for comedic effect, best illustrated when, in discussing the recently departed Lucy, Hopkins announces, "No, no, no, not exactly. I just want to cut off her head and take out her heart." These lines need to be played straight to instill within viewers a sense of dread and pathos over the horrific fate still to befall poor Lucy. Instead, only half-hearted chuckles result as Hopkins undermines the emotional potential of the scene in his unsuccessful pursuit of laughs. "Sir" Anthony Hopkins seems to have forgotten while filming that this was a serious take in the Dracula canon, not Mel Brooks' *Dracula, Dead and Loving It.*

IT CAME FROM ...

Man of Many Parts:
Stitching Together Frankenstein

Frankenstein (1910)

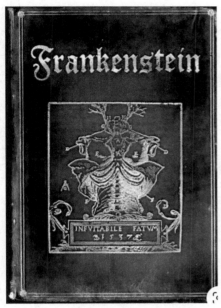

Original first edition of Frankenstein

This is a historically significant and interesting curio in the Frankenstein canon. Credited as the first filmed adaptation of Shelley's novel, the fact that a copy exists over a century later is amazing and fortuitous for fans and historians alike.

Produced by Edison Studios (yes, *the* Thomas Edison) and directed by J. Searle Dawley in four days, the film runs a scant 12 minutes. Bowing to the pressures of religious and other "moralist" groups of the day where the fledgling film industry was concerned, Edison required a considerably toned-down version of Shelley's tale. A disclaimer contained in the March 15, 1910 issue of Edison's *Kinetogram* publication enlightens potential viewers:

To those familiar with Mrs. Shelly's (sic) story it will be evident that we have carefully omitted anything which might of any possibility shock any portion of the audience. In making the film, the Edison Co. has carefully tried to eliminate all actual repulsive situations and to concentrate its endeavors upon the mystic and psychological problems that are to be found in this weird tale. Wherever, therefore, the film differs from the original story it is purely with the idea of eliminating what would be repulsive to a moving picture audience.

One wouldn't expect much from a story given a running time of only 12 minutes, but within this time, Dawley delivers the entire (pun intended) bare bones of the Frankenstein mythos: Dr. Frankenstein creates a Monster, subsequently rejects said creation, and in turn Frankenstein and those he loves are made to suffer at the hands of the Monster before it is vanquished.

The stories and novels behind Classic Horror, Fantasy and Science Fiction Films

The performances amount to little, being over-theatrical, typical for silent films. And Charles Ogle, as Frankenstein's creation, resembles more Lon Chaney's hunchback Quasimodo (who would come 13 years later) than Mary Shelley's vision, or the iconic Karloff visage.

A grain of wheat amongst all the chaff in this film, however, is the Monster's creation. Resulting from alchemy rather than electricity (that would become the standard with James Whale's 1931 version), watching the Monster slowly materialize before one's eyes is a spectacular effect! (The effect was achieved via filming a Monster dummy ablaze, then reversing the footage to make it appear as if the creature was slowly generating.)

All said—the above-mentioned scene is the exception—Edison Studio's *Frankenstein* is more interesting for its survival as a film and distinction as the first film adaptation of Mary Shelley's novel than for most anything within the film itself.

IT CAME FROM ...

Frankenstein (1931)

The granddaddy of them all, the film that both launched the career of then-unknown actor Boris Karloff and contributed greatly to sinking that of Bela Lugosi's, who just earlier that very same year was propelled to stardom through his iconic portrayal of the world's most famous vampire, *Dracula*.

Various stories abound regarding how Karloff came to the role. Universal Pictures hoped to immediately follow up on the success of *Dracula* with an adaptation of Mary Shelley's novel. One of the more popular stories tells of how Lugosi, hoping to play the role of Dr. Frankenstein, becomes indignant over being asked to play the Monster instead. The thought of a role with no lines, and being almost unrecognizable under much make-up, was unthinkable to the prideful Lugosi, and so he turned it down. (Other versions on this tale tell of a disastrous screen test or the complete rejection of Lugosi for any part when British director James Whale was brought in by Universal to replace original director Robert Florey.) Equally numerous are the stories surrounding Karloff's landing of the role. One story posits that Karloff begged Whale for a screen test, another that Whale "discovered" Karloff in a Universal com-

missary, and yet another that Whale's boyfriend saw Karloff's performance in the film *Criminal Code* and recommended the actor to Whale.

For the sake of this discussion, however, Karloff's real path to the role is irrelevant. What matters is that he did land the role and both actors' subsequent careers were forever changed as a result. Karloff used the role as a launching pad to a moderately successful career through the remainder of his life, while Lugosi, whether losing out on the role by choice or not, found himself forever typecast (when he could find work) as Dracula or other such boogeymen in films of declining quality until his death in 1956.

Whale's *Frankenstein* set the template for subsequent films for decades to follow. Probably to ensure a box-office success comparable to that of *Dracula* earlier that year, Whale produced a straight-out horror film.

Boris Karloff as the Monster in *Frankenstein* **(1931)**

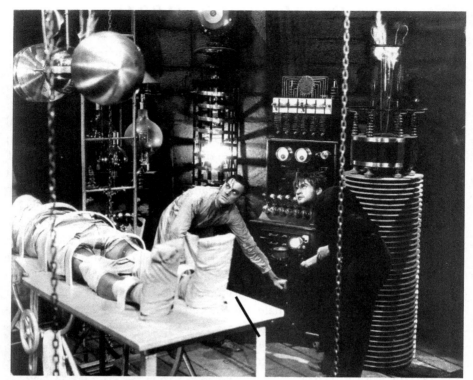

Here, Karloff's Monster rampages and kills, not from the understandable and sympathetic motivations provided by Shelley (stemming from a "child" abandoned by his "father"), but rather from a screenwriter taking the "easy route" by having the Monster a recipient of an abnormal brain. This concept of a defective or evil brain (for there were to be numerous transplants to follow) as motivation for the Monster's actions robs the entire Universal *Frankenstein* series, not to mention the vast majority of Frankenstein films produced by other studios, of the opportunity to pursue the more interesting moral and philosophical implications inherent in the novel. But truth be told, studios produce what audiences desire. (Although just consider a *Love Letters* or *My Dinner with Andre* film featuring Henry Frankenstein and his creation! *My Dinner with Frankenstein!*)

Whale and company additionally set the template for future films on another important aspect regarding the Monster. Taking Shelley's frustratingly ambiguous single line, "… I collected the instruments of life around me, that I might infuse a spark of being into the lifeless thing that lay at my feet," the film introduces the concept of lightning, or more generally as the series progressed, electricity, as the source of the Monster's life. ("Your father was Frankenstein, but your Mother was da lightnink!") This allows for a more *grounded*-in-science explanation for the creature's seemingly eternal life than had been offered pre-

viously. More so, the Monster's spectacular electrical birth certainly provides for an *electrifying* visual experience for viewers, thanks to the efforts of electrical special effects genius, Kenneth Strickfaden.

Regarding performances, only two are of note. Colin Clive is superb as Henry Frankenstein, deftly and believably oscillating between normalcy and near lunacy. I hesitate to comment on Karloff's performance here as it is universally lauded. Karloff admittedly deserves kudos for a performance that is by turns sympathetic and horrifying, additionally so, given the constraints of make-up and costume. However, to extend the laurels further, as some fans do, to posit that no one could have done as fine a job as Karloff in the role (I feel) goes a bit far. Generating viewer sympathy through a smile, supplicating hand gestures, or beatifically gazing up for the "first" time at sunlight is not, I feel, beyond the ability of *any* actor worth his salt.

Missing from Whale's *Frankenstein* are two major plot points from Shelley's novel—that of the Monster's demand for a female companion, as well as his schooling in humanity through a blind man in his sequel, *Bride of Frankenstein*. However, while certainly interesting in its own right, *Bride* and all subsequent films in the Universal *Frankenstein* canon are not covered here. *Bride*, while lauded by many (not I) as superior to Whale's original, stretches the black comedy too far. (And don't get me started on the Monster talking or the existence of a completely illogical, castle-destroying "lever.") The remaining films in the Universal series are unworthy of note, due either to an all-too similarity in plot, or that the Monster subsequently becomes little more than window dressing as the film series progresses.

The stories and novels behind Classic Horror, Fantasy and Science Fiction Films

The Curse of Frankenstein (1957)

Hammer Film Productions hit its stride with this, their first Eastman color Gothic. As a retelling of Shelley's novel it is no more faithful than the 1931 James Whale film (or *Young Frankenstein*, for that matter), but it does start Hammer's most interesting and thoughtful film series. Most of the films that followed were infinitely superior to this initial effort, with special kudos to *The Revenge of Frankenstein* (1958), *Frankenstein Created Woman* (1967), and the grim *Frankenstein Must Be Destroyed* (1969).

Prior to his death at the guillotine (and looking like an audition reel for *A Tale of Two Cities*), Frankenstein (Peter Cushing) tells his priest-confessor that he is not guilty of various murders, rather, it was a Monster of his own creation. As a framing device, this doesn't quite work as Frankenstein relates several murders he committed in the course of making his creature, but no matter. Like Shelley's novel, the terror bits are muted and sparingly served, though the performances are uniformly good and the whole enterprise is served with the earnest professionalism that marked Post-War British moviemaking.

The main reason to watch *The Curse of Frankenstein* today is to watch Peter Cushing at his best. With his fire-and-ice delivery, Cushing is alternately charismatic and sinister in the role of obsessed doctor, and it is a performance that grows richer and more complex with each succeeding film. Made at the height of his powers as an actor—before illness and premature aging made him almost unrecognizable—all of his thespic tricks are on display: the hard consonants, the restrained febrile energy, the pointing finger, and the slow de-

Christopher Lee in Hammer's *The Curse of Frankenstein* (1957).

livery that turns staccato in a heartbeat. A dandy on-and-off screen, Cushing's Frankenstein is a gore-spattered Beau Brummel, a suave and smiling sociopath. One wonders what he could have done with better material and better films.

The various monsters that Frankenstein creates over the course of the Hammer series are never the centerpiece of the narrative (with the exception of *Frankenstein Created Woman*), and here the Monster is pretty much an afterthought. (He is not even featured in the original trailer.) The make-up, too, is a let-down after so many decades of the Universal conception of the Monster, but since the character never signifies in any real emotional way, it matters little.

IT CAME FROM …

The key strength of *The Curse of Frankenstein* is its visceral, charnel-house vibe.

Like Hammer's *Dracula*, *The Curse of Frankenstein* is a competent but middling film that had significant impact. (Only two Hammer films of the period achieve something of classic status, *The Mummy* [1959] and *The Brides of Dracula* [1960]). Both Dracula and Frankenstein films reinvigorated Gothic cinema, and suddenly period pieces were successful with young people. They would generate a spate of such films in Britain, the United States, and the Continent that continued all the way to *The Exorcist* (1973), before fading away until Dracula once again poured fresh blood into the genre with *Bram Stoker's Dracula* (1992).

This is essential viewing for the Frankenstein completest, but stick around for the later and better Frankenstein films.

The stories and novels behind Classic Horror, Fantasy and Science Fiction Films

Horror of Frankenstein (1970)

Sometimes a film is so wrong-headed in its conception and so ham-fisted in its execution that it becomes oddly successful in its own twisted way. Such is *Horror of Frankenstein*.

As the 1960s waned into the 1970s, Hammer decided to re-energize its Gothic films by losing such middle-aged stars as Peter Cushing and replacing them with younger, more "modern" types. A retelling of *The Curse of Frankenstein* (and not of Shelley's novel), writer and director Jimmy Sangster decides to send up the material with heightened violence and tons of sex. The result is a film so bizarre and of its time as to become a perfect snapshot of late-1960s excess.

To replace Cushing, Hammer pegged actor Ralph Bates. A much younger man than Cushing (only 30 at the time of *Horror of Frankenstein*), young Master Bates has a rather jaded, decadent screen presence that reads both older and oddly reptilian. Hammer was grooming Bates as leading man material, showcasing him in this, as well as *Taste the Blood of Dracula* (1970), *Dr. Jekyll and Sister Hyde* (1971), and *Lust for a Vampire* (1971). But movie audiences never warmed to him and he eventually became a staple on British television.

The Bates Frankenstein blithely goes through the film murdering relatives and school chums, taking a breather only to seduce a bevy of buxom supporting players. Sex is the primary narrative driver, with the creation of life (by more artificial means) fading into the background.

When Frankenstein does finally make his Creature, it is body-builder (and later Darth Vader) David Prowse, flexing pecs while walking around in a pair of athletic underwear. This weird anticipation of *The Rocky Horror Picture Show* constantly seems poised to be some kind of plot point (a muscle-bound Monster in such an over-sexed picture has to mean *something*), but the Monster does little more than kill off Frankenstein's enemies and lovers when the time is ripe.

The movie only really comes to life with the appearance of Dennis Price

Darth Vader was still far, far away for David Prowse when he portrayed The Creature in *Horror of Frankenstein*.

as a grave robber. A gifted light comedian, one gets the feeling that Price knew he was slumming and decided to have as much fun as humanly possible. When Frankenstein kills him by dumping him in an acid bath, the movie sadly runs out of whatever steam it had.

Curiously, Frankenstein's Monster dies accidently in the same acid bath, leaving his creator to survive without punishment, despite his many murders. What, one wonders, was Hammer thinking with that? Keep him for a sequel?

IT CAME FROM ...

Dan Curtis' Frankenstein (1973)

For the period of the mid-1960s through the early 1970s, one name was synonymous with television horror: Dan Curtis. Primary among his distinctions, Curtis introduced two iconic figures into the horror pantheon: Barnabas Collins (via the supernatural "soap opera" *Dark Shadows*, 1966-1971) and Carl Kolchak (from the ratings-smashing TV movie, *The Night Stalker*, 1972). Curtis additionally produced a number of made-for-television horrors, many being adaptations from Gothic horror literature. The first of these, *The Strange Case of Dr. Jekyll and Mr. Hyde*, premiered in 1968, starring Jack Palance (who would return years later for Curtis' *Dracula* in 1974). The year 1973 in partic-

ular was comparable to a year-long Christmas for monster fans, as Curtis released the much-anticipated follow-up to *Stalker*, *The Night Strangler*, an adaptation of Oscar Wilde's *The Picture of Dorian Gray*, as well as the subject of this chapter, *Frankenstein*.

Curtis' adaptation (scripted by Sam Hall and Richard Landau) remains one of the most faithful to date of Shelley's tale. The only significant story point missing here is the framing sequence of Frankenstein's pursuit of his creation through the frozen north. Due, assuredly, to budgetary restrictions, its omission is not missed. However, from the creation sequence that opens the film through the deaths of both Frankenstein and his creation, fans of Shelley's novel will recognize all remaining major plot points. Particularly welcome here is the film's inclusion of the oft-neglected sequence in which Frankenstein's creation learns of speech, reading, and the ways of humanity through his observation of a poor family while holed up in an abandoned structure adjacent to their cottage. Being the rare adaptation that sticks with Shelley's vision of an intelligent "Monster" that speaks, the sequence bolsters the film immeasurably for providing an explanation for the creation's mental development as well as allowing for a "softer" side in which to garner viewers' sympathies.

16 Oakland Tribune Tues., Jan. 16, 1973

Bob MacKenzie

. . . On Television . . .

Do the Monster Mash

The poor old Frankenstein monster. They just won't let him rest. Tonight ABC trots him out again for the first of two parts of "Frankenstein," a new TV version, at 11:30. This is one of the "Wide World of Entertainment" features. Part two follows tomorrow night.

According to my calculations, this will be the twentieth film treatment, and that's if you don't count "The Munsters." We haven't had a rock-musical version yet, so the cycle isn't complete.

Tonight's treatment of the story employs a big brute named Bo Svenson as the monster, with Robert Foxworth as Dr. Victor Frankenstein and Susan Strasberg as his girl friend. The good doctor has a pair of aides named Otto and Hugo who go about gathering up the bits of anatomy from the graveyards. Personally, I was fond of Igor. But this version takes the story as much from the Mary Shelley novel as from the old movies.

MacKenzie

To give you the flavor of the thing, I couldn't do better than quote from ABC's description of the action:

"At first pleased with his success, Victor is horrified when the monster accidentally kills Otto and later flees from the laboratory. Bewildered and afraid, the monster hides in the woods as Victor tries to find him. At the same time, Elizabeth, shunted aside, wonders if she can ever be happy with Victor."

If that reminds you of "As the World Turns," wait till tomorrow night, when the monster demands that Victor make him a lady monster he can settle down with.

I have not seen this ABC version of the story. But I have seen all the movie versions except one, and that one was made in 1910 and all the prints are lost, so it doesn't count.

I have a still shot from the ABC version, which appears to show Svenson as the monster, with no electrodes under his ears. This shows no respect for tradition. Everybody knows the monster has electrodes under his ears and wears a size 15 shoe.

Bo Svensen

While Hall and Landau's script is exemplary, Curtis' *Frankenstein* ultimately suffers in its execution. Primarily, the lack of money afforded this production—from the film's cramped and flimsy sets to effects that are significantly less than special—is painfully evident throughout. (Frankenstein could have just as well used a Duracell battery to power his creation in place of the "birth by lightning" that viewers are given.) Additionally, Glenn Jordan's direction seems by-the-book and "dialed in," helping little in upping the ante surrounding mood and suspense, or, god forbid, finding imaginative ways to obscure the aforementioned budgetary embarrassments.

In the lead roles, Robert Foxworth as Victor Frankenstein and Bo Svenson as the Monster both surprise, albeit for different reasons. The usually solid and dependable Foxworth here wildly overacts. Wild-eyed, loud, and over-expressive, you'd think the actor was performing for the back of the theater, rather than a television film. Yes, you'd expect any "mad" scientist to be somewhat manic, but Foxworth too often takes it over-the-top. It is a disappointing, one-dimensional performance that distracts. Svenson, on the other hand, gives what I feel is one of the best performances of Frankenstein's creation to date. Svenson's "Monster" is anything but—instead the actor delivers a character possessing, by turns child-like innocence, intelligence, and rationality, and, when the circumstance requires, hatred and rage. Not knowing anything of Svenson's body of work before viewing this film for the first time, I came away immensely impressed.

In the supporting roles, there is little to say, as the actors (including Susan Strasberg as Elizabeth), turn in perfunctory performances. One notable exception is the work of John Karlen. A Curtis regular in both the *Dark Shadows* TV soap and the franchise's first feature release, *House of Dark Shadows*, Karlen here turns in a nuanced, sympathetic performance as the doomed Otto. A far cry from the less-than-rational Willie Loomis in *Shadows*, Karlen here is a stand out, and his early exit from the story is to the film's loss.

Dan Curtis' *Frankenstein* may contain a number of problems but is still worth viewing for its faithfulness to Shelley and for the very fine performances of Svenson and Karlen.

IT CAME FROM ...

Frankenstein: The True Story (1973)

Well, color me foolish! Never having seen this made-for-television adaptation until preparing for this chapter, I've gone decades thinking that *"True Story"* meant the most faithful adaptation of the famed novel to date. Little did I suspect that scripters Don Bachardy and Christopher Isherwood had other plans—for while Frankenstein does indeed bring a creation to life, Ms. Shelley would recognize little else in this mad three-hour romp!

As a reimagining, rather than adaptation, of Shelley's tale, it would be pointless (not to mention lengthy) to detail all the areas where *True Story* differs. Rather, let's look instead at the highlights. Overall, the film is a handsome production, displaying and making full use of what must have been a lavish budget. The sets are grand, costumes gorgeously Victorian, and for once in a television production, the special effects are, in fact, special. But it is particular story points that merit mention, though … where to start? In a twist on previous Frankenstein films, our "Monster," upon creation, is not hideously ugly; instead, he's the breathtakingly beautiful Michael Sarrazin. However a handsome Monster could hardly provide the conflict necessary to sustain a three-hour production, and so the script takes the twist yet further. Borrowing from Oscar Wilde, we discover that, like Dorian Gray's hidden portrait, our creature is slowly deteriorating. As Sarrazin's visage grows increasingly grotesque, other characters react in kind, and thus … anticipated mayhem ensues. This twist by scripters Bachardy and Isherwood is a very nice touch. In perhaps a yet even more surprising twist, *True Story* provides us with our first "green" Monster! Harnessing sunlight rather than electricity, Frankenstein's creature gains life from … solar power! (*So* much better for the environment!) Lastly, no discussion of *True Story* would be complete without mention of the film's climax. Adjectives are insufficient here, and so just imagine: a battle between the creature and his "bride," taking place in

John Polidori (James Mason) about to experience a shocking moment in *Frankenstein: The True Story* (1973).

a grand ballroom in front of horrified bystanders; Jane Seymour losing her head (literally!); and an ill-fated voyage upon a sailing vessel where Elizabeth is murdered and James Mason not only loses a hand (hints of Inspector Krogh in *Son of Frankenstein*), but is subsequently hoisted to the top of a sail mast where a cackling Sarrazin gleefully observes as Mason literally becomes not a shadow, but a skeleton of his former self. It's mad, it's delirious, and … it's fantastic. Required viewing.

Regarding our players, Leonard Whiting disappoints in the central role of Victor Frankenstein. Bland and seldom convincing, it is more Whiting's inability (or perhaps poor choices) to convey the needed emotional range required for such a complex role. Really, his character's reaction when regaining consciousness to discover his success in creating life amounts to the emotional equivalent of "Huh. That's nice." Where is just a *touch* of Colin Clive's "It's alive, it's alive!" mania? More so, Frankenstein's reaction upon the discovery of his dead and *frozen* wife aboard the sailing vessel is … nothing. No rage, no tears, nada—an apt summary of Whiting's Frankenstein. Michael Sarrazin, a 1969 Golden Globe nominee (Most Promising Newcomer—Male), shows little of that promise here as Frankenstein's creation. For most of the film, Sarrazin just shambles through the motions, bringing nothing interesting or fresh to the role. Nicola Pagett, as Victor's wife Elizabeth, brings a welcome strength and courage to the character seldom seen. Particularly, in Elizabeth's final confrontation with the Monster, Pagett's work here is quite superb. Then we have

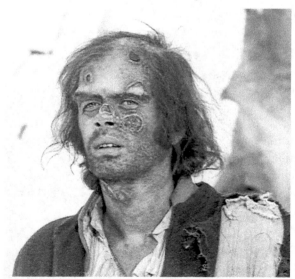

James Mason. In a superbly mad cross between Dr. No and Dr. Pretorious (with a touch of Inspector Krogh thrown in), the actor steals not only every scene he is in, but the film as well.

Frankenstein: The True Story may not be a Shelley purist's cup of tea, but accepting it for what it is, the film makes for fine entertainment—the disappointment resulting from its lead actors' lapses notwithstanding. James Mason's delightful turn as Dr. "Poly-Dolly" and the film's insane final half hour alone make *True Story* worth a watch.

Michael Sarrazin as the Creature begins to decay in the made-for-television *Frankenstein: The True Story* **(1973).**

IT CAME FROM ...

Mary Shelley's Frankenstein (1994)

Fresh off the commercial and critical success (dubious in this writer's mind, explained in detail in our *Dracula* chapter) of *Bram Stoker's Dracula* two years previous, famed director Francis Ford Coppola next turned his sights on bringing Mary Shelley's classic to the screen. Choosing this time to only produce, Coppola turned the directing duties over to actor/director Kenneth Branagh.

Lavish and beautiful to behold, the film overall is a very faithful adaptation of Shelley's novel, until about the final 20 minutes, when the film diverts and goes seriously off the rails. The film is bookended by the novel's framing story—an almost-frozen-dead Victor, discovered by mariners in the Arctic seas, bear witness to Victor's incredible story of the pursuit of the murderous brute to which he gave life. Usually discarded by other Frankenstein films, this sequence encourages the viewer with the thought of at last having the definitive telling of Shelley's story. However, the film annoyingly diverts from Shelley here by ending the film explicitly depicting the Creature's self-immolation; in so doing, gone is any ambiguity regarding the Creature's fate and the fear (hope?) that he may yet live.

Screenwriters Frank Darabont and Steph Lady keep the primary "soul" of the source material, the morality tale of Victor Frankenstein's abdication of responsibility for what he has created, and the resulting consequences. The film *attempts* to tackle the moral dichotomy between creator and creation by includ-

ing the novel's numerous discussions between Frankenstein and the Creature. In the novel, while both parties hurl accusations at each other, at least these moralistic debates are nuanced and impassioned (if, at times, admittedly overwrought), allowing for understanding and compassion by the reader for each side. In the film, DeNiro and Branagh are certainly impassioned, but sadly to the extreme, more yelling at than debating each other, in turn losing much of the emotional core of the

The ever-obsessed Victor Frankenstein (Kenneth Branagh) prepares to create life in *Mary Shelley's Frankenstein* (1994).

The creature (Robert De Niro) and Elizabeth (Helen Bonham Carter) in *Mary Shelley's Frankenstein*

book. Despite this, it's refreshing that these passages are included at all—as most films in the Frankenstein canon totally disregard this aspect of the story in favor of traveling the easier (and admittedly safer box-office) route of an out-of-control, rampaging Monster. (*Mary Shelley's Frankenstein* certainly has its share of DeNiro rampages, but unlike other films, at least these stem from understandable motivations.)

For all its positive qualities, *Mary Shelley's Frankenstein* ultimately is undone by director Branagh's inability to rein in his urges to go "big," when perhaps keeping the novel's subtlety would have been the better route. In scene after scene, viewers are treated to loud, overly dramatic and over-the-top sequences. While the Creature's "birth" immediately comes to mind, nowhere is Branagh's excess more evident than the film's out-of-control ending. Here, in the film's greatest departure from the novel, Victor brings Elizabeth, dead at the hands of the Creature, back to life (through overly gruesome means). The first absurdity here stems from the almost apparent assembly-line ease in which Victor can now bestow life. Compounding the nonsense, the now reanimated Elizabeth, whose horrific visage approaches that of the Creature's, finds herself with two suitors—Victor and the Creature both attempt to win her affections. (This sequence, already stretching the limits of credulity, made me half expect Elizabeth to hand out a rose to the winner, like *The Bachelorette*.) Not absurd enough, you say? How about Victor dancing with his corpse bride, her limp legs dragging, her arms flailing to-and-fro, as Victor accelerates the pace in the most (perhaps only?) necrophilic waltz ever committed to film?

One thinks of what the film might have been had Branagh not succumbed to dramatic overreach. Screenwriter Darabont would certainly have you believe this. In succeeding years since the film's release, the writer has, at every opportunity, distanced himself from the film's arguable failure by laying blame solely at Branagh's feet. In one such case, an interview with Stu Kobak for *Films on Disc* (publication date unknown), Darabont states:

> Oy, my Waterloo, my worst experience. Actually, the script was great; the movie was a mess. You can't really judge the script based on what you saw on the screen. It got rephrased and messed with every inch of the way.

Darabont's defense only works to a point. I mean, what you see on the screen *is in the script.* If you write a scene where:

> And here we are treated to the most sweepingly romantic and hair-raisingly demented image of the film: Frankenstein dances with his dead bride, showing her the way, begging her to remember, please remember …And the worst part … The very worst thing of all? There on the shelf is a large formaldehyde jar containing Justine's severed head. Watching them through the glass with dead, sightless eyes. Watching them dance. Still a wallflower? No. She's finally finishing her dance with Victor … most of her, anyway. Under the circumstances, it'll have to do … and the waltz goes on, madder and madder, sweeping in glorious circles as a dazzling array of LIGHTNING bathes them in its wild, jittering spotlight.

Just what do you *think* a director is going to do with something like this?

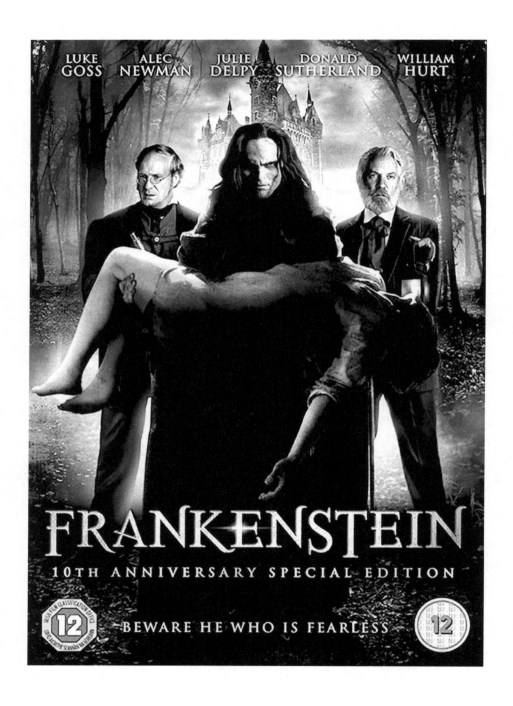

IT CAME FROM ...

Frankenstein (2004)

Easy to admire and impossible to love, the *Frankenstein* miniseries made for Hallmark is the single most faithful version of Mary Shelley's novel. As such, it is blessed with the novel's many high spots, and cursed by its many misfires. It never quite comes to life (sorry), but it is rewarding viewing and certainly worth your time.

The film maintains Shelley's device of framing the story with Frankenstein telling his story to a ship's captain (Donald Sutherland) in the frozen wastes of the arctic. Frankenstein tells of his studies under Professor Waldman (William Hurt) and of his eventual success in creating a creature (Luke Goss). Abandoned by Frankenstein and spurned by humanity, the Creature goes on a killing spree, murdering members of Frankenstein's family until he capitulates and makes a mate for his creation.

This is the one film that manages to do what other, bigger-budgeted films—*Mary Shelley's Frankenstein* or *Frankenstein: The True Story*—failed to do so completely: realize a faithful adaptation of the novel. And while that laudable ambition is realized, sadly, the result leaves something to be desired.

It's not that the film directed by Kevin Connor (*The Land That Time Forgot* and *At The Earth's Core*) is bad; it's just flat. The actors go about, mouthing their Romantic-era dialogue, but never does it seem to catch fire. This may be because the film has an awkward staginess that cripples the proceedings. One gets the feeling that Connor respected the material so much that he never allowed his actors to cut loose. One wishes that Connor approached the movie with the same sense of fun he used in his Edgar Rice Burroughs adaptations—none of those films were great, but they were fun in a *Classic Comics* sort of way. Also, too often the actors seem to be declaiming their parts, rather than playing them. It takes a "big" actor to pull off this type of material, and no one in the cast seems willing to go big.

Alec Newman (potentially Barnabas Collins in a proposed revamp of *Dark Shadows*) is fine as Frankenstein, a youthful medical student obsessed with creating life. Goss is very disappointing as the Creature. Though tall and imposing – and looking quite like Shelley's description – he never imbues the role with any menace. Worse still, his high and somewhat reedy voice does him no favors; all too often, he sounds like a nervous college kid reading the book aloud.

Sutherland steals the film with his brief turn as Captain Walton, and Hurt, as usual, fades into the background as Waldman. (One gets the feeling that Hurt is the only major screen star that appears in every film hoping that you don't notice him.)

Definitely worth a look for lovers of Shelley's novel, but easier to admire than to like.

Victor Frankenstein (2015)

Simply the gayest mainstream movie ever made.

Victor Frankenstein, like *Horror of Frankenstein* before it, is both a snapshot of its time and something that has to be seen to be believed.

Directed by Paul McGuigan and written by Max Landis, *Victor Franken-stein* apes both the BBC series *Sherlock* and the Guy Ritchie take on Holmes, centering the story around the bromance between Victor (James McAvoy) and his hunchbacked assistant (Daniel Radcliffe). If you are looking for a straight (pardon the pun) take on Shelley's novel, you've come to the wrong place.

In short: Victor Frankenstein rescues a brilliant hunchback from cruel circus owners (as one does), and cures him of his hump. The hunchback then happily helps Frankenstein in his quest to create life. The initial attempt is a beast made up of dead animal parts that goes on a rampage soon after Victor imbues it with life.

This brings Inspector Turpin (Andrew Scott, Moriarty in *Sherlock*) knocking on their door. In the meantime, the hunchback is reacquainted with Lorelei (Jessica Brown Findlay), an old circus friend, who is now the pampered beard of a closeted homosexual aristocrat. (You think I'm making this up, don't you?)

Frankenstein and his hunchback decide to cut their losses and now build a man. They plan on a giant, one with two hearts, two sets of lungs, two … well, two of everything important (draw your own conclusions). As this project is underway, Frankenstein is enticed to build a race of supermen by an evil and decadent aristocrat, Finnegan (Freddie Fox), who looks like a cross between Oscar Wilde's lover Lord Alfred Douglas and Draco Malfoy.

The hunchback finds his predecessor, Igor, dead in the basement (his eyes missing, because Frankenstein needs them), and is freaked by the unending harassment by Turpin. Trying to convince his mentor that they still have one another, Frankenstein rebuffs the hunchback, and Frankensteion leaves with his new friend, Finnegan (I swear).

IT CAME FROM …

The hunchback and his beloved Lorelei race to Finnegan's castle to save Frankenstein, Turpin in pursuit. It all ends happily (well, not for Turpin, Finnegan, or the Monster), with Frankenstein going off into the sunset, telling his hunchback that he was always his greatest creation.

Well. Where to begin?

A cross between Mary Shelley's *Frankenstein* and George Bernard Shaw's *Pygmalion, Victor Frankenstein* is one of those truly terrible movies that achieves its own kind of greatness. That *Victor Frankenstein* is a gay retelling is so obvious that soon the subtext becomes jokey text; one wonders why McGuigan and

Landis just didn't go whole *Brokeback Frankenstein* and shoot for the stars.

The tone is set early, when McAvoy takes Radcliffe home. McAvoy's first action is to push him against the wall, pull off his shirt from behind and pierce him with a phallic needle. "This is going to hurt just a little bit," he says before draining his "rather large fluid sack." When Radcliffe screams that it hurts, Frankenstein deadpans, "You'd be surprised how often I hear that" before saying, "I'm pulling out." From there on, it is a delicious wallow in impassioned looks, lots of one man standing behind another quite closely while talking, and quality time among the corpses. The joke reaches its apogee when Fox's Finnegan appears (looking for all the world as if he left Oscar Wilde waiting in the cab).

I certainly cannot damn the film. It is too delirious, too energetic, and too entertaining to be dismissed. It's just so damned ... odd.

McAvoy is splendid as Frankenstein, and it is his best film performance to date. His kind of scenery chewing is the type of brio that would have saved Hallmark's 2004 *Frankenstein* from oblivion, and one hopes that he some day gets the chance to sink his choppers into an Edgar Allan Poe piece. Radcliffe does what he does best: looking dewy-eyed and vulnerable before ultimately manning up and saving the day. Scott has a field day with Turpin, eventually losing a hand in the action (a throwback, one imagines, to Inspector Krogh in *Son of Frankenstein*—odd how echoes of Krogh appear in later films), and his off-center intensity plays nicely against the histrionics of McAvoy.

Certainly not to every taste—and a major disappointment upon release—*Victor Frankenstein* is one of my favorite genre films of the last decade and a great deal of fun.

Appendix

Below we provide a fairly comprehensive list of horror, science fiction, and fantasy films based (however closely/loosely) from other material. Each entry contains the title, author, publisher, and publication date of the source material. A minimum of three separate sources validates each entry.

A

Alien (1979) Said to be inspired (no official credit given in film) by the story "Black Destroyer" by A.E. van Vogt. First published in the July 1939 issue of *Astounding Science Fiction* magazine.

And Now the Screaming Starts! (1973) Based on the novel *Fengriffen: A Chilling Tale* by David Case. First published by Hill & Wang, 1970.

The Andromeda Strain (1971) Based on the novel *The Andromeda Strain* by Michael Crichton. First published by Alfred A. Knopf, Inc., 1969.

Around the World in 80 Days (1956) Based on the novel *Le tour du monde en quatre-vingts jours* (*Les Voyages Extraordinaires* [*The Extraordinary Voyages*] series #11) by Jules Verne. First published in book form by Pierre-Jules Hetzel, 1873.

Asylum (1972—anthology consisting of four stories):

Segment 1—based on the story "Frozen Fear" by Robert Bloch. First published in the May 1946 issue of *Weird Tales* magazine.

Segment 2—based on the story "The Weird Tailor" by Robert Bloch. First published in the July 1950 issue of *Weird Tales* magazine.

Segment 3—based on the story "Lucy Comes to Stay" by Robert Bloch. First published in the January 1952 issue of *Weird Tales* magazine.

Segment 4—based on the story "Mannikins of Horror" by Robert Bloch. First published in the December 1939 issue of *Weird Tales* magazine.

At the Earth's Core (1976) Based on *At the Earth's Core* by Edgar Rice Burroughs. First published in the April 4-25, 1914 issues of *All-Story Weekly* magazine.

Audrey Rose (1977) Based on the novel *Audrey Rose* by Frank De Felitta. First published by G.P. Putnam's Sons, 1975.

The Awakening (1980) Based on the novel *The Jewel of Seven Stars* by Bram Stoker. First published by William Heinemann, 1903.

B

Back from the Dead (1957) Based on the novel *The Other One* by Catherine Turney. First published by Henry Holt and Company, 1952.

The Bad Seed (1956) Based on the novel *The Bad Seed* by William March. First published by Rinehart & Company, 1954.

The Beast from 20,000 Fathoms (1953) Based on the story "The Beast from 20,000 Fathoms" (aka: "The Foghorn") by Ray Bradbury. First published in the June 23, 1951 issue of the *Saturday Evening Post* magazine.

The Beast with Five Fingers (1946) Based on the story "The Beast with Five Fingers" by William Fryer Harvey. First published in the anthology *The New Decameron, Second Day* by Robert M. McBride & Company, 1920.

The Beast Within (1982) Based on the novel *The Beast Within* by Edward Levy. First published by Arbor House in 1981.

The Beastmaster (1982) Based (no official credit given in film) on the novel *The Beast Master* by Andre Norton. First published by Harcourt Brace & Company, 1959.

The Birds (1963) Based on the story "The Birds" by Daphne du Maurier. First published in the October 1952 issue of *Good Housekeeping* magazine.

The Black Cat (1934) Suggested by the story "The Black Cat" by Edgar Allan Poe. First published in the August 19, 1843 issue of the *United States Saturday Post.*

Black Sunday (*Maschera del demonio, La*) (1960) Based on the story "The Viy" by Nikolai Gogol. First published in the collection *Mirgorod* (vol. 1), 1835. Publisher unknown.

Blade Runner (1982) Based on the novel *Do Androids Dream of Electric Sheep?* by Philip K. Dick. First published by Doubleday, 1968.

Blood from the Mummy's Tomb (1971) Based on the novel *The Jewel of Seven Stars* by Bram Stoker. First published by William Heinemann, 1903.

The Body Snatcher (1945) Based on the story "The Body Snatcher" by Robert Louis Stevenson. First published in the December 1884 *Pall Mall Gazette* Christmas "Extra" edition.

Burn Witch Burn (1962) Based on the novel *Conjure Wife* by Fritz Leiber, Jr. First published in the April 1943 issue of *Unknown Worlds* magazine.

Burnt Offerings (1976) Based on the novel *Burnt Offerings* by Robert Marasco. First published by Delacorte Press, 1973.

C

The Canterville Ghost (1944) Based on the story "The Canterville Ghost" by Oscar Wilde. First serialized in the February 23-March 2 1887 issues of *Court and Society Review* magazine.

Cape Fear (1962) Based on the novel *The Executioners* by John D. MacDonald. First published by Simon and Schuster, 1957.

Carrie (1976) Based on the novel *Carrie* by Stephen King. First published by Doubleday, 1974.

Charly (1968) Based on the story "Flowers for Algernon" by Daniel Keyes. First published in the April 1959 issue of *The Magazine of Fantasy & Science Fiction.*

Christine (1983) Based on the novel *Christine* by Stephen King. First published by Viking, 1983.

A Christmas Carol (all versions) Based on the story "A Christmas Carol" by Charles Dickens. First published by Chapman & Hall, 1843.

The Clairvoyant (1934) Based on the novel *The Clairvoyant* by Ernst Lothar. First published by Martin Secker (London), 1931.

The Climax (1944) Based on the play *The Climax* by Edward Locke. First performed on stage at Weber's Music Hall, NY April 12, 1909.

A Clockwork Orange (1971) Based on the novel *A Clockwork Orange* by Anthony Burgess. First published by William Heinemann, 1962.

The Collector (1965) Based on the novel *The Collector* by John Fowles. First published by Jonathan Cape (UK), 1963.

The Crawling Eye (aka: *The Trollenberg Terror*; 1958) Based on the British television serial *The Trollenberg Terror* by Peter Key. First aired in six half-hour episodes, 1956.

The Crime of Dr. Crespi (1935) Suggested by the story "The Premature Burial" by Edgar Allan Poe. First published in *The Philadelphia Dollar Newspaper*, July 31, 1844.

Cujo (1983) Based on the novel *Cujo* by Stephen King. First published by Viking, 1981.

Curse of the Crimson Altar (1968) Inspired by the story (no official credit given in film) "The Dreams in the Witch House" by H.P. Lovecraft. First published in the July 1933 issue of *Weird Tales* magazine.

Curse of the Demon (1958) Based on the story "Casting the Runes" by M.R. James. First published in the collection *More Ghost Stories*, Edward Arnold (London), 1911.

Curse of the Werewolf (1961) Based on the novel *The Werewolf of Paris* by Guy Endore. First published by Farrar and Rinehart, 1933.

D

The Dark Secret of Harvest Home (TV-1978) Based on the novel *Harvest Home* by Thomas Tryon. First published by Alfred A. Knopf, 1973.

The Day of the Triffids (1962) Based on the novel *The Day of the Triffids* by John Wyndham. First serialized (five parts) as "Revolt of the Triffids" in the January-February 1951 issues of *Collier's Weekly*.

The Day the Earth Stood Still (1951) Based on the story "Farewell to the Master" by Harry Bates. First published in the October 1940 issue of *Astounding*.

The Dead Zone (1983) Based on the novel *The Dead Zone* by Stephen King. First published by Viking, 1979.

The Deadly Bees (1966) Loosely based on the novel *A Taste for Honey* by H.F. (Gerald) Heard. First published by Vanguard Press, 1941.

Demon Seed (1977) Based on the novel *Demon Seed* by Dean R. Koontz. First published by Berkley Publishing, 1973.

Destination Moon (1950) Based on the novel *Rocket Ship Galileo* by Robert Heinlein. First published by Scribner's, 1947.

The Devil and Daniel Webster (1941) Based on the story "The Devil and Daniel Webster" by Stephen Vincent Benet. First published in the October 24, 1936 issue of *The Saturday Evening Post*.

The Devil Commands (1941) Based on the novel *The Edge of Running Water* by William Sloane. First published by Farrar & Rinehart, 1939.

The Devil Doll (1936) Based on the novel *Burn Witch Burn* by Abraham Merritt. First serialized (six parts) in the Oct 22-Nov 26, 1932 issues of *Argosy Weekly*.

Diary of a Madman (1963) Based on the story "Le Horla (The Horla)" by Guy de Maupassant. First published (abridged version) in *Gil Blas*, October 26, 1886.

Die! Die! My Darling! (1965) Based on the novel *Nightmare* by Elizabeth Linington (as Anne Blaisdell). First published by Harper and Brothers Publishers, 1961.

Die, Monster, Die! (1965) Based on the story "The Colour out of Space" by H.P. Lovecraft. First published in the September 1927 issue of *Amazing Stories* magazine.

Donovan's Brain (1953) Based on the novel *Donovan's Brain* by Curt Siodmak. First serialized in the September-November 1942 issues of *Black Mask* magazine.

Don't Look Now (1973) Based on the story "Don't Look Now" by Daphne du Maurier. First published in the collection *Not After Midnight*, by Victor Gollancz (London), 1971.

Dr. Jekyll and Mr. Hyde (all versions) Based on the story "Strange Case of Dr. Jekyll and Mr. Hyde" by Robert Louis Stevenson. First published by Longman's, Green & Co., (London) 1886 (some reports have Charles Scribner's Sons preceding the UK edition by a few days).

Dr. Renault's Secret (1942) Based (no official credit given in film) on the novel *Balaoo* by Gaston Leroux. First published in the October 9-December 18, 1911 issues of *Le Matin*.

Dr. Strangelove or: How I Learned to Stop Worrying and Love the Bomb (1964) Based on the novel *Two Hours to Doom* (aka: *Red Alert*) by Peter Bryan George (as Peter Bryant). First published by Boardman (London), 1958.

Dracula (various) Based on the novel *Dracula* by Bram Stoker. First published by Archibald Constable and Company (UK), 1897.

Dune (1984) Based on the novel *Dune* by Frank Herbert. First serialized in *Analog* magazine ("Dune World," Dec 1963-Feb 1964; "Prophet of Dune" Jan-May, 1965).

The Dunwich Horror (1970) Based on the story "The Dunwich Horror" by H.P. Lovecraft. First published in the April 1929 issue of *Weird Tales* magazine.

E

Earth vs. the Flying Saucers (1956) Suggested by the book *Flying Saucers from Outer Space* by Donald E. Keyhoe. First published by Holt, 1953.

The Exorcist (1973) Based on the novel *The Exorcist* by William Peter Blatty. First published by Harper & Row, 1971.

The Exorcist III (1990) Based on the novel *Legion* by William Peter Blatty. First published by Simon & Schuster, 1983.

Eye of the Devil (1967) Based on the novel *Day of the Arrow* by Philip Lorraine. First published by Collins (London), 1964.

F

Fahrenheit 451 (1966) Based on the novel *Fahrenheit 451* by Ray Bradbury. First published by Ballantine, 1953. (Novel expanded from his short story "The Fireman," first published in *Galaxy Science Fiction* magazine, 1951.)

Fiend Without a Face (1958) Based on the story "The Thought Monster" by Amelia Reynolds Long. First published in the March 1930 issue of *Weird Tales* magazine.

Firestarter (1984) Based on the novel *Firestarter* by Stephen King. First published by Viking, 1980.

The First Men in the Moon (1919) Based on the novel *The First Men in the Moon* by H.G. Wells. First serialized in the November 1900-August 1901 issues of *The Strand Magazine*.

Flowers in the Attic (1987) Based on the novel *Flowers in the Attic* by V.C. Andrews. First published by Simon & Schuster, 1979.

The Fly (1958) Based on the story "The Fly" by George Langelaan. First published in the June 1957 issue of *Playboy*.

The Food of the Gods (1976) Based on the novel *The Food of the Gods and How it Came to Earth* by H.G. Wells. First serialized in the December 1903-June 1904 issues of *Pearson's Magazine*.

The Fool Killer (1965) Based on the novel *The Fool Killer* by Helen Eustis. First published by Doubleday, 1954.

Frankenstein (1931) Based on the novel *Frankenstein; or the Modern Prometheus* by Mary Wollstonecraft Shelley. First published by Lackington, Hughes, Harding, Mavor & Jones (London), 1818.

Freaks (1932) Suggested by the story "Spurs" by Clarence Aaron 'Tod' Robbins. First published in the February 1923 issue of *Munsey's Magazine*.

From the Earth to the Moon (1958) Based on the novel *De la Terre a la Lune* (*Les Voyages Ex-traordinaires* [*The Extraordinary Voyages*] series #4) by Jules Verne. First serialized in the September 14-October 14, 1865 issues of *Journal des Debats politiques et litteraires*. First published in book form by Pierre-Jules Hetzel, 1865.

The Fury (1978) Based on the novel *The Fury* by John Farris. First published by Playboy Press, 1976.

G

A Game of Death (1945) Based on the story "The Most Dangerous Game" by Richard Connell. First published in the January 19, 1924 issue of *Collier's*.

The Great Impersonation (1935) Based on the novel *The Great Impersonation* by E. Phillips Oppenheim. First published by Little, Brown & Co., 1920.

Gulliver's Travels (1939) Based on the novel *Travels into Several Remote Nations of the World in Four Parts. By Lemuel Gulliver, First a Surgeon, and then a Captain of Several Ships* by Jonathan Swift. First published by Benjamin Motte, 1726.

H

The Haunted Palace (1963) Based on the story "The Case of Charles Dexter Ward" by H.P. Lovecraft. First published (in abridged form) in the May and July 1941 issues of *Weird Tales* magazine. (Title comes from the poem "The Haunted Palace" by Edgar Allan Poe.)

The Haunting (1963) Based on the novel *The Haunting of Hill House* by Shirley Jackson. First published by Viking, 1959.

Hellraiser (1987) Based on the story "The Hellbound Heart" by Clive Barker. First published in the collection *Night Visions 3* by Dark Harvest, 1986.

The Hound of the Baskervilles (1939) Based on the novel *The Hound of the Baskervilles* by Arthur Conan Doyle. First serialized in the August 1901-April 1902 issues of *The Strand* magazine.

The House of the Seven Gables (1940) Based on the novel *The House of the Seven Gables* by Nathaniel Hawthorne. First published by Ticknor, Reed, and Fields, 1851.

House of Usher (1960) Based on the story "The Fall of the House of Usher" by Edgar Allan Poe. First published in the September 1839 issue of *Burton's Gentleman's* magazine.

The House That Dripped Blood (1970: Anthology consisting of four stories):

Segment 1—based on the story "Method for Murder" by Robert Bloch. First published in the July 1962 issue of *Fury* magazine.

Segment 2—based on the story "Waxworks" by Robert Bloch. First published in the January 1939 issue of *Weird Tales* magazine.

Segment 3—based on the story "Sweets to the Sweet" by Robert Bloch. First published in the March 1947 issue of *Weird Tales* magazine.

Segment 4—based on the story "The Cloak" by Robert Bloch. First published in the May 1939 issue of *Unknown* magazine.

How the Grinch Stole Christmas! (1966) Based on the book *How the Grinch Stole Christmas!* by Theodor ("Dr. Seuss") Geisel. First published by Random House, 1957.

The Howling (1981) Based on the novel *The Howling* by Gary Brandner. First published by Fawcett, 1977.

The Hunchback of Notre Dame (1923) Based on the novel *Notre-Dame de Paris* (English title: *The Hunchback of Notre Dame*) by Victor Hugo. First published by Charles Gosselin Libraire, 1831.

IT CAME FROM ...

The Hunger (1983) Based on the novel *The Hunger* by Whitley Strieber. First published by William Morrow and Company, 1981.

I

The Illustrated Man (1969) Based on the book *The Illustrated Man* by Ray Bradbury. First published by Doubleday & Company, 1951.

The Incredible Shrinking Man (1957) Based on the novel *The Shrinking Man* by Richard Matheson. First published by Gold Medal, Fawcett Publications, 1956.

The Innocents (1961) Based on the novel *The Turn of the Screw* by Henry James. First serialized in the January 27-April 16, 1898 issues of *Collier's*.

Interview with the Vampire (1994) Based on the novel *Interview with the Vampire* by Anne Rice. First published Alfred A. Knopf, 1976.

Invasion of the Body Snatchers (1956) Based on the novel *The Body Snatchers* by Jack Finney. First serialized in the Nov 26, Dec 10, and Dec 24, 1954 issues of *Collier's Weekly*.

Invasion of the Saucer Men (1957) Based on the story "The Cosmic Frame" by Paul W. Fairman. First published in the May 1955 issue of *Amazing Stories* magazine.

The Invisible Man (1933) Based on the novel *The Invisible Man* by H.G. Wells. First serialized in the June 12-August 7, 1897 issues of *Pearson's Weekly*.

The Island of Dr. Moreau (1977) Based on the novel *The Island of Dr. Moreau* by H.G. Wells. First published by Heinemann (UK), 1896.

Island of Lost Souls (1933) Based on the novel *The Island of Dr. Moreau* by H.G. Wells. First published by Heinemann (UK), 1896.

It (TV: 1990) Based on the novel *IT* by Stephen King. First published by Viking, 1986.

J

Januskopf, Der (1920) Based on the story "Strange Case of Dr. Jekyll and Mr. Hyde" by Robert Louis Stevenson. First published by Longman's, Green & Co., (London) 1886 (some reports have Charles Scribner's Sons preceding the UK edition by a few days).

Jaws (1975) Based on the novel *Jaws* by Peter Benchley. First published by Doubleday, 1974.

Journey to the Center of the Earth (1959) Based on the novel *Voyage au Centre de la Terre* (*Les Voyages Extraordinaires* [*The Extraordinary Voyages*] series #3) by Jules Verne. First published by Pierre-Jules Hetzel, 1864.

The Jungle Book (1967) Based on the book *The Jungle Book* by Rudyard Kipling. First published by MacMillan, 1894.

L

The Lady and the Monster (1944) Based on the novel *Donovan's Brain* by Curt Siodmak. First serialized in the September-November 1942 issues of *Black Mask* magazine.

Lair of the White Worm (1988) Based on the novel *The Lair of the White Worm* by Bram Stoker. First published by William Rider and Son, Limited of London, 1911.

The Land that Time Forgot (1975) Based on the novel *The Land That Time Forgot* by Edgar Rice Burroughs. First published in the August 1918 issue of *Blue Book* magazine.

Last Man on Earth (1964) Based on the novel *I Am Legend* by Richard Matheson. First published by Gold Medal (Fawcett), 1954.

The Legend of Hell House (1973) Based on the novel *Hell House* by Richard Matheson. First published by Viking Press, 1971.

Lifeforce (1985) Based on the novel *The Space Vampires* by Colin Wilson. First published by Random House, 1976.

The Lodger (1927) Based on the novel *The Lodger* by Marie Adelaide Belloc Lowndes. First published by Methuen (London), 1913. Expanded from the short story of same name, first published in the January 1911 issue of *McClure's*.

Logan's Run (1976) Based on the novel *Logan's Run* by William F. Nolan and George Clayton Johnson. First published by Dial Press, 1967.

Lord of the Flies (1963) Based on the novel *Lord of the Flies* by William Golding. First published by Faber and Faber, 1954.

The Lord of the Rings: The Fellowship of the Ring (2001) Based on the novel *The Fellowship of the Ring* by J.R.R. Tolkien. First published by George Allen & Unwin, Ltd., 1954.

The Lord of the Rings: The Return of the King (2003) Based on the novel *The Return of the King* by J.R.R. Tolkien. First published by George Allen & Unwin, Ltd., 1955.

The Lord of the Rings: The Two Towers (2002) Based on the novel *The Two Towers* by J.R.R. Tolkien. First published by George Allen & Unwin, Ltd., 1954.

Lost Horizon (1937) Based on the novel *Lost Horizon* by James Hilton. First published by Macmillan & Co. (London), 1933.

The Lost World (1925) Based on the novel *The Lost World* by Arthur Conan Doyle. First serialized in April-November 1912 issues of *Strand Magazine*.

Lust for a Vampire (1971) Based on the story "Carmilla" by Joseph Sheridan Le Fanu. First serialized in the December 1871-March 1872 issues of *The Dark Blue* magazine.

M

The Magician (1926) Based on the novel *The Magician* by Somerset Maughm. First published by Heinemann, 1908.

The Man Who Could Work Miracles (1936) Based on the story "The Man Who Could Work Miracles" by H.G. Wells. First published in 1898 in *The Illustrated London News*.

The Man Who Fell to Earth (1976) Based on the novel *The Man Who Fell to Earth* by Walter Tevis. First published by Gold Medal (Fawcett), 1963.

The Manchurian Candidate (1962) Based on the novel *The Manchurian Candidate* by Richard Condon. First published by McGraw-Hill, 1959.

Marooned (1969) Based on the novel *Marooned* by Martin Caidin. First published by Dutton, 1964.

The Martian Chronicles (1980) Based on the book *The Martian Chronicles* by Ray Bradbury. First published by Doubleday, 1950.

The Masque of the Red Death (1964) Based on the story "The Masque of the Red Death" by Edgar Allan Poe. First published in the May 1842 issue of *Graham's Magazine*.

Master of the World (1961) Based on the novel *Maître du monde* (*Les Voyages Extraordinaires* [*The Extraordinary Voyages*] series #53) by Jules Verne. First serialized in the July 1-December 15, 1904 issues of *Magasin d'Education et de Recreation (Magasin)* magazine. First published in book form by Pierre-Jules Hetzel, 1904.

Misery (1990) Based on the novel *Misery* by Stephen King. First published by Viking, 1987.

The Most Dangerous Game (1932) Based on the story "The Most Dangerous Game" by Richard Connell. First published in the January 19, 1924 issue of *Collier's Weekly*.

Mr. Sardonicus (1961) Based on the story "Sardonicus" by Ray Russell. First published in the January 1961 issue of *Playboy*.

IT CAME FROM ...

Murders in the Rue Morgue (1932) Based on the story "The Murders in the Rue Morgue" by Edgar Allan Poe. First published in the April 1841 issue of *Graham's Magazine.*

Mysterious Island (1951) Based on the novel *L'Île mystérieuse* (*Les Voyages Extraordinaires* [*The Extraordinary Voyages*] series #12) by Jules Verne. First serialized in the January 1, 1874-December 15, 1875 issues of *Magasin d'Education et de Recreation (Magasin)* magazine. First published in book form by Pierre-Jules Hetzel, 1874.

Mystery of Marie Roget (1942) Based on the story "The Mystery of Marie Roget" by Edgar Allan Poe. First serialized in *Ladies' Companion* in three installments, November and December 1842 and February 1843.

N

The Nanny (1965) Based on the novel *The Nanny* by Merriam Modell (writing as Evelyn Piper). First published by Atheneum Publishers, Inc., 1964.

Navy vs. the Night Monsters (1966) Based on the novel *The Monster From Earth's End* by Murray Leinster. First published by Fawcett Publications, Inc., 1959.

The Night of the Hunter (1955) Based on the novel *The Night of the Hunter* by Davis Grubb. First published by Harper & Brothers, 1953.

Night of the Lepus (1972) Based on the novel *The Year of the Angry Rabbit* by Russell Braddon. First published by Heinemann (London), 1964.

Night of the Living Dead (1968) Inspired by (no official credit given in film) the novel *I Am Legend* by Richard Matheson. First published by Gold Medal (Fawcett), 1954.

The Night Stalker (TV-1972) Based on the (then unpublished) novel *The Kolchak Papers* by Jeffrey Grant Rice. First published (as *The Night Stalker*) by Pocket Books, 1973.

Nightbreed (1990) Based on the novella *Cabal*, by Clive Barker. First published by Poseidon Press, 1988.

1984 (1956, 1984) Based on the novel *Nineteen Eighty-Four,* by George Orwell. First published by Secker and Warburg (London), 1949.

Nosferatu (1922) Based on the novel *Dracula* by Bram Stoker. First published by Archibald Constable and Company (UK), 1897.

O

The Oblong Box (1969) Based on the story "The Oblong Box" by Edgar Allan Poe. First published in the September 1844 issue of *Godey's Lady's Book* magazine.

The Old Dark House (1932) Based on the novel *Benighted* by J.B. Priestly. First published by Heinemann (UK), 1927.

Omega Man (1971) Based on the novel *I Am Legend* by Richard Matheson. First published by Gold Medal (Fawcett), 1954.

On the Beach (1959) Based on the novel *On the Beach* by Nevil Shute. First serialized as "The Last Days on Earth" in *The Sunday Graphic* (London weekly) in four installments (April 7, 14, 21, and 28), 1957.

The Other (1972) Based on the novel *The Other* by Thomas Tryon. First published by Alfred A. Knopf, Inc., 1971.

P

The People That Time Forgot (1977) Based on the novel *The People That Time Forgot* by Edgar Rice Burroughs. First published in the October 1918 issue of *Blue Book Magazine.*

Pet Sematary (1989) Based on the novel *Pet Sematary* by Stephen King. First published by Doubleday, 1983.

The Phantom of the Opera (1925) Based on the novel *Le Fantôme de l'Opéra* (*The Phantom of the Opera*) by Gaston Leroux. First serialized in the French newspaper, *Le Gaulois* (September 23, 1909—January 8, 1910).

Phantom of the Rue Morgue (1954) Based on the story "The Murders in the Rue Morgue" by Edgar Allan Poe. First published in the April 1841 issue of *Graham's Magazine*.

The Picture of Dorian Gray (1945) Based on the novel *The Picture of Dorian Gray* by Oscar Wilde. First published in the July 1890 issue of *Lippincott's Monthly Magazine*.

Pit and the Pendulum (1961) Based on the story "The Pit and the Pendulum" by Edgar Allan Poe. First published in *The Gift: A Christmas and New Year's Present for 1843*, 1842.

Planet of the Apes (1968) Based on the novel *La Planète des Singes* (*Planet of the Apes*) by Pierre Boulle. First published by Le Cercle du Nouveau Livre/Rene Julliard, 1963.

The Premature Burial (1962) Based on the story "The Premature Burial" by Edgar Allan Poe. First published in the July 31, 1844 issue of *The Philadelphia Dollar Newspaper*.

Psycho (1960) Based on the novel *Psycho* by Robert Bloch. First published by Simon & Schuster, 1959.

Q

The Queen of Spades (1949) Based on the story "Pikovaya Dama" by Alexander Pushkin. First published in *Biblioteka dlya chteniya* magazine, 1834.

Queen of the Damned (2002) Based on the novel *The Queen of the Damned* by Anne Rice. First published by Alfred A. Knopf, 1988.

R

The Raven (1935) Suggested by the poem "The Raven" by Edgar Allan Poe. First published in February 1845 issue of *The American Review*.

The Raven (1963) Based (loosely!) on the poem "The Raven" by Edgar Allan Poe. First published in February 1845 issue of *The American Review*.

Re-Animator (1985) Based on the story "Herbert West—Reanimator" by H.P. Lovecraft. First serialized in the February-July 1922 issues of *Home Brew*.

Rebecca (1940) Based on the novel *Rebecca* by Daphne du Maurier. First published by Gollancz (UK), 1938.

Rollerball (1975) Based on the story "Roller Ball Murder" by William Harrison. First published in the September 1973 issue of *Esquire* magazine.

Rosemary's Baby (1968) Based on the novel *Rosemary's Baby* by Ira Levin. First published by Random House, 1967.

The Running Man (1987) Based on the novel *The Running Man* by Stephen King (as Richard Bachman). First published by Signet, 1982.

S

Salem's Lot (TV-1979) Based on the novel *'Salem's Lot* by Stephen King. First published by Doubleday, 1975.

The Satan Bug (1965) Based on the novel *The Satan Bug* by Alistair MacLean (writing as Ian Stuart). First published by Collins (UK), 1962.

Scrooge (all versions) Based on the story "A Christmas Carol" by Charles Dickens. First published by Chapman & Hall, 1843.

Séance on a Wet Afternoon (1964) Based on the novel *Séance on a Wet Afternoon* by Mark McShane. First published by Cassell (UK), 1961.

Seconds (1966) Based on the novel *Seconds* by David Ely. First published by Pantheon Books, 1963.

IT CAME FROM ...

The Sentinel (1977) Based on the novel *The Sentinel* by Jeffrey Konvitz. First published by Simon & Schuster, 1974.

7 Faces of Dr. Lao (1964) Based on the novel *The Circus of Dr. Lao* by Charles Finney. First published by Viking Press, 1935.

Seven Footprints to Satan (1929) Based on the novel *Seven Footprints to Satan* by Abraham Merritt. First serialized in the July 2, 9, 16, 23, and 30, 1927 issues of *Argosy All-Story Weekly* magazine.

She (1965) Based on the novel *She (A History of Adventure)* by H. Rider Haggard. First serialized in the October 2, 1886-January 8, 1887 issues of *The Graphic* magazine.

She Devil (1957) Based on the story "The Adaptive Ultimate" by Stanley G. Weinbaum (as John Jessel). First published in the November 1935 issue of *Astounding Stories* magazine.

The Shining (1980) Based on the novel *The Shining* by Stephen King. First published by Doubleday, 1977.

The Silence of the Lambs (1991) Based on the novel *The Silence of the Lambs* by Thomas Harris. First published by St. Martin's Press, 1988.

The Skull (1965) Based on the story "The Skull of the Marquis de Sade" by Robert Bloch. First published in the September 1945 issue of *Weird Tales* magazine.

Slaughterhouse-Five (1972) Based on the novel *Slaughterhouse-Five, or The Children's Crusade* by Kurt Vonnegut, Jr. First published by Delacorte Press, 1969.

Something Wicked This Way Comes (1983) Based on the novel *Something Wicked This Way Comes* by Ray Bradbury. First published by Simon & Schuster, 1962.

Somewhere In Time (1980) Based on the novel *Bid Time Return* by Richard Matheson. First published by Viking Press, 1975.

Soylent Green (1973) Based on the novel *Make Room! Make Room!* by Harry Harrison. First serialized in the August-October, 1966 issues of *SF Impulse* magazine.

Spirits of the Dead (1968: Anthology consisting of four stories):

Segment 1—based on the story "Metzengerstein" by Edgar Allan Poe. First published in the January 14, 1832 issue of the *Saturday Courier* newspaper.

Segment 2—based on the story "William Wilson" by Edgar Allan Poe. First published in *The Gift for 1840*, 1839.

Segment 3—based on the story "Never Bet the Devil Your Head" by Edgar Allan Poe. First published in the September 1841 issue of *Graham's* magazine (published as "Never Bet Your Head, A Moral Tale").

The Stand (TV-1994) Based on the novel *The Stand* by Stephen King. First published by Doubleday, 1978.

The Stepford Wives (1975) Based on the novel *The Stepford Wives* by Ira Levin. First published by Random House, 1972.

Svengali (1931) Based on the novel *Trilby* by George du Maurier. First serialized in the January-August, 1894 issues of *Harper's New Monthly Magazine*.

T

Tales of Terror (1962: Anthology consisting of three stories):

Segment 1—based on the story "Morella" by Edgar Allan Poe. First published in the April 1835 issue of the *Southern Literary Messenger*.

Segment 2—suggested by the stories "The Black Cat" and "The Cask of Amontillado" by Edgar Allan Poe. First published in the August 19, 1843 issue of the *United States Saturday Post* and the November 1846 issue of *Godey's Lady's Book*, respectively.

Segment 3—based on the story "The Facts In the Case of M. Valdemar" by Edgar Allan Poe. First published in the December 1845 issue of the *American Review* (published as "The Facts of M. Valdemar's Case").

Target Earth (1954) Based on the story "Deadly City" by Paul W. Fairman (writing as Ivar Jorgenson). First published in the March 1953 issue of *If* magazine.

These Are the Damned (aka: *The Damned*; 1963) Based on the novel *The Children of Light* by H.L. Lawrence. First published by Macdonald, 1960.

The Thing From Another World (1951) Based on the story "Who Goes There?" by John W. Campbell (as Don A. Stuart). First published in the August 1938 issue of *Astounding Science-Fiction* magazine.

Things To Come (1936) Based on the novel *The Shape of Things to Come* by H.G. Wells. First published by Hutchinson (UK), Macmillan (USA), 1933.

This Island Earth (1955) Based on the novel *This Island Earth* by Raymond F. Jones. First serialized in three segments in *Thrilling Wonder Stories* magazine: "The Alien Machine" (June 1949), "The Shroud of Secrecy" (December 1949), "The Greater Conflict" (February 1950).

To the Devil ... A Daughter (1976) Based on the novel *To the Devil—A Daughter* by Dennis Wheatley. First serialized in an abridged form in the October 1952 issue of the *Sunday Empire News*.

The Tomb of Ligeia (1965) Based on the story "Ligeia" by Edgar Allan Poe. First published in the September 1838 *American Museum* magazine.

Torture Garden (1967: Anthology consisting of four stories):

Segment 1—based on the story "Enoch" by Robert Bloch. First published in the September 1946 issue of *Weird Tales* magazine.

Segment 2—based on the story "Terror Over Hollywood" by Robert Bloch. First published in the June 1957 issue of *Fantastic Universe* magazine.

Segment 3—based on the story "Mr. Steinway" by Robert Bloch. First published in the April 1954 issue of *Fantastic* magazine.

Segment 4—based on the story "The Man Who Collected Poe" by Robert Bloch. First published in the October 1951 issue of *Famous Fantastic Mysteries* magazine.

20,000 Leagues Under the Sea (1954) Based on the novel *Vingt mille lieues sous les mers (20,000 Leagues Under the Sea)* by Jules Verne. First published in book form by Pierre-Jules Hetzel, 1870.

Twice Told Tales (1963: Anthology consisting of three stories):

Segment 1—based on the story "Dr. Heidegger's Experiment" by Nathaniel Hawthorne. First published (as "The Fountain of Youth") in the January 1837 issue of *The Knickerbocker* magazine.

Segment 2—based on the story "Rappaccini's Daughter" by Nathaniel Hawthorne. First published in the December 1844 issue of the *United States Magazine and Democratic Review*.

Segment 3—based on the novel *The House of Seven Gables* by Nathaniel Hawthorne. First published by Ticknor, Reed, and Fields, 1851.

2001: A Space Odyssey (1968) Inspired by the story "Sentinel of Eternity" by Arthur C. Clarke. First published in the Spring 1951 issue of *10 Story Fantasy* magazine.

U

The Undying Monster (1942) Based on the novel *The Undying Monster: A Tale of the Fifth Dimension* by Jessie Douglas Kerruish. First published by Heath Cranton (UK), 1922.

The Unholy Three (1925) Based on the story "The Terrible Three" by Clarence Aaron 'Tod' Robbins. First serialized in the July 14-August 4, 1917 issues of *All-Story Weekly* magazine.

The Uninvited (1944) Based on the novel *Uneasy Freehold* by Dorothy Macardle. First published by Peter Davies (UK), 1941.

V

The Vampire Lovers (1970) Inspired by (no official credit given in film) the story "Carmilla" by Joseph Sheridan Le Fanu. First serialized in the December 1871-March 1872 issues of *The Dark Blue* magazine.

Vampires (aka: *John Carpenter's Vampires*; 1998) Based on the novel *Vampire$* by John Steakley. First published by Roc Books, 1990.

Village of the Damned (1960) Based on the novel *The Midwich Cuckoos* by John Wyndham. First published by Michael Joseph (UK), 1957.

Village of the Giants (1965) Loosely based (no official credit given in film) on the novel *The Food of the Gods and How It Came to Earth* by H.G. Wells. First serialized in the December 1903-June 1904 issues of *Pearson's Magazine*.

W

War of the Worlds (1953) Based on the novel *The War of the Worlds* by H.G. Wells. First serialized in the April-December 1897 issues of *Pearson's Weekly* (UK).

Weird Woman (1944) Based on the novel *Conjure Wife* by Fritz Leiber. First published in the April 1943 issue of *Unknown Worlds* magazine.

Whatever Happened To Baby Jane? (1962) Based on the novel *Whatever Happened to Baby Jane?* by Henry Farrell. First published by Rinehart, 1960.

When Worlds Collide (1951) Based on the novel *When Worlds Collide* by Philip Wylie and Edwin Balmer. First serialized in the September 1932-February 1933 issues of *Blue Book* magazine.

Willard (1971) Based on the novel *Ratman's Notebooks* by Stephen Gilbert. First published by Michael Joseph (UK), 1968.

Willy Wonka and the Chocolate Factory (1971) Based on the novel *Charlie and the Chocolate Factory* by Roald Dahl. First published by Alfred A. Knopf, 1964.

The Witches (1966) Based on the novel *The Devil's Own* (aka: *The Little Wax Doll*) by Norah Lofts (as Peter Curtis). First published by Macdonald (UK), 1960.

The Wizard of Oz (1939) Based on the novel *The Wonderful Wizard of Oz* by L. Frank Baum. First published by George M. Hill Company, 1900.

Bibliography

Books

Amis, Kingsley. *The James Bond Dossier.* Jonathan Cape, 1965.

Auerbach, Nina. *Daphne du Maurier: Haunted Heiress.* Philadelphia, Pennsylvania: University of Pennsylvania Press, 2002.

Bennett, Charles, and John Charles Bennett, ed. *Hitchcock's Partner in Suspense: The Life of Screenwriter Charles Bennett.* Lexington, KY: The University Press of Kentucky, 2014.

Bloch, Robert. *Once Around the Bloch: An Unauthorized Autobiography.* New York: Tom Doherty Associates, Inc., 1993.

Bradbury, Ray. *Bradbury Speaks: Too Soon from the Cave, Too Far from the Stars.* New York: HarperCollins Publishers, 2005.

Briggs, Julia (contributor). *Penguin Encyclopedia of Horror and the Supernatural.* New York: Viking Press, 1986.

Collins, Vere, ed. *Ghosts and Marvels: a selection of uncanny tales from Daniel Defoe to Algernon Blackwood.* London, UK: Oxford University Press, 1925.

Cunningham, Jesse G., ed. *Science Fiction: The Greenhaven Press Companion to Literary Movements and Genres.* Greenhaven Press, 2002.

Daniels, Les. *Superman: The Complete History: The Life and Times of the Man of Steel.* Chronicle Books, 1998.

Davis, Paul. *The Life and Times of Ebenezer Scrooge.* Yale University Press, 1990.

Dille, Robert C. *The Collected Works of Buck Rogers in the 25th Century.* Chelsea House Publishers. 1969.

Du Maurier, Daphne. *Daphne du Maurier's Classics of the Macabre.* Garden City, New York: Doubleday & Company, Inc., 1987.

Earnshaw, Tony. *Beating the Devil: The Making of the Night of the Demon.* Sheffield, UK: Tomahawk Press, 2005.

Engel, Joel. *Rod Serling: The Dreams and Nightmare of Life in the Twilight Zone.* Contemporary Books, 1989.

Finney, Charles G. *The Old China Hands.* New York: Doubleday, 1961.

Gabler, Neal. *Walt Disney: The Triumph of the American Imagination.* Knopf, 2006.

Gibson, William. *Burning Chrome.* Arbor House, 1986.

Gordon, Bernard. *Hollywood Exile or How I Learned to Love the Blacklist: A Memoir.* Austin, TX: University of Texas Press, 1999.

Guida, Fred. *A Christmas Carol and Its Adaptations: Dickens'- Story on Screen and Television.* McFarland & Company, 2006.

Harman, Claire. *Myself and the Other Fellow: A Life of Robert Louis Stevenson.* New York: HarperCollins Publishers, 2005.

Hartwell, David G. *Age of Wonders: Exploring the World of Science Fiction.* Tor Books, 1984.

Hearn, Michael Patrick. *The Critical Heritage Edition of the Wizard of Oz.* New York, Schocken, 1986.

Hickman, Gail Morgan. *The Films of George Pal.* New York: A. S. Barnes and Company, 1977.

Higham, Charles, and Joel Greenberg. *The Celluloid Muse: Hollywood Directors Speak*. Chicago, IL: Henry Regnery Company, 1969.

Kendrick, Walter. *The Thrill of Fear: 250 Years of Scary Entertainment*. Grove Weidenfeld, 1991.

King, Stephen. *Danse Macabre*. New York: Berkley Books, 1983.

Larson, Randall, ed. *The Robert Bloch Companion: Collected Interviews 1969-1986*. Mercer Island, WA: Starmont House, Inc., 1989.

LaValley, Al, ed. *Invasion of the Body Snatchers: Don Siegel, Director*. London: Rutgers University Press, 1989.

Madison, Bob, ed. *Dracula: The First Hundred Years*. Baltimore, MD: Midnight Marquee Press, 1997.

Mank, Gregory William. *Bela Lugosi and Boris Karloff: The Expanded Story of a Haunted Collaboration, With a Complete Filmography of Their Films Together*. Jefferson, NC: McFarland & Company, Inc., Publishers, 2009.

Marco, John. Introduction. *The Circus of Dr. Lao*. By Charles Finney. Lincoln, NE: University of Nebraska Press, 2002.

McCarthy, Kevin, and Ed Gorman, eds. *They're Here ... Invasion of the Body Snatchers: A Tribute*. New York: Berkley Boulevard, 1999.

Porfirio, Robert, Alain Silver, and James Ursini, eds. *Film Noir Reader 3: Interviews with Filmmakers of the Classic Noir Period*. New York: Limelight Editions, 2002.

Ricca, Brad. *Super Boys: The Amazing Adventures of Jerry Siegel and Joe Shuster—the Creators of Superman*. St. Martin's Griffith. 2014.

Rogers, Katharine M. *L. Frank Baum, Creator of Oz: A Biography*. New York, St. Martin's Press, 2002.

Rosner, Lisa. *The Anatomy Murders: Being the True and Spectacular History of Edinburgh's Notorious Burke and Hare and of the Man of Science Who Abetted Them in the Commission of Their Most Heinous Crimes*. Philadelphia, PA: University of Pennsylvania Press, 2010.

Sander, Gordon F. *Rod Serling: The Rise and Twilight of Television's Last Angry Man*. Knopf, 1992.

Scott, Allan, and Chris Bryant. *Don't Look Now: Screenplay*. UK: Sight and Sound, 1997.

Sellers, Michael D. *John Carter and the Gods of Hollywood*. Universal Media, 2012.

Siegel, Don. *A Siegel Film: An Autobiography*. London: Faber and Faber Limited, 1993.

Skal, David J. *Hollywood Gothic: The Tangled Web of Dracula From Stage to Screen*. US: W.W. Norton 1991.

Skal, David J. *The Monster Show: A Cultural History of Horror*. US: W.W. Norton, 1993.

Snelling, O.F. *James Bond: A Report*. New American Library, 1965.

Steinbrunner, Chris and Penzler, Otto. *The Encyclopedia of Mystery and Detection*. McGraw-Hill Books, 1976.

Stuart, Mel, and Josh Young. *Pure Imagination: The Making of Willy Wonka and the Chocolate Factory*. New York: St. Martin's Press, 2002.

Sturrock, Donald. *Storyteller: The Authorized Biography of Roald Dahl*. New York: Simon & Schuster, 2010.

Tye, Larry. *Superman: The High-Flying History of America's Most Enduring Hero*. Random House, 2012.

Usborn, Richard. *Clubland Heroes*. Constable, 1952.

Van Ash, Cay and Sax Rohmer, Elizabeth. *Master of Villainy: A Biography of Sax Rohmer*. Tom Stacey, 1972.

Welden, Glen. *The Caped Crusade: Batman and the Rise of Nerd Culture*. Simon & Schuster, 2016.

Welden, Glen. *Superman: The Unauthorized Biography*. Wiley, 2013.

Weller, Sam. *The Bradbury Chronicles: The Life of Ray Bradbury*. New York: HarperCollins Publishers, 2005.

Weller, Sam. *Listen to the Echoes: The Ray Bradbury Interviews*. Brooklyn, NY: Melville House Publishing, 2010.

Zicree, Marc Scott. *The Twilight Zone Companion*. Bantam Books, 1982.

Magazines and Newspapers

Barrett, Robert R. "How John Carter Became Flash Gordon." *Burroughs Bulletin* #60, 2004.

Bradley, Matthew. "The Illustrative Man: An Interview with SF Legend Ray Bradbury." *Outre* Fall 1995: 26+.

Culhane, John. "Nostalgia: The Vogue for the Old." *Newsweek*, December 26, 1970.

French, Lawrence. "Ray Bradbury on Something Wicked This Way Comes." *Fangoria* May 1983: 28+.

Jacobs, Robert. "The Writer's Digest Interview: Ray Bradbury." *Writer's Digest*. February 1976: 18-25.

Kaminsky, Stuart. "On Invasion of the Body Snatchers." *Cinefantastique* Winter 1973: 16-23.

Kaplan, Peter W. "Yip Harburg: Beyond The Rainbow." *The Washington Post*, February 28, 1981.

Kleiman, Dena. "It's Yesteryear Time Again." *The New York Times*, September 2, 1977.

Knight, Damon. "The Body Snatchers." *Original Science Fiction Stories* September 1955: 118-120.

Maitland, Leslie. "Remember Last Year's Nostalgia?" *The New York Times*, August 27, 1976.

Rebello, Stephen. "Something Wicked This Way Comes." *Cinefantastique* June-July 1983: 28-49.

Skotak, Robert and Holton, Scott. "Space 1955: This Island Earth." *Starlog Magazine*, August 1978.

Zito, Salena. "Nostalgia and the American Dream Aren't Airy Fantasies." *The Washington Examiner*, January 25, 2019.

Websites

AbeBooks. <https://www.abebooks.com/>.

Anders, Charley Jane. *Tomorrowland is Baby Boomer Nostalgia At Its Most Dreary*. May 22, 2015. <https://io9.gizmodo.com/tomorrowland-is-baby-boomer-nostalgia-at-its-most-drear-1706221215>.

Cartoon Research. Bob Camplett's John Carter of Mars. <https://cartoonresearch.com/index.php/bob-clampetts-john-carter-of-mars>.

Edgar Allan Poe Society of Baltimore, The. 01 May 1997. 05 Jan. 2014 <http://www.eapoe.org/index.htm>.

Eubank, Joanna. "Tucson Notable: Star editor's book piqued the imagination." 03 June 2015. 14 January 2019. <https://tucson.com/news/blogs/morgue-tales/tucson-notable-star-editor-s-book-piqued-the-imagination/article_0bac839e-0972-11e5-88b2-ebe01d89d573.html>.

Films on Disc. Kobak, Stu. "Redeeming the Writer: A Conversation with Frank Darabont." 19 January 2019. <http://www.filmsondisc.com/Features/darabont/darabont.htm>.

Gilbert, Jan. "An Interview with Allan Scott." 04 July 2011 <http://www.kamera.co.uk/an-interview-with-allan-scott>.

Goodman, Amy and Ernie Harburg. *A Tribute to Yip Harburg: The Man Who Put the Rainbow in The Wizard of Oz.* November 25, 2004. <https://www.democracynow.org/2004/11/25/a_tribute_to_yip_harburg_the>.

History Blog, The. Ed. Livius. "Watch the first film Frankenstein restored." 31 October 2018. 16 January 2019. <http://www.thehistoryblog.com/archives/date/2018/10>.

Internet Speculative Fiction Database. Vers. 4.00. Apr. 2006. <http://www.isfdb.org>.

Jordison, Sam. "Don't Look Now: Reading the film." 27 October 2011. 03 June 2014. <http://www.theguardian.com/books/2011/oct/27/dont-look-now-film-du-maurier>.

Paris Review, The. Weller, Sam. "Ray Bradbury, The Art of Fiction No. 203." Spring 2010. <https://www.theparisreview.org/interviews/6012/ray-bradbury-the-art-of-fiction-no-203-ray-bradbury>.

Raymond, Eric S. "A Political History of SF." <http://www.catb.org/~esr/writings/sf-history.html>.

Reader's Guide to John Wyndham's The Day of the Triffids, The. Ed. Paul Thompson. 02 June 2012 <http://triffids.wuthering-heights.co.uk/index.htm>.

Roald Dahl. Ed. Quentin Blake. 2019. <https://www.roalddahl.com>.

Scott, Allan, and Greg Jameson. "Allan Scott Interview." 29 June 2011. 05 June 2014. <http://www.entertainment-focus.com/film-section/film-interviews/allan-scott-interview>.

Stille, Andrew. "Diary of a Screenwriter: Writing 'Psycho': Interview with Joseph Stefano." 02 June 2014 <http://diaryofascreenwriter.blogspot.com/2013/08/writing-psycho-interview-with-joseph.html>.

Vincent, Bev. "Identifying First Editions." July 2018. <https://www.stephenking.com/other/identifying_first_editions.pdf>.

Wilcox, Roger M. "The Highly Unofficial Logan's Run FAQ." May 24, 2000. <http://www.rogermwilcox.com/LogansRun.html>.

CD/DVD

"The Making of Psycho." Dir. Laurent Bouzereau. 1997. *Psycho 50ᵗʰ Anniversary Edition.* DVD. Universal Studios Home Entertainment, 2010.

Schecter, David. "The Day of the Triffids." Booklet. *This Island Earth (and Other Alien Invasion Films).* CD. Radio Symphony Orchestra of Slovakia. Cond. Masatoshi Mitsumoto. Monstrous Movie Music, 2006.

Smith, Adam, and Nicolas Roeg. Audio Commentary. *Don't Look Now Special Edition*. DVD. Optimum Home Releasing, 2006.

Screenplays
Lady, Steph; Darabont, Frank. "Frankenstein." 2nd Revised Draft, February 8, 1993.
MacDonald, Philip. "The Body Snatcher." Film script, 1944.
Mainwaring, Daniel. "The Body Snatchers." Final revised film script, 1955. Wisconsin Center for Film & Theater Research.
Stefano, Joseph. "Psycho." Revised film script, 1959.

Interviews
Crabbe, Buster. Personal interview. September 1976.
Bradbury, Ray. Personal interview. 29 May 1993.

The stories and novels behind Classic Horror, Fantasy and Science Fiction Films

Meet the Authors

About Jim Nemeth:

By day, Jim Nemeth is a technical writer within the fields of computer software and biotechnology.

As a professional writer, in 1993, Jim won 1st Prize in a national magazine's short-story writing contest for which novelists Ray Bradbury and Robert Bloch were judges. Winning held special meaning for Jim, as Robert Bloch remains his favorite writer and main literary influence. Jim has had essays, articles, and reviews printed in a variety of magazines, including *FilmFax*, *Mad About Movies*, and *Monsters From The Vault*. Additionally, he contributed to *Peter Cushing: Midnight Marquee Actors Series* (Midmar Press, 2004).

A long-time community activist, Jim is particularly committed to the causes of animal rescue and breast cancer research.

It Came From … The Stories and Novels Behind Classic Horror, Fantasy and Science Fiction Films is his first book.

Born and raised in Chicago, Jim now lives with his husband in historic Marblehead, Massachusetts.

About Bob Madison:

Bob Madison is a seasoned communications professional with extensive experience in the nonprofit and corporate spheres. He has 20+ years of experience with leading corporations and nonprofits, such as Hoffmann-La Roche, Porter Novelli, Golin/Harris, and the American Liver Foundation.

His short story "Red Sunset" received starred reviews in publications like *Locus Magazine*, and he is the author of *American Horror Writers* (2000), and editor of *Dracula: The First Hundred Years* (1997). Other writing credits include numerous articles for *Wonder Magazine*, *FilmFax*, *Cult Movies*, and a comic strip adaptation of Conan Doyle's *The Lost World* for *The Dinosaur Times*, illustrated by Gray Morrow.

Madison is also a frequent talk show guest and lecturer, having appeared twice on WABC-TV's *Good Morning America*, WOR's *Joey Reynolds Show* and WABC's *Morning News*, among others. He has also been featured in documentaries for several DVDs, including the classic movie versions of *Frankenstein*, *The Bride of Frankenstein*, *Dracula*, and *Abbott and Costello Meet Frankenstein*.

Bob Madison resides in Southern California with his husband, Russell Frost. He is still unable to build his interocitor.

*Midnight Marquee books
are available at
Amazon.com, Oldies.com
and all other book sellers*s.

Lightning Source UK Ltd.
Milton Keynes UK
UKHW052307100920
369682UK00014BA/1459